About the editors

Anissa Hélie is assistant professor in history at John Jay College of Criminal Justice, New York. She is involved with various women's organizations and transnational networks, serving as director of the Women Living Under Muslim Laws International Coordination Office from 2000 to 2005. She has held research and teaching positions at Amherst and surrounding colleges, and is a board member of the Urgent Action Fund for Women's Human Rights and *Reproductive Health Matters* journal. She is co-author (with Jan Bauer) of *Documenting Women's Rights Violations by Non-State Actors: Experiences of Activists from Muslim Communities* (2006).

Homa Hoodfar is a professor of anthropology at Concordia University, Montreal. She has extensively studied survival and empowerment strategies among those marginalized by legal constraints. She has also researched women in local and national politics, with a particular focus on Egypt, Iran, Afghanistan, Pakistan, and among Canada's Muslim communities. Her publications include: 'Health as a context for social and gender activism: Female volunteer health workers in Iran' (2010); 'Women, religion and the "Afghan education movement" in Iran' (2008); *Between Marriage and the Market: Intimate Politics and Survival in Cairo* (2005); and *The Muslim Veil in North America: Issues and Debates* (2003).

Sexuality in Muslim Contexts

RESTRICTIONS AND RESISTANCE

*Edited by Anissa Hélie
and Homa Hoodfar*

Zed Books
LONDON | NEW YORK

Sexuality in Muslim Contexts: Restrictions and Resistance was first published in 2012 by Zed Books Ltd, 7 Cynthia Street, London N1 9JF, UK and Room 400, 175 Fifth Avenue, New York, NY 10010, USA

www.zedbooks.co.uk

Editorial Copyright © Anissa Hélie and Homa Hoodfar 2012
Copyright in this collection © Zed Books 2012

The rights of Anissa Hélie and Homa Hoodfar to be identified as the editors of this work have been asserted by them in accordance with the Copyright, Designs and Patents Act, 1988

FSC
www.fsc.org
MIX
Paper from
responsible sources
FSC® C013604

Designed and typeset in Monotype Bembo Book
by illuminati, Grosmont
Index: rohan.indexing@gmail.com
Cover design: www.roguefour.co.uk
Printed by CPI Group (UK) Ltd, Croydon CR0 4YY

Distributed in the USA exclusively by Palgrave Macmillan, a division of St Martin's Press, LLC, 175 Fifth Avenue, New York, NY 10010, USA

A catalogue record for this book is available from the British Library
Library of Congress Cataloging in Publication Data available

ISBN 978 1 78032 286 5 hb
ISBN 978 1 78032 285 8 pb

Contents

ACKNOWLEDGEMENTS   vii

GLOSSARY   ix

INTRODUCTION Policing gender, sexuality
and 'Muslimness'
Anissa Hélie

PART I Tools of policing: the politics of history,
community, law

1 The politicization of women's bodies in
Indonesia: sexual scripts as charters for action   17
Vivienne Wee

2 Iranian women and shifting sexual ideologies,
1850–2010   52
Claudia Yaghoobi

3 Moral panic: the criminalization of sexuality
in Pakistan   79
Hooria Hayat Khan

4 The promise and pitfalls of women challenging
Muslim family laws in India and Israel   98
Yüksel Sezgin

5 Sexuality and inequality: the marriage contract
  and Muslim legal tradition   124
  Ziba Mir-Hosseini

PART II Sites of contestation: reclaiming public spaces

6 Purity, sexuality and faith: Chinese women
  ahong and women's mosques as shelter and
  strength   151
  Maria Jaschok with Shui Jingjun

7 Veiled transcripts: the private debate on public
  veiling in Iran   182
  Shadi Sadr

8 Kicking back: the sports arena and sexual politics
  in Iran   208
  Homa Hoodfar

9 Morality policing and the public sphere:
  women reclaiming their bodies and their rights   234
  Homa Hoodfar and Ana Ghoreishian

10 'Living sexualities': non-hetero female sexuality
  in urban middle-class Bangladesh   269
  Shuchi Karim

11 Risky rights? Gender equality and sexual
  diversity in Muslim contexts   294
  Anissa Hélie

ABOUT THE AUTHORS   335

INDEX   339

Acknowledgements

During a workshop in December 2008 organized as part of the Women's Empowerment in Muslim Contexts (WEMC) research project in Tehran, a heated discussion among scholars and activists arose around defining the field of 'sexuality'. In their view, when sexuality was understood in a broad way participants could engage the public much more: their ability to discuss and mobilize around sexuality issues was enhanced whenever 'sexuality' encompassed larger issues – such as the reform of marriage law, reproductive rights, women's control over their bodies, the right of women and individuals to enjoy their sexuality, the importance of consensual sexual relations (including same-sex), as well as issues of dress code and compulsory veiling. They believed that the narrowing of the field, particularly after the Cairo conference (1994), and the increased focus on sexual orientation had actually disadvantaged LGBTTI groups, at least in the increasingly conservative Muslim contexts. They were sure that feminists faced similar problems in the rest of the Middle East and North Africa region, if not in many other Muslim contexts.

These concerns remained with me, even though I was aware that the reasons for the shrinking space for wider discourses on sexual rights and sexual minorities stemmed in large part from the rise of neoliberal economic policies, religious conservatism and fundamentalism, particularly under the leadership of the Vatican and proponents of Wahhabi Islam. When WEMC teams met in February 2009 in Hong Kong to discuss cross-cutting issues between the countries involved in the research, I presented the Iranian team's concerns. Instantly this opened up the debate. Indonesian team members had even more to say on the topic. In particular, they reflected on how political Islamists used the narrow equating of sexuality with LGBTTI to shut down any broader conversation on sexual autonomy, which in the end hindered holistic political advocacy for the rights of both women and stigmatized sexualities. Pakistani team members shared similar stories, particularly in areas where Taliban ideology had penetrated deep.

As a result of this workshop, with the support of Shirkat Gah Women's Resource Center (Lahore, Pakistan) and Concordia University (Montreal, Canada), we organized a subsequent workshop in April 2009 in Montreal and invited several experts in the field, including Anissa Hélie, to flesh out a broader conceptual framework on sexuality in Muslim contexts, exploring the intersections of various dimensions of sexuality, 'Muslimness' and women's lives. This book is the result of that process. Anissa Hélie graciously accepted the invitation to join the book project and played a central role in making it happen. Anissa Hélie wishes to thank John Jay College of Criminal Justice, where she is an assistant professor in the history department, for the support it has extended to her: the teaching release was crucial and allowed her to focus on this project.

Anissa and I are indebted to many women who took part in the WEMC research project workshops, as well as contributors who joined us later to share their work with us. We are grateful to Shirkat Gah for its continued support for this project, and for providing us with the financial resources to make this book possible. We would like to thank Ariane Brunet, who agreed to participate in the April 2009 workshop, and who patiently hosted several subsequent working meetings, providing us with her valuable comments and insights along the way. Most especially we thank Farida Shaheed, whose timely interventions and continuous support were instrumental in transforming ideas into action. Without her this book would simply not have materialized. We are also appreciative of the efforts of our contributors, who patiently agreed to rework their chapters and address our comments; of Rima Athar, who was indispensable in coordinating this project, keeping in touch with our contributors, working on multiple drafts, and pulling together the final manuscript; and of Marlene Caplan, who worked under pressure of our deadlines as our external editor to improve our diverse styles of writing.

Glossary

'Awrah   Shameful; private parts – for men, it is often defined as the area between knees and navel; for women, all the body apart from hands, feet and face. [In Indonesian and Farsi, *aurat*.] The term is linked to concepts of modesty (specifically what should not be seen in public), a notion that is subject to ongoing debates with the bodily parts that are considered *'awrah* being redefined in various Muslim contexts.

Abaya   A kind of overall worn as a style of veiling in some Muslim communities.

Ador   Caresses. [Bengali]

Ahadith   Plural of Hadith; sayings ascribed to the Prophet.

Ahkam   Plural of *hukm*, rulings, law.

Ahong   Female Muslim religious leader (i.e. women imams) in Mandarin from the origin of Farsi/Persian word *akhond*.

Amrad   A term/concept referring to male teenagers who are often praised/ objects of desire by older men for their youthful attractiveness and who may be involved in same-sex conduct.

Aqd al-nikah   Marriage contract, religious marriage ceremony. Literally 'contract of coitus'. Also often referred to as *nikah*.

Ayatollah   Highly and formally educated Shi'i Muslim legal scholars.

Bajaar er meye   Market girl. [Bengali]

Basij   A militia force in Iran, set up in 1979 to protect the principles of the Islamic Revolution.

Basiji   A member of *basij* organization in Iran, heralded by the state as 'vanguards of the revolution'.

Bon   Sister. [Bengali]

Burqa An enveloping outer garment worn by women in some Muslim communities (most prevalent in Afghanistan and part of India) to cover their bodies head to toe in public places. It usually also includes a face veil.

Caliph A successor in the caliphate political system established by early Muslims at the early stage of Islam. In theory it was an elite (Medina) consultative system which represented Muslim unity.

Chador A cape-like head-to-toe covering worn by women in Iran and certain parts of other Muslim countries.

Dar-ul Qazas Network of Islamic courts. The expression is used in most Arab and Farsi contexts.

Dayanim at battei din Religious courts [in Palestinian context].

Eid of *Ghadir Khom* The celebration of the day that Shia Muslims believe the Prophet appointed his son-in-law, Ali Ibn Abi Talib, as his successor.

Fatwa A non-binding opinion on a point of religious law rendered by a *mufti* (learned scholar) in response to questions submitted to him by a private individual or a *qadi*.

Fiqh Jurisprudence; generally used to refer to Muslim laws as developed by jurists in various schools of law.

Fitna Chaos, a threat to the social order. [In Indonesian and Farsi, *fitnah*.]

Fitra Nature – human nature. [In Indonesian, *fitrah*.]

Fudao Female morality. [Mandarin]

Funü jiefang Women's liberation. [Mandarin]

Ghairat 'Honour', sexual honour and jealousy.

Hadith Sayings ascribed to the Prophet. Plural: *Ahadith*.

Hailifan Religious trainees. [Mandarin]

Hajj A pilgrimage to Mecca, Saudi Arabia. It is one of the five pillars of Islam.

Halal Permitted, lawful.

Haram Prohibited, unlawful.

Haya Shame, modesty.

Hidayatnama Marriage guidelines for brides and grooms under Muslim laws and traditions.

Hijab A headscarf for women, veil. Literally 'barrier'.

Hijra Individuals and communities of feminine transgender identity prevalent across South Asia; gender-nonconforming; transgendered. [Bengali]

Houshi Afterlife. [Mandarin]

Hukum Judgment, legal verdict.

'Ibadat Worship, pertaining to devotional matters.

Iddat The waiting period that a Muslim woman must observe following the divorce, or death, of her husband under Muslim family codes.

During *iddat*, the woman cannot marry another man in order to establish paternity.

'Iffat Chastity, decency.

Ijab & qabul 'Offer and acceptance' of the terms and conditions of a marriage contract.

Ijtihad Independent reasoning.

Imam Ali The son-in-law of the Prophet Muhammad, and according to Shi'i belief his first and only legitimate successor.

Iqa' A unilateral act.

'Iwad A wife's compensation to the husband for agreeing to a divorce. Sometimes erroneously referred to as divorce by 'mutual consent', despite the wife buying her release.

Izzat Honour, respect.

Jalabia A traditional loose long dress and overall that women and men wear in many Arab countries.

Jama' Sexual intercourse.

Jiaoshi Female teachers. [Mandarin]

Jie Purity. [Mandarin]

Jihad Struggle, striving to achieve a goal. Although today it is often understood as a military war to advance Islam or Muslim causes, in its original meaning it often refers to struggles against one's own selfish desires and striving to be a good Muslim.

Jilbab Refers to the tight headscarf that covers at least the hair, ears and neck, but it can be much longer. Contrasts to *kerudung*, which is a looser scarf which may not fully enclose hair and neck. [Indonesian]

Jingge Islamic songs of moral instruction.

Jingtang Mosque-based Islamic education. [Mandarin]

Jinshi Human life marked by transitoriness. [Mandarin]

Juzíyya Fragmented.

Kafir A derogative term for 'non-Muslim'.

Karahiya Reluctance, strong dislike. One of the grounds on which a woman can demand divorce from her husband under Muslim laws.

Kebaya A style of blouse first worn in Indonesia some time during the fifteenth or sixteenth century. The style since evolved through various influences.

Khala Aunt. [Bengali]

Khalwat Seclusion; close proximity between a man and a woman who are not close relatives.

Khitān Cutting of female genital parts. [Indonesian]

Khul' A form of divorce available to Muslim women.

La ikrah-a fi'ddin 'There is no compulsion in religion'; a popular concept and phrase among Muslims, promoted by many religious leaders, indicating that religious belief cannot be forced on people.

Mahr/Meher Dower. An intrinsic part of Muslim marriage contracts; a material gift that a man gives or pledges to give the wife at the time of marriage.

Mahram 'Forbidden'; refers to members of the opposite sex (who have reached puberty) with whom marriage and sexual intercourse are forbidden.

Makrumah Venerated.

Mazhab/Madhab Different Islamic schools or sects.

Mosaheqeh Female same-sex relations. [Farsi]

Mosque Muslim house of worship.

Mu'amilat Social/contractual acts; duties to people.

Mubah Religiously neutral.

Mufti A formally appointed high-ranking religious leader in Sunni Muslim contexts.

Muhtaseb In the contemporary era, refers to the 'Office for Propagating of Virtue and Prevention of Vice'. Historically, however, it was a Muslim institution mainly responsible for overseeing market transactions and taxation.

Mujahideen Conventionally, refers to people who fight in the name of Muslim ideology. See also *jihad*.

Mullah The common title given to lay and lower-rank religious leaders.

Murtad Apostates.

Musawah Equality. Also the name of a transnational campaign working to establish transnational guidelines for Muslim family laws based on gender equality.

Mutawwa'in Saudi Arabian moral police force. See also *muhtaseb* for its origins.

Nafaqa Maintenance of wife and children.

Nari-premi Love for women. [Bengali]

Nari shomo-premi Women-loving women. [Bengali]

Nikah Marriage ceremony.

Nikahnama Marriage contract document.

Niqab A face covering worn by women which leaves only the eyes visible; worn by various ethnic groups more commonly in the Gulf.

Nowruz New year celebrations on the first day of spring. Originates from Zoroastrianism; celebrated in Afghanistan, the Balkans, Iran and Kurdistan.

Nü ahong Female religious leaders. [Mandarin]

Nürenjing The book of religious scripture from which specifically women learn. [Mandarin]

Nushuz Disobedient (usually used in reference to wives who do not obey their husband).

Obbhyash A 'tendency' or practice; refers specifically to same-sex male sexual behaviour. [Bengali]

Polygyny A gendered relationship of ownership, whereby a woman's body as property is accessible only to her husband as property-owner, who may have more than one property (i.e. multiple wives). As opposed to polygamy, which could be relationships of ownership over either sex.

Purdah Literally veil or curtain; veiling and/or seclusion of women; sometimes interpreted as an entire code of conduct for women from Muslim communities.

Qadi A judge.

Qaṭ'i Immutable.

Qiancheng Pious or devout. [Mandarin]

Qisas Retribution.

Qiwama A husband's (mixture of) dominion and protection over his wife.

Qudah at mahakim shar'iyya Religious courts.

Qur'an The holy book of Islam, regarded as divine by those who believe it to consist of the exact words of God (Allah) as revealed to the Prophet Muhammad.

Rubandeh A face-covering worn by women. [Farsi] See *niqab*.

Sakhi Intra-female friendship. [Bengali]

Samaj Human society; any one of the divisions of biological history; a community; a nation or race; a collective body of people having something in common, a class, a community an association; a gathering, especially a social one. [Bengali]

Sancong The 'three subordinations' of a woman: to her father before marriage, to her husband in marriage, and to her son in widowhood. [Mandarin]

Shahvat Sexual desire, lust, passion. [Bengali]

Shakha Male bonding. [Bengali]

Shari'a A term commonly but erroneously used to refer to the body of religious 'laws' that are said to be derived from Islam. Contrary to popular belief, there is no single, homogeneous set of Muslim laws or practices which can be labelled *shari'a*; it is important to recognize the great diversity among Muslim communities and schools of law.

Shari'a/Shariat Courts Courts that use Muslim laws as the basis of their judgments.

Shi'i/Shi'a Ten per cent of all Muslims belong to the Shi'i sect. For them, after the death of the Prophet the leadership of the Muslim community passed not to the elected caliphs but to his descendants, the Imams. Shi'i are a majority population in Iran and Iraq, and there are substantial minorities in several other countries, primarily in Asia.

Shifu Master. [Mandarin]

Shiniang Title of an *ahong's* wife. [Mandarin]

Shomo-kaami Same-sex desire; *shomo* = same; *kaami* = desiring/lustful/ lover. [Bengali]

Shomo-premi Love for the same. [Bengali]

Shongshar Family household. [Bengali]

Side Women's virtues, manifest in her industrious labour, modest appearance, refined speech, and seemly behaviour. [Mandarin]

Sigheh A religious agreement between two persons. It is often known as a reference to temporary marriage, but in Iran many women use this as a way of consolidating their relations with other women as 'sisters'.

Sitr Covering, in terms of dress; concealing.

Sufi A person adhering to Sufism, which stresses the mystical and spiritual dimension of Islam.

Sunna/Sunnah The practice (acts, deeds/omissions and words) of the Prophet Muhammad.

Sunni Followers of the Sunna; the majority Muslim denomination, with four main schools of *fiqh*: Hanafi, Maliki, Shafi'i and Hanbali.

Ta'a See *Tamkin*.

Tabir Curtain.

Talabeh A student at a religious seminary. In Iran it can refer to a female student.

Talaq Repudiation, unilateral divorce exercised by Muslim men.

Talaq-e tafwiz Option for delegated divorce.

Tamkin/Ta'a Obedience, submission; the wife's duty in marriage, and the husband's right.

Tawhid The oneness of God.

Ulama Highly educated and knowledgeable persons in issues of Muslim laws as well as other intellectual matters, such as philosophy.

Wahhabi A very orthodox and sectarian interpretation of Islam that is primarily practised in Saudi Arabia but is increasingly exported into other regions through Salafist networks.

Wali A Guardian, a marriage guardian; commonly recognized as the father or paternal grandfather who has authority to contract a marriage on behalf of a girl.

Xiuti Shame. [Mandarin]

Yicong A wife's obedience and submission to her husband. [Mandarin]

Zina Sexual intercourse outside of legal marriage (*nikah*).

INTRODUCTION

Policing gender, sexuality and 'Muslimness'

Anissa Hélie

This book looks at emerging trends that affect women's sexuality, with a particular focus on Asia and the Middle East, and documents both the curtailing of sexual rights occurring in diverse Muslim societies and the strategies designed to counter these developments. Yet this focus in no way suggests that the policing of gender and sexuality is unique to Muslim societies: rather, bodily rights, sexual conduct and gender expression are regulated in all societies. Throughout the world, a range of actors – from families to communities to governments – refer selectively to 'Western values', 'Christian values', 'African values', 'Jewish tradition' or 'Muslimness' to justify stigmatization and repression.

Nonetheless, there is a widespread tendency to posit gender equality and emancipation within the sexual realm as products of modern – or 'Western'-inspired – reforms. On the one hand, conservatives and Islamists in Muslim communities reject gender equality and gender plurality as impositions from 'the West'. On the other hand, Western discourses (from popular media to mainstream journalism to academic writing) often stigmatize Muslim communities for limitations placed on both women's rights and bodily rights. The authors here reject this reductive perspective. They recognize that such an approach not only ignores the sexual plurality that existed in Muslim communities and cultures prior to encounters with 'the West',[1] but also fails to recognize the way women in Muslim societies have designed empowerment strategies within their own societies that draw on existing traditions. The assumption that any movement towards sexual emancipation in Muslim communities must be linked to 'Western' influence carries the risk that advocacy around women's empowerment[2] and sexual rights will continue to be dismissed as foreign and imported from/imposed by 'the West'.

Instead, the essays in this anthology discuss the means people in Muslim societies employ to negotiate sexuality in their specific contexts: all contributors explore infringements on expressions of sexuality, and document the ways through which social actors confront a range of challenges, using a variety of means.

While rejecting the assumptions that Muslim societies are unique in policing women's sexuality, and that any movement towards greater emancipation is linked to Western influence, the essays in this volume nevertheless recognize that sexuality remains one of the cornerstones through which 'Muslimness' is enforced. Thus, it is critical to question the very concept of 'Muslimness'. What is it supposed to convey? Who defines it? And how is it used to legitimize the control of sexuality, with women and stigmatized sexualities being particularly targeted?

These are important questions at a time when widespread references to the 'Muslim world' (which is by no means the monolithic whole suggested by this formula) tend to obscure the complex historical, cultural, economic and political legacies that shape specific Muslim societies. The notion of a 'Muslim world' also ignores the fact that the meanings attached to 'Islam' vary not only between different societies but within them, with individuals or groups adopting different beliefs and practices.

In the same vein, the concept of 'Muslimness' erroneously suggests homogeneity among communities whose understandings of Islam may vary widely. Far from being designed to transcend existing differences, the discourse of 'Muslimness' purposely ignores diversities that exist and operate across and within Muslim communities, and projects a diasporic identity centred on an 'imaginary transnational Muslim culture' (Hélie-Lucas 2004). Often promoted by actors linked to political Islam, this essentialist representation is a political construct that portrays 'Muslimness' as unified and Islam as monolithic in order to establish a set of totalizing 'truths'.

First, Islam is no longer understood simply as a question of belief (as related to personal faith); instead, it becomes an all-encompassing identity – one that should shape an individual's sense of self, as well as the collective code of conduct. In addition, the notion of 'Muslimness' supports the transformation of Muslim-*majority* countries into 'Muslim countries'; in the process, long-standing contributions of non-Muslim religious minorities, as well as those of secular-minded people, are minimized or erased. In this view, anyone born in a Muslim-majority culture is automatically assumed to be a believer who should be made to behave according to prevailing cultural norms. Further, this definition of 'Muslimness' is posited as impossible to challenge because it is cast as deriving from an ahistorical 'Muslim identity' which is divinely ordained. The consequence is that alternative visions of what it may mean to be a Muslim are dismissed as culturally irrelevant; they may even be denounced as blasphemous, a charge that can lead to severe sanctions imposed on individuals or entire communities (including the death sentence).

In short, the conventional, commonly used construction of 'Muslimness' derives from a conservative political agenda that seeks to implement an ideal 'Islamic society'. This definition relies heavily on sexual repression, of women and stigmatized sexualities in particular. Thus the idea of 'Muslimness' tends to strengthen exclusionary discourses and to emphasize that personal behaviour and social norms – especially in the sexual arena – should reflect 'Muslim values'.

The chapters in this volume focus on the many ways that culture, expressions of religiosity and sexual conduct manifest themselves through time and space. Contributors also document recent trends in various Muslim-majority countries where religious arguments are used to deny the complexity and fluidity with which customs, religion and sexuality intersect. Indeed, as noted above, the current policing of sexuality is often justified through discourses of moral codes, cultural 'authenticity' and religion. In Muslim communities around the world, conservative forces and actors linked to the religious right rely on selective interpretations of Islam to oppose sexual diversity and gender equality. Challenging such trends, this book relies on the premiss that all major religious traditions, as understood and practised in today's world, can promote either emancipatory or conservative standpoints. Within each religious tradition, a broad range of interpretations of religious scriptures, combined with diverse and locally defined cultural values, can lead either to promotion or to denial of sexual rights for all.

This volume embraces a broad view of sexuality and sexual rights – in contrast to most of the existing scholarship, which tends to privilege either the question of women's sexual and bodily rights (with all women assumed to be heterosexual) or the rights of sexual and gender minorities.[3] Given that the field of sexuality has been recently dominated by issues relating to sexual orientation (and, to a lesser degree, to questions of gender identity), current debates often de-emphasize or ignore the links between compulsory heterosexuality and other forms of control of women. This book intends to broaden the lens through which sexuality is analysed. For example, it is commonly understood that a trans-identified person or a bisexual individual can be seen as challenging established 'Muslim norms'. It is less widely recognized that, depending on the context, a woman may be seen as similarly challenging such norms if she is divorced; if she refuses to marry altogether; if she mingles outside her caste, class, ethnic or religious group; if she refuses to observe the prevalent dress code; or if she seeks work.

Since 'sexuality is influenced by the interaction of biological, psychological, social, economic, political, cultural, ethical, legal, historical and religious and spiritual factors' (WHO 2010), numerous elements other than sexual orientation remain tightly linked to local understandings of sexuality and to notions of modesty or promiscuity. The linkages between sexuality and female dress codes, or between sexuality and the gendered provisions of marriage laws, are made explicit in the case studies presented here. The contributors understand both the centrality of sexuality as a site of control and the varied methods of operation of conservative forces in Muslim contexts. Their broad framework of analysis brings into visibility the connections between the repression of women's sexuality and the repression of stigmatized sexualities. At a time when human rights advocates deplore the fragmentation of progressive efforts in the arena of sexual and reproductive rights,[4] the perspectives presented here highlight the potential for larger coalitions that would promote a shared understanding that the notion of sexual rights must truly encompass sexual rights for all.

Finally, although this volume explores how people in Muslim societies engage with sexuality differently in a variety of contexts, religious identity is not its main focus. While it is certainly true that discrepancies between the discourses promoted by religious leaders and the actual practices of believers can lead to dynamic tensions and negotiations, religion is far from the only parameter impacting the politics of sexuality and gender empowerment. Despite pervasive claims positing Islam as the main marker of identity in Muslim communities, women, men and trans persons from Muslim contexts are reclaiming the right to shape their own cultures, within as well as outside religious frameworks. As elsewhere, they are engaged in defining not only their (sexual, cultural, gendered) subcultures, but their societies as a whole.

The volume highlights the diversity of concerns, obstacles, opportunities and forms of resistance within the so-called Muslim world. As noted, this mapping exercise is critical at a time when conservative coalitions of both non-state actors and governments insist on enforcing narrowly defined sexual norms, which are often promoted as Muslim values or Asian values. Furthermore, the rise of Islamist rhetoric is made more powerful through its manipulation of Western democracies, which are sometimes blinded by (or even opportunistic about) misguided arguments favouring cultural relativism. The ongoing competition between legal arguments upholding gender equality and arguments linked to religious freedom is a significant marker of current and serious threats to stigmatized sexualities and women's individual and collective rights. Yet, concurrent with these troubling indications, there is an unprecedented wave of organizing around sexuality issues, and evidence of ongoing local efforts. Recognizing the ability of local actors to challenge oppressive structures, this volume seeks to make women's and LGBTT people's agency more visible, providing testimonies about their ongoing engagements with sexuality, and about the tensions produced in the course of that struggle.

The writings here offer a combination of insights, ranging from the perspectives of advocates and activists grounded in specific contexts to academic analyses coming from a variety of disciplines, including history, anthropology, gender studies, law and political science. In contrast with much of the available research that tends to concentrate on case studies linked to a specific cultural or historical setting,[5] the chapters also reflect the constraints and opportunities of a broader variety of socio-political contexts: the book's geographical focus encompasses Iran, Pakistan, Bangladesh, India, Indonesia, Israel, China, Saudi Arabia, Algeria and Malaysia, with additional examples pertaining to Lebanon, Turkey and Morocco. The authors map the restrictions individuals – women in particular – face, as well as the avenues they find for change. A central focus of the book is the ways women analyse, address and resist the mechanisms of sexual control; while the essays here report on gender ideologies promoted by states and/or customary traditions, they emphasize women's and LGBTT people's contestations.

Country case studies, for instance, provide evidence of indigenous strategies that women, as well as people stigmatized for their gender expression or sexuality, have designed – either collectively or as individuals – to mobilize for bodily rights. The various chapters are thematically unified in their emphasis on the varied paths that local actors pursue towards empowerment. The authors' combined scholarship suggests that there is a range of ways to reach this goal: from individual to collective, oppositional to coalition-building. One key argument is that transformative resistance is more likely to lead to social change where social actors develop strategies that are grounded in their specific settings. Several chapters present research from field work carried out through the Women's Empowerment in Muslim Contexts programme (WEMC),[6] offering concrete data drawing from women's grassroots understanding of sexuality as including 'perhaps less obvious areas of sexual control such as dress codes, marriage contracts, criminalization of sexuality'. Several chapters stress the impact of customary practices on women's lives and agency, as well as the impact of non-state actors[7] in policing their communities. The book reflects these concerns through explorations of both historical processes and current contexts.

Part I, 'Tools of Policing: The Politics of History, Community, Law', combines chapters pertaining to widely different political contexts, including Muslim states such as Indonesia, Iran, Pakistan and Muslim-minority communities in Israel and India. Historical constructions of gender and sexuality are addressed in two different settings: Vivienne Wee focuses on Indonesia, and Claudia Yaghoobi on Iran. Both authors sketch the evolution of past and current constructions of gender and sexuality, and both stress the links between gendered sexual norms and broader cultural and political processes.

Wee reports on the drive to police sexuality currently enacted by both the Indonesian government and Islamist non-state actors. She shows that this policing, while 'justified' by references to Islam, in fact draws from earlier periods. She evokes, for example, Dutch colonial officials' attempts to 'reform' indigenous populations by introducing indecency laws to curb their supposedly wild sexuality. She also notes policies enacted by the Suharto regime to control political opponents. Wee argues that the progressive obscenification of women's bodily parts has much to do with political agendas.

In a similar vein, Yaghoobi explores the links between modernity and the gradual casting of homosociability as a backward social practice which occurred in Iran in the late nineteenth century. Yaghoobi also considers strategies designed by Iranian women's rights advocates during the period from the Constitutional Revolution of 1905 to the post-1979 Islamic Revolution, concluding with a brief overview of the role played by sexuality in the more recent Green movement.

The chapter by Hooria Hayat Khan, on Pakistan, reflects on the issue of policing within and by communities. It includes a discussion of the crucial roles of customary practices in defining what constitutes acceptable women's sexuality, and in sanctioning those who dare to defy tribal norms. Khan's case study is anchored in Balochistan, but it illuminates how sexual norms are enforced by non-state actors in a variety of other settings, particularly in contexts where legal and cultural spheres overlap. While women have occasionally been able to use customary traditions to enhance their rights[8] (hence illustrating that local customs do not always work to women's disadvantage), Khan's data raise the urgent question of what happens to women, in particular, where states are unwilling or unable to enforce even marginally progressive laws and, instead, allow harsh traditions to prevail.

Part I also includes two chapters focusing on formal legal frameworks. Yüksel Sezgin offers a comparative examination of restrictive legal norms and of women's resistance in two non-Muslim-majority countries. Focusing on marriage and divorce among Muslim minorities in Israel and India, Sezgin highlights the degree to which strategies around women's sexuality are intricately entangled with identity politics in contexts where women attempt to increase their autonomy while at the same time demonstrating their allegiance to their community. The realities of Israel's treatment of its 'Arab citizens' renders the situation of Palestinians in Israel (Muslims and others) much more drastic in all respects, but the Indian Muslim minority also experiences heavy forms of discrimination within the Hindu-majority state.[9] Sezgin explores how tensions between women's rights and majority-minority politics leads to complex strategizing within ethno-religious communities, particularly regarding the (dis)advantages of using either secular or religious strategies to effect change at the community level in terms of women's access to divorce and maintenance.

Ziba Mir-Hosseini proposes a general analysis of the legitimization of women's unequal status in Muslim legal traditions, with a focus on marriage contracts and dress codes. Grounding her discussion on classical jurists' rulings, Mir-Hosseini raises the analogy between marriage regulations and slavery – an institution which, while 'repugnant to modern sensibilities', was prevalent enough to influence pre-modern interpretations of religious scriptures. Recognizing the variety of conceptual frameworks that regulate both marriage and dress codes, she argues that this range of opinion produces welcome tensions and allows feminist scholarship to challenge gender inequality from a religious perspective. These reinterpretation efforts, she contends, are particularly crucial given the regressive gender policies enacted in various Muslim contexts since the 1980s.

Together, the chapters of Part I establish clearly that tools of policing tend to be both varied and overlapping: states, communities and religious institutions all use history, culture and identity – including the concept of 'Muslimness' – as powerful frameworks to control women's (and men's) bodies and minds.

In the chapters of Part II, 'Sites of Contestation: Reclaiming Public Spaces', contributors identify public spaces as both sites of negotiation and sites of contestation. In doing so, they illuminate the fact that the behaviour of 'private' bodies within 'public' spaces is as crucial to politico-religious forces seeking to curtail sexual rights as it is to individuals or organized collectives who seek to resist specific policing practices. Contributions in Part II address trends that have emerged with regard to a variety of public spaces; most report on contemporary expressions of resistance that are innovative, diverse and powerful. They record the reclaiming of public spaces by both women and stigmatized sexualities in locales as varied as China, Iran, Pakistan, Bangladesh, Saudi Arabia, Algeria and Malaysia.

China, despite having an estimated Muslim population of 21 million, is often overlooked in research relating to Muslim contexts. Maria Jaschok and Shui Jingjun focus on China's long-established tradition of female preachers, specifically on women's mosques in the Northern region. The data on two female *ahong* describe how these individuals deal with expectations surrounding their role as spiritual leaders, who must convey notions of purity and modesty, while highlighting how their public persona provides them with the necessary authority to negotiate the sexual arena of their own private lives. This discussion is also relevant to the broader debate regarding women as religious leaders, particularly as female imams face opposition from male religious authorities from Morocco[10] to the USA.[11]

Equally relevant to current developments (with the Iranian government reviving attempts to tighten the regulation of Internet cafés and planning to launch a 'national Internet' that would limit access to the World Wide Web),[12] Shadi Sadr attests to the vibrancy of online debates in Iran. Focusing on cyberspace as a public space occupied by a majority of urban middle-class and young voices, she presents the findings of an innovative research project aiming to document citizens' diverse assessments of the regime's policies on veiling. In reviewing the lively blog discussions, she contrasts public and private discourses on the *hijab* issue in a context of strictly censored state media. She also calls attention to the fact that dress codes – one of the regime's most visible assertions of power since the imposition of compulsory *hijab* in 1983 – are being subverted and redefined as political statements in defiance of the Iranian authorities.[13]

Focusing on the same Iranian context where women's bodies are framed as always erotic and often obscene, Homa Hoodfar examines sports events as critical public venues for the assertion of autonomy. Echoing Sadr's Internet-based controversies, Hoodfar's discussion of the Open Stadiums Campaign also documents 'non-organized' ways of resisting the exclusion of women from the public sphere. She reviews the limitations imposed by the post-1979 regime on women's participation in sport (as both practitioners and viewers) and shows how over the last three decades Iranian women have, through reclaiming the sports arena in a context of strict gender segregation, invested political meaning into terrains that were not previously defined as overtly 'political'.

The chapter by Homa Hoodfar and Ana Ghoreishian maps out various forms of morality policing and shows how the regulation of sexuality has effectively shrunk the public spaces available to women in a variety of contexts. While the authors emphasize context-specific strategies designed by women to promote agency and to boost visibility, this chapter also testifies to the broader, cross-regional trend that aims at controlling female bodies in the public arena. Hoodfar and Ghoreishian offer case studies of moral policing enacted as part of state legislations (as in Saudi Arabia and Iran) as well as case studies of moral policing enforced primarily by non-state actors (as in Algeria and Malaysia), for example through religious leaders pronouncing *fatwas*. Whether institutionalized or not, these forms of gendered policing increasingly gain currency as a legitimate enforcement of 'Muslimness'.

Shuchi Karim focuses on Bangladesh and specifically on the experiences of women with non-normative sexualities in middle-class urban areas, Dhaka in particular. Karim relies on data collected through interviews with individuals ranging from professionals to commercial sex workers. She explores how women deal with internalized gender roles in a context marked by heteronormativity and an emphasis on marriage and childbearing – and how at the same time they are able to negotiate their lives in a society where homosociability and sex segregation can offer alternatives spaces to follow one's desires.

Anissa Hélie contrasts the emphasis on victimization of both 'Muslim women' and 'gay Muslims' in mainstream Western discourses with actual strategies designed by advocates of gender equality and sexual rights, including reinterpretation efforts in South Africa and Indonesia, and organizing geared towards public visibility in Lebanon, Turkey and Morocco. Deconstructing the false dichotomy between an 'enlightened West' and 'oppressive Muslim contexts', she insists on the need to take into account various factors that impact the ability of both individuals and collectives to claim bodily rights. Drawing the links between limitations placed on women's rights and discrimination based on sexual orientation and gender identity, Hélie argues that broader coalitions should be build if gender equality is to be achieved.

The contributions to Part II acknowledge that expressions of resistance need not necessarily be spectacular, and that individual, even seemingly modest, achievements play a role in challenging mainstream constructions of 'Muslimness'. Overall, *Sexuality in Muslim Contexts: Restrictions and Resistance* provides evidence of sustained and ongoing local efforts – ranging from individual assertions of leadership to judicial lobbying, to religious reinterpretation, to alliances across identity lines – and attests to the fact that social actors in Muslim societies are engaged in redefining, resisting and subverting narrow constructions of sexuality and gender.

Notes

1. Commonly associated with nineteenth-century Western colonization, the notion of 'encounters with the West' is historically debatable given the scope of global economic and cultural exchanges that have taken place since the early days of Islam.
2. We rely here on the understanding of women's empowerment put forward by the Women's Empowerment in Muslim Contexts research programme consortium (WEMC, see note 6), which defines empowerment as 'women's increased capacity to take autonomous decisions that challenge power relations which are detrimental to them'. See www.wemc.com.hk/web/index.htm (accessed 10 January 2012).
3. The collections by Ilkkaracan are an exception to this rule. See *Deconstructing Sexuality in the Middle East – Challenges and Discourses* (2008); and *Women and Sexuality in Muslim Societies* (2000).
4. For a discussion on this issue, see for example Reproductive Health Matters 2011.
5. Recently, much valuable research has explored the issue of sexuality in specific Muslim contexts, such as India or Iran – see, for example, Vanita 2002; Vanita and Kidwai 2002; Najmabadi 2005, 2012; Amer 2008; Babayan and Najmabadi 2008; Afary 2009. For work emphasizing specifically male sexuality, see for example Ouzgane 2006; and El-Rouayeb 2009.
6. From July 2006 to June 2010 WEMC was a multi-country research, communication and capacity-building programme, carried out in China, Indonesia, Pakistan and Iran, as well as among two cross-border populations – Afghan refugees and returnees, and Indonesian migrant women

workers. Focusing on the nexus between culture, religion and democratic rights, WEMC documented, analysed and multiplied women's successful strategies to negotiate and transform disempowering socio-economic and legal structures, engendering long-term changes in policy and practice supportive of women's empowerment in Muslim contexts. See www. wemc.com.hk/web/index.htm.

7. 'Non-state actors' refers to individuals or groups who are not linked to state institutions (such as law enforcement, judiciary, etc.) and include, for example, families or community members.

8. The ambitious Women and Law collective research, carried out in 1991–2001 by the international solidarity network Women Living Under Muslim Laws (WLUML) in over twenty countries, has documented various examples of women taking advantage of customary practices to claim their rights (WLUML 2006). An illuminating example from the Khyber Pakhtunkhwa province in Pakistan, collected during the course of the Women and Law research by the Shirkat Gah research team, Lahore, shows how a rural woman used her native ingenuity simultaneously to obtain a divorce from her husband and to annul her husband's marriage to another woman. When she learnt that her husband was going to take a second wife, she asked her husband to divorce her, but he refused. Since she failed either to prevent his second marriage or to obtain a divorce, this woman devised an innovative strategy. She was breastfeeding her baby at the time and offered her husband and new wife tea in which she had added a few drops of her own milk. Once they drank it, she confronted them with a long-standing tradition in her community which established that no man can marry a woman who had nursed him, and that individuals who were nursed by the same woman cannot enter into marriage. By drinking her milk, her husband became 'forbidden' to her (as his putative 'mother'); and at the same time the husband and second wife also (as putative 'siblings') became *haram* to each other. The husband was outraged and approached the local *maulvi* and elders, who agreed that the woman was correct and that having drunk her milk both marriages stood dissolved. While this story can be read as evidence of autonomy, it also illustrates an issue raised in Khan's chapter, namely the difficulty for some women to access formal rights and formal courts.

9. For a gender perspective on the most recent large-scale attacks on the Muslim community in 2002 in Gujarat, see for example the discussion on sexual violence by International Initiative for Justice in Gujarat (2003) in *Threatened Existence: A Feminist Analysis of the Genocide in Gujarat*, co-authored by S. Abeysekara, U. Chakravarti, R. Copelon, A. Hélie, G. Mischokowski, V. Nainar, F. Naqvi, M. Velayudan and N. Yuval-Davis.

10. Following the state-sponsored one-year religious training of female imams (initiated in 2005 by the Moroccan Ministry of Habous and Islamic Affairs), the first promotion of *morchidates* in 2009 saw their role restricted by a *fatwa* issued by the High Council of Ulama forbidding the new graduates from leading prayers, including to entirely female audiences (Eddouada 2009; Lamlili n.d.).

11. For relatively recent developments in the US context, see for example the controversy around Amina Wadud leading prayers in 2005 in New York City.

12. Note that the Iranian government has tried to curtail Internet access for years – this is only the latest attempt, most likely in anticipation of the spring 2012 parliamentary elections (Deghan 2012).

13. Many Iranian women, particularly urban women, subvert compulsory veiling on a daily basis, for example by adopting highly visible (i.e. potentially 'immodest') scarves, or by letting strands of hair show. Interestingly, in December 2009, young men also attempted to ridicule the prescribed dress codes for women: reacting to the arrest of a Green Movement leader, Majid Tavakoli (whose veiled picture was circulated by the authorities in an attempt to humiliate him), hundreds expressed their solidarity by posting on the Internet portraits of themselves wearing a *hijab*.

References

Afary, J. (2009) *Sexual Politics in Modern Iran*. Cambridge: Cambridge University Press.

Amer, S. (2008) *Crossing Borders: Love between Women in Medieval French and Arabic Literatures*. Philadelphia: University of Pennsylvania Press.

Babayan, K., and Najmabadi, A. (eds) (2008) *Islamicate Sexualities: Translations across Temporal Geographies of Desire*. Cambridge MA: Harvard University Press.

Reproductive Health Matters (2011) 'Repoliticizing sexual and reproductive health and rights', *Reproductive Health Matters* 19(38), November: 4–10.

Deghan, S.K. (2012) 'Iran clamps down on internet use', *Guardian*, 5 January, www.guardian.co.uk/world/2012/jan/05/iran-clamps-down-internet-use?CMP=twt_gu (accessed 6 January 2012).

Eddouada, S. (2009) 'Morocco's "mourchidates" and contradictions', *Reset – Dialogues on Civilizations*, 17 April, www.resetdoc.org/story/00000001323 (accessed 1 January 2012).

El-Rouayeb, K. (2009) *Before Homosexuality in the Arab-Islamic World, 1500–1800*. Chicago: University of Chicago Press.

Hélie-Lucas, M. (2004) 'What is your tribe? Women's struggles and the construction of Muslimness', *Women Living Under Muslim Laws Dossier 26*, www.wluml.org/node/480 (accessed 30 December 2011).

Ilkkaracan, P. (ed.) (2000) *Women and Sexuality in Muslim Societies*. Istanbul: Women for Women's Human Rights.

Ilkkaracan, P. (ed.) (2008) *Deconstructing Sexuality in the Middle East: Challenges and Discourses*. Farnham: Ashgate.

International Initiative for Justice in Guajarat (2003) *Threatened Existence: A Feminist Analysis of the Genocide in Gujarat*. www.onlinevolunteers.org/gujarat/reports/iijg/2003 (accessed 1 January 2012).

Lamlili, N. (n.d.) 'Femmes imams: Une révolution manquée', *Tel Quel*, www.telquel-online.com/228/maroc2_228.shtml (accessed 1 January 2012).

Najmabadi, A. (2005) *Women with Mustaches and Men without Beards: Gender and Sexual Anxieties of Iranian Modernity.* Berkeley: University of California Press.

Najmabadi, A. (2012) *Sex in Change: Configurations of Sexuality and Gender in Contemporary Iran.* Durham NC: Duke University Press.

Ouzgane, L. (ed.) (2006) *Islamic Masculinities.* London: Zed Books.

Vanita, R. (2002) *Queering India: Same-Sex Love and Eroticism in Indian Culture and Society.* New York: Routledge.

Vanita, R., and Kidwai, S. (eds) (2002) *Same-sex Love in India: Readings from Literature and History.* New Delhi: Macmillan.

WHO (World Health Organization) (2010). 'Gender and human rights – working definition', 16 January, www.who.int/reproductivehealth/topics/gender_rights/sexual_health/en (accessed 30 December 2011).

WLUML (Women Living Under Muslim Laws) (2006) *Knowing Our Rights – Women, Family, Laws and Customs in the Muslim World*, 2nd edn. London: Women Living Under Muslim Laws.

PART I

Tools of policing:
the politics of history, community, law

The politicization of women's bodies in Indonesia: sexual scripts as charters for action

Vivienne Wee

Sexual scripts, indigenous contexts and Islamism

How have women's bodies in Indonesia been politicized by disputed sexual scripts over time? The term 'sexual scripts' refers to two political dimensions: an external interpersonal dimension that generates a discourse shared by two or more persons, and an internal intrapersonal dimension whereby participants internalize such discourse as motivations for action (Gagnon and Simon 2005: 14).[1] I examine sexual scripts as charters for action in Indonesia, including indigenous contexts, external sources of inspiration, and competing normative proposals for the shaping of Islam and Indonesia.[2]

In indigenous contexts prior to conversions to Islam (since the twelfth century) and European colonization (since the sixteenth century), men and women in tropical Southeast Asia enjoyed relative freedom from constraining clothes and gender segregation. With both sexes accorded near-equal importance in the prevalent bilateral kinship system, there was/is relatively little concern with a woman's virginity, the number of her sexual partners, the biological paternity of her child or the production of male heirs (Winzeler et al. 1976: 628). In my research in Indonesia and among Indonesian migrant workers, I encountered many instances of families tolerating premarital sex, women becoming pregnant before marriage, and women migrants bearing children out of wedlock and having their children at home brought up by relatives (see Sim 2006). This indicates relative social acceptance of women's sexual autonomy, in keeping with the relative gender equality of a bilateral kinship system.[3]

Women in the Indonesian archipelago had relative bodily freedom without fear of harassment or rape. Even in the twentieth century, among non-Muslim and non-Christian indigenous populations, women could bare their breasts in the same way as men could bare their chests, without insinuating sexual impropriety. This corroborates the correlation of relative gender equality with rape-free societies, as argued by Sanday (1997).[4] In Riau villages in the 1970s and 1980s, I saw Muslim women wearing sarongs that covered their breasts, leaving shoulders and arms bare, for bathing at public wells, some draping a towel on their backs to cover their shoulders, with no harassment for their state of dress/undress. However, constraints are increasingly imposed by a sexual script that obscenifies customary dress codes and bodily routines as immoral.

Although conversion to Islam began in the Indonesian archipelago in the twelfth century, it did not reach all areas uniformly. Despite the country having the world's largest population of Muslims (about 177.53 million in 2000), the Muslim majority represents only 88 per cent of the population, alongside Christians, Hindus, Buddhists, Confucians, animists and others (Suryadinata et al. 2003: 104). There is diversity even among Muslims, with Islamic traditions derived from 'the Arab world, Persia, India and … the Muslim trading communities of southern China', as well as from varied teachings brought back by Indonesian Muslims studying abroad (Fox 2004: 2–3; see also Riddell 2001, and Azra 2004).

This religious diversity relates to the political diversity that preceded Dutch colonization. Apart from the empires of Srivijaya (twelfth–thirteenth centuries) and Majapahit (fourteenth–fifteenth centuries) that unified sizeable parts of the archipelago, there were diverse tribal societies, Muslim sultanates and Hindu kingdoms (Munoz 2006). No higher level of political unity unified the Muslim sultanates. Religious interpretations varied between sultanates and between the reigns of different rulers, often influenced by foreign Muslims (Federspiel 2007).

To illustrate, in Sulawesi (in the east of the archipelago), 'in the nineteenth century there were still several queens ruling in Bugis states, long after they had disappeared from other parts of the Muslim world' (Andaya 2003: 79). These queens appeared in public 'like the men', rode, ruled and met foreigners 'without the knowledge or consent of their husbands' (Brooke and Munday 1848: 75, cited in Andaya 2003: 79).

In contrast, in Riau (in the west of the archipelago), during the reign of Raja Ali as underking (1845–57), women were ordered to cover their heads (Andaya 2003: 85).

Raja Ali abhorred those who indulged in pleasures which led to loose behaviour between men and women and those who sang and crooned *pantun* (rhyming verses) with veiled invitations to adultery. Sometimes he ordered the instruments of those who serenaded near the houses of decent people to be confiscated, so that their young girls would not be corrupted and so that there was nothing unseemly in the state (Matheson 1972: 137).

Raja Ali's brother, Raja Abdullah, the next underking, was even stricter.

> According to a Dutch report of January 1858, a woman whose husband was absent had taken a young man into her house and was discovered. Without further ado, she was declared guilty of adultery and strangled. ... In response to Dutch objections, ... Abdullah argued that religious law lay outside colonial jurisdiction. (Andaya 2003: 90)

The Riau examples indicate the growing influence of the movement initiated by Muhammad Ibn Abdul-Wahhab (1703–1787) in Arabia. Wahhab's followers condemned 'unlawful commerce with women' and 'infamous lust' (Burckhardt 1831: 111, cited in Andaya 2003: 84). The Wahhabi capture of Mecca and Medina in 1803 was a landmark event widely publicized in the Indonesian archipelago (Andaya 2003: 84; Hadler 2008: 979). Before this event, by the end of the eighteenth century, an *islah* (reformist) movement had already begun in parts of the Indonesian archipelago, especially West Sumatra. This movement differentiated between elements identified as 'Islamic' and those identified as 'un-Islamic', urging Muslims to purge the latter from their religious practices (Zakariya 2011: 197–9). The movement was radicalized in 1803 when three pilgrims returning from Wahhabi-ruled Mecca advocated the use of force to bring about 'an Islamic community' (Zakariya 2011: 199). Such a community was characterized by 'the abandonment of cock fighting, gambling and the use of tobacco, opium, *sirih* and strong drink; white clothes symbolizing purity were to be worn, with women covering their faces and men allowing their beards to grow' (Dobbin 1987: 132). An English visitor to the West Sumatran highlands in 1818 noted that the men were clad 'in white or blue, with turbans, and allowing their beards to grow, in conformity with the ordinances of Tuanku Pasaman, the religious reformer. ... The women, who are also clad in white or blue cloth, ... conceal their heads under a kind of hood, through which an opening is made sufficient to expose their eyes and nose alone' (Raffles 1830: 349–50).

The Wahhabi nation-making vision creates a constituency based on sexual morality by regulating gender relations and controlling women's bodies (El-Fadl 2001). This political use of sexuality is not unique; the control of sexuality as a site of power shaped European civilization (Foucault 1976). By imposing sexual morality, a power structure can be developed through the regulation of persons and activities, resulting in a chain of regulatory relations that permeates society.[5] As noted in Hoodfar and Ghoreishian (Chapter 9 in this volume), 'the mechanisms and institutions charged with "forbidding the wrong", whether upheld by states or private citizens, have emerged as serious impediments to gender equality. They are used to regulate and control "morality" and operate as the bedrock for many policies and practices that seek to create a gender apartheid system, rendering women subjects of their male kin and limiting their public roles.' The religious vigilantism that currently exists in Indonesia derives from two centuries of Wahhabi-influenced violence that included 'physical attacks, abduction and even assassination', all legitimized in the name of religious purification (Abd A'la 2008: 283).

Dutch colonization destroyed the religiously diverse sultanates in the Indonesian archipelago, thereby opening a space for anti-colonialism to develop around a more uniform, Wahhabi-influenced, interpretation of Islam. Pilgrims to Mecca 'would have been brought into contact with other Muslims who were virulently anti-European' (Andaya 2003: 84–5). Anti-colonial resistance elsewhere also provided inspiration, including the Wahhabi call to jihad (holy war) when the French invaded Egypt in 1798 and the efforts by Indian Muslims to halt the advance of the *kafir* (non-Muslims) in India (Burckhardt 1968: 207–9, cited in Andaya 2003: 85). Wahhabism led to a significant shift in Muslim discourses worldwide, ushering in a new politics of everyday control:

> An attentiveness to private life and daily behavior was a common and novel discourse in the Islamic world in the late eighteenth century.... Through the early 1700s, Islam and the ulama had been primarily concerned with states and with kingship. These new reformist Islamic movements were more involved with the everyday lives of ordinary people; *fatwa* addressed issues of family life, sex, and appropriate conduct. (Hadler 2008: 978)

Sexual dimensions of Dutch colonialism

In 1602 the Dutch East India Company was established with a monopoly from the Netherlands government to colonize Asia (Ames 2008: 102–3). Dutch men were considered as *noblesse de la peau* ('nobility of the skin'), privileged to form sexual liaisons with and even marry brown-skinned native women (Gouda 2008: 164–5).[6] In contrast, any white-skinned woman who had a sexual encounter with a brown-skinned man was legally stripped of her European status.[7] Dutch women's sexual agency was thus penalized, even though its potential was implicitly acknowledged by such laws.

Dutch colonial policies regulated indigenous women's bodies according to different agendas. In various parts of Bali from the late nineteenth century to 1927, the Dutch government required Balinese women to cover their breasts 'to protect the morals of Dutch soldiers (and adolescent sons)' (Wiener 2005: 74). But as the Dutch began to promote tourism to Bali (and elsewhere), 'women's bare breasts became a selling point, encouraging [male] tourists to visit Bali and indulge their fantasies about paradise and easy sex' (Wiener 2005: 68). Either way, the Balinese women were treated as the desired objects of white men, whether soldiers or tourists. Ironically, the Balinese women were compelled by the Dutch to wear the *kebaya*, a blouse made of a translucent material and 'designed to signify, if not enhance the torso of the woman' (Cattoni 2004: 4). Dutch policies thus obscenified Balinese women's breasts. The means used to hide the breasts banned from public view instead calls attention to that part. Obscenification thereby imbues a bodily part with the power to arouse desire through its very existence, whether hidden or revealed.

Politicizing polygyny as anti-colonialism

Localized resistance to colonization took the form of royalist revival-ism without pan-archipelagic aspirations (Wee 2002). But Islamist nationalism and pluralist nationalism were the pan-archipelagic forms of resistance that shaped Indonesia, with different political visions of the post-colonial state. By 'Islamism', I refer to 'a political discourse ... that attempts to centre Islam within the political order' (Sayyid 2003: 17).

The first Islamist federation, the Great Islamic Council of Indone-sia, was formed in 1938 specifically to promote polygamy (Cribb 2004: 814). The colonial government's proposed law of 1937 on 'voluntary monogamous marriage' had to be rescinded due to the united oppo-sition of such organizations as Muhammadiyah and Sarekat Islam, both founded in 1912, and Nahdlatul Ulama (NU), founded in 1926 (Locher-Scholten 2000: 188). Prior to this, views were already polar-ized at the first Indonesian Women's Congress (1928):

> The Christian organizations and the non-religious organizations on the one hand, and the Islamic women's groups on the other hand, however, were deeply and decisively divided on the central issue: polygamy. The Christian and non-religious women's organizations saw polygamy as an unpardonable humiliation for women, against which they actively fought; the Islamic organizations only wanted to improve the conditions under which polygamy was allowed to occur, not to abolish the institution itself. (Wieringa 1985: 8–9)

Although some members of Islamically identified women's wings voiced private misgivings, they never did so publicly:

> Personally, I have never agreed with polygamy. I would never have allowed it. But, it is a religious rule, so what can we say against it?

> Polygamy is a religious rule, we couldn't change that. But we did feel that it didn't give men license to take one woman after another. It should not be abused! Men have to adhere strictly to the conditions under which it is allowed. Now if a woman does not get any children, yes, then it was necessary. But if not ... then he is just fooling around. Religion doesn't allow that. (Two dissenting women, cited in Robinson 2009: 44).

Rasoena Said, a school principal and 'female nationalist', also said that while she recognized the evil of polygamy, she nevertheless 'protested against the state interfering in Islamic law' (Locher-Scholten 2000: 200). But Christian and non-religious organizations consistently opposed polygamy in public, including the pan-Indonesian Kongres Wanita Katolik (Catholic Women's Congress), the left-wing All Indonesia Centre of Labour Organizations[8] and the secularist Association of Greater Indonesia[9] (van der Kroef 1953: 124–5).

Following Lestari (2008: 10), I mostly use the term 'polygyny', rather than 'polygamy', which wrongly implies that both men and women can be polygamous. Polygyny may be understood as a gendered relationship of ownership, whereby a woman's body as property is accessible only to her husband as property-owner, who may have more than one property (i.e. multiple wives).

Accessibility was also restricted through a curtain (*tabir*) to hide women from men's gaze at public meetings even of supposedly 'moderate' organizations, such as NU and Muhammadiyah (Blackburn 2008: 88). However, 'NU women resisted the tabir separating men and women in public meetings, and it was abandoned in 1959' (Machrusah 2005: 21–2, cited in Robinson 2009: 53). The curtain implies that women exposed to men's gaze would have been obscenified as indecent and thus fair game. A respondent from West Java told me that in the 1950s the women in her family had to hide themselves from militants in the Darul Islam movement, then fighting to make Indonesia an Islamic state. The women feared that if sighted, they could be seized by the men 'as wives'.

The notion that men need not control their sexual urges continues to be viewed by some as God-ordained. Nita, a woman member of the Islamist Prosperous Justice Party,[10] said (2003):

> Allah knows the weaknesses of humanity and makes rules for this. Therefore, for humans for whom one wife is not enough, Islam opens the opportunity for polygamy. … If a man really wants to have children, but his wife has been told by a doctor that it is not possible for her to have children, then Islam permits polygamy. Also for a man who has high sexual needs, Islam permits polygamy. Because it is not possible for a woman to serve the man all day long, so a man may take another wife. (cited in Rinaldo 2011: 55)

Nita thus identifies 'humanity' and 'humans' with men, whose sexual and reproductive needs must be met by women as service providers with no desires of their own. But one Muslim woman bravely rejected polygyny in public: Siti Rohana, a religious teacher and champion of girls' education. On radio, she criticized a male leader for trying to justify polygyny as a means of 'combating illicit sex' and for seeing 'women as created by Allah to satisfy the desires of men':

> If you know that a woman is a human, you will certainly know how she feels if her husband takes another wife. ... If a wife goes looking for another husband, what would her husband do?... It is a falsehood to say that polygamy restricts illicit sex. Illicit sex arises from desire that cannot be governed by an individual. But a human who is not a man but a woman must govern her desires. (Harian Radio, March 1929, cited in Blackburn 2004: 121)

Siti Rohana thus rejected the subjugation of women as men's sexual servants. Although seventy-four years separate Siti Rohana and Nita, they nevertheless represent the two sides of the debate. Until the 1980s, all the Islamically identified organizations publicly supported polygyny as a 'religious rule'. Although some opponents were also Muslims, such as Siti Rohana, they were in the minority and were not supported by any organization that identified itself as 'Islamic'. Polygyny was a metaphor for 'men's power within marriage' and 'the willingness of a male-dominated state to uphold that power' (Blackburn 2004: 113). The core question concerns gender-equitable rights. Are male and female equally human with equal rights to sexual desire and fulfilment or is only the male considered sexually 'human', with the female a mere service provider created to serve him?

Instigating moral panic to justify anti-communism

The political utility of a sexual script extended beyond Islamist agendas. In 1965, when General Suharto established his New Order regime by killing between 500,000 and 2,000,000 alleged communists, the legitimizing myth included a sexual script that equated communism with sexual immorality, which thus had to be stamped out. In particular, members of the left-wing Gerwani[11] – the 'Indonesian Women's Movement' – were alleged to have indulged in sexual debauchery that resulted in the killing of six generals (Wieringa 2002, 2009). Despite lack of evidence from the autopsy, the armed forces alleged that Gerwani women gouged out the generals' eyes, cut off their genitals and committed sexual acts with their corpses, while dancing naked (Wieringa 2009: 10). Gerwani women detained by the army said that they were tortured, raped, forced to confess to these allegations, as well as stripped naked and photographed as 'proof' of sexual debauchery, without ever being brought to court (Wieringa 2009: 11). In 2006, Gerwani women survivors publicly recounted how, without any legal process, they were detained for years, suffering physical, psychological and sexual violence (McGregor 2008: 11–12). Pondering 'why the socialist women's movement is so much more demonized' than, say, the farmers' union, Wieringa (2009: 16) asks: 'If nation building in modern times ... is a project of the imagination, what kind of masculinist imagination has been at work here?'

The answer is that certain political interests were served by constructing a threat of national collapse due to sexual immorality. The moral panic thus generated led to religiously identified organizations calling for a holy war against the communists, declaring their 'extermination ... an obligatory religious duty' and 'the will of Allah', with a signed agreement between NU and the army for cooperation in 'the extermination of leftist people' (Wieringa 2009: 10). Unified in moral panic, an anti-communist alliance was mobilized, including right-wing secularists, Muslims, Catholics, Protestants and Hindus (McGregor 2008: 4; Robinson 1995: 279). The nation-building myth thus mutated from fighting Dutch colonizers trying to impose monogamy to fighting sexually immoral communism.

This moral panic exhibited the characteristics identified by Goode and Ben-Yehuda (1994: 33–41) as well as Garland (2008: 11):

1. Heightened concern over the behaviour of a certain group and the consequences of that behaviour for the rest of society – the fear of national collapse due to Gerwani women's alleged sexual immorality.
2. Increased hostility to the perpetrators of the behaviour in question – arrest, detention, torture, rape, killing of Gerwani/Communists.
3. Substantial agreement or consensus about the seriousness of the threat – the anti-Communist alliance formed among different social groups.
4. Disproportionality or an assumption that there are more people involved in the problematic behaviour than the number known

 – the widespread belief that beyond the Gerwani women detained, unknown numbers of Communists were also sexually immoral.

5. A volatile short-term episode, which may lead to a routinized, institutionalized moral concern about the problematic behaviour – the shorter-term sequence of events, including large-scale massacre,[12] followed by a longer-term routinization of anti-Communism in national culture.

6. A moral dimension in the social reaction – sexual morality re-asserted by the anti-Communist alliance.

7. The idea that the deviant conduct is symptomatic of a larger malaise – the idea that women as autonomous citizens become immoral, which thus requires alteration of the very basis of women's political participation, leading to the replacement of women's organizations by state-sponsored wives' organizations. (Sen 1999)

Significantly, what had attracted many women to Gerwani was its opposition to polygyny. A Gerwani survivor stated: 'Most women were drawn to our organization because of our stand on polygamy.... They hated the polygyny of their men.... What appealed most to the young people was the right to marry as they wish and to the women the struggle against polygyny' (Wieringa 2002: 10, 13).

Another Gerwani survivor wondered whether they had been persecuted because of this: 'If one of our members consented to become the second wife... she was thrown out of Gerwani' (Wieringa 2002: 181). The perverse sexual script of Suharto and his allies thus stigmatized a women's organization that opposed polygyny, which continued to be accommodated as a moral practice within Indonesian law.

The politics of polarization

In 1973, a Marriage Law bill was radically revised to appease those claiming to represent 'Islam'. In its original form, the bill proposed to abolish polygamy, establish civil registration as the only legal signifier of a marriage, require use of a civil court only (rather than an Islamic court) and allow inter-religious marriage. These proposals provoked street riots in Jakarta, and attracted accusations from Muslim leaders that the bill was an exercise in 'Christianization'. Consequently, these provisions had to be withdrawn in order for the bill to be passed. The revised bill, which became the Marriage

Law, allowed court-sanctioned polygamy and required marriage to be based on religion (O'Shaughnessy 2009: 30).

The fact that self-proclaimed 'Muslim leaders' obtained such concessions demonstrates their power under the supposedly secularist New Order, showing that the post-Suharto increase of Islamist power did not emerge out of nothing. The 1974 Marriage Law[13] forbids non-religious civil marriages, sets 16 as the legal minimum age of marriage for girls, and permits polygyny if the first wife approves, or even without her permission if she is infertile, disabled, has an incurable disease or is not fulfilling her sexual obligations. No provision is made for the wife if her husband has similar deficiencies. Men are thus privileged to marry additional wives to compensate for deficiencies in existing wives. Nursyahbani Katjasungkana, co-founder of the Indonesian Women's Association for Justice (LBH APIK),[14] describes the Marriage Law as an embodiment of gender inequality that permits men to do things forbidden to women (Blackburn 2004: 134).

Calls for Marriage Law reform have been largely unsuccess-ful. But in 1983, Dharma Wanita (Women's Duty), a large state-sponsored organization for civil servants' wives, successfully lobbied for Regulation PP 10/1983, which requires male civil servants to obtain workplace superiors' approval before marrying a second wife, contingent upon the existing wife's permission (Suryakusuma 1996: 97–118). Unsurprisingly, Islamist organizations opposed this regulation. More recently, in 2000, Dharma Wanita, representing some 3 million wives of civil servants, rejected a proposal by the minister of religious affairs to revoke this regulation, because 'most of the state employees still have very low morals and discipline' and because there are 'legitimate concerns' for the future of polygynous families that are expected to share a husband's limited salary, thereby citing practical, not religious, grounds (*Jakarta Post* 2000).

Polygyny has been debated for more than five decades but its current incidence is unknown because the Indonesian government does not compile national data on marriage (Kurnia 2009). The known percentages of polygynous men are:

- The entire archipelago: 2.6 per cent (1930 census)
- Java: 1.5 per cent (1920 census); 1.9 per cent (1973 Fertility–Mortality Survey)

Since most Indonesians live on Java (63.83 per cent in 1971; 60.12 per cent in 2000), these figures indicate that polygyny is rarely practised (see Suryadinata et al. 2003: 5). The 1973 Survey showed that the highest percentages of polygynous men are in Sumba (13.5 per cent) and Flores (12 per cent), both with patrilineal systems, and small, mostly Christian, populations (see Jones 1994: 269). Polygyny may thus relate more closely to kinship than to religion, as men in patrilineal systems wish to maximize their male heirs by impregnating more than one woman contemporaneously. In contrast, Java is largely bilateral with no corporate descent groups and no incentive to produce male heirs (see Gordan 1980; Needham 1980; Sairin 1982). Among mostly Muslim populations, the highest incidence of polygyny occurs among the matrilineal Minangkabau (12 per cent). Since the Minangkabau husband customarily visits his wife's matrilineal home without residing there, this enables him to be a husband to multiple wives; he is also absolved from supporting them economically as they are already property owners (Keddie 1987: 18).

While many Indonesian men may marry secondary wives through a secret informal ceremony,[15] recognized by neither Islamic nor national law, the incidence of this is unknown. The result is a gap between the known incidence of polygyny and 'polygamy talk', a situation of 'marginal practice, ubiquitous discourse' (van Wichelen 2009: 174). More important than actual incidence, however, is the politicization of public discourse through instigating the public to take sides on this issue. This is the politics of polarization at work, with 'differences around conceptions of morality ... becoming sources of polarization' (Rinaldo 2011: 47).[16] Believers and non-believers are polarized, with a constituency of supporters mobilized against clearly identified opponents. The fault line produced is between those who adhere to a sexual script said to be 'Islamic' and those who hold different views of gender, sexuality and Islam, not between the polygamous and the monogamous. At stake are different normative proposals for what Islam and Indonesia should be.

The Convention on the Elimination of All Forms of Discrimination Against Women (CEDAW)

The Indonesian government signed CEDAW in 1984, committing itself to removal of all discrimination against women, at least in principle. However, the Indonesian Country Report (1996) admitted to the Committee that 'the continued legality of polygamy is evidence of the continuing inequality of women before the law' (Blackburn 2004: 134). The situation has not improved since. The CEDAW Committee (CEDAW 2007: para. 8) noted that 'the Convention has not been fully and systematically incorporated throughout Indonesian law'. The Committee identified ongoing discriminations, including:

- Failure 'to rescind local laws that discriminate against women on the basis of religion, including laws regulating dress codes, which are disproportionately enforced against women' (para. 12).
- 'The requirement that a woman obtain her husband's consent regarding sterilization and abortion, even when her life is in danger' (para. 16).
- A discriminatory Marriage Law that 'perpetuate stereotypes by providing that men are the heads of households and women are relegated to domestic roles, allow polygamy and set a legal minimum age of marriage of 16 for girls' (para. 18).
- 'The medicalization of the practice of female genital mutilation... [with] no law prohibiting or penalizing the practice of female genital mutilation in Indonesia' (para. 20).
- 'Cultural perceptions connected with female genital mutilation ... as a violation of the human rights of women and girls that has no basis in religion' (para. 21).
- Exploitation of 'the prostitution of women' (para. 24).
- 'Lack of a law prohibiting sexual harassment in the workplace' (para. 34).
- 'Lack of family planning education and ... difficulty in accessing contraceptives, which result in a high rate of abortions and teenage pregnancies' (para. 36).

Despite such challenges, the obligation of the Indonesian state to comply with CEDAW is important to women's rights advocates, providing a platform for national advocacy and for informing the international community of Indonesian women's realities, especially through independent reports submitted to the CEDAW Committee (see Komnas Perempuan 2007).

The 1991 Compilation of Islamic Laws versus gender-equitable interpretations of Islam

The 1991 Compilation of Islamic Laws,[17] enacted on President Suharto's instruction, reinforces the gender hierarchy by defining a husband as a guide leading his wife, who is 'to loyally serve her husband in all matters, physical and spiritual, within the limits allowed by Islamic law' (Article 83(1), cited in O'Shaughnessy 2009: 36). Musawah (2009) notes that the Compilation disadvantages women beyond the 1974 Marriage Law, with the bride's consent no longer deemed necessary as marriage is redefined as a contract between two men – her father and the groom. As noted by Bennett (2007: 376), there is 'widespread reluctance to acknowledge Muslim women's right to refuse sexual intercourse within marriage, based on the belief that a woman's consent to marry is synonymous with her consent to have sex with her husband on request'. If the bride's consent is considered unnecessary for marriage, then the wife's consent to marital sex would be equally irrelevant. According to the Compilation, a wife who refuses to have sex with her husband is considered as having committed *nushuz* (rebellion) and can be justifiably beaten and deprived of maintenance (Musawah 2009).

Zina (sex outside marriage) is highlighted in the Compilation as the primary reason for divorce (Article 116(a), which is treated as irreconcilable (Article 163(2)). Supposedly forbidden to both men and women, 'in reality *zina* for men is not condemned or punished, but is often ignored or tolerated. It is women who are primarily targeted as responsible for upholding the moral code of Islam by disciplining their desire in order to avoid *zina*' (Bennett 2005: 22).

Since the 1980s, the male-biased interpretations of religious texts informing the Compilation have been contested by dissenting religious scholars, who have formed several organizations to promote gender-equitable interpretations of religious texts.[18] Their alternative interpretations have advanced public understanding that what is presented as *shari'a*, divine revelation, is actually *fiqh*, historical schools of jurisprudence that are man-made, not God-ordained, and thus relevant only to specific historical contexts, rather than being universally applicable (see Mir-Hosseini and Hamzić 2010: xvi).

In this light, Husein Muhammad, a religious scholar who describes himself as 'feminist', criticizes classical *fiqh* for its gender inequality:

'It is an irony that classical *fiqh* gave only men opportunities to achieve sexual enjoyment while women had to control, hide and oppress theirs ... as we can find in the issue of female *khitan* [circumcision]' (Muhammad 2001: 39, translation quoted in Muttaqin 2008: 82).

Husein Muhammad also criticizes classical *fiqh* for unfairly applying the idea of *fitnah* (social disorder arising from the wrongful arousal of passion) only to women, as if they can arouse men's sexual desires but not vice versa. He notes that this gender bias prevents women from becoming imam (prayer leaders) who can lead a mixed congregation (see Muhammad 2001: 37–8, cited in Muttaqin 2008: 82).

As Siti Rohana did in 1929, Husein Muhammad criticizes the privileging of men's desires, with women eliminating their desires and withdrawing from the public sphere so as not to arouse men. Nevertheless, Islamists still use the prioritization of men's desires to justify polygyny. In 2006, when President Susilo Bambang Yudhoyono tried to extend PP10/1983 (hindering male public servants from practising polygyny) to other men, Islamist parties protested, arguing that restricting polygyny would lead men to commit *zina*, since they cannot be expected to control their sexual desires and should thus be allowed to satisfy themselves with four wives (Wiyana et al. 2006).

The counter-argument made by dissenting religious scholars[19] is that it contradicts central Islamic values for marriage to be reduced to a contract based on a master–servant hierarchy, allowing a husband to force his wife to satisfy him sexually even against her will. They object to marriage becoming a device to prevent people from committing *zina*. Rather, they argue, marriage should be an indivisible part of humanity's worshipful relationship to God, part of *tawhid* (the oneness of God) where all are equal before God, not a power relationship where one Muslim oppresses another Muslim (see Muttaqin 2008: 83; Kassim 2010: 256–7; Sikand 2010).

Resisting the disciplining of unruly women

Defining female genital cutting as a 'religious duty'

Despite alternative interpretations of Islam, moral panics about women's sexual autonomy continue to be generated, leading to the increasing politicization of women's bodies, including reinforcement of female genital mutilation (FGM). The Population Council Jakarta (2003) found FGM widely believed to be a religious duty. But when probed, the religious leaders interviewed admitted that different Islamic schools (*mazhab*) have different views. On 20 April 2006, the Ministry of Health banned FGM, adopting the World Health Organization's position that injuring female genital organs for non-medical reasons has no health benefit whatsoever. However, on 7 June 2008, the Indonesian Council of Ulama[20] issued a *fatwa* (opinion supposedly based on religious laws):[21]

1. Concerning the 'legal status of female circumcision (*khitān*)':
   a. The circumcision of 'either male or female is *fitrah* (human nature) and an Islamic notion'.
   b. 'Female circumcision is *makrumah* (venerated) and performing that circumcision is considered as a recommended obedience ('*ibādah*) to Allah.'
2. The 'prohibition of female circumcision is thoroughly against the *shari'a* (Islamic law) because circumcision either for male or female is *fitrah* (human nature)'.
3. 'The limitation and guidance of female genital operation':
   a. 'It is sufficient to cut or to remove the tiny portion of preputium/... skin' that covers the clitoris.
   b. 'The operation must not exceed the part mentioned' – for example, by hurting or removing any part of the clitoris other than the preputium through incision or excision that will cause harm.
4. Recommendations:
   a. The Ministry of Health is asked to adopt this *fatwa* as guidance to enact decrees and other regulations concerning female circumcision.
   b. It is recommended that the Ministry of Health should give medical practitioners a directive counselling them about female genital circumcision as stated in this *fatwa*.

The Indonesian Council of Ulama thus declared the Ministry of Health in contravention of the *shari'a* and asked the Ministry to adopt its *fatwa* as guidance. In March 2010, NU, 'the country's largest Muslim organization, issued an edict supporting FGM/C [female genital mutilation/circumcision], though a leading cleric told the NU's estimated 40 million followers "not to cut too much"' (IRIN Humanitarian News 2010). In November 2010, the Ministry of

Health issued a new regulation, authorizing doctors, midwives and nurses to perform FGM, now defined as 'the act of scratching the skin covering the front of the clitoris, without hurting the clitoris' (Article 4.2(g)).[22] The Ministry thus reversed its 2006 position and complied with the *fatwa* of the ulama.

Countering the claim that FGM is part of 'Islamic law', Siti Musdah Mulia from the Islamic State University Syarif Hidayatullah in Jakarta said that it has no basis in Islamic teachings (Faizal 2011). Maria Ulfah Anshor, another religious leader, who was the former chairperson of Fatayat NU, said that the underlying motivation is to 'make men more excited in bed... [while the] women themselves ... don't get any excitement at all' (IRIN Humanitarian News 2010). The chair of the Assalaam Foundation, which sponsors free annual mass circumcision for the public to celebrate Prophet Muhammad's birth, confirmed the sexual script: 'One, it will stabilize her libido. ... Two, it will make a woman look more beautiful in the eyes of her husband. And three, it will balance her psychology' (Corbett 2008).

While a woman's clitoris is cut to reduce her sexual pleasure, the rest of her body is increasingly obscenified as a source of *fitnah*. Moral panic arising from fear of *fitnah* underpins the enclosure of, first, a woman's hair, then ears, neck, arms, legs, then the very shape of her body, extending even to her voice.

Reformulating and restricting dress codes for women

Women's dress codes have changed drastically in the last forty years. In the 1970s and 1980s, women wore dresses, blouses and short skirts, including the *kebaya* (a figure-hugging translucent blouse), with their hair uncovered, without being considered sexually immoral. They played sports (basketball, volley ball, badminton, etc.) wearing sports attire. For example, in Riau, women formed village teams to play against each other. Even women religious teachers just covered their hair loosely with a shawl (*selendang*). It was only when women prayed that they wore white prayer clothes, covering their hair, ears, neck and body, with hands exposed. But none was expected to wear prayer clothes when not praying.

Suharto's government prohibited headscarves among female government employees and schoolgirls in state schools, prescribing as uniform 'a knee-length skirt and a short-sleeved blouse or jacket [with] no long-skirted, veiled option' (Smith-Hefner 2007: 397). This situation changed in the 1990s. As recounted by Alatas (2007), a 'headscarf revolution' was inspired by the Iranian Revolution of 1979 and the ideology of the Muslim Brotherhood of Egypt, disseminated through translated books. Alatas rates the latter as more influential, because its ideology was communicated through campus workshops, especially at Salman Mosque of the Institute of Technology in Bandung (ITB) where 'missionary warriors' were trained. From 1979 until 1990, several hundred upper secondary schoolgirls were thereby motivated to wear headscarves to state-run schools in Java, West Sumatra and Aceh, leading to expulsions (actual or threatened) and court cases.

One case led to a judgment in favour of ten veiled schoolgirls, who won on appeal at the High Court in 1990. Significantly, the schoolgirls' attorney was Nursyahbani Katjasungkana, a leading secularist feminist, who had taken on the case to oppose Suharto's authoritarian regime. At that time, because of the regime's ban on headscarves, many dissidents, including secularists, supported the wearing of headscarves as a signifier of opposition. But despite this wider political connotation, because the headscarf derives from a sexual script that obscenifies women's hair, this led to the obscenification of other bodily parts.

On 16 February 1991, the Department of Education and Culture formally allowed schoolgirls to wear headscarves to state schools.[23] Since then it has become increasingly prevalent for women to cover their hair as part of everyday dress code. A respondent, who was then studying at ITB, described to me the changes she witnessed:

> By the mid-1990s, it became increasingly necessary for women to cover their ears, which were now considered as *aurat* (a private part). In tertiary institutions, including non-Islamic universities, all female students started to wear headscarves to cover not just their hair, but also their ears and neck. Some even wore the *jubah* (robe), which extended to the upper thighs, to cover the waist, hips and buttocks so as to hide the shape of the female figure. Beneath the *jubah*, they wore long skirts to hide the shape of their legs. A small group at ITB, consisting of students majoring in mathematics, geography and technology, start wearing socks to cover their feet. Once the female students started to cover up their bodies, they no longer participated in sports. Many students belonged to particular

religious groups under certain religious teachers. Some groups, such as
Darul Arqam, required their members to wear only black, but other
groups still allowed colours. If the students are members of such groups,
it is their teachers who will match make them [i.e. marry them off] to
each other. The girls in such groups were taught not to look at men at
all and to hide themselves from men's gaze, unless the latter are their
husbands and other family members. Such students eventually constituted
the cadre of the Islamist political parties.

What is considered as *aurat* has expanded in the 2000s. In some
schools under Islamist influence, girl students are now forbidden to
sing or speak in public as the female voice is redefined as *aurat*. The
Islamist penetration of schools has largely happened under the radar
of public scrutiny, as the schools are relatively closed environments
regulated by principals and teachers. Indicative of growing public
concern, a study on the Islamist radicalization of public schools in
seven cities in Java and Sumatra has been completed by the Indonesian Institute for Civil Society (INCIS).[24] The pressure on girls and
women to cover ever more bodily parts and to mute their voices is
likely due to Islamist perceptions of social disorder as continuing
unabated despite large numbers now covering their heads, which is
therefore seemingly insufficient.

One may ask why women would be attracted to Islamist groups,
if restrictions are all they offer. Brenner's (1996: 689) argument on
'the discipline of veiling' is relevant: '[Wearing the headscarf gives
women a] sense of self-mastery and identity in a time of great social
flux.... Women who veil believe that it helps them to establish
control over their lives.' Smith-Hefner's (2007: 401) respondents
also say that 'veiling helps them feel "calm" ... and more in control
of their feelings and behaviour, particularly in interactions with
members of the opposite sex'.

Themes of heightened self-confidence and moral self-control run
through all of the veiling narratives I collected from young women.
While they recognize that veiling imposes certain limitations on
their behaviour, those who have made the commitment to veil say
they weighed their decision carefully and view the limitations as
positive, not negative.

I would develop this argument further by contextualizing the
'discipline of veiling' in the Islamist argument that exposure of

women's *aurat* creates *fitnah*. By covering their *aurat*, however defined, women achieve not only 'self-mastery', but also other-mastery: mastering men's passions and thereby bringing social order. This elevates women to a position of moral superiority, with the potential power of bringing order to an otherwise chaotic world.

The view that a woman who does not cover her *aurat* is 'deliberately tempting men' – to quote a respondent of Brenner (1996) – and thereby causing social disorder has been preached in sermons, books, workshops, websites, and elsewhere for some time. Women who believe this may feel guilty for not having covered up. So, after they decide to cover up, they may feel at peace for having done their bit to save the world, as it were. As a respondent commented to me, women who adopt the wearing of headscarves often try to persuade other female relatives to do so, not only because they think it is the right thing to do, but also because they feel better after covering up.

However, even when women voluntarily cover themselves, this may be deemed inadequate. For example, in Yogyakarta the headscarf has become a fashion statement for some, with headscarves made of 'expensive gauzy, silk, and chiffon fabrics with colourful, eye-catching patterns and embroidered lace or bead trim', and 'tied behind the head in glamorous movie-star fashion' (Smith-Hefner 2007: 413). The executive director of the Council of Indonesian Jihad Fighters[25] reacted: 'The wearing of sexually alluring *jilbab* [is] a serious threat to the Islamic social order for which the council is struggling ... [as] veiling is a preliminary but important step toward the implementation of Islamic law' (Smith-Hefner 2007: 414).

There is violent policing of women by vigilante groups in many areas (see Smith-Hefner 2007: 413–14; Simanjuntak 2009), including pulling off women's headscarves if considered too stylish (e.g. in Yogyakarta and elsewhere) or cutting up their trousers if considered too tight (e.g. in West Aceh). '*Khalwat* vigilantism' is also increasing – *khalwat*[26] meaning close proximity between a man and a woman who are not close relatives (Newman 2009). Unmarried couples, even if only sitting or walking together, may be beaten (e.g. in many parts of Java), whipped (e.g. in Bulukumba, South Sulawesi) or stripped naked and paraded (e.g. in Aceh; see also Newman 2009; WEMC–Solidaritas Perempuan 2009; Mir-Hosseini and Hamzić

2010). The Aceh municipal religious police subject girls and women detained for *khalwat* to virginity tests. Even though both sexes get detained for *khalwat*, to quote a women's rights activist, 'women are the ones who are stigmatized. Men just walk away' (Broecker 2010: 38). Women who are seen as undisciplined are thus disciplined by those claiming to represent society's moral force. Mir-Hosseini (Chapter 5 in this volume) points out that the view of women's sexuality as a source of *fitnah* 'grants men the right to control women's movements'.

Introducing discriminatory legislation to police women's bodies

After a devastating tsunami in Aceh province in December 2004, the Islamic Defenders' Front,[27] Soldiers of the Holy War,[28] Council of Indonesian Jihad Fighters, and other Islamists declared the tsunami God's punishment of women for flaunting their bodies and not obeying their husbands. Because nearly two-thirds of the approximately 167,000 dead were women,[29] many with clothes torn off by the tsunami, their naked bodies were said to 'prove' that they had not covered their *aurat*, hence causing the disaster[30] (APWLD 2006: 50; Suraiya Kamaruzzaman 2005: pers. comm.). After the tsunami, many Islamist groups 'flocked to Aceh' (Clarke et al. 2010: 42). Five years later, in 2009, Aceh's regional legislature proposed to expand its existing Muslim Criminal Code (enacted in 2003) to increase punishments for *zina* to 100 cane lashes for the unmarried and stoning to death for those married. As of December 2011, this proposal has not become law, due to the governor of Aceh's objection.

The view that social order is founded on the disciplining of women can be a charter for disciplining society when it is seen as incapable of disciplining unruly women. In 2008, the Law on Pornography[31] was passed. The bill, drafted in 1999 by a coalition of Islamist parties, resulted in ten years of debate (Tedjasukmana 2008). While the law that was eventually passed seems to be a dilution of the bill, due to the strong opposition encountered, it nevertheless offers open-ended scope for prosecutions. The first clause defines pornography as 'sexual material made by people in the form of pictures, sketches, illustrations, photographs, writings, voices, sounds, motion pictures, animations, cartoons, poems, conversations, body movements, and other forms of messages through various mass media or public displays that can arouse sexual desires and/or violate public moral values'. This loose definition of 'pornography' is applicable to anything deemed arousing or against 'public moral values', with heavy penalties of up to fifteen years' imprisonment and fines of up to Rp 7.5 billion (US$837,054; see Pasandaran 2010). 'The law is wide open to interpretation and could even apply to voice, sound, poetry, works of art or literature. Anything that supposedly raises the libido could be prosecutable' (Kaden Krishna Adidharma, a Balinese opponent of the law, cited in Tedjasukmana 2008).

Opponents of the law argue that existing legal provisions are sufficient to deal with public indecency, needing only more effective implementation, not a new law. However, proponents – mostly Islamically identified organizations with a few non-religious organizations – regard existing provisions as inadequate.[32] No non-Muslim religious organization supports the law. 'The law imposes the will of the majority that embraces Islam, is a form of religious discrimination and against the spirit of tolerance taught by the country's founders. It is an effort to divide the country' (Theophilus Bela, chairman of the Christian Communication Forum, quoted in Tedjasukmana 2008). In appeasement, the chair of the Indonesian Council of Ulama said that the law presents a moral solution that only happens to coincide with Islamic law (Komnas Perempuan 2011: 28–9). But opponents – civil society activists, artists, religious minorities, and non-Muslim populations in four provinces – still view it as an Islamist imposition.[33] The fault line resembles the division in the 1930s around polygamy. The difference is that while the organizations identified as 'Islamic' are still mostly on one side, there are now other Islamic-identified organizations on the opposing side. The polarization is now more clearly among Muslims, with increasingly public opposition by dissident scholars and lay Muslims, including men (Semarak Cerlang Nusa 2011). The dissenting scholars prioritize justice as 'immutable (qaṭ'i) and non-negotiable', rejecting fragmented (juzíyya) text-derived rulings on women's rights that contradict the 'underlying principles and foundations' of Islam (Mas'udi 1993: 188; 2002: 17–19). Despite the persistence of Islamist agendas, Indonesia has not become an Islamic state, and contestations have actually increased. Although Islamist forces have been powerful enough to shape certain laws and policies, other Indonesians who value gender equality, including theologically knowledgeable Muslims, do constitute a countervailing force.

Three petitions for a judicial review of the Law on Pornography were filed in 2009 by rights activists, cultural organizations and experts. Constitutional grounds for the review were that this law is discriminatory towards women, ignores the rights and psychological state of child victims by requiring an evidentiary process, restricts citizens' constitutional rights, undermines the freedom of religion and belief, and threatens cultural diversity (Komnas Perempuan 2010b). No argument was made for the right to exercise one's sexual autonomy free of coercion from the state. Even so, on 25 March 2010, the Constitutional Court of the Republic of Indonesia declared the petitioners' reasoning ungrounded and affirmed that the Law on Pornography does not violate the constitution, because community norms take precedence over individual rights and freedoms. The only female judge, Maria Farida Idrati, issued a 'dissenting opinion'. She criticized 'the loose definition of pornography, the overall lack of legal clarity, the attempts to usher in a singular, culturally insensitive vision of public morality, as well as provisions which discriminate against women and sexual and gender minorities', noting that the definition 'allows for the criminalization of women's attire and even "body movements" deemed inappropriate, thus curtailing women's constitutionally guaranteed freedom of expression' (Mir-Hosseini and Hamzić 2010: 62).

Advocates for women's rights are responding robustly. For example, in 2008 Solidaritas Perempuan launched a campaign 'Stop the criminalization and inhuman punishment of women!'[34] Another example is the slogan 'Your porno mind is not my body's fault!' coined and publicized by LBH APIK to say that women are not responsible for men's pornographic thoughts.

Concerns about the law have been reinforced by two incidents. On March 2010, the law was used in Bandung (West Java) to jail four female dancers, a café manager, and the organizer of a New Year dance show. This prompted concern among human rights advocates that (i) women would be targeted, and (ii) the 'rubber law' – to quote Eddy Hiariej of Gadjah Mada University – would be implemented elastically to criminalize anything arbitrarily labelled 'pornographic'

(Osman and Andriyanto 2010). The second incident occurred in July 2010 when a 15-metre sculpture entitled *Three Women* in Bekasi (West Java) was destroyed by Islamist militants as 'pornographic' (Tedjasukmana 2010).

The rights of lesbians, gays, bisexuals and transsexuals (LGBT) are also attacked. Article 4(1)(a) in the Law on Pornography defines lesbianism and (male) homosexuality as 'deviant behaviour', punishable by between one and twelve years' imprisonment or a fine of between Rp 500 million and Rp 6 billion (US$55,804–US$669,643). The law has emboldened Islamist vigilantes to attack LGBT groups. In March 2010 in Surabaya, the International Lesbian and Gay Association (ILGA) Asia Conference, involving 150 activists representing 100 organizations from sixteen Asian countries, was halted by the Islamic Defenders' Front and other Islamists. Non-LGBT civil society groups rallied to support the LGBT activists under siege, including a group self-identified as 'Muslim' as well as the Indonesian Human Rights Commission. Although the local host, GAYa NUSANTARA, had its office sealed off by the vigilantes until 21 April 2010, it resumed its advocacy for LGBT rights thereafter (Poore 2010a, 2010b, 2010c).

In September 2010 in Jakarta, Islamist vigilantes also tried to stop the annual Q! Film Festival, which shows international films about homosexuality and HIV/AIDS. Despite some cancelled screenings, the festival successfully continued (Jakarta Post 2010). In October 2010, the Indonesian Council of Ulama urged the national censorship board to ban any movie that (supposedly) promotes homosexuality and endorsed denouncements of the festival by the communications and information technology minister and the culture and tourism minister (Sagita 2010). The Q! Film Festival was successfully organized again in September 2011, with the help of the Indonesian Human Rights Commission, Law Advocacy Help and other human rights NGOs, including the LGBT group Arus Pelangi. Pre-emptive arrangements included screening in Jakarta plus five other cities, reduced media exposure and registration of viewers (Fridae 2011). Such strategies of resistance are thus important:

- Solidarity by different types of human rights activists to support those attacked, such as the non-LGBT groups who rallied around the LGBT activists under siege.

- Resilience by those who are attacked, such as GAYa NUSANTARA and the Q! Film Festival organizers, who persevered with their work.
- Pre-emptive arrangements such as those made for the 2011 Q! Film Festival – diffusing activities over a wider geographical area, preventing information from being communicated to hostile forces and consolidating membership through registration.

Despite the risks, many organizations continue to advocate for LGBT rights. For example, on 29 October 2010, Institut Pelangi Perempuan (IPP) launched its comic book about the Yogyakarta Principles,[35] with its website showing Kamilia, IPP's executive director, holding this comic book.[36] Precautions against attacks have not stopped IPP's public activities, including a 'Lez School' for members and a women's boxing club. The latter even attracts heterosexual women who are drawn to the sport, evidently comfortable with IPP as a lesbian organization, sparring with lesbian fellow boxers and the notion that women can take up a contact sport like boxing.[37]

Rewriting sexual scripts as alternative charters for action

Siti Musdah Mulia,[38] one of the religious scholars promoting gender equality, has publicly stated her opinion on LGBT rights. She considers homosexuality as God-given and therefore 'natural'. Sin occurs only if people commit sexual violence, paedophilia or other crimes. Although she advocates same-sex marriage to avoid premarital sex, she acknowledges that it is unlikely to happen. She said, 'Nevertheless, gay people should not feel guilty either. Just leave it all to God, it's his prerogative to judge' (Diani 2010).

Musdah Mulia's view of God as all-understanding and merciful differs from the view of God as rigid and punitive. All else aside, the dispute over sexual scripts is also about the nature of God and how human beings should relate to God – directly or only indirectly through intermediaries claiming to represent him. Gellner (1968) observes that intermediaries become important when the rest of society lacks direct access to religious knowledge. This is why, other than trying to shape national laws and policies, Islamist leaders also seek to control local communities – through so-called 'Muslim villages' and new 'colonies', for example, in South Sulawesi (Fealy and White 2008: 186–8). Women in such communities are the bearers and carers of expected multitudes of obedient followers, as implied in the Islamist slogan 'Many children, many benefits, come let us build colonies!'[39] While situational instability may lead eventually to a pendulum swing towards a more direct form of religiosity, as argued by Gellner (1968), advocates for women's rights are not passively waiting for that to happen, but are actively striving towards a gender-equitable vision of Islam and Indonesia with women enjoying equal sexual rights.

Contestations over sexual scripts are inherently political, involving the question of women's very existence. Do women exist as human beings with rights over their own bodies? Or do they exist only as bodies subjected to the dictates, pleasures and agendas of others? Control over women is often presented as 'protection', but this rhetoric cloaks a threat of violence as it implies that only 'good' women deserve to be 'protected'. The identification of 'good' women and 'bad' women rests with power-holders in gendered power structures – authors of the sexual scripts that women must follow, if they are to qualify as 'good'. The rewriting of such scripts means a rejection of the power structures that reduce women to bodies for use. But do the entrenched power structures allow women to escape control? Historical evidence of structural violence – whether couched as religious purification, anti-communism or public morality – indicates the severity of the risk faced by rebellious women, a risk that they can overcome only through profound knowledge of opposing forces and through the strategic mobilization of women at large, with the support of male allies. The fact the rebellions persist, despite enormous dangers, shows that even as structures of control grow in power, women's resistance to such structures also intensifies.

Notes

1. In the USA, 'the sexual views espoused by the religious Right are now embodied in an identifiable social movement' (Gagnon and Simon 2005: 257).
2. This chapter draws on field research in Indonesia since 1979, particularly in Riau, West Sumatra and Jakarta, and on collaborative research with

Indonesian colleagues in the programme 'Women's Empowerment in Muslim Contexts' (2006–10), including:
* Fatayat Nadlatul Ulama: Neng Dara Affiah, Nur Rofiah and others.
* Solidaritas Perempuan: Risma Umar, Andi Cipta, Ni Loh Gusti Madewanti, Marhaeni Nasution, Wahidah Rustam and others.
* Semarak Cerlang Nusa: Sri Wiyanti Eddyono, Dini Anitasari Sabaniah, Indry Octaviani, Melly Setyawati and others.
* LSPPA: Sri Marpinjun and others.
* Koalisi Perempuan Indonesia: Lolly Suhenty, Juni Warlif and others.
* Rahima: Ciciek Farha, Leli Nurohmah, Fatimah Hasan and others.

3. Unilineal kinship systems are found in Sumatra, eastern Indonesia and northern Southeast Asia.
4. Sanday's (1997) analysis of 156 tribal societies reveals a continuum comprising rape-free, rape-present and rape-prone societies.
5. Heyworth (2006) discusses this process in late Anglo-Saxon England.
6. In 1942, of the population of 90 million in the Indonesian archipelago, an estimated 'eight or nine million inhabitants had one or more European ancestors' (Gouda 2008: 165).
7. This included Dutch women in the Netherlands who married men from the Dutch East Indies (Gouda 2008: 168).
8. Sentral Organisasi Buruh Seluruh Indonesia.
9. Persatuan Indonesia Raya.
10. Partai Keadilan Sejahtera.
11. Gerakan Wanita Indonesia.
12. This sequence of events was referred to by the New Order as 'G30S' (Gerakan 30 September, Movement of 30 September) or 'Gestapu' (Gerakan satu Oktober, Movement of 1 October).
13. Undang-Undang 1/1974 tentang Perkawinan.
14. Lembaga Bantuan Hukum – Asosiasi Perempuan Indonesian untuk Keadilan.
15. Variously called *nikah siri, kawin siri, nikah dibawah tangan, kawin diam-diam.*
16. Hunter (1991) argues that such polarization is increasing in American society.
17. Instruksi Presiden 1/1991 tentang Penyebarluasan Kompilasi Hukum Islam.
18. These organizations include: Fatayat Nadlatul Ulama (Fatayat NU), Perhimpunan Pengembangan Pesantren dan Masyarakat (P3M), Forum Kajian Kitab Kuning (FK3), Fahima, Yayasan Puan Amal Hayati, Rahima and Aalimat (see Muttaqin 2008; Arnez 2010; Komnas Perempuan 2010a).
19. These include Siti Musdah Mulia, Siti Ruhaini Dzuhayatin, Husein Muhammad, Syafiq Hasyim, Neng Dara Affiah, Nur Rofiah and others.
20. Majelis Ulama Indonesia.
21. Cited in Muttaqin 2011: 9.
22. No. 1636/MENKES/PER/XI/2010.
23. SK No. 100/C/Kep/D/1991.
24. See www.direktori-perdamaian.org/english/org_detail.php?id=729.

25. Majelis Mujahidin Indonesia.
26. Literally 'seclusion'.
27. Front Pembela Islam.
28. Laskar Jihad.
29. Oxfam (2005: 3) identified various factors for the gender disparity.
30. While other religionists also claim that natural disasters are punishments for sinfulness (Lang and Wee 2005), of significance here is the gender-specific blaming of dead women victims.
31. Undang-Undang 44/2008 tentang Pornografi.
32. Religious proponents include NU, Muhammadiyah, the Indonesian Council of Ulama, the Islamic Defenders' Front, Hizbut Tahrir Indonesia (HTI), and other Islamist groups. Except for Fatayat NU, the women's wings of NU, Muhammadiyah and HTI (Muslimat NU, Aisiyah, and Muslimah HTI) also support the law, together with Wanita Indonesia, another religious women's group. Non-religious proponents are Congress of Indonesian Women (Kongres Wanita Indonesia), Commission for the Protection of Children, Alliance for the Protecting Indonesian Children, as well as a newly formed Society for Rejecting Pornography (see Komnas Perempuan 2011: 24–5).
33. Opponents include three organizations self-identified as 'Islamic', as well as the Catholic Representative Conference of Churches in Indonesia and the Protestant Union of Churches in Indonesia. Other opponents are non-religious organizations, including three women's organizations – Coalition of Indonesian Women (Koalisi Perempuan Indonesia), Solidaritas Perempuan and Foundation for the Journal of Women – and the National Alliance for Unity in Diversity. The provincial governments of Bali, Yogyakarta, Papua and North Sulawesi also oppose the law and have stated that they will not implement it.
34. See www.violenceisnotourculture.org/index.php?q=wrrc/indonesia (accessed 7 November 2011).
35. The Yogyakarta Principles are 'a set of international principles relating to sexual orientation and gender identity … which affirm binding international legal standards with which all States must comply'. See www.yogyakartaprinciples.org (accessed 6 November 2011).
36. See www.pelangiperempuan.or.id/berita/the-yogyakarta-comic-as-an-innovative-educational-tool-for-lgbtiq-youth (accessed 6 November 2011).
37. Personal communication with Kamilia, 2011.
38. She is the 2010 recipient of the Yap Thiam Hien human rights award and co-founder of the Indonesian Conference on Religion and Peace (ICRP), established in 2000 to promote inter-faith dialogue between religions. See http://icrp-online.org/profil (accessed 6 November 2011).
39. *Banyak anak, banyak rezeki, mari kita buat koloni!* (Risma Umar, Andi Cipta, Ni Loh Gusti Madewanti,and Wahidah Rustam of Solidaritas Perempuan 2010: pers. comm.).

References

Abd A'la (2008) 'The genealogy of Muslim radicalism in Indonesia: A study of the roots and characters of the Padri movement', *Journal of Indonesian Islam* 2(2): 267–99.

Alatas, A. (2007) 'Kasus Jilbab (Bagian 1, 2, 3)', http://alwialatas.multiply. com/journal/item/34 (accessed 1 November 2011).

Ames, G.J. (2008) *The Globe Encompassed: The Age of European Discovery, 1500–1700.* London and New York: Pearson.

Andaya, B. (2003) 'Gender, Islam and the Bugis Diaspora in nineteenth- and twentieth-century Riau', *Sari* 21: 77–108.

Arnez, M. (2010) 'Empowering women through Islam: Fatayat NU between tradition and change', *Journal of Islamic Studies* 21(1): 59–88.

APWLD (Asia Pacific Forum on Women, Law and Development) (2006) *Tsunami Aftermath: Violations of Women's Human Rights in Nanggroe Aceh Darussalam, Indonesia.* Jakarta and Banda Aceh: National Secretariat of Solidaritas Perempuan, Bungoeng Jeumpa Aceh Community of Solidaritas Perempuan, APWLD.

Azra, A. (2004) *The Origins of Islamic Reformism in Southeast Asia: Networks of Malay–Indonesian and Middle Eastern 'Ulama' in the Seventeenth and Eighteenth Centuries.* Honolulu: University of Hawai'i Press.

Bennett, L.R. (2005) *Women, Islam and Modernity: Single Women, Sexuality and Reproductive Health in Contemporary Indonesia.* London: RoutledgeCurzon.

Bennett, L.R. (2007) 'Zina and the enigma of sex education for Indonesian Muslim youth', *Sex Education* 7(4), November: 371–86.

Blackburn, S. (2004) *Women and the State in Modern Indonesia.* Cambridge: Cambridge University Press.

Blackburn, S. (2008) 'Indonesian women and political Islam', *Journal of Southeast Asian Studies* 39(1): 83–105.

Brenner, S. (1996) 'Reconstructing self and society: Javanese Muslim women and the "veil"', *American Ethnologist* 23(4), November: 673–97.

Broecker, C. (2010) *Policing Morality: Abuses in the Application of Shari'a in Aceh, Indonesia.* New York: Human Rights Watch.

Brooke, J., and Munday, R. (1848) *A Narrative of Events in Borneo and Celebes Down to the Occupation of Labuan.* London: J. Murray.

Burckhardt, J.L. (1831) *Notes on the Bedouins and Wahábys collected during his travels in the East.* London: Henry Colburn and Richard Bentley.

Burckhardt, J.L. (1968) *Travels in Arabia.* New York: Frank Cass.

Cattoni, V. (2004) 'Reading the Kebaya', paper presented at the 15th Biennial Conference of the Asian Studies Association of Australia, 29 June–2 July, Canberra, http://coombs.anu.edu.au/SpecialProj/ASAA/biennial-conference/2004/Cattoni-V-ASAA2004.pdf (accessed 3 November 2011).

CEDAW (2007) 'Concluding comments of the Committee on the Elimination of Discrimination against Women: Indonesia'. United Nations: Committee on the Elimination of Discrimination against Women, 39th session, 23 July–10 August.

Clarke, M., Ismet F., and Kennedy, S. (eds) (2010) *Post-disaster Reconstruction: Lessons from Aceh*. London: Earthscan.

Corbett, S. (2008). 'A cutting tradition', *New York Times*, 20 January, www.nytimes.com/2008/01/20/magazine/20circumcision-t.html (accessed 1 November 2011).

Cribb, R. (2004) 'Madjlisul Islamil a'laa Indonesia (MIAI) [Great Islamic Council of Indonesia]', in K. Gin Ooi (ed.), *Southeast Asia: A Historical Encyclopedia, from Angkor Wat to East Timor*, Volume 3: *ABC–CLIO*, 814–15.

Diani, H. (2010) 'Being gay, Muslim and Indonesian', *Jakarta Globe*, 16 April, www.thejakartaglobe.com/home/being-gay-muslim-and-indonesian/331310 (accessed 6 November 2011).

Dobbin, C. (1987) *Islamic Revivalism in a Changing Peasant Economy: Central Sumatra, 1784–1847*, 2nd edn. London: Curzon Press.

El-Fadl, K.A. (2001) *Speaking in God's Name: Islamic Law, Authority and Women*. Oxford: Oneworld.

Faizal, E.B. (2011) 'Stop female genital circumcision, activists say', *Jakarta Post*, 25 June, www.thejakartapost.com/news/2011/06/25/stop-female-genital-circumcision-activists-say.html (accessed 1 November 2011).

Fealy, G., and White, S. (2008) *Expressing Islam: religious life and politics in Indonesia*. Singapore: Institute of Southeast Asian Studies.

Federspiel, H.M. (2007) *Sultans, Shamans, and Saints: Islam and Muslims in Southeast Asia*. Honolulu: University of Hawai'i Press.

Foucault, M. (1976) *Histoire de la Sexualité*, 3 vols. Paris: Gallimard. (History of Sexuality, 3 vols, trans. Robert Hurley. New York: Vintage Books, 1988–90.)

Fox, J.J. (2004) 'Currents in contemporary Islam in Indonesia', paper presented at Harvard Asia Vision 21, 29 April–1 May, Cambridge, Massachusetts. http://rspas.anu.edu.au/papers/anthropology/04_fox_islam_indonesia.pdf (accessed 3 November 2011).

Fridae. (2011) 'Q! Film Festival returns to Jakarta and 5 other cities, Sept 30–Oct 8', Fridae: Empowering Gay Asia, 26 September, www.fridae.asia/newsfeatures/2011/09/26/11209.q-film-festival-returns-to-jakarta-and-5-other-cities-sep-30-oct-8?n=aut (accessed 6 November 2011).

Gagnon, J.H., and Simon, W. (2005) *Sexual Conduct: The Social Sources of Human Sexuality*, 2nd edn. Piscataway NJ: Transaction.

Garland, D. (2008) 'On the concept of moral panic', *Crime Media Culture* 4(1): 9–30.

Gellner, E. (1968) 'A pendulum swing theory of Islam', in *Annales de Sociologie Marocaines*. Rabat: Institut de Sociologie, 5–14.

Goode, E., and Ben-Yehuda, N. (1994) *Moral Panics: The Social Construction of Deviance*. Oxford: Blackwell.

Gordan, J.L. (1980) 'The marriage nexus among the Manggarai of West Flores', in J.J. Fox and M. Adams (eds), *The Flow of Life: Essays on Eastern Indonesia*. Cambridge: Harvard University Press, 48–67.

Gouda, F. (2008) *Dutch Culture Overseas: Colonial Practice in the Netherlands Indies, 1900–1942*. Singapore: Equinox Press.

Hadler, J. (2008) 'A historiography of violence and the secular state in Indonesia:

Tuanku Imam Bondjol and the uses of history', *Journal of Asian Studies*, 67(3), August: 971–1010.

Heyworth, M. (2006) 'Be rihtre æwe: legislating and regulating marital morality in late Anglo-Saxon England'. Ph.D. thesis, Centre for Medieval Studies, University of Sydney. http://ses.library.usyd.edu.au/bitstream/2123/1020/2/02whole.pdf (accessed 12 September 2011).

Hunter, J.D. (1991) *Culture Wars: The Struggle to Define America*. New York: Basic Books.

Indonesian Country Report (1996) *Indonesian Country Report to the United Nations Committee on the Elimination of Discrimination Against Women*, CEDAW/C/5/Add.36/Rev.1. 1996. New York: United Nations.

IRIN Humanitarian News (2010) 'Indonesia: female genital mutilation persists despite ban', United Nations Office for the Coordination of Humanitarian Affairs, 2 September, www.irinnews.org/report.aspx?reportid=90366 (accessed 1 November 2011).

Jakarta Post (2000) 'Dharma Wanita "rejects removal of polygamy ban"', 13 December, www.thejakartapost.com/news/2000/12/13/dharma-wanita-039rejects-removal-polygamy-ban039.html (accessed 28 October 2011).

Jakarta Post (2010) 'FPI disrupts gay film festival', 29 September, www.thejakartapost.com/news/2010/09/29/fpi-disrupts-gay-film-festival.html (accessed 28 October 2011).

Jones, G.W. (1994) *Marriage and Divorce in Islamic South-East Asia*. Kuala Lumpur: Oxford University Press.

Kassim, Z.R. (ed.) (2010) *Women and Islam*. Santa Barbara CA: Praeger.

Keddie, N. (1987) 'Islam and society in Minangkabau and in the Middle East: comparative reflections', *Sojourn* 2(1), February: 1–30.

Komnas Perempuan (2007) *Crucial Issues Related to the Implementation of the CEDAW Convention in Indonesia*. Independent report prepared by the National Commission on Violence Against Women presented on the occasion of Indonesia's Combined Fourth and Fifth Periodic Reports to the CEDAW Committee. Jakarta.

Komnas Perempuan (2010a) 'Press conference on the results of the national ALIMAT meeting: realizing true public participation', 4 March, www.komnasperempuan.or.id/en/2010/03/press-conference-on-the-results-of-the-national-alimat-meeting-realizing-true-public-partcipation (accessed 6 November 2011).

Komnas Perempuan (2010b) 'The National Commission on Violence Against Women's conclusions on the judicial review of the Pornography Law', www.komnasperempuan.or.id/en/2010/03/the-national-commission-on-violence-against-women%E2%80%99s-conclusions-on-the-judicial-review-of-the-pornography-law (accessed 6 November 2011).

Komnas Perempuan. (2011) *Seksualitas dan demokrasi: kasus perdebatan UU Pornografi di Indonesia*. Jakarta: Komnas Perempuan.

Kratz, E.U., and Amir, A. (trans. and eds) (2002) *Surat keterangan Syeikh Jalaluddin by Fakih Saghir*. Kuala Lumpur: Dewan Bahasa dan Pustaka.

Kurnia, N. (2009) 'Berbagi suami (Love for share): the discourse of polygamy in a recent Indonesian film', *Intersections: Gender and Sexuality in Asia and the*

Pacific 19, February, http://intersections.anu.edu.au/issue19/kurnia.htm#n2 (accessed 2 November 2011).

Lang, G., and Wee, V. (2005) 'Religions and the tsunami disaster in Southeast Asia', *ASA Sociology of Religion Newsletter* XI(2), Winter: 3, 8.

Lestari, E. (2008) 'The discourses on polygyny: A contemporary debate in Indonesia', M.A. thesis, Institute of Social Studies, Graduate School of Development Studies, The Hague.

Locher-Scholten, E. (2000) *Women and the Colonial State: Essays on Gender and Modernity in the Netherlands Indies, 1900–1942.* Amsterdam: Amsterdam University Press.

Machrusah, S. (2005) 'Muslimat and Nahdlatul Ulama: Negotiating gender relations in a traditional Muslim organisation in Indonesia', M.A thesis, Australian National University, Canberra.

Mas'udi, M.F. (1993) 'Menuju keberagamaan yang pluralistic: reorientasi pemikiran keagamaan Nahdlatul Ulama – Muhammadiyah' (Towards pluralistic religiosity: Reorientation in the religious thought of Nahdlatul Ulama – Muhammadiyah), in Y. Ilyas (ed.), *Muhammadiyah dan NU: reorientasi wawasan keIslaman* (Muhammadiyah and NU: Reorientations of Islamic insights). Yogyakarta: LPPI UMY, LPKSM NU, PP Al-Muhsin.

Mas'udi, M.F. (2002) *Islam and Women's Reproductive Rights.* Kuala Lumpur: Sisters in Islam.

Matheson, V. (1972) 'Mahmud, sultan of Riau and Lingga', *Indonesia* 13: 119–46.

McGregor, K.E. (2008) 'Syarikat and the move to make amends for the Nahdlatul Ulama's violent past', ARI Working Paper no. 107, September. Singapore: Asia Research Institute.

Mir-Hosseini, Z., and Hamzić, V. (2010) *Control and Sexuality: The Revival of Zina Laws in Muslim Contexts.* London: Women Living Under Muslim Laws.

Muhammad, K.H. (2001) *Fiqh perempuan: refleksi kyai atas wacana agama dan gender* (Islamic jurisprudence of women: A kyai's reflection on women and religion). Yogyakarta: LKIS.

Munoz, P. (2006) *Early Kingdoms of the Indonesian Archipelago and the Malay Peninsula.* Singapore: Éditions Didier Millet.

Musawah. (2009) 'Indonesia', in *Home Truths: A Global Report on Equality in the Muslim Family*, www.musawah.org/np_indonesia.asp (accessed 6 November 2011).

Muttaqin, E.Z. (2011) 'Female genital circumcision in Islam: A study of Indonesian 'Ulamā Council's fatwa on female genital circumcision', http://zaymuttaqin.wordpress.com/2011/01/20/female-genital-circumcision-in-islam-a-study-of-indonesian-%E2%80%98ulama-council%E2%80%99s-fatwa-on-female-genital-circumcision (accessed 31 October 2011).

Muttaqin, F. (2008) 'Progressive Muslim feminists in Indonesia from pioneering to the next agendas', M.A. thesis, Center for International Studies, Ohio University.

Needham, R. (1980) 'Principles and variations in the structure of Sumbanese society', in J.J. Fox and M. Adams (eds), *The Flow of Life: Essays on Eastern Indonesia.* Cambridge MA: Harvard University Press, 21–47.

Newman, S.J. (2009) 'Patrolling sexuality', *Inside Indonesia* 96, April–June, www.insideindonesia.org/edition-96-apr-june-2009/patrolling-sexuality-19041197 (accessed 27 November 2011).

O'Shaughnessy, K. (2009) *Gender, State and Social Power in Contemporary Indonesia: Divorce and Marriage Law*. Abingdon: Routledge.

Oxfam (2005) 'The tsunami's impact on women', Oxfam Briefing Note, March, www.oxfam.org/sites/www.oxfam.org/files/women.pdf (accessed 6 November 2011).

Osman, N., and Andriyanto, H. (2010) 'Sexy dancers jailed by Indonesia's porn law as activists fume', *Jakarta Globe*, 13 March, www.thejakartaglobe.com/home/bandung-sexy-dancers-get-25-months-each/363477 (accessed 3 November 2011).

Pasandaran, C. (2010) 'Anti-porn statute to remain law of the land in Indonesia', *Jakarta Globe*, 26 March, www.thejakartaglobe.com/home/anti-porn-statute-to-remain-law-of-the-land-in-indonesia/365771 (accessed 3 November 2011).

Poore, G. (2010a) 'LGBT activism under attack in Surabaya, Indonesia: Part 1', IGLHRC Blog, International Gay and Lesbian Human Rights Commission, 1 April, http://iglhrc.wordpress.com/2010/04/01/threats-to-lgbt-in-surabaya-part-1 (accessed 7 November 2011).

Poore, G. (2010b) 'LGBT activism under attack in Surabaya, Indonesia: Part 2', IGLHRC Blog, International Gay and Lesbian Human Rights Commission, 2 April, http://iglhrc.wordpress.com/2010/04/02/lgbt-activism-under-attack-in-surabaya-indonesia (accessed 7 November 2011).

Poore, G. (2010c) 'Letter to Indonesian Human Rights Commissioners: Appreciation and call for solidarity', IGLHRC Blog, International Gay and Lesbian Human Rights Commission, 18 May, www.iglhrc.org/cgi-bin/iowa/article/takeaction/resourcecenter/1127.html (accessed 7 November 2011).

Population Council Jakarta (2003) 'Female circumcision in Indonesia: Extent, implications and possible interventions to uphold women's health rights', Jakarta: Population Council with support from the Ministry for Women's Empowerment.

Raffles, T.S. (1830) *Memoir of the Life and Public Services of Sir Thomas Stamford Raffles, F.R.S. &C.* London: John Murray.

Riddell, P. (2001) *Islam and the Malay–Indonesian World: Transmission and Responses.* Honolulu: University of Hawai'i Press.

Rinaldo, R. (2011) 'Gender and moral visions in Indonesia', *Asia Pacific: Perspectives* 10(1), May: 44–60.

Robinson, G. (1995) *The Dark Side of Paradise: Political Views in Bali.* Ithaca NY: Cornell University Press.

Robinson, K. (2009) *Gender, Islam and democracy in Indonesia.* London: Routledge.

Sagita, D. (2010) 'MUI gives thumbs down to Q! Gay Film Festival', *Jakarta Globe*, 1 October, www.thejakartaglobe.com/home/mui-gives-thumbs-down-to-q-gay-film-festival/399020 (accessed 7 November 2011).

Sairin, S. (1982) *Javanese Trah: Kin-based Social Organisation.* Yogyakarta: Gajah Madah University Press.

Sanday, P.R. (1997) 'The socio-cultural context of rape', in L.L. O'Toole, J.R. Schiffman and M.L. Kiter Edwards (eds), *Gender Violence: Interdisciplinary Perspectives*, 2nd edn. New York: New York University Press, 52–66.

Sayyid, B.S. (2003). *A Fundamental Fear: Eurocentrism and the Emergence of Islamism*. London: Zed Books.

Semarak Cerlang Nusa. (2011) 'Inisiatif dan strategi laki-laki dalam penghapusan poligami di Indonesia', Jakarta: Semarak Cerlang Nusa Consultancy, Research and Education for Social Transformation, Institute for Women Empowerment, Women Living Under Muslim Laws.

Sen, K. (1999) 'Women on the move', *Inside Indonesia* 58, April-June, www.insideindonesia.org/edition-58–apr-jun-1999/women-on-the-move-2209690 (accessed 3 November 2011).

Sikand, Y. (2010) 'Indonesia: Developing a discourse of gender justice in Islam', *Countercurrents*, 24 June, www.wluml.org/node/6451 (accessed 1 November 2011).

Sim, A. (2006) 'The sexual economy of desire: Girlfriends, boyfriends and babies among Indonesian women migrants in Hong Kong', paper presented at the International Workshop on Sexuality and Migration in Asia, Asian MetaCentre for Population and Sustainable Development Analysis, National University of Singapore, 10–11 April.

Simanjuntak, H. (2009) 'Women banned from wearing trousers', *Jakarta Post*, 28 October, www.thejakartapost.com/news/2009/10/28/women-banned-wearing-trousers.html (accessed 27 November 2011).

Smith-Hefner, N. (2007) 'Javanese women and the veil in post-Soeharto Indonesia', *Journal of Asian Studies* 66(2), May: 389–420.

Suryadinata, L., Arifin, E.N., and Ananta, A. (2003) *Indonesia's Population: Ethnicity and Religion in a Changing Political Landscape*. Singapore: Institute of Southeast Asian Studies.

Suryakusuma, J.I. (1996) 'The state and sexuality in New Order Indonesia', in L.J. Sears (ed.), *Fantasizing the Feminine in Indonesia*. Durham NC: Duke University Press, 92–119.

Tedjasukmana, J. (2008) 'Indonesia's new anti-porn agenda', *Time*, 6 November, www.time.com/time/world/article/0,,1857090,00.html (accessed 6 November 2011).

Tedjasukmana, J. (2010) 'Indonesia's artists vs. Muslim extremists', *Time*, 7 July, www.time.com/time/world/article/0,8599,2001698,00.html (accessed 6 November 2011).

van der Kroef, J.M. (1953) 'Conflicts of religious policy in Indonesia', *Far Eastern Survey* 22: 121–5.

van Wichelen, S. (2009). 'Polygamy talk and the politics of feminism: Contestations over masculinity in a new Muslim Indonesia', *Journal of International Women's Studies* 11(1): 173–87.

Wee, V. (2002) 'Ethno-nationalism in process: Ethnicity, atavism and indigenism in Riau', *Pacific Review* 15(4): 497–516.

WEMC–Solidaritas Perempuan. (2009) 'Report on a successful campaign to halt sharia laws in South Sulawesi', Women's Empowerment in Muslim Contexts e-Bulletin, September, www.wemc.com.hk/web/e-bulletin/09–2009/index. htm (accessed 27 November 2011).

Wiener, M. (2005) 'Breasts, (un)dress, and modernist desires in the Balinese–tourist encounter', in A. Masquelier (ed.), *Dirt, Undress, and Difference: Critical Perspectives on the Body's Surface*. Bloomington, Indiana University Press, 61–95.

Wieringa, S. (1985) 'The perfumed nightmare: Some notes on the Indonesian Women's Movement', Institute of Social Studies Working Paper, The Hague.

Wieringa, S. (2002) *Sexual Politics in Indonesia*. London: Macmillan.

Wieringa, S. (2009) 'Sexual slander and the 1965–1966 mass killings in Indonesia: Political and methodological considerations', ARI Working Paper no. 125, Asia Research Institute, Singapore.

Winzeler, R.L., Cohen, R., Hunt, R., Hutterer, K.L, Izard, M., Panoff, M., Riggs, F.W., van der Kroef, J.M, and Webb, M.C. (1976) 'Ecology, culture, social organization, and state formation in Southeast Asia [and comments and reply]', *Current Anthropology* 17(4), December: 623–40.

Wiyana, D., Agustina, W., Nurhayati, B., and Nurhayati, N. (2006) 'Aa Gym's surprise polygamy', *Tempo* 15(VII), 12–18 December, www.asiaviews.org/index.php?option=com_content&view=article&id=1951:headlinealias1951&catid=1:headlines&Itemid=2 (accessed 30 October 2011).

Zakariya, H. (2011) 'From Makkah to Bukit Kamang? The moderate versus radical reforms in West Sumatra (ca. 1784–1819)', *International Journal of Humanities and Social Science* 1(14), October: 195–203.

2

Iranian women and
shifting sexual ideologies, 1850–2010

Claudia Yaghoobi

Sexual ideology is a significant arena in the construction of societal identity, and nowhere more so than in Iran. Investigating how shifts in sexual ideology are expressed within accepted social norms can reveal some of the forces that bring about such social transformations, as well as bring to light the impacts that such shifts have on the lives of individual citizens, particularly members of less empowered segments of society (Foucault 1978). Thus, an overview of changes in both perception and articulation of sexuality in Iran, from the nineteenth century to the first decade of the twenty-first century, can open a window to the primary subject of this chapter – the processes involved in the diminished social and legal status of Iranian women and their resistance in light of these changes.

Sexuality and sexual mores in Iran have transformed substantially from the nineteenth century, where gender segregation was the norm and sexual practices played a less direct role in people's identity. While most people married and had children, same-sex practices, for example, were not stigmatized and were quite widely practised, as evidenced by historical research as well as sources such as poetry and Sufi literature (Najmabadi 2005; Afary 2009). With modernity, social engineering by the state and public discourse launched by intellectuals have continued to transform the definition of 'acceptable' sexuality; in contrast with earlier public space gender segregation, between 1900 and 1979 the state and intellectuals rather rapidly paved the way for heterosexuality and hetero-sociability (the mingling of men and women) to become the social norm.

However, the establishment of the Islamic Republic following the Iranian Revolution in 1979 changed the social landscape yet again, through a range of state-sponsored policies intended to rebuild a gender-segregated/apartheid society. Policies included the introduction of a restrictive dress code for women, the gender segregation of public spaces, and the annulment of the modest reforms to family law that Iranian women had secured after sixty-seven years of struggle that began with the 1906 Constitutional Revolution. The Islamic regime unabashedly championed male heterosexuality; promoting polygyny as a prized practice, making divorce once again a unilateral male right, and legalizing unlimited temporary marriages for men (Paidar 1995; Afary 2009). At the same time new legal provisions were introduced that made consensual sexual relations outside marriage and same-sex relations a crime against the state. People found guilty of such crimes became liable to severe punishments, including state-sanctioned judicial killings (for example, adultery became punishable by death by stoning). Considerable resources went into organizing moral police forces, whose job was to reinforce adherence to these new regulations. While the post-1979 regime in Iran is often misconstrued as monolithic, this chapter in no way reinforces such an analysis; rather, it focuses on laws and policies promulgated under the regime precisely because their focus – the control of sexuality – has provided consensus-building among a set of relatively diverse and even oppositional religious actors and policymakers.

Increasingly over the last few decades, as the number of convictions for the crimes defined by these laws has increased, more Iranians have been drawn into the discourse around the issue of sexuality, including sexual orientation, and the advisability of the state's unrelenting attempts to control and shape it. Thus, as scholars have documented, sexuality today has become more politicized than ever before in the history of Iran (Yaghmaian 2002; Afary 2009; Mahdavi 2009). Rebellious young people, who make up approximately 70 per cent of the total population today – and, among them, young women in particular – view their bodies and the articulation of their sexuality as a site of resistance against the government.[1]

While on the one hand this undoubtedly reflects highly personal perspectives, it is simultaneously an explicit expression of political opposition to the Islamic regime. Indeed this new and widespread form of resistance (Varzi 2006; Naw 2008; Mahdavi 2009) – along with more organized and formal resistance efforts such as the Stop Stoning Forever and One Million Signatures campaigns (Hoodfar and Sadeghi 2009) – primarily demands the removal of discriminatory laws against women, so that women gain the same rights and control over their bodies and minds as male citizens. Furthermore, the draconian treatment of homosexuality has made the question of sexual orientation, and of whether the state has any right to interfere in the affairs of two consenting adults regardless of whether the relationship is heterosexual or homosexual, more prominent than at any other time in the second half of the twentieth century.

This chapter is mainly concerned with the impact of historical changes on sexuality discourse and practice, and with the ways Iranian women have struggled to carve spaces of empowerment within the constrained/repressive environment. The chapter has three main foci. First, based on existing literature, I highlight how sexuality was defined in the urban, pre-modern context and the role(s) played by the community and socio-religious institutions in governing sexuality prior to the twentieth century. Second, against this background I then outline the impact of modernity and ideas of modernization on sexual ideology and on the establishment of hetero-sociability and heterosexuality as the norm, while also highlighting the role that women played in this transformation between 1900 and 1979. This section aims to address how the introduction of modernization and a Western model of modernity changed sexual ideology from 1900 onward. During this period, women both within and outside the state structure pushed to expand education for women and facilitate their access to the public sphere. More importantly, they pushed for the reform of the family law, a major demand of women since the constitutional revolution. Finally, the chapter briefly deals with contemporary concerns that have arisen since the 1979 revolution and the establishment of the Islamic Republic. I will review the state's attempts to regulate sexuality through a legislative focus on 'morality' and the introduction of harsh penalties for those, especially women, who do not comply. Here I specifically explore how the current expression of sexuality in youth circles is framed as part of resistance to the regime. It appears that in pre-revolutionary Iran many women welcomed the advent of state-sponsored modernity, including 'modern' sexuality, in part because it expanded sexual autonomy and personal opportunities, for heterosexual women in particular (Sanasarian 1982; Paidar 1995). In contrast, a number of women (i.e. not only urban, educated women – see Mahdavi 2009) have now become highly articulate in reclaiming agency over their bodies and sexuality, as well as outspoken in their criticisms of state interference in their private, intimate matters.

Sexuality in pre-modernity urban Iran, 1850–1925

At any historical juncture, conventional definitions of appropriate male and female sexual expression and desire are based primarily on the established norms and standards of a given community and society. Pre-modern Iranian society attempted to maintain a patriarchal structure in part by suppressing female sexuality and underscoring male sexual primacy. Discussing sex, particularly with young women in nineteenth-century Iran, was outside the norms of the patriarchal hegemony. Consequently, Iranian women, who commonly were married quite young, had very limited knowledge about sex and no right to express their opinions over, or to explore, their sexuality (Afary 2009: 7–8). Further, the importance of female virginity prior to marriage as a signifier of family honour added to the oppressive sexual power relations and the tensions around marriage (Vieille 1978: 455). On the wedding night, a groom was under immense pressure to prove his virility, while the bride was terrified lest for some reason she did not 'prove' her virginity (Afary 2009: 28).[2] Generally older men and sometimes powerful matriarchs controlled the most important rites of passages, such as marriage, in the lives of young females (and males). Although both Islamic and pre-Islamic Sasanian (224–651) law considered the age of puberty and thus marriage to be 9 years old for girls, Shi'a and Sunni laws allowed fathers/guardians to promise a minor girl to whomever they wished before puberty. While neither young girls nor boys had the opportunity to choose their spouse, if men could afford it they could marry more than one wife and even engage in temporary marriages; thus, at least theoretically, they could have a degree of autonomy that was denied to women. Furthermore, men had the formal unilateral right of divorce, while women were granted such a right only in very limited and rare circumstances (Mir-Hosseini 1996; Afary 2009).

Nonetheless, despite women's lack of formal power to defy their fathers'/guardians' decisions, recent research does show that some did manage to circumvent unwanted arranged marriages through various strategies, such as showing their discontent to the suitor's family or acting in ways that were deemed very inappropriate (Afary 2009: 23–5). Elite women, through family influence and connections, were more often able to initiate and obtain divorce (Afary 2009: 40). Within marriage, a husband had absolute legal and customary rights over his wife's body; she was expected to fulfil his sexual desires regardless of her own wishes. In another clear assertion of women's bodies as male property, women's visibility was restricted: a wife could only show herself to her husband and certain categories of male kin. Here as well, however, women's lack of formal power over their sexuality did not mean an absence of resistance nor an absolute compliance within the bounds of marriage. For example, women could, in some cases, take advantage of provisions that allowed them to demand sexual fulfilment within marriage. Lack of sexual 'prowess' on the part of a husband actually allowed a woman to sue for divorce. Indeed, in some schools of Islamic law a woman can get an immediate divorce if she claims fear of *fitna* (social disorder), which implies that he does not satisfy her sexually (Fluehr-Lobban 2004). However, in most Muslim societies, it is not socially acceptable for women to provoke a divorce on this ground. Regardless, men were concerned about their reputations for virility and masculinity, and worried that women could spread gossip concerning their sexual inability.

Women found other ways to resist their sexual oppression and to break the silences imposed on them by social mores and legal prescriptions. One way was to use the very veil that symbolized patriarchal control to resist their exclusion from public life. In urban centres, from approximately the age of 9, girls were expected to wear a loose-fitting outfit called *chador* in public. In addition to *chador*, urban women wore a face covering, *rubandeh* (or *niqab*), which in most cases only revealed the eyes. Women from lower and lower-middle classes went about the city without facing much constraint, as long as they were veiled. There is also compelling evidence that elite women, who were subject to more restrictions, also used a veil (often that of their lower-class maids) to enter public places without the knowledge of their husbands or guardians. This offered women the possibilities of visiting a doctor, socializing with other women on their own, or even trying to interact with men in public, by discreetly revealing a part of their body or face to them (Afary 2009: 44–7). The anonymity that the veil afforded women thus enabled them to subvert limitations and exercise a certain degree of sexual freedom.[3] A similar impulse can be found among women who cross-dressed and appeared in male clothing in urban centres (Afary 2009).

When unable to transcend the limitations placed on their sexual desires (by manipulating the imposition of the veil, destabilizing its implied 'modesty' or cross-dressing), women did at least sometimes manage to express their sexual frustration indirectly, including through culturally condoned female-centred rituals that allowed them to assert their needs and agency. Thus, for example, Afsaneh Najmabadi (2005) argues that traditional practices allegedly performed as rituals to bring about pregnancy should in fact be read as expressions of women's sexual agency and resistance. In one of these rituals, called 'untying the knot of the trousers', women collectively sing the following: '*Havan-i man dastah mikhwad / mard-i kamar bastah mikhvad* (My mortar needs a pestle / it desires a man with a tied belt)' (Najmabadi 2005: 25). The song, Najmabadi argues, addresses women's sexual frustration and expresses their breaking with the conventions that encourage them to remain silent about their sexuality.

Other strategies included women renouncing or refusing sexual relations with men altogether or entering into sexual relationships with other women. Women also used some of the religious rituals and avenues open to them to expand both their networks and the boundaries of friendship and support to non-kin groups. Through visiting shrines, particularly the shrines of female saints, women could develop *sighehs*, or 'bonds of sisterhood'. These were similar to 'bonds of brotherhood' that often included homoerotic relations among men (Khansari 1999; Najmabadi 2005; Babayan 2008; Afary 2009). Despite the fact that overt same-sex sexuality was inexpressible and that even heterosexual expressions were meant to be restrained, male and female homoerotic sexual expressions, though deemed inappropriate for women, were widely practised in pre-nineteenth-century Iranian society (Najmabadi 2005; Afary 2009) among people of different classes, ages and locations. Thus, while it is plausible to view the bonds of sisterhood as enabling sexual and homoerotic dimensions, the extent to which this happened is not clear and we need further research in this area. What is clear, however, is that *sighehs* included emotional bonds of solidarity outside women's immediate kin groups.

Yet another strategy for women to express their non-compliance with male dominance over their sexuality was to join Sufi circles, many of which were open to women from the late eighth century on. Renouncing marriage and staying celibate was a common practice among female Sufis. This, however, indicated 'a complete double standard [for men and women] with regard to the concept of earthly love', which was considered a 'bridge to the divine' in Sufism (Afary 2009: 100). Sufi men were encouraged to experience earthly love as a doorway to ultimate divine love; whereas Sufi women were expected to renounce all types of earthly desire (Lewis 2000; Afary 2009). Nonetheless, although male sexuality was given more importance and recognition even in Sufi circles, the renowned scholar of Islam Annemarie Schimmel (1975: 432) comments that 'Sufism, more than stern orthodoxy, offered women a certain amount of possibilities to participate actively in the religious and social life.' Certain Sufi shrines were exclusively open to women worshippers. Further, women could attend Sufi lectures and support or become members of certain Sufi orders (Schimmel 1975: 432–4). There were even a number of popular Sufi women, such as Rumi's favourite female disciple, Fateme Khatun, who was his friend Salah al-Din's daughter (Smith 1928; Schimmel 1975; Lewis 2000: 211–12; Wines 2000: 64).

Although documented literature on female Sufis and women's sisterhood bonds in Sufi circles is scarce, the most thorough source is the late-seventeenth-century *Kolsum Naneh*, written by Molla Aqa Jamal Khansari (b. 1605). The book includes a chapter entitled 'On Sisterhood Sighehs'. Sisterhood bonds would be tied after a period of negotiations between the two women. The ritual would begin with a woman who sought a 'sister' asking a love broker to negotiate the matter by taking 'a tray of sweets ... in the middle of [which] was a dildo or doll made of wax or leather. If the beloved agreed, she threw a white scarf over the tray'; otherwise, she would use a black one (Afary 2009: 102). There were special days when vows of sisterhood were usually contracted, such as Nowruz (Persian New Year) and the 'Eid of Ghadir Khom – the day when according to Shi'a belief the Prophet Muhammad designated Ali as his successor. Customary practices such as socializing for several months, sending love tokens to one another, and exploring compatibility would happen before tying bonds. Husbands often resented sisterhood bonds, which they perceived as threatening to their marriage. However, the segregated nature of social life was such that in many cases a husband's resentment would not stop the adopted sisters from secretly meeting and spending time with each other; sometimes the process did precipitate a divorce. In such cases many of these sisters remained in the relationship and did not remarry (Khansari 1999: 60–3, 89–91; Afary 2009). Although Khansari's work is evidence of this form of female companionship, within which women experienced a degree of power and freedom as well as deep emotional relations, it does not provide enough information about the extent to which women were sexually or erotically involved.

Kathryn Babayan (2008) also argues that women used traditional venues and social patterns incorporated into customary practices to establish long-lasting relationships with one another. In her essay 'In Spirit We Ate Each Other's Sorrow', Babayan (2008) analyses the writings of a late-seventeenth-century Isfahani widow regarding the separation from her female companion. The elite Isfahani woman embarks on a pilgrimage to Mecca after her husband's death. Her grief and distress over the death of her husband, in conjunction with the powerfully affective religious rituals and prayers of the pilgrimage, renew the widow's sorrow over her separation from her female companion. She decides to travel and pay her a visit; however, the woman's situation, including that she is married, means the widow must once again leave her dear friend. Babayan argues that the widow's writings demonstrate clearly how her own subjectivity was significantly impacted by the dominant discourses of the time on desire and the institution of *sigheh*. The widow's longing to reunite with her former female companion is evidence of the powerful female space created through the sisterhood *sighehs* in Isfahani society. However, as Babayan notes, writings of the time such as the widow's portray how prevailing moralistic views discredited this female companionship, forcing women bound by such ties to live apart, and likely regulating their sexuality (Babayan 2008: 239–74). The widow's writings, it can be argued, illustrate how society and community suppressed female expressions of sexuality and displacement of prevailing male authority. The widow's seventeenth-century account nevertheless reveals her struggle to assert her agency despite this.

Female same-sex relations were prevalent in harems at the time. The memoirs of Qajar Princess Taj al-Saltaneh (1848–1896), the information given by the court gynaecologist and obstetrician Dr Polak (1982), and the work of Qajar and early Pahlavi period historian Jafar Shahri (1990) all illustrate that many women engaged in homoerotic relations (*mosaheqeh*). According to Shahri (2009, vol. VI: 328–9), two categories of women entered sisterhood bonds: those who were unwillingly deprived of male companionship, and those who were predisposed to or seduced by same-sex eroticism. Shahri's use of the term 'seduced' may be misleading; we can equally assume that women chose same-sex relationships over the limited options available within the dictates of their society. Counter to Shahri's portrayal of women as passive or reactive in terms of sexual relations, we can argue that women were deliberate in their choice to pursue same-sex relationships.

It is important to address briefly male same-sex practices, as these were constructed differently, and had social consequences distinct from those involving women. While female homoeroticism was considered improper, male same-sex relations, so long as they were discreet, were a tolerated cultural practice in pre-twentieth-century Mediterranean Muslim societies. Similar to European pre-modern notions, Iranian men were not necessarily identified by their sexual activities, and male same-sex relations were practised within the frameworks of various categories of social relations; in pre-modern Iranian society they tended to involve pairs from different age groups, classes or social standing (Najmabadi 2000, 2004, 2005:

16–22; Afary 2009). Afary refers to pre-nineteenth-century male same-sex relations in Iran as 'status-defined homosexuality', whereby adult men sexually engaged with adolescent boys (*amrad*). The adult was assumed to be the initiator and agent, the *amrad* the passive recipient of the older man's affection/sexual interest. The *amrad* was in fact not supposed to take pleasure in the sexual activity. The relationship might include courtship and mentorship between the adult man and the *amrad* until he reached adulthood. Men who had sexual relationships with other men or with adolescent boys could be married and have a family as well; heterosexual marriage prevailed as the ideal relationship between sexes, and having an *amrad* in no way precluded a man from having a wife. The *amrad* was expected to outgrow the relationship once he reached adulthood, and to marry and father children, while concurrently able to enter into a same-sex relationship as the active, mature partner. The passive partner in such relationships was often the object of derision, arguably because of his equation with the stereotypical submissive female role (Schmitt and Sofer 1992; Murray and Roscoe 1997; Afary 2009: 79). Similar to same-sex female relationships, those between men encompassed certain courtship rules. However, unlike female companionship, male same-sex relationships were tolerated and relatively acceptable within the prevailing moral norms and social forces.

The patriarchal structure of society through the 1800s prioritized male sexuality, and accepted men's hetero- and homosexual practices within a framework of generally strong surveillance of citizens' sexuality through various socio-religious and community institutions. There is thus a great deal of documentation concerning male homoeroticism of the time. Classical Persian literature and Sufi poetry from the twelfth to the fifteenth century is also filled with themes of male same-sex relations and homoerotic allusions and symbolism. In addition, while numerous codes of conduct concerning male homosexuality exist in the literature of the period, their absence regarding same-sex relations between women strongly suggests that these were considered inappropriate and disdainful. Indeed, female sexuality is almost invisible in documents of the period; it was not articulated publicly and was defined only with reference to male sexuality. However, as we have seen from the little documentation and research that does exist, despite overwhelming constraints and strong incentives to comply with traditional gender norms, women managed to find ways to exercise sexual and social autonomy.

Sexuality and the introduction
of modernity, 1925–79

The Qajars, who ruled Iran from 1794 to 1925, entered into many economic arrangements with European states – a process through which Iran largely lost its economic independence. Along with the exchange of goods and ideas, gradually, over the course of the nineteenth century, interaction with Europeans engendered certain changes concerning gender and sexuality. Europeans were scandalized by, and wrote extensively about, the extent of male 'homosexuality' in Iran, which by now had become defined as a perverse practice in much of Europe. Iranians for their part were astonished at the public display of European women's bodies, and the institutionalized monogamy of the West. Some Iranian men viewed the clean-shaven European men, who wore tight-fitting clothes, as *amrads* despite their age, although they eventually realized that in fact the Europeans were intensely homophobic.

The increasing dominance of European-influenced notions of modernity considerably changed the dominant sexual ideology. The comparatively open display of heterosexual affection in European public spaces and the Europeans' abhorrence for public manifestations of same-sex attraction brought about new national debates and widespread discussions between Iranians on gender and sexuality. Both in Iran and in the region some intellectuals, without questioning patriarchy per se, began viewing women's education and more equitable family structures as the key sources of European advancement, and began advocating for a more woman-friendly social system. In these debates hetero-sociability was presented as the norm and both homosexuality and polygamy were constructed as perverted, backward traditions that had to be pushed to the margins and eradicated.[4] Iranian diaspora newspapers in London, Istanbul, Bombay, and other cities began to advocate for women's education and other gender reforms including monogamy and mandatory heterosexuality. Intellectuals inside the country launched these debates among other enlightened segments of the population (Paidar 1995; Najmabadi

2000, 2004; Amin 2002).[5] These public debates struck a chord amidst the increasing soul-searching by Iranians, who sought to analyse the reasons behind Iran's loss of autonomy to European powers. In this context, Iran saw a modest gradual expansion in education for women, and the appearance of men and women together in public became more fashionable among the elites and educated strata in Iran (Najmabadi 2005: 54). The introduction of modernity to urban, upper- and middle-class constituencies also had a broader impact in terms of women's involvement in political matters: intellectuals attentive to debates on liberal democracy highlighted how the arbitrary rule of the monarch effectively strangled Iran while ceding increasing rights to European powers. They advocated for the development of a different and more publicly accountable political system. Yet other intellectuals launched debates arguing for secularism and a rule of law providing equality of citizens. In this context women began actively participating in national debates around gender and family law reform. Gradually, the imagining of a different society widened among urban social groups. This led to women playing a significant part in the successful nationwide street protests in 1887 against the tobacco monopoly granted to British companies by the Shah of Iran. Women marched front and centre with men towards the Shah's palace, and a number of women were amongst those killed in the protest (Keddie 1967; Afary 1996). This not only politicized more women to participate in national debates and activism for change; it also legitimized their presence in constitutional reformist circles, and women began organizing their own associations, primarily around nationalist causes and demands for the introduction of a democratic constitution (Afary 1989).

This burgeoning political consciousness and activism led to the successful Constitutional Revolution (1906–11), a turning point in the life of the nation, particularly for women and for gender relations (Afary 1989, 1996; Paidar 1995). Though conservative religious *ulama* had formed a coalition with modernists and nationalists and successfully managed to deny women's political rights in the name of religion, women continued to agitate for reform and for the expansion of women's education, which they saw as key to their emancipation and to the end of women's relegation to the private sphere and their valuation solely as mothers. Recognizing that raising awareness and questioning the status quo were prerequisites to changing gender relations, women organized to open schools for girls, hospitals for women, and remained active in national political debates (Paidar 1995). These activities were crucial in shaping a context in which wider numbers of women could formulate further political demands for education, marriage reform and political participation, and push them onto the national agenda (Afary 1989: 66; Paidar 1995).[6]

Women launched publications showcasing women's rights issues, including *Danesh* (Knowledge) in 1910, *Zaban-e Zanan* (Women's Voice) in 1919, and *Alam Nesvan* (Women's Universe) in 1920, and contributed to various modernist newspapers and publications (Sanasarian 1982: 28–40). Various organizations and societies for women were established, both before and after the Constitutional Revolution: the Women's Freedom Society in 1906; the National Ladies Society in 1910; Jamiet Nesvan Vatankhah Iran (Patriotic Women's League of Iran) in 1922; Jamiet Payke Saadat Nesvan (Messenger of Women's Prosperity) in 1927. The main thrust of most of the publications and organizations was to raise women's awareness and urge them to struggle to achieve the rights long denied them (Sanasarian 1982: 28–40). With the fall of the Qajar dynasty in 1925 and the establishment of the modernist monarchy under Reza Pahlavi (1925–42), a new era dawned for women activists; they were increasingly co-opted into the state structure, where they could more effectively promote women's education and gender reform from within the system.

The new regime's preoccupation with modernizing the country included a gender ideology which profoundly impacted on the creation of modern Iranian womanhood. Pahlavi's policies in this arena focused on the promotion of heterosexuality as the only acceptable form of sexuality, and the ending of gender segregation and female seclusion, through women's education, their integration into the workforce and de-veiling (Paidar 1995; Hoodfar 1997; Amin 2002). Following other modernist states in the region, especially Turkey, the new regime introduced a national dress code in 1929, according to which men and women were expected to wear 'Western style' clothing. In 1936, Pahlavi issued a police-enforced ban on veiling in public (Paidar 1995; Hoodfar 1997), and offered state employment and educational opportunities for urban women willing to abandon their veils. However, while the regime aimed to promote a modern way of life supposedly modelled on 'the West', it did not introduce any reforms to the prevailing polygynous structure of marriage in Iran. Indeed, as numerous Iranian men, including Reza Shah himself and many other political elites, had multiple wives, marriage reform was not on the agenda.

The state's modernization agenda lacked support from significant sections of the population, including conservative and religious groups. While initial opposition centred on women's education, the most controversial reform was the de-veiling of women: this further alienated larger segments of the urban population, including many women from diverse class backgrounds who believed in veiling as a religious requirement. Among these strata, families of young girls from more traditional backgrounds, regardless of their economic class, generally did not permit their daughters to attend modern schools beyond the primary level, and continued to observe the veil even if in its less restricted form (Hoodfar 1997). Further, the age of marriage among these demographics remained low (often before or at the onset of puberty). While some groups softened their views on education, there remained a major gap between modernist sectors of society and the more religious and conservative sectors, with a small constituency in the middle which supported more indigenous notions of modernization and gender reforms. In short, whereas pre-nineteenth-century sexual and gender norms were primarily defined by the standards set by the community and socio-religious institutions, the Pahlavi era marked the beginning of a period of state intervention, to which many were opposed.

A number of factors – ranging from the unveiling of women; their increased presence in public spaces, partly motivated by a more widespread acceptability of education for women; and the encouragement of normative hetero-sociability – disrupted male homo-social spaces. Tehran University, which had opened in 1934, admitted twelve women in 1936. However, Badr ol-Moluk Bamdad (1977: 98–9), one of the earlier historians of Iran's women's movement writes that although girls 'had deliberately and prudently prepared themselves for entry, the boys were completely disconcerted. For most of them mixing with girls was something unforeseen.' Even male professors avoided looking into girls' eyes while answering their academic questions. With time, the removal of strict segregation of the sexes and women's increased presence in public gave young men and women the opportunity to see and socialize with each other before marriage, even if under the strict supervision of family. It thus gradually became acceptable for young men and women to have some degree of participation in the selection of their future spouses (Afary 2009: 160–62).

These reforms did have some impacts on the prevailing patriarchal culture, by giving a little more space to women, and by limiting the power of fathers and agent kin over them. However, in the family sphere women's status was relatively unaffected. While a reform was introduced raising the minimum age of marriage (15 years for girls and 18 for boys), in practice overall gender relations within the family structure remained unequal and women remained subjects of their husbands. Many women activists thus viewed an equitable family structure as the foundation for truly equal citizenship for women, and devoted their activism and consciousness-raising above all to family law reform (Sayyah 1975; Sanasarian 1982).

Although the modernist regime advocated active female participation in society, it did not appreciate democracy or citizen-led initiatives, and ensured that gender reforms were decreed by the state alone. For instance, in 1932 the Patriotic Women's League, a progressive association for women, sponsored the Oriental Women's Congress in Tehran, which called for changes in women's rights to vote, compulsory education for girls, equal pay at work, abolition of polygamy, education for adult women, and improvement of men's morals (Sanasarian 1982: 66–7). Immediately after the congress, in an attempt to homogenize women's organizations and to co-opt their aspirations, Reza Shah closed down the Patriotic Women's League along with other women's organizations and formed the new government-controlled and sponsored Ladies' Centre (*Kanun-e Banuan*), led by his daughter Princess Shams.

Nonetheless, whether they worked from within the state structure or independently, women remained focused on the reform of family law and women's political rights, both of which were subject to much resistance by conservative social forces led by religious clerics. Finally, more than fifty years after the success of the Constitutional

Revolution, women's sustained efforts resulted in the 1963, all-male, nationwide referendum, which granted women political rights, including the right to vote and to stand for elections (Paidar 1995). In the following election six women entered the lower house of the parliament, and two were appointed to the senate. After this success, all energies were focused on family law. After many years of intensive lobbying, in 1967 a mild reform to the Family Protection Law was finally introduced where the unilateral right of men to divorce was curbed. Divorce now had to be registered through the family court, and the right to polygyny became subject to the agreement of the first wife or the family court. More importantly, within divorce the custody of children, which had automatically gone to the father after the initial period of infancy, was now decided at the discretion of the court, with the best interests of the child in mind. The law was again revised in 1973 to improve its provisions, increasing the age of marriage to 18 for women (Afary 2009). Although gender reforms in Iran are often presented as a matter of state intervention, an examination of the history of political movements makes clear that it was women's awareness of their rights, their collective efforts in consciousness-raising, and their assertiveness that gave the regime its power to address and reformulate gender discourses.

The combined impact of these reforms and of women's increased political visibility in the 1960s led to the emergence of a new generation of assertive women with confidence and a firm belief in their equality with men and as citizens. They were more outspoken about their sexuality and their right to sexual freedom and to sexual pleasure. Examples of women breaking sexual taboos can be found in the poetry of Forough Farrokhzad (1935–1967). This new generation of urban, educated, politically savvy women identified with Farrokhzad's sexually provocative poems, which became the subject of many debates in intellectual circles.[7] Nonetheless her fame and considerable popularity among the large number of young women who followed her example was an indication of an emerging consciousness, which, even if it was not articulated as such by its pioneers, can be viewed as the Iranian second wave of feminism that moved beyond women's legal rights alone and incorporated the notion of the individual right to love and sexual pleasure.

With the Pahlavi era (1925–79), women found increasing ways to access the public sphere through education and state jobs, which gave them some economic independence. However, despite all the changes that took place during the Pahlavi regime in the more modern sectors and larger cities, many pre-nineteenth-century customs and practices, such as the institution of marriage, remained the same among the conventional middle classes, as well as in the low-income strata and rural communities.

Further, despite gradual acceptance of women in public life and their increasing role in the labour market, conservative social forces, comprising a large segment of the nation, remained hostile to these changes, which they viewed as Westernization in the name of modernity. As the regime became more autocratic and the space for basic democratic rights, freedom of expression and citizens' participation lessened, more people, including a sizable portion of the educated middle classes and intellectuals, joined the chorus of opposition.

As the arena of women's rights increasingly became the site for the regime and oppositional forces to challenge each other through the 1960s and 1970s, despite different ideological views, leading Islamist clerics, lay Muslim thinkers, as well as many secular leftist intellectuals came to share a strong hostility towards aspects of modernist gender norms. While the ayatollahs upheld the traditional hierarchy and reiterated that God had appointed men as guardians of women and that the reforms were un-Islamic, nationalist intellectuals such as Jalal Al-e Ahmad (1923–1969), a highly influential writer and public persona who supported the unveiling of women, their education, their employment and divorce rights, was at the same time critical of burgeoning Western-style consumerism and the entertainment industry, and was against the public display of eroticized female bodies. Like Al-e Ahmad, Ali Shari'ati (1933–1977), a French-educated sociologist and probably the most influential intellectual at the time concerning the use of Islam to mobilize Iranian youth, agreed with more rights for women, but within a framework of an indigenous modernity. Through redefining the religious role of Muslim women and modernity, he encouraged women's social and political participation, rejecting a gender-segregated society where women were seen only as homemakers. Instead, he encouraged modern Iranian women to reconsider Fatimah, the

Prophet Muhammad's daughter, and his granddaughter Zainab, as ultimate role models given their dedication to issues of social justice and their political and social activism. Like Al-e-Ahmad, he criticized the promotion of superficial aspects of women's lives and culture as imperialist modernization, and encouraged women to look up to women intellectuals, scientists and political activists in the West, rather than to Hollywood starlets, who he claimed turned women into objects of desire and agents of capitalist consumerism. In short he opposed both the Western model of gender roles and that of traditional religious conservatives, framing both as objectifying women and robbing them of their autonomy (Afary 2009: 234–5). Not only did his views attract many secular, educated women who strongly objected to the lack of democracy and freedom of expression, but his expounding on new interpretations of women's roles, within a religious framework, allowed many women of conventional and conservative backgrounds to define a political role for themselves in a manner neither 'Western' nor in the tradition of their mothers. Thus a new notion of female identity emerged, which drew its legitimacy not from modernity but from a new understanding of Islam. In this new Islamic vision women had a duty to participate in public life and struggle against tyranny, injustice and poverty.

Since the Pahlavi regime had made the 'woman question' an integral part of its reforms, it became a major component in various political movements and platforms. Even Islamist parties realized that appropriating the idea of modern womanhood would aid their cause. They encouraged women from the traditional middle classes to become politically active and mobilized women's support through customary religious institutions where women gathered to propagate their conservative view of womanhood.[8]

These various political strands had clearly mobilized women hoping to bring about major changes in their society. However, the lack of public space for open discussion and practice of diverse political ideas and beliefs concerning gender roles and rights meant that most women, regardless of their ideological tendencies, idealized what 'a new society' could offer women legally or socially. They thus focused on opposing the existing regime, rather than on articulating their gender-based demands or formulating plans for how gender rights would realistically be operationalized within the new society.

Clearly none of the oppositional groups, which had joined forces despite their vastly different analysis of the issues and their different visions of a new society, saw women's oppression as located in the social, economic, political and cultural conditions of Iranian society (Shahidian 1994; Paidar 1995). For women activists, for the most part, imperialist manipulation and consumerism had simply replaced patriarchal oppression of women as the force to oppose. Leftist women posited that the changes in the position and status of women did not truly benefit women, but functioned as a mere facade of progressiveness for the regime, and with this focus they avoided any meaningful discussions of sexuality. As Hammed Shahidian notes (1994: 229–34), the Iranian left's criticism of women's sexual objectification was based largely on a denial of female rights to enjoy their personal autonomy and sexuality, and they did not see the need for an autonomous women's movement. Neither did they articulate how the left envisaged overcoming the historical oppression of women.

The complicated alliance between the left(s) with their anti-imperialist position, the liberal and nationalist forces with their demand for democracy, and religious and conservatives who wanted to return to a gender-segregated society of the past, eventually brought about what was probably one of the most popular revolutions in modern history: the 1979 Iranian Revolution.[9] Breaking with convention, hundreds of thousands of women demonstrated alongside Iranian men; their mobilization played a considerable role in the success of the revolution, but they participated as citizens in support of the general demands of the nation, not as a constituency with gender demands of their own. Indeed, in the revolution's aftermath, and through the complicated power struggle that emerged between the allied groups, it was the religious actors who took leadership of the movement and assumed power (Arjomand 1988). Not surprisingly this had serious implications for the 'woman question'.

Reformulation of sexuality
under the Islamic Republic

Whereas modernity and social changes between 1900 and 1979 established hetero-sociability and heterosexuality as social norms, the Islamic Republic has aimed to rebuild a gender apartheid society, through the introduction of dress code, segregation of public spaces and, more importantly, cancelling the modest reforms to Family Protection Law which Iranian women had secured after decades of struggle. The Islamic regime promoted unilateral male heterosexual autonomy; supporting and even promoting polygyny; making divorce once more a unilateral right of men, and allowing men to contract unlimited temporary marriages. At the same time, they criminalized both consensual sexual relations outside of marriage and homosexual relations, with severe punishments including stoning and execution. Considerable resources went into organizing moral police forces, whose mission was to reinforce these new laws.

Many women outside the conservative religious social milieu who had supported the revolution were stunned to find themselves in a worse situation than before. When Ayatollah Khomeini announced compulsory veiling on 7 March 1979, women showed their resistance through a spontaneous and dramatic demonstration on 8 March, incidentally International Women's Day and normally not a day of any significance in Iran.[10] While this slowed down the implementation of compulsory veiling and opened space for some critical analysis, the regime nonetheless continued its plans to implement gender segregation.

In fact this show of force and criticism of the revolutionary regime heightened hostility towards feminists and secular women in general, as well as towards the many Muslim women activists who continued to hold Shari'ati's vision of a democratic Muslim society, and set in motion the process of their marginalization through various policies and increased public harassment. Conversely, religious and traditional women who supported the conservative ideologies of the state were encouraged to be socially and politically active, an opportunity they lacked prior to the revolution due to family restrictions and religious beliefs. However, with the regime claiming Islam as the principal guiding force driving their policies, conservative families and communities lost some of the legitimacy to limit women's freedom of movement, since the Islamic state rhetoric decreed social and political action as serving Islam. The highly politicized Islam promoted by the regime became a means to resist Western modernization and young conservatives became agents of its implementation.

However, the opening of the political and social arena to conservative women had many unintended consequences for a regime
attempting to re-create an imaginary 'Islamic society' based on
gender segregation and women's place in the home. Young Islamist
women began demanding their rights to higher education. They
became active in Islamist organizations, joined the literacy, health, or
reconstruction programmes, enlisted in the Basij (a militia set up to
protect the principles of the revolution), supported the war effort, and
even began choosing their husbands through these networks, rather
than complying with arranged marriages. Some even entered the
battlefield in various capacities during the Iran–Iraq war (1980–88).
These unconventional roles to some extent allowed conservative
women to assert their equality with men, and provided them with
the personal and financial autonomy that the liberal Pahlavi regime
had failed to offer them.

However, as the regime's gender policies unfolded throughout
the 1980s, many women who had initially supported the regime
became disillusioned and questioned the legitimacy of certain policies
presented in the name of religion. With more and more women
educated in religious matters and re-examining the religious texts,
more women-centred interpretations of the Qur'an emerged. This
process was assisted by the critical and rights-based writings of
secular women, especially prominent lawyers such as Mehrangiz
Kar and Shirin Ebadi, who, although apparent adversaries of Islamist
women, articulating gender equality through a secular framework,
shared largely similar demands with them (Hoodfar 1999). In particular, they shared demands for the reform of the family law, which
for all practical purposes had legally reduced women to subjects of
their husbands and denied them full citizenship rights. As a result
of these public discourses, a generation of religious reformers that
included certain prominent male religious leaders emerged, which
began interpreting the religious texts in a more woman-friendly and
less sexist way (Mir-Hosseini 1999).

In the process, the question of sexuality grew increasingly politicized in Iran. By the 1990s and 2000s young people, 'the children of
the Islamic Republic' (Yaghmaian 2002: 3), whom Varzi (2006: 11)
considers 'the target of the Islamization project', had created new
opportunities to express themselves and their sexuality in ways that

contradicted the Islamic regime's teachings. They adopted Western styles of dressing, and adopted new lifestyles based on watching MTV, listening to Pink Floyd and reading Pablo Neruda and Milan Kundera (Yaghmaian 2002; Khosravi 2008). Despite continual arrests and punishments by moral police, younger women in particular question compulsory veiling and challenge the regime daily by wearing unconventional *hijab*, tight and colourful manteaux and make-up as they stroll the busy streets and sit in public cafés. In today's Iran, the youth, particularly secular, middle-class urbanites, engage in activities that risk sanctions, hanging out with friends of the opposite sex, looking for potential partners on the streets, attending Western-style mixed-gender parties, and engaging in non-marital sexual relations (Mahdavi 2009). They reject the regime's stigmatization of homosexuality and argue for the right to consensual adult sex, despite awareness of the ramifications of their social behaviour and the threat of state punishments. In her book *Passionate Uprisings* (2009), Pardis Mahdavi documents the various ways that young Iranian men and women (mostly urban, middle class and university-educated) use their bodies and sexualities as a major means to challenge the repressive policies of the Islamic regime in everyday life (Mahdavi 2009). Though the youth are undoubtedly motivated in part by enjoyment, their behaviour is equally an expression of political opposition to the Islamic regime and an explicit voicing of their agency over their sexuality. To social observers these changes are an indication of a sexual and social revolution happening in Iran.

While the above forms of resistance are mostly individualized, when simultaneously adopted by large numbers of youth they are a major manifestation of resistance and challenge to the regime around its gender vision and sexual ideology. Besides these individualized forms of defiance, however, there exists more formal and organized resistance. For instance, the Stop Stoning Forever campaign launched by young women activists inside Iran continues to create international embarrassment for the regime, calling attention to its brutal and unjustifiable use of stoning as a means of execution – for alleged sexual offences in particular. Similarly, the One Million Signatures campaign is another effort that draws huge numbers of supporters from many towns and cities, and from both rural and urban populations (Hoodfar and Sadeghi 2009). The campaign's primary demands are revision of the Iranian constitution to remove all discriminatory clauses against women, and reforms to family law to make marriage a partnership between two equals, with women granted the same rights and control over their bodies as men. Women now expect more intimacy and greater emotional and sexual closeness in marriage, which is no longer seen as merely for procreation.

The debates around sexual orientation and homosexuality have never been so widespread in the country, at least since the second half of the twentieth century. Further, the focus is now on the sexual rights of consenting adults, regardless of whether the relations are hetero- or homosexual. The virtual world continues to expand as a major forum for the discussion of sexuality, sexual rights and freedoms, and sexual pleasures. Cyberspace is also a venue where the regime's ideological/pseudo-scientific stance that men have greater sexual needs than women is challenged and sometimes ridiculed. Secret gay subcultures have also emerged, particularly in urban centres, and some have cyberspace publications and online forums in Persian. Legal recognition of homosexuality by the state is one of the topics they address. Several underground organizations in support of freedom of sexual orientation have formed inside and outside the country, and have developed transnational links.

Conclusion

Public discourse and state intervention in Iran have continued to shape and transform what is 'acceptable' sexuality. In the nineteenth century, prior to the modernization period, sexual moral concerns and contestations were mostly shaped through community actors and socio-religious institutions, and men and women found routes through which to carve out a degree of autonomy for themselves. The state, prior to the twentieth century, was more concerned with paedophilia, the rape of boys, and lack of consent, and less about female sexuality, dress code or male and female homosexuality. During the Pahlavi era, industrialization, secularization and Westernization became the main goals of the state, and the promotion of heterosexuality and hetero-sociability, along with the presence of women in public life, were an integral part of the regime's modernization vision and process. This played out through a focus on the imposition of Western styles of dress and unveiling, the expansion of education and the opening of public spheres to women. While many women welcomed these changes, large segments of the conservative strata remained aloof and did not greatly benefit from them. Nonetheless, although democracy was not part of the regime's modernization plan, women seized the opportunity to work within and outside the state structure to bring about major changes, including family law reform, giving women slightly more rights in divorce and custody issues and limiting the practice of polygyny.

Since the 1979 revolution, the regime of the Islamic Republic has been concerned with the regulation of sexuality, mainly through so-called 'Islamic' dress codes, the reversal of family law reforms and the promotion of polygyny and temporary marriage. While male sexuality within a strict heterosexual framework is highlighted and promoted as natural, female sexuality has again been pushed to the margins. Homosexual relationships are condemned and forced into secrecy. The state's attempts to contain and regulate sexuality, its treatment of women, and the stigmatization and handing out of severe punishments to sexual minorities, have led some Islamic and secular women activists to join forces and embark on a women's rights movement, lobbying and launching debates in both religious and secular circles, in the physical public arena and in cyberspace. Youth, who now make up around 70 per cent of the population, have engaged in their own movement through various individualized actions such as inventing clothing styles that contradict the regime's prescriptions, engaging in sexual relations outside of marriage, and questioning the neutrality of 'heterosexuality' as well as the state's definition of sexuality. In short, Iran is going through what might well be called a sexual liberation of sorts. Many social observers have commented on the irony that, in many ways, sexual liberation in Iran is emerging under and in response to the Islamic Republic, in a manner that even many secular states would have difficulty fathoming. In assessing the scope of this public resistance we must remember that, as is often the case, women, who are often more oppressed, are the ones who carry the heaviest social and political cost of these challenges.

Notes

1. In 2009, Iran's urban population was about 55 million (75%). The Iranian age structure was very interesting: 0–14 years, 24% (18 million); 15–29 years, 35% (26 million); 30–44 years, 23% (17 million); 45–59 years, 12% (9 million); 67–74 years, 5% (4 million); 75 years and over, 1% (1 million). It means that 80 per cent of Iranians are less than 45 years old. In fact, 60 per cent are less than 30 years old, and 70 per cent are less than 35 years old. See http://iransnews.wordpress.com/2011/04/09/irans-population-tells-the-truth; www.amar.org.ir/default-52.aspx.

2. Sexuality was not discussed even between married couples. For instance, defloration on the wedding night could place a considerable amount of pressure on the couple and be traumatic, decreasing their sexual intimacy. Moreover, 'Despite ample advice attributed to the Prophet and religious luminaries such as Imam Ghazali and Majlesi, who recommended foreplay in order for men to arouse women's desire before coitus, many men were ignorant of these practices' (Shahri 1990, Vol. I: 259).

3. Such strategies are known and used in other Muslim societies where veiling is imposed on women. For instance, see Fernea 1969 on Iraq.

4. Debates on heterosexuality were almost entirely meant to put an end to the male–male relations, since female same-sex relations were unspeakable publicly.

5. Print media were introduced rather late in Iran. Many of the Iranian publications were printed outside Iran, in Europe and in neighbouring countries.

6. For information on women's press during this period, see Sheikh al-Islami 1972 and Qavami 1973.

7. Conventionally, Iranian women poets assumed a male identity in expressing their sexual desires. While Farokhzad was not the first women poet to break with this tradition, her poetry and its simplicity struck a chord with many women (and men) and made her among the most celebrated poets of twentieth-century Iran, despite her very short life. See Milani 1982 and Talattof 1997 for more on her life.

8. Groups of conservative women who held more conventional views of Islam also entered the inner circle of Ayatollah Khomeini's supporters.

9. Along with the recent revolutions in Tunisia and Egypt in 2011.

10. An estimated 20,000 women participated in this protest rally, which remains to this day the largest women's demonstration in Iran; www.youtube.com/watch?v=pxGYLk92edY&feature=player_embedded.

References

Afary, J. (1989) 'On the origins of feminism in early 20th-century Iran', *Journal of Women's History* 1(2), Fall: 65–87.

Afary, J. (1996) *The Iranian Constitutional Revolution of 1906–11: Grassroots Democracy, Social Democracy, and the Origins of Feminism.* New York: Columbia University Press.

Afary, J. (2009) *Sexual Politics in Modern Iran*. Cambridge: Cambridge University Press.

Amin, M.C. (2002) *The Making of the Modern Iranian Women: Gender, State Policy, and Popular Culture 1865–1946*. Gainesville: University of Florida Press.

Arjomand, S.A. (1988) *The Turban for the Crown: The Islamic Revolution in Iran*. New York: Oxford University Press.

Babayan, K. (2008) '"In spirit we ate each other's sorrow": Female companionship in seventeenth century Safavi Iran', in K. Babayan and A. Najmabadi (eds), *Islamicate Sexualities: Translations across Temporal Geographies of Desire*. Cambridge: Harvard University Press, 239–74.

Bamdad, B. (1977) *From Darkness into Light: Women's Emancipation in Iran*, trans. F.R. Bagley. New York: Exposition Press.

Fernea, E.W. (1969) *Guests of the Sheikh: An Ethnography of Iraqi Village*. New York: Anchor Books.

Fluehr-Lobban, C. (2004) *Islamic Societies in Practice*. Gainesville: University Press of Florida.

Foucault, M. (1978) *The History of Sexuality*, 3 vols, trans. Robert Hurley. New York: Vintage.

Hoodfar, H. (1997) 'The veil in their minds and on our heads: The persistence of colonial images of Muslim women', in D. Lloyd and L. Lowe (eds), *Politics of Culture in the Shadow of Capital*. Durham NC: Duke University Press.

Hoodfar, H. (1999) *The Women's Movement in Iran: Women at the Crossroad of Secularization and Islamization*. Montpellier: Women Living Under Muslim Laws.

Hoodfar, H., and Sadeghi, F. (2009). 'Against all odds: The building of a women's movement in the Islamic Republic of Iran 1979–2007', *Development* 52(8): 1–11.

Keddie, N.R. (1967) *Religion and Rebellion in Iran: The Tobacco Protest of 1891–1892*. New York: Humanities Press.

Khansari, M.J. (1999) *Kolsum Naneh*. Cologne: Ghassedek Press.

Khosravi, S. (2008) *Young and Defiant in Tehran*. Philadelphia: University of Pennsylvania Press.

Lewis, F.D. (2000) *Rumi: Past and Present, East and West. The Life, Teaching and Poetry of Jalal al-Din Rumi*. New York: Oneworld Publications.

Mahdavi, P. (2009) *Passionate Uprisings: Iran's Sexual Revolution*. Stanford CA: Stanford University Press.

Milani, F. (1982) 'Forugh Farrokhzad: A feminist perspective', in J. Kessler and A. Banani (eds), *Bride of Acacias: Selected Poems of Forugh Farrokhzad*. Delmar NY: Caravan Books.

Mir-Hosseini, Z. (1996) 'Divorce, veiling and feminism in post-Khomeini Iran', in H. Afshar (ed.), *Women and Politics in the Third World*. London: Routledge.

Mir-Hosseini, Z. (1999) *Islam and Gender: The Religious Debate in Contemporary Iran*. Princetin NJ: Princeton University Press.

Murray, S.O., and Roscoe, W. (1997) *Islamic Homosexualities: Culture, History and Literature*. New York: New York University Press.

Najmabadi, A. (2000) '(Un)veiling Feminism: Islamic feminism or feminist challenges to Islam', *Social Text* 18(3), Fall: 29–45.

Najmabadi, A. (2004) 'The morning after: Travails of sexuality and love in modern Iran', *International Journal of Middle Eastern Studies* 36: 367–85.

Najmabadi, A. (2005) *Women with Mustaches and Men without Beards: Gender and Sexual Anxieties of Iranian Modernity*. Berkeley: University of California Press.

Naw, D.H. (2008) 'Iranian chic'. www.irandokht.com/editorial/index4. php?area=per&sectionID=3&editorialID=1028.

Paidar, P. (1995) *Women and the Political Process in Twentieth-Century Iran*. Cambridge: Cambridge University Press.

Polak, J.E. (1982). 'Jahrbuch des Verbandes Iranischer Akademiker', *Der Bundesrepublik Deutschland und Berlin* 2: 31–44.

Qavami, F. (1973) *Karnameh-ye Zanan-e Mashur-e Iran*. Tehran: Vezarat-e Amuzesh va Parvarish Press.

Sanasarian, E. (1982) *The Women's Rights Movement in Iran: Mutiny, Appeasement, and Repression from 1900 to Khomeini*. New York: Praeger.

Sayyah, F. (1975) *Naghad va Siahat: Majmueh Maghalat va Taghrirat* (The Collected Writings of Fatemeh Sayyah), ed. Mohammad Golbon. Tehran: Tus Publications.

Schimmel, A. (1975) *Mystical Dimensions of Islam*. Chapel Hill: University of North Carolina.

Schmitt, A., and Sofer, J. (1992) *Sexuality and Eroticism among Males in Muslim Societies*. New York: Haworth Press.

Shahidian, H. (1994) 'The Iranian left and the "woman question" in the revolution of 1978–79', *International Journal of Middle East Studies* 26(2), May: 229–34.

Shahri, J. (1990) *Tarikh-e Ejtema'i-ye Tehran dar Qarn-e Sizdahom* (The Social History of Tehran in the Thirteenth Century). Tehran: Rasa Publications.

Sheikh al-Islami, P. (1972) *Zanan-e Ruznameh-nigar va Andishmandi-e Iran*. Tehran: Maz Graphics Press.

Smith, M. (1928) *Rabi'a the Mystic and Her Fellow Saints in Islam*. Cambridge: Cambridge University Press.

Talatoff, K. (1997) 'Iranian women's literature: From pre-revolutionary social discourse to post-revolutionary feminism', *International Journal of Middle East Studies* 29: 531–58.

Varzi, R. (2006) *Warring Souls: Youth, Media, and Martyrdom in Post-Revolution Iran*. Durham NC: Duke University Press.

Vieille, P. (1978) 'Iranian women in family alliance and sexual politics', in L. Beck and N.R. Keddie (eds), *Women in the Muslim World*. Cambridge MA: Harvard University Press.

Wines, L. (2000) *Rumi: A Spiritual Biography*. New York: Crossroad.

Yaghmaian, B. (2002) *Social Change in Iran: An Eyewitness Account of Dissent, Defiance, and New Movement for Rights*. New York: SUNY Press.

3

Moral panic: the criminalization of sexuality in Pakistan

Hooria Hayat Khan

In 2008, the district of Jafferabad, a remote and highly under-developed area of Pakistan's Balochistan province, bore witness to a horrific slaying of women accused of transgressing normative sexual behaviour. The incident took place in a tribal setting where the writ of the state is, at best, weak and ineffectual, and in a social environment where daring to choose one's own husband can result in being murdered at the hands of male elders and kinsman. In this region, a woman's exercise of her legal right to free choice contravenes tribal tradition. Initial reports that stray dogs had uncovered the bodies of women said to have been buried alive for wanting to choose their life partners shocked the nation, provoking countrywide protests by women's rights activists and others demanding justice and an end to brutal customs.

The town of Usta Mohammad, also in Balochistan, was a research site for the project 'Women's Empowerment in Muslim Contexts: Gender, Poverty and Democratization from the Inside Out'[1] (WEMC), investigating issues relating to women's status and drawing lessons from the various strategies women use to empower themselves in the context of rural Pakistan. Subsequent investigations into the incident by WEMC researchers revealed that in fact two young women had been accosted by young men from their tribe, abducted and assaulted, before being killed as a form of retributive tribal justice. As is customary, the women were not given a

Muslim burial, as further disgrace for being considered 'adulterous women'. They were unceremoniously interred in the clothes they were wearing when killed. Their families were not informed until well after their murders.

WEMC research indicates that the young women were apprehended during a rendezvous at a local hotel, and the head of the Umrani tribe to which they belonged was informed of the situation. The tribal head ordered that the women be brought to his house, where they were assaulted for two days before being shot dead and thrown into a shallow grave on the outskirts of the town. Two older women, who had accompanied the young women and were employed by their families, were also apprehended and later returned to their families, where they were killed by their male kin at the insistence of the tribal head. A fifth woman, a go-between who had arranged the rendezvous, escaped and her whereabouts are unknown.

Even though such traditional attitudes and practices are not entirely unopposed within traditional communities, the father of one of the two younger murdered women told the tribal head he had no right to order the murder of his daughter. Normally such criticism is unheard of, as tribal 'justice' is not open to question within the communities where it operates. The father argued that his daughter should have been handed over to the men of her family to be dealt with as they saw fit, but the father's protests were silenced. Tradition was invoked, and he was labelled 'dishonourable' for protesting the murder of his daughter in light of her behaviour. The police were reluctant to file a case against the perpetrators since the tribal leader had strong political ties with a provincial minister in parliament from the same tribe.

This was also the reason why the case was initially not reported to the media. Local residents, fearful of retaliation in case they were named as sources by the local media, sent the information to an international human rights organization abroad, which circulated it. The coverage prompted outrage both in Pakistan and beyond. Protests by civil society groups and human rights organizations throughout Pakistan eventually led to the issue being raised in the Senate (the upper house of the bicameral parliament). When a female senator decried the killings as acts of barbarity and a gross violation of human rights, Senator Zehri of Balochistan justified them as part of centuries-old Baloch tribal tradition to curb obscenity and maintain honour in the community. Zehri urged the House to stop politicizing the issue, arguing it was a matter of safeguarding an age-old value system. Though the Senate ultimately did pass a resolution condemning the incident, the government's response was slow and woefully inadequate. Women's rights activists condemned Senator Zehri and anyone else defending traditions that condoned the murder of women. They called for Zehri's resignation and denounced the use of tribal retribution targeting so-called 'honour' violations. The brutality of the incident, in conjunction with the outcry from women's rights groups, sparked a debate about tribal traditions within Balochistan itself – an area notable for its adherence to a strict tribal code and for enforcing traditional views, when necessary with violence.

The chief justice of the Balochistan High Court took *suo motu* notice[2] based on a newspaper report detailing the incident, and directed the police to register a case and start an investigation into the murders. In 2010, four of the twenty individuals accused were sentenced to life imprisonment.

The incident and everything surrounding it raises many urgent questions. What is it that compels families and communities to murder their own women who exercise autonomy in terms of marriage choices? How is it that nothing short of the death of such women can restore 'honour' to the family or the community? Was there was no other alternative available to deal with the accusations levelled against the women? Had these women been able to flee, would the state have been able to protect them and guarantee their lives? Is the legal system able to guarantee such women their rights? How has culture become an acceptable justification for brutal extrajudicial punishments? Why does the formal state machinery renege on its promise to protect the life and liberty of its citizens and capitulate to arguments based on cultural practices? And, finally, why is it that women's decisions regarding their own bodies and sexuality lead to such moral panic?

It is also important to try to understand the meaning of these women's actions. Knowing that they were overstepping the bounds of acceptability, was their defiance a protest against a system they strongly felt was unfair; an attempt to contest rigid tribal rules? Did they weigh the risks and potential cost of their actions? Finally, we must consider the state response to their murders. The incident and subsequent events that transpired show how deep-rooted the biases and discriminatory attitudes towards women are in Pakistan.

What happened to these women in Balochistan is not an isolated incident. Each year in Pakistan, numerous women are killed in the name of honour.[3] This begs the question of why there is so great a preoccupation with sexuality that it warrants a confluence of mechanisms to control women's autonomy. Perhaps allowing women the freedom to choose a life partner or lover is perceived as so threatening and challenging to the status quo that it evokes profound panic, not only within communities but also within state institutions. Any dissidence concerning attitudes, customs, laws, and so forth, is seen as potentially disruptive and destabilizing and therefore rejected. There appears to be a deep-seated fear of a woman's sexual power; her uncontrolled sexuality is perceived as dangerous and capable of causing *fitna*[4] (social disruption). Thus, for the greater good of (male-dominated) society, it is seen as necessary to restrain women; and to achieve this, sexuality is equated with shame, guilt and blame. Fear of women's sexuality as a challenge to the status quo and to male power perpetuates vigilant maintenance of the mechanisms controlling women's behaviour. Deviation from sexual social norms might set a dangerous precedent, and the act of one woman would have the potential to stir every Pakistani daughter.

This essay examines how the sexuality of women in Pakistan has been criminalized both within the parameters of the criminal legal system and within the cultural context of society. The objective is to look at women's sexuality through the lens of the legal system and dominant interpretations of culture and, through these, to trace the central theme of control over women. The essay will focus on the overlap between these two spheres (legal and societal), their interaction with one another, and how they serve to uphold the social and moral order through a combination of social norms and legal provisions. It starts by looking at cultural constructions around the issue of sexuality and links them with the law as the essay progresses.

Cultural notions of control

The ideas of *izzat*[5] (honour/respect) and *purdah* (veil/segregation) and their interconnectedness are key concepts in understanding masculine and feminine perspectives of socially and culturally acceptable behaviour in Pakistan. 'Honour' is a powerful construct within South Asia as a whole; it determines the respectability and status of a family within society and, therefore, is jealously guarded by its male members. It also encompasses a woman's chastity, which is considered an important marker not only of her family's honour but also of the masculinity of the male members of her family. On a wider canvas, a woman's chastity also signifies the honour and masculinity of the community; its honour is embodied by her.

This equation of women with honour and the unequivocal notion that men's honour resides in the bodies of women require that women stay within the confines of what is deemed culturally acceptable in order to avoid any 'inappropriate' interaction that could threaten the reputation of the family. Honour is lost if the character or chastity of a woman is thrown in doubt. It thus becomes imperative to control every facet of a woman's behaviour through codes of conduct that are internalized and then routinely followed without question by women. Nevertheless, as evident from the aforementioned incident in Balochistan and from other cases that will subsequently be examined in this chapter, there are women who, exceptionally and at great peril to their lives, rebel against these strict codes. They do this fully aware that retribution will be violent and entirely disproportionate to the severity of their 'crime', and that they stand to lose their lives.

The cultural conception of honour manifests within a gender construct where women and their sexuality reflect the honour of their family, and men are the protectors of that honour:

> Because of this vesting of such a socially crucial male interest in the body of a woman, men accord themselves complete authority and control over their female family members in order to protect their interest... Consequently, when a woman takes her sexuality into her own hands, or even exercises independent freedom to act, she disturbs this conception, and the male responsible for controlling her then becomes 'ungendered'. A man may be considered effeminate by his peers if he does not take authoritative action to re-assert his authority over a transgressing woman;

it is through an act of violence toward the woman that he demonstrates the power of his masculinity. (Hussain 2006: 223)

The fact that such crimes are committed on the basis of suspicion or even mere rumour shows that actual guilt or innocence is irrelevant. All that is required is that the honour of the family/community is perceived to have been slighted. This also helps to explain why sexual violence is perpetrated as a way of attacking another community – a tactic employed by both Hindu and Muslim communities during partition of the Indian subcontinent in 1947, with women belonging to the 'other' community being abducted and raped. Played out on women's bodies, these acts were in a sense attacks on the masculinity of the community and on its ability to defend its members and its honour. State action to recover abducted women could also be seen as the state reasserting its masculinity, though in many cases the women victims would have been shunned by their families on account of having been 'spoiled' (Alwis and Kumari 1996: 163).

The threat and practice of violence have been successful means of controlling women's sexuality across the subcontinent (Coomaraswamy 2005: XI). Acts of violence as punishment serve two important functions: they deter other women in the family who may contemplate challenging the rules and norms established by elders, and reinforce the authority and 'masculinity' of the patriarch and other male kin, who are de facto the custodians of women's bodies. These mechanisms of control not only operate within the confines of the family and community; they pervade the very fabric of society and are also reflected in state institutions. They are thus norms that dictate the private morality of individuals and work quickly to address any deviance.

Legal notions of control

The legal environment of any country is a product of the relationship between the legal, cultural and political spheres and is crucial as it outlines the rights and privileges available to citizens and the extent to which these rights will be protected. The primary function of any legal system is regulation for the sake of public order. To a greater or lesser extent, all legal systems reflect the shared values of morality and justice within a society. Notions of morality and justice are fluid, however, in that they do change over history, and it is imperative that the legal system adapts and evolves to reflect changing social realities. When prevailing notions of justice and morality, as regulated within a legal system, are contested by segments of the populace, the law becomes a political matter.

The operative boundaries of Pakistan's legal system are blurred because the system interacts with a host of other factors that include custom, culture and religion. This interplay manifests in both the enactment of legislation and, more importantly, in the subsequent interpretation and enforcement of law by the state. Individual actors in the justice system, including members of parliament and judges, bring their own cultural interpretations and biases, which reflect communal and societal ideas around female roles and associated gendered social norms and practices. That the legal system is gendered is indisputable; it actively fortifies dominant notions of morality and of patriarchal cultural norms.

In theory, the legal system of Pakistan provides for equality before the law. Why is it, then, that a state which guarantees the equal treatment of its citizens ends up excluding women from these parameters? There are numerous examples of existing cultural and traditional frameworks that obstruct women from actually experiencing equal legal status with men. But there are factors other than culture and tradition that engender the state to behave in the way it does. In a broader framework, as the feminist and political theorist Carole Pateman (1988) contends, the social contract between the individual and the state, which emerged as a result of the creation of the nation-state, formalized a patriarchal social order. She argues that even though the social contract guarantees the rights and freedom of all citizens, in practice it is solely the adult male who is considered to be competent to enter into a relationship or contract with the state. Women, Pateman suggests, were excluded as parties to the original contract because they were not considered to possess the necessary capacities. Men are therefore conceived as the state's true subjects, while women are in practice objects of the state who require men to function as the medium through which they are able to access rights.

Laws which attempt to control and regulate sexuality, both overtly and covertly, are fundamentally political in nature as they reveal the distribution of power within society and expose the contradictions that accompany the notion of equality before the law. An analysis of the law conducted through the prism of culture/tradition clearly reveals the imposition of a social order through the formal justice system. Laws considered particularly disadvantageous to women have inherent in them dictates of morality that seem to apply more to women than to men. Women who challenge these laws are seen as questioning the moral and cultural social norms; the contest is in fact between the notion of legal equality and the social subordination of women.

On the question of consent

Any issue that involves a woman's sexuality or its control is problematic, as Pakistan's legal system permits concessions to culture and tradition and often allows for what is culturally permissible to play a more prominent role than the law itself. The question of marriage based on personal choice is a glaring example where retaining male control trumps legal rights, as clearly manifested in cases brought before the court in which women, exercising their legal entitlements but defying social norms, have married against the wishes of their families.

An adult woman, possessing legal capacity, is legally entitled to give or withhold consent when contracting her marriage – a right granted both by the state of Pakistan and by the majority religion, Islam. In deference to social customs and traditions, however, this right is delegated to her male guardian,[6] and there is a social stigma attached to contracting one's marriage without the consent of one's guardian. This legal right is thus often withheld from women, for fear of women being 'corrupted' and disturbing the social/moral balance. Thus a woman's family will resort to extreme measures to prevent her from choosing her own husband. Even where women bring cases to court in order for their legal entitlements to be upheld, judges often struggle to strike a balance between the right that accrues to a woman (and is capable of being enforced), on the one hand, and the reluctance to allow women any measure of control, on the other. The controversy described below involving Saima Waheed,[7] a legal major who married without parental consent, shows the extent to which public opinion is roused about this matter and the sheer terror that surrounds the idea of young women defying the control that male family members exert over their lives.

In February 1996 Saima Waheed, a 22-year-old woman, defied her parents to marry a man of her own choice who was not of the same social standing as her family. The marriage was registered in accordance with the requirements prescribed by the Muslim Family Law Ordinance of 1961. Nevertheless her father challenged the validity of the marriage, initially by filing a First Information Report with the police, alleging his daughter had been abducted, and subsequently filing a case with the Lahore High Court contesting validity on the grounds the marriage was contracted without the guardian's consent. The case itself was fairly straightforward and could have been decided easily on merit alone, but it ended up being a tussle between socio-cultural norms and the law.

Although a majority judgment of the Court conceded the validity of Saima's marriage and held that a valid *nikah*, or betrothal, can be contracted without the consent of the guardian, it is important to consider the authorities that the Court relied on, as well as the language used during arguments and in rendering the judgment. Neelum Hussain's (1997) content analysis of the court proceedings does this, and illuminates the friction that can exist between guaranteed rights and social norms, especially when the accepted moral underpinnings of society are deemed to be under threat:

> Islamic tradition and cultural norms as 'authoritative sources' were selectively manipulated by the prosecuting council and the whole was contexted [sic] in traditional male/female binaries supported by cultural and religious norms which designate the man as the decision maker and woman as the passive object of his desire. Stereotypes of the 'good' and 'bad' woman were brought into play and the asexual, obedient woman, viewed through the lens of ideologically class gendered notions of appropriate behaviour, was vociferously upheld as a central marker of morality, decency, shame and national, specifically Muslim identity. Saima's exercise of a right, sanctioned by both the law of the land and granted to her under Islam, was seen as a transgressive act and as such interpreted as a sign of moral degeneracy, shamelessness and loss of cultural purity. (Hussain 1997: 202)

Examining the debate that came to surround this case, Hussain insightfully states that 'the Saima case is an instance that demonstrates the strategic use of morality and the reformulation of concepts of the licit and the illicit as a means of regulating and disciplining the social' (1997: 210).

Though the court ultimately ruled that the marriage was legal, it nevertheless at the same time clearly conveyed the message that a marriage sanctioned with the consent of parents is moral, decent and desirable. By implication, a 'love marriage', which suggests a degree of female sexual autonomy, threatens 'the safety of an orthodox male order' (Hussain 1997: 218). Fundamentally, the Saima case highlighted the tension between a woman's right to free choice and the patriarchal order that underpins Pakistan's cultural identity and legitimizes control over women. Any threats to existing patterns of authority within the family had the judges scrambling to denounce such actions, all the while conceding the legal validity of the marriage itself. It would seem, therefore, that in the judges' minds, there was a very real danger of other girls doing what Saima had done.[8]

Essentially, it appears that any reference to a woman's right immediately prompts a deliberation from the perspective of a male-oriented interpretation of religion[9] and culture. This highly constrictive reading of the law leads to legal interpretations that in practice dangerously curtail rights and undermine entitlements, because the emphasis is on conformity to social, rather than legal, norms.

Of crimes and honour

Judges also seem to lose sight of the law in favour of social and cultural precepts when addressing 'honour' killings and crimes. In simple terms, these are murders usually carried out by male relatives of a woman accused of sexual inappropriateness, and consequently of tarnishing the 'honour' of her family. As stated earlier, honour is heavily vested in the chastity of women. Any so-called 'immorality' linked to a woman damages her male kinsmen's social standing and honour, which men are considered to have the right, indeed the duty, to defend. 'Honour' punishments are viewed by many Pakistanis as inviolate customary practices, and the fact that they have persisted relatively unchecked testifies to their social acceptability as a mechanism for controlling women's behaviour, sexuality and autonomy.

In so far as it is the state's responsibility to protect its citizens, it has shown itself unable or unwilling address the endemic violence perpetrated against women in the name of honour. This failure is predicated on a variety of factors, some of which have been mentioned, and also includes loopholes within existing legal provisions that allow lenient sentences for perpetrators of 'honour' crimes. The 'Islamization' of criminal law under General Zia ul-Haq's regime (1977–88) confounded the prevailing confusion regarding differing statutory provisions and different regimes of punishment. The judiciary's reading of the law also reinforces dominant interpretations of culture and religion and goes so far as to justify and condone recourse to violence.

At the time of independence Pakistan inherited the penal code promulgated by the British colonial government. Under the code, killing would not be considered murder if the accused could show he had been deprived of self-control by 'grave and sudden provocation'[10] resulting from the actions of the deceased. This provided judges considerable discretion with regard to sentencing. Judgments prior to the annulment of the provision in 1990 clearly show that judges viewed perceived dishonour by the accused as an acceptable mitigating factor coming under the category of 'grave and sudden provocation'. This resulted in the conversion of death sentences to life or lesser sentences and at times even in acquittal.[11] A review of case law indicates that when a homicide involved a man's honour, invariably the provocation was deemed grave enough to justify leniency. In cases around a woman's alleged sexual impropriety, honour and its defence resonated in legal arguments that sought to justify killing in terms of men's obligation to avenge their honour.

In 1990 the Federal Shari'at Court,[12] the second highest appellate court for matters under *shari'a* or Islam-derived laws, ruled that provisions concerning murder, including grave and sudden provocation, were not in conformity with Islamic injunctions and had to be replaced. The Court's critique highlighted the differences concerning murder and bodily harm between the penal code promulgated during colonial rule based on principles of common law, and Islam-derived legal concepts the Court was exhorting the government to usher in.

Under the revised law, murder is no longer primarily considered to be an offence against the state; instead the offence is deemed to have been committed against the victim's family, and the family chooses whether or not to prosecute. This legal framework allows the accused to negotiate with the heirs of the victim,[13] any of whom can waive their right of retribution (*qisas*) in the name of Allah or compromise with the perpetrator, with or without monetary compensation. When all the heirs (male or female) have not waived their right of *qisas* or agreed to a compromise with or without monetary compensation, the court has discretion to sentence the accused up to fourteen years in jail, depending upon the facts and circumstances of the case. With regard to the exercise of these rights there is no legal discrimination between the male and female heirs so long as they are adults. Where the heirs of the victim are minors, their mother would be considered lower in hierarchy, compared to the paternal male family members, in terms of being the authority to exercise the above-mentioned rights.[14] As so-called 'honour' killings normally take place within the family structure and the family is complicit in the crime, reaching a settlement with the accused happens more often than not, meaning such crimes often go unpunished. Moreover, certain categories of family – parents, grandparents and spouses that have children with the deceased – are exempt under the law from capital punishment and are only liable to pay monetary compensation, though the courts have the discretion to impose a maximum sentence.[15] The state in such cases clearly abdicates its responsibility by not prosecuting instances that should be classified as state offences. Rather than working to uphold the law, the system in practice leaves matters in the hands of individuals and families who may be complicit in, or guilty of, murder.

At the same time, the Federal Shari'at Court also declared that the defence of provocation, no matter how grave and sudden, would not lessen the intensity of the crime. From an Islamic perspective, a murderer is only to be exempted from the death penalty if it is proven that the victim committed a crime for which the punishment is death, or where the killing was in self-defence. Prima facie, this position by the Court made it very difficult to rely on the defence of 'grave and sudden provocation' in the case of 'honour killings'. Where a woman accused of having committed adultery is

murdered, the accused would have to fulfil the evidentiary requirements of proof (the attestation of four eyewitnesses to the act of
adultery) under Islamic law to be exempt from the death penalty.[16]
Furthermore, killing an unmarried person, even if caught in the act
of sexual intercourse, would not be justified even if the requisite
standard of proof was met, as that offence is not punishable by death
under the law.

Despite this, with the passage of time, the courts reverted to
allowing provocation as a mitigating circumstance for reduced
sentences based on the victim's alleged sexual misconduct. In essence,
the victim stands trial and if found 'guilty' of sexual inappropriateness his or her murder is subsequently justified. In cases where 'grave
and sudden provocation' is raised as a defence, courts have held that
if the victim in question is not completely innocent of any social
'misconduct', the death penalty is not applicable.[17]

These legal loopholes that ensure leniency in the form of reduced
sentences and exonerations clearly illustrate that the courts are
complicit in preventing women from exercising their legal rights
and freeing themselves from the control of their families, tribes and
customs in matters of sexuality. In 2005, the Lahore High Court
reduced the death sentence of a man convicted of killing his sister's
suspected lover to fourteen years,[18] stating:

> No court of law would encourage 'honour killings'. But people do get
> provoked on such questions either suddenly or otherwise, when they
> remain under the obsession of *ghairat* [honour] and unleash their negative
> impulse at the first available opportunity. They need to be punished.
> But then we have our own culture and background and customs...[that]
> attract the principles of diminished liability/extenuation.[19]

Statements like these in theory uphold the law, but at the same
time the decision that is delivered has the effect of rendering the
law meaningless and undermining its substantive content. These
judgments have the duality of stating the law but contradicting it
at the same time.

A woman's sexuality is thus considered to be the domain of her
male relatives, who are ultimately considered primarily responsible
for its regulation and control. As noted repeatedly, crimes committed to address women's alleged sexual misconduct are justified on

the basis of a man's right to redeem his honour. The law also takes into account the social harm that such a loss of honour engenders, such that the balance needs to be restored. In a 2006 case, the court used similar arguments to reduce a death sentence for murder of a woman's suspected paramour to life imprisonment.[20] The court stated that even though family 'honour killings' are to be discouraged that 'does not mean that the benefits of mitigation are not to be given at all to the accused in whose house someone trespasses and invades privacy in fulfilment of a lust'.[21]

In essence, allowing a lighter penalty redefines the crime as somehow justifiable. It gives the impression that the woman killed must have done something to bring it upon herself and so, instead of being the victim, the woman is recast as contributing an important element of the crime. She becomes the woman who had to be killed to safeguard the honour of the family and protect the morality of society. Her death is an extrajudicial execution where she herself is held responsible for what happened to her along with being the perpetrator of an important element of the crime.

The treatment of 'honour' crimes by the police and the judiciary clearly reflect social norms about female and male sexuality, the role of the sexes in marriage, and so on. In a case where a father murdered both his daughter and the person she was allegedly having illicit relations with, the court held that

> In a Muslim society, the knowledge of illicit liaison of a female of the family with some other person is so painful, disturbing and a cause of mental torture that it cannot be explained in words. Such things are not accepted in our Muslim society and a *ghairat mand* [honourable] father/brother loses all his patience and even mental balance. His actions [following] such an incident are but natural and need proper [recognition] by the Courts.[22]

The Court went on to state:

> the Courts neither favour nor allow anyone to [take the law into his own hands] and thereby thwart the legal process. If citizens start settling their own accounts, even for a noble cause or under provocation, social upheaval and chaos [would obliterate] the established judicial system. To meet such an eventuality, such persons must be punished *but with leniency.* [emphasis added][23]

The engagement of the legal system with religion and culture is evidently complex and challenging. Both elements are treated with deep respect, and Islam is understood to be indisputable. If a legal process is perceived to contradict an age-old custom or a religious edict, it stands to risk its authority. The law's deference to religion and culture undercuts the state's responsibility to its citizens (especially female citizens), creating a dissonance between what the law guarantees in theory and what it delivers in practice. Particularly with regard to the control of women's sexuality, dominant religious and cultural perspectives trump the law. These cardinal reference points are at odds with rights granted and in theory guaranteed by the state. The prevalence of vigilante justice and the state's ambivalence towards it support the premiss that there is an inherent conflict between law and culture with regard to the guarantee and protection of rights under law.

Conclusion

The murders of four women in Jafferabad and their aftermath illustrate the kind of 'moral panic' generated over women's sexuality and the perception of female sexual conduct outside the rigidly proscribed boundaries of arranged marriage. Women's sexuality is perceived to have the potential to instigate chaos if not rigidly controlled, and allowing women to make their own sexual or marital choices is seen as threatening the status quo. The preoccupation with the maintenance of male authority engenders mechanisms of control to keep women subordinate. These include behavioural restrictions, constraints on mobility, the denial of legal entitlements and the use of brute force. The only place where women may claim their bodily rights is in a court of law, where in theory all citizens are guaranteed their rights by the state and its institutions. However, we have seen that misogynist interpretations of *shari'a* and cultural biases affect court proceedings and verdicts, and the courts seem to valorize men's status as custodians of women.

Pakistan's current legal system incorporates characteristics of custom, tribal law, *shari'a* and the legislation introduced by British colonial rulers. Regardless of the sources of law, the concept of male custodianship is a prominent feature of the way crimes against women are dealt with by the legal system. This is a reflection of the traditional notion that a woman belongs to her father, her brother, her husband and eventually her son. Her body is not her own; her choices are made for her. This notion of male ownership over a woman's body manifests most brutally in crimes committed to avenge assault on a family's honour through a woman's alleged immoral behaviour. Killing a woman because she is perceived to have somehow shamed her family through her behaviour is a crime wherein the state, through its leniency in applying the law, concedes that men are entitled to control women's personal bodily choices and to punish perceived transgressions. The formal state machinery is complicit in reinforcing violent extrajudicial mechanisms of control, and in fact goes to some lengths to discount women's legal rights.

Women have been questioning and objecting to oppressive and discriminatory laws as well as practices which are justified and therefore shielded in the name of either religion or culture. There have always been exceptions where women have flouted social and customary practices in favour of autonomy and the freedom to decide for themselves, even if it comes at the cost of their lives. Incidents of runaway marriages that come to court or 'honour killings' where a woman was found to have committed the transgression of choosing for herself, all attest to women rebelling against the system. In so far as changing attitudes are concerned, the women's movement and civil society organizations have tirelessly worked to bring about more awareness about dominant social issues, and to change the existing mindset towards women and girls. In many instances, these efforts have brought about positive change at the governmental level, as reflected in policies and plans that are more supportive of women, as well as at the community level where spaces have opened up for dialogue that is leading to a greater degree of acceptance. Work is slowly extending to more remote areas such as Jafferabad, the location of this essay's opening story. The research and discussions initiated by the research teams with the local community catalysed the formation of a local community-based women's organization, Nissa Women Welfare and Social Development Organization. Since its inception, Nissa has been successfully advocating for women's rights and empowerment in this conservative area that is very loyal to its customs and traditions. In a major break with tradition, Nissa facilitated the return and resettlement of five couples who had run away upon marrying without the consent of their elders. Thanks to Nissa's interventions these couples have been enabled to return and continue living within their community without the threat of retribution and being killed. Hailed as a positive step in changing existing attitudes about women and their designated role within society, it is all the more remarkable since Nissa supported the first couple to return home soon after the horrific incident of the four women being murdered by their tribesman for alleged sexual misdemeanour.

For women to enjoy their legal entitlements, the law needs to roll back its attitude of deference to religion and custom and intervene when grave injustices are being committed. A first step towards changing the current scenario would be to usher in legal reform to ensure that the state assumes far greater responsibility for the protection of all its citizens, especially women. The way forward is for rights activists and law practitioners to bring about a change in the language of the law so that it may not be undermined by social pressure and cultural interpretations of how women's lives should be ordered and organized. It is the courts of law to which women turn to contest misogynist readings of tradition and call upon the instruments of the state to affirm their secular rights as citizens of the state. This point needs to be qualified, however. Laws reformed on paper would have little effect unless there is a move towards better implementation by the judiciary and acceptance by the populace at large. This, in all likelihood, is going to be problematic. As mentioned earlier, the law reflects dominant values within society. If the law changes but that change is at odds with accepted notions of morality within society, there is a strong possibility that there would be no successful implementation or acceptance of it.

Notes

1. The WEMC project (2006–10) was funded by the UK Department for International Development and involved research in three other countries: Indonesia, China and Iran, as well as cross-border research on Indonesian migrant workers and Afghan refugees. For more information, see www.wemc.com.hk.
2. *Suo motu* is a Latin legal term meaning 'on its own motion'. It is used when the court takes notice of a matter on its own initiative.

3. The 2009 report of the Human Rights Commission of Pakistan (HRCP) shows that there has been a sharp surge in violence against women: 1,404 women were murdered in 2009. Of these, 647 were so-called 'honour killings', while 757 were killed for other reasons. Most of the crimes in the name of honour are not prosecuted, or perpetrators benefit from a high acquittal rate.

4. *Fitna* also translates as 'beautiful woman' – the connotation of the *femme fatale* who causes men to lose their self-control (Mernissi 1987: 31).

5. The term *izzat* can be used to mean both respect and honour, whereas the term *ghairat* is one that is specifically used to denote honour.

6. The right to choose one's marriage partner has led to considerable debate concerning the question of guardianship in marriage. With regard to the general *shari'a* rules on guardianship there is an important distinction between guardianship with the right of compulsion and guardianship without the right of compulsion. The latter is exercised when the woman contracting a marriage is an adult and possesses legal capacity. Under the Hanafi school, which Pakistan subscribes to, the power of the guardian to contract a marriage for his children comes to an end when the child attains the age of puberty.

7. *Hafiz Abdul Waheed* v. *Asma Jahangir*, PLD 1997 Lahore 301.

8. There have been similar cases where courts have allowed the validity of the marriage to stand. The Saima Waheed case was different in that it was high profile and drew a lot of publicity and attention. Her family pursued this case because it felt that her marriage to someone who did not belong to the same background as her had compromised their social standing.

9. Islam in fact does not justify murdering women in the name of honour and upholds an adult woman's right to marry whom she pleases.

10. Exception 1 to Section 300 of the Pakistan Penal Code stated: 'Culpable homicide is not murder if the offender, while deprived of the power of self-control by grave and sudden provocation, causes the death of the person who gave the provocation or causes the death of any other person by mistake or accident.'

11. Even after the provision was revoked, according to the National Commission on the Status of Women (NCSW) in 2004 the acquittal ratio for people accused of 'honour killings' was 43.13 per cent in Balochistan, 71.97 per cent in Punjab, 91.4 per cent in Sindh and 92.9 per cent in the North West Frontier Province (now known as Khyber-Pakhtunkhwa).

12. *Federation of Pakistan* v. *Gul Hassan Khan*, PLD 1989 S.C 633.

13. Those who inherit from the deceased under the Muslim law of inheritance.

14. Practically, however, case law does not reflect such a distinction and mothers as guardians do exercise these rights on behalf of minors.

15. Section 306 of the Pakistan Penal Code provides for an exemption from capital punishment where (a) the offender is a minor or is insane, (b) where the offender causes the death of his child or grandchild, how low-so-ever, and (c) where the *wali* of the victim is a direct descendant, how low-so-ever, of the offender. *Wali* has been defined to mean the heirs of the victim.

16. In *The State* v. *Abdul Waheed* (1992 PCrLJ 1596) the accused confessed to shooting the victim, who had interceded while the accused was attempting to shoot his sister. There was no eyewitness account of the incident and the case rested on the confession of the accused. Since there was no evidentiary proof that his sister was in fact guilty of adultery the court converted his initial sentence of seven years' imprisonment to a death sentence.

17. *Abdul Haque* v. *The State*, PLD 1996 S.C 1.

18. *Muhammad Nawaz* v. *The State*, 2005 PCrLJ 937.

19. *Muhammad Nawaz* v. *The State*, 2005 PCrLJ 937.

20. *Zulifiqar Ali* v. *The State*, 2006 MLD 1676.

21. *Zulifiqar Ali* v. *The State*, 2006 MLD 1676.

22. *Akbar* v. *The State*, 1997 P.Cr L J 1887.

23. *Akbar* v. *The State*, 1997 P.Cr L J 1887.

References

Coomaraswamy, R. (2005) *'Honour': Crimes, Paradigms, and Violence Against Women*. London: Zed Books.

Hussain, M. (2006) '"Take my riches, give me justice": A contextual analysis of Pakistan's honour crimes legislation', *Harvard Journal of Law and Gender* 29: 223–46.

Hussain, N. (1997) *Narrative Appropriation of Saima: Coercion and Consent in Muslim Pakistan, Engendering the Nation-State*. Lahore: Simorgh Women's Resource and Publication Centre.

Jayawardena, K., and de Alwis. M. (1996) *Embodied Violence: Communalising Women's Sexuality in South Asia*, New Delhi, Kali for Women.

Mernissi, F. (1987) *Beyond the Veil: Male–Female Dynamics in Modern Muslim Society*, rev. edn. Bloomington: Indiana University Press.

Pateman, C. (1988) *The Sexual Contract*. Cambridge: Polity Press.

4

The promise and pitfalls of women challenging Muslim family laws in India and Israel

Yüksel Sezgin

Across nations one of the most common ways that women's sexuality and personal autonomy are controlled is through family law, particularly marriage and divorce. In essence, many such laws are in place to govern autonomous and individual expressions of sexuality, most often through the use of moral arguments located within ethno-religious traditions. Yet matters of family law are often analysed in terms of state- or nation-building and religious practices. Indeed, as Carole Pateman (1988) has shown, family law remains one of the least democratic legal and social institutions, despite women's struggles, with limited success, for family law reform. Resistance to democratizing family law is often most pronounced among elements within ethno-religious communities, which hold a minority position vis-à-vis the state and are thus excluded from the state's political power structure. This has meant that women within such communities have to develop nuanced strategies to extend their sexual and personal autonomy without alienating their community. A comparison of the cases of India and Israel – where the Muslim minorities' relationships with the state are extremely politicized – provides insight into the ways in which women are contesting the governance and control of their sexuality through the reshaping of marriage and divorce laws.

In both Israel and India, marriage and divorce are regulated according to the family laws of ethno-religious communities: Muslims are thus subject to *shari'a*, Christians to canon law, Jews to *halakhah*, Hindus to Hindu law and so forth. In Israel, religious family laws are applied directly by communal judges at religious courts (e.g. *qudah* at *mahakim shar'iyya* or *dayanim* at *battei din*), whereas in India they are implemented by civil judges at secular courts. Israel does not have a uniform civil family code applicable to all citizens; in family law the Israeli government recognizes only religious law. The Indian state, however, which claims to be a socialist, secular and democratic republic, does provide citizens with a secular alternative: the Special Marriage Act of 1954 allows individuals who do not want to be subject to religious laws to contract civil marriage and divorce.

Such legal systems, where individuals are subject to the jurisdiction of their ethno-religious communities in matters of family law, are known as personal status systems. Historically, personal status systems were employed by imperial powers (e.g. the Ottoman Empire, the French in Syria, the Dutch in Indonesia, etc.) to categorize their colonial subjects into ethno-religious groupings, excluding subaltern groups from power by denying them terms of equal membership in the political community (Mamdani 1996; Mirow 2004). Currently, personal status laws continue to regulate familial relations and to exert control over women's sexuality and bodily freedoms in many countries, from Indonesia to Morocco; they are thus more than antiquated systems of legal and political ordering.

Nearly all postcolonial governments that inherited these poly-centric structures from colonial predecessors have intervened in personal status systems in the process of state- and nation-building. Prolongation of old personal status systems after independence would not only have resulted in further ossification of the colonial categories of race, gender and ethnicity, but also subverted the attempts of postcolonial leaders to strengthen through unity their newly formed nations and redefine the terms of membership in the political community. Therefore, most governments have restructured colonial versions of personal status laws with the aim of inculcating particular ideological visions and notions of subjectivity in their citizens, while ethno-religious communities have generally fiercely resisted government meddling in order to preserve their juridical autonomy and communal identity (Sezgin 2009, 2010). However, it would be inadequate to analyse matters of personal status or family law only from the perspective of state- or nation-building, as such laws are intimately related to the rights and freedoms of individuals, particularly women, who live under their regulations.

Whether in colonial or postcolonial contexts, the restructuring of personal status systems has always been dominated by men. Women's inputs were rarely sought and almost never taken into consideration as men negotiated and renegotiated among themselves the rules pertaining to marriage, divorce and maintenance that regulated women's sexuality and controlled their bodies. Men have been the sole interpreters of the 'holy' scriptures on matters concerning what was required of a woman to release her from the bond of marriage, when she could be declared a disobedient wife and denied her maintenance, how many days she must wait following divorce before making herself available to another man, how many silver coins must be paid to a non-virgin bride prior to engaging in sexual relations with her husband, and so forth. In other words, personal status systems have always been manipulated to preserve traditional male privileges by institutionalizing discriminatory characteristics and gender inequalities of major religious traditions. Thus, one premiss of this essay is that all religiously based personal status systems, whether Muslim, Jewish or Hindu, have been constructed through androcentric readings of sacred texts and traditions, and thus heavily discriminate against women in matters pertaining to marriage and divorce, subjugating their sexuality and establishing a regime of control over their bodies.

While all of the above-mentioned legal traditions oppress women through their family laws, this chapter focuses particularly on some of the common problems women encounter under Muslim family laws in India and Israel, where Muslims live as religious minorities, though under very different historical circumstances. Although nowadays it is fashionable to single out Islam as inherently misogynistic, this chapter claims nothing of the sort; nor is it an analysis of women's rights under Islam in general; rather, it considers so-called Muslim family laws as they are interpreted and applied by male-dominated secular and religious institutions in these two non-Muslim states. If women are discriminated against and denied equal treatment under current Muslim family laws, how can gender equality be achieved in Muslim societies? Are Muslim women doomed to suffer under these systems? Are they simply passive subjects, silently accepting the subjugation of their sexuality and violations of their fundamental rights under a patriarchal legal system, as is often presented in much of the media? Or do Muslim women devise strategies of resistance? If so, what tactics, particularly in Muslim-minority settings, are they using to navigate the maze of personal status systems? How do women struggle to change interpretations of religious texts? Are there ways to integrate international women's rights standards (e.g. CEDAW) into religion-based personal status systems? These are some of the questions that the present chapter seeks to begin to answer by analysing emerging Muslim women's rights movements in Israel and India. Mapping out their strategies and tactics will help us see how women can further empower themselves within these anachronistic legal frameworks and challenge state-imposed religious rules and institutions that have communalized their bodies and oppressed their sexuality.

How do Muslim family laws affect women's rights and sexuality?

Many Muslims believe, and many scholars of contemporary Islam now accept, that when Islam was first revealed in the seventh century, it significantly advanced women's status by granting them revolutionary rights and freedoms which had not previously existed in Arabian society (Esposito and DeLong-Bas 2001; Tucker 2008). However, the persistence of pre-Islamic tribal customs coupled with patriarchal interpretations of Islamic law are believed to have under-mined the egalitarian principles of Islam and fostered a misogynistic legal tradition that has denied women equal rights in the name of Allah (Mernissi 1991; Wadud 1999; Barlas 2004; Souaiaia 2008). It is beyond the scope of this essay to confirm or reject this assertion; however, like many other scholars of Islam (Stowasser 1994; Mir-Hosseini 1999; Wadud 1999), I do hold that Muslim family laws are not sacrosanct, but are masculine legalities built upon androcentric interpretations of sacred texts, historical narratives and traditions. As such they often discriminate against women, violate their fun-damental rights and liberties, and deny them the power to control their own bodies and sexuality. The laws pertaining to divorce are particularly demonstrative of women's subordination under Muslim family laws. With this in mind, the following addresses the question of how Muslim family laws in Israel and India affect women's rights, focusing on intricacies of divorce and other aspects of breakdown of family union such as postnuptial maintenance, and looks at specific strategies Muslim women in minority settings have devised to empower themselves and respond to rights violations under religious law.

Status of women under Muslim family law in Israel

Muslim citizens of Israel are subject to the purview of *shari'a* courts, which have exclusive jurisdiction over marriage and divorce, and have concurrent jurisdiction with civil family courts in regard to all other family matters (e.g. custody, maintenance, succession, etc.). The position of Muslim women under the current family law system is precarious on two levels.

First, since Israel – like other Muslim-minority states (e.g. India) – lacked the legitimacy and political motivation to intervene directly in substantive Islamic law and enact a new code to replace the Ottoman Law of Family Rights (1917), Israeli *shari'a* courts continue to apply the Ottoman law, allowing men polygynous marriages and the unilateral right to divorce without recourse to the court (*talaq*). Even though the Israeli legislature, through penal interventions,[1] banned such discriminatory practices as polygyny, *talaq* and underage marriage, religious courts have found ways to protect male privileges and circumvent the secular law, which they claim contravenes the Islamic law (Layish 1975). For instance, the current president of the Shari'a Court of Appeals, Sheikh Ahmad Natour, has repeatedly instructed the *qadis* of *shari'a* courts to disregard Israeli civil law prohibiting *talaq* and confine their decisions to Islamic jurisprudence and precedents, arguing that this is necessary to protect Muslim identity under Jewish rule, even though such practices have been banned or curbed in many Muslim-majority countries in the region.[2]

Second, as many commentators point out, for ideological and political reasons, Israeli law enforcement agencies often view matrimonial issues as internal affairs of the Arab community[3] and neglect to enforce civil laws[4] that primarily aim to protect women against discriminatory practices.[5] The state's failure and unwillingness to uphold its own laws vis-à-vis its Muslim citizens has further weakened women's position with regard to communal institutions and diminished their capacity to demand substantive changes in Muslim family laws. Thus, for the most part, Palestinian women have remained silent on issues relating to substantive laws of marriage and divorce, which are often viewed as the pillars of Muslim autonomy and identity in the Jewish state. Instead, as I will shortly demonstrate, they have for the most part limited their demands for reform to aspects of law and such secondary issues as spousal maintenance (*nafaqa*) and custody.

According to the 1917 Ottoman law (Articles 92–101), maintenance, which is minimally understood to include at least food, clothing and shelter, is an unequivocal obligation of the husband within Islamic marriage (Layish 1975: 91–111; Zahalka 2010: 151–73). However, there are certain circumstances under which a wife may be denied her right to maintenance. For instance, like the Jewish *halakhah*, which denies maintenance to a woman who refuses to have sex with her husband, Islamic law also holds that a rebellious wife (*nushuz*), who leaves the marital home without her husband's permission, will lose her right to maintenance. The amount of postnuptial maintenance is normally determined by the parties themselves through negotiations. In the absence of consensus, the *qadi* appoints representatives of the parties (*mukhbirun*) and the court to determine the exact amount of award. As far as spousal maintenance payments are concerned, Israeli *shari'a* courts, like other religious courts, have historically been very conservative. One Palestinian scholar demonstrates that maintenance awards ordered by *shari'a* courts have been significantly lower than average maintenance awards ordered by civil family courts (El-Taji 2008: 88). In this regard, Palestinian feminists' main agenda item has been to increase the amount of maintenance Muslim women receive in the event of separation or divorce (Abou Ramadan 2006: 32). The strategy adopted to attain this objective was to give Arab women the alternative option to bring their maintenance cases to civil family courts by removing the maintenance from the list of issues over which *shari'a* courts had exclusive jurisdiction.

Because Israel does not have a secular maintenance law[6] the civil family courts still need to determine maintenance cases according to 1917 Ottoman law. However, as is the case for all communities governed by respective family law, Muslim family law applied by secularly trained civil court judges, most of them Jewish, differs in practice from its application by Muslim *qadis* at *shari'a* courts. This is because the legal culture, ideology, and the rules of evidence and procedure at civil courts differ from those at *shari'a* court, and civil courts also abide by standards of secular international law even though implementing religious law (Abou Ramadan 2006: 43). Against this background, as we will explore later, Muslim women activists from 1996 to 2001 pushed for legislative change that would transfer maintenance and custody from the jurisdiction of *shari'a* court to civil family court, which they believed would be fairer and friendlier to women.

Status of women under Muslim family law in India

Muslim Personal Law in India, known as Anglo-Muhammadan law, is a hybrid system incorporating principles of English common law, local customs and Islamic law. In contrast with Israel, in India Muslim family laws are applied exclusively by secularly trained judges in civil courts, who are likely to be non-Muslim, and most likely to be Hindu. For Indian Muslim women the most oppressive aspect of the current Muslim Personal Law system is what is known as 'triple *talaq*', whereby a man may divorce his wife by uttering *talaq* three times. Even though this type of divorce proceeding is heavily frowned upon within classical Islamic law, it is the most common form of divorce within the Indian Muslim community; unlike in Israel, the Indian state has never intervened – perhaps for political reasons and fear of backlash – to curb the customary Muslim male prerogative of unilateral, extrajudicial divorce (*talaq*).

As demonstrated by the Shah Bano[7] case in 1985, the practice of *talaq* can condemn Muslim divorcees to years of suffering and destitution. According to Muslim family law in India, in the event of divorce a woman is entitled to the deferred part of her *mahr*[8] and maintenance for three months, or, if pregnant, until she gives birth; otherwise there is no further financial obligation on the part of a husband to a wife. Though Section 125 of the Criminal Procedure Code of 1973 requires that men provide for their wives in case of divorce where women are destitute and unable to support themselves, Muslim men are excluded, ironically under a law called the Muslim Women (Protection of Rights in Divorce) Act (1986), which limits the husband's postnuptial maintenance obligation to the *iddat*[9] period alone (Agnes 2001; Menski 2001). The enactment of this 1986 law has discriminated against Muslim women, denying them the financial guarantees bestowed on Hindu, Parsi and Christian women in the event of divorce. As will be shown below, following recent successes concerning maintenance and despite resistance from within the Muslim community, Indian Muslim women continue to fight gender discrimination and injustices perpetrated by religious and secular laws, to further secure their right to 'a reasonable and fair provision'.

Muslim women's responses to rights violations and sexual subjugation

As demonstrated, current Muslim family laws in both Israel and India are detrimental to women's rights and freedoms, and both governments have proved unable or unwilling to reform personal status systems to protect women against encroachments of so-called religious norms and authorities. However, this does not mean that women are resigned to sit on the sidelines, quietly enduring repression. On the contrary, they are fiercely fighting to advance their rights and freedoms, contesting hegemonic narratives of gender and subjectivity to reclaim control of their bodies and redefine their roles as rights-bearing, equal citizens within both domestic and public spheres.

In religiously based personal status systems, where the systematic denial of women's fundamental rights is framed in terms of obeying God's orders, debate centres on which interpretation of the Holy Qur'an or Hadith is the authentic one (Gaay Fortman et al. 2010). Hence, it is not surprising that in many Muslim societies women respond by forming hermeneutic communities that challenge official interpretations of religious precepts and offer alternative women-friendly readings of law. Such attempts to reform the system involve discourses framed by both Islam and vernacular readings of international women's rights standards, meticulously grafting ideas of gender equality onto culture, tradition and religious beliefs and teachings (Haddad 1978; An-Naim 1992; Merry 2006a, 2006b; Levitt and Merry 2009; Rajaram and Zararia 2009). In this process of 'indigenization', the so-called alien discourses of rights and equality are appropriated and firmly grounded in the morals and traditions of religious communities.

These hermeneutic activist groups do not simply engage in scriptural analysis and debate; they are agents of change working to define and redefine the legal status of women. In doing so, they build cross-communal alliances that transcend ethno-religious divides (e.g. Muslim–Jewish alliances in Israel, Muslim–Hindu alliances in India), lobby for judicial and legislative change, mobilize courts, educate the public and seek change by framing gender issues in terms that resonate with the dominant culture. Although they generally use moderate means and strive for incremental change by working within existing institutions, some reformist groups do end up marginalized, calling for more extreme measures demanding abolition of existing family law systems, and even establishing alternative legal institutions. In other words, as governments and religious authorities fail to respond to repeated calls for reform, some disillusioned groups cease to use state-run family law institutions and set up their own judicial bodies, applying their own version of law to members of their self-proclaimed communities. Such 'self-ruling communities' are epitomized by associations such as the All India Muslim Women Personal Law Board (AIMWPLB), which, after years of dissatisfaction with the version of *shari'a* imposed by the male-dominated All India Muslim Personal Law Board (AIMPLB), set up a *mahila adalat* (women's court) to offer religiously acceptable solutions to such problems as triple *talaq*.

As noted earlier, personal status systems in effect control women's sexuality and bodies by subjugating their desires and wills to the purview of communal and religious authorities. In effect, women's bodies are objectified as communal property, all in the name of obeying God's orders and protecting the community's morals, values and identity. Especially in settings where the ethno-religious minority community is denied a national 'homeland' or sovereign territory (e.g. Palestinian citizens of Israel, Muslim citizens of India), the bodies of females are territorialized – they come to represent the 'motherland' the community longs for, in addition to being the 'otherland' that the majority community longs to subjugate. Family laws thus in effect demarcate the borders of the community, by regulating whom women may marry and have children with. The survival of the community and the endurance of the nation depend upon the defence of its boundaries; tampering with its border markers – the family laws – simply cannot be tolerated by its male members.

As I will shortly demonstrate, in the context of Muslim family laws in Israel and India, interventions by majority-dominated institutions (e.g. legislative, judicial) have often been perceived as hostile acts and thus fiercely resisted. In fact, more often than not they have backfired, solidifying patriarchal authoritarianism and intensifying communal resolve to resist change in family laws. In this atmosphere, women's rights groups operating within the community in collaboration with like-minded majority groups to pressure mainstream 'enemy' institutions (e.g. courts, the parliament etc.) to reform personal status laws and community conventions have often been accused of treason and discredited by self-proclaimed guardians of tradition and identity. As secular remedies thus become increasingly suspect as hostile attempts to weaken the community, hermeneutics has become the favoured route to reform for Muslim-minority women to advance their rights from within an Islamic, culturally acceptable framework. Bearing this in mind, the following section looks at the activities of Islamic hermeneutic groups in Israel and India, exploring some of the strategies and tactics successfully employed by them to reinstate Muslim women's claim to their bodies and to their rights under religious family laws.

Internal reform at Israeli *shari'a* courts

As mentioned earlier, Palestinian women have been primarily concerned with issues of maintenance under the *shari'a* system and focused their energy and resources to equalize the legal status of Muslim women to that of Jewish and Druze women through 'the option of recourse in maintenance suits to the new civil family courts' (Shahar 2006: 130).

In 1995, several Israeli and Palestinian (Jewish, Muslim and Christian) civil and women's rights organizations came together to form the Working Group for Equality in Personal Status Issues.[10] The group's primary goal was to amend the Law of Family Courts (1995) as it pertained to Muslim women by giving them the option to choose between religious and civil courts to adjudicate matters concerning family law other than marriage and divorce, such as maintenance, custody, and so on. In 1997, the group initiated a bill to amend the Law of Family Courts of 1995, with the support of Nawwaf Masalha, a male Palestinian member of the Knesset (Abou Ramadan 2006). Throughout the process, the Working Group galvanized public opposition to the inequalities suffered by Palestinian Muslim women by publicizing National Insurance Institute statistics showing that spousal and child maintenance payments awarded to Muslim women by the *shari'a* courts were significantly lower than those awarded to Jewish and Druze women by the civil family courts (Shahar 2006: 130). After four years of horse-trading in parliament, the amendment (Law No. 5) was finally passed in November 2001 by a vote of 51 to 23. Seven Arab members of parliament voted for the bill, three abstained and four voted against (El-Taji 2008: 95–6).

As expected, the new law caused some profound schisms between the pro-reform groups and conservative elements within the Muslim community. Even some leftist and liberal members of the community joined conservatives in opposing the law, which they perceived as an assault on the national, cultural and institutional autonomy of the Muslim minority in Israel (El-Taji 2008: 89–90). Nonetheless, most remarkable about this reform process was the alliance of Muslim and Jewish conservatives, both outside and within the Knesset, that formed in opposition to the coalition of Muslim and Jewish women's organizations. Outside parliament, *qadis* allied with the Palestinian Islamic Movement against the pro-reform groups (Abou Ramadan 2006: 42–6), while in the Knesset the Islamist and conservative Palestinian representatives joined with Orthodox Jewish parties to forestall and thwart the proposed legislative reform. The conservative front in parliament was eventually defeated by a counter-alliance of secular and centrist parties. As noted by Nasreen Alemy-Kabha, the former coordinator of the Working Group for Equality in Personal Status Issues, 'Orthodox religious parties saw this initiative as an assault on religion by secularist forces', and joined the Islamists in opposing the reform.[11]

Even though the passage of Law No. 5 of 2001 was an important achievement for Israeli Muslim women, nearly ten years after its passage the question remains as to whether the new legislation has actually resulted in women bringing their cases of concurrent jurisdiction to the civil family courts. Although Israeli family courts do not provide any statistics regarding the ethnic and religious background of petitioners, anecdotal evidence suggests that far fewer Muslim women are coming to civil court than envisioned in 2001 by the architects of the law. As argued by proponents of the law, this is mostly due to inherent structural problems and limitations of the civil court system. For example, in 2005 there was only one Palestinian judge and one Palestinian social worker in all thirteen family courts in the country. Though there are now two Palestinian judges and six Palestinian social workers, the current coordinator of the Working Group says this is still far from sufficient.[12]

Moreover, proceedings at family courts are conducted in Hebrew, and courts do not provide pro bono translation services for Arabic-speaking citizens. Although in the last three years the Working Group has been providing free translation and legal aid services to Palestinians at the Haifa and Nazareth family courts, the lack of Arabic-speaking personnel familiar with the culturally specific concerns of Palestinian families continues to make these courts an alien and unwelcoming environment for many Arab women.[13] And, as some suggest, the social and political sanctions for using Israeli courts for family matters traditionally dealt with under *shari'a* also discourage many women from accessing civil family courts to resolve their maintenance or custody disputes.[14] All in all, the legislative change has not yet produced many of its intended outcomes.

However, there have been some unintended and indirect positive effects resulting from the Working Group's efforts. Fearing the erosion of their jurisdiction in favour of the civil family courts, Israeli *shari'a* courts introduced a number of reforms to improve the status of women concerning maintenance, child custody and even divorce (Abou Ramadan 2003a, 2003b, 2005, 2006). In this regard, the maintenance reform is especially notable. The process adopted by the Shari'a Court of Appeals, under the leadership of Qadi Natour, was identical to that used a century earlier by the British to reform Islamic law in the Sudan: a legal circular or *marsoum qadai*.[15] The circular (No. 2), issued amidst calls for intervention by the Knesset, ordered *qadis* to rely upon written evidence, such as tax returns or insurance documents, instead of *mukhbirun* (informants), to determine the amount of spousal maintenance. In the months following the promulgation of the new circular, maintenance awards made to Muslim women by the Shari'a Court in West Jerusalem rose by nearly 50 per cent (Shahar 2007: 209). In fact, some claim that *shari'a* courts now award the highest average sums of maintenance in the country (Zahalka 2010). As both Shahar (2007) and Abou Ramadan (2006) have shown, the *marsoum* engaged not only with the Palestinian feminists by adopting a more women-friendly stance on maintenance, but also with the Israeli government by emphasizing the independence, originality and textual authority of the *shari'a* courts. In fact, the circular made no mention whatsoever of the State of Israel, despite the fact that the state appointed and paid the salaries of *qadis*. On the contrary, the *marsoum* referred to the Islamic courts as the Shari'a Courts of 'Palestine', which, *qadis* claimed, recognized no legislative or political authority above the 'holy' *shari'a*.

Even though the pressure exerted by women's groups during the campaign for Law No. 5 seems to have forced *shari'a* courts in Israel to embrace a more women-friendly approach, discrimination and unequal treatment of women remain a major problem under the current system. Some women attribute this to the lack of female voices at the *shari'a* courts, and advocate for the appointment of female *qadis*. The current coordinator of the Working Group noted that women's groups have already raised the issue with the nomination committee for *shari'a* judges and received the vocal support of several key members for inclusion of female *qadis* in the future.[16] Muslim feminists remain hopeful that the Israeli authorities will follow the revolutionary example set by the Palestinian Authority,[17] and soon appoint female judges to *shari'a* courts. However, women also recognize that the idea of female *qadis* will be fiercely opposed by not only Islamic conservatives but also orthodox Jewish parties, which will be fearful of the impact of such a drastic change on the rabbinical system.

The initiative leading to amendment of Law No. 5 in 2001 was the first and most successful attempt of Israeli Muslim women's organizations to reform Muslim family laws and exert more control over their bodies and livelihoods. However, as shown, the 2001 reform has also starkly exposed the inadequacy of the secular approach to the issue of reform in Muslim family laws in Israel. Thus, women have drawn two important lessons from the 2001 experience. First, they learned that in the eyes of most of the Palestinian population any change brought through collaboration with 'enemy' institutions (e.g. the Knesset or Israeli civil courts) discredits the organizations and individuals pushing for reform. Second, they also experienced first-hand the deep distrust among Palestinians towards Israeli institutions; the inaccessibility of Hebrew-dominated legal institutions for the Arabic-speaking population; and the unwillingness of the Israeli state to uphold its own laws aimed at protecting women's rights within the Arab community, all of which undermine any reform and lessen its applicability and effectiveness. Thus, following the 2001 reform, some women's groups, despairing of the limitations of the secular approach, have begun looking for remedies to problems in Muslim family law within an Islamic framework, seeking women-friendly interpretations of classical sources of *shari'a* such as the Qur'an and Sunna. To date, the leading advocate of this approach is the organization Nissa wa Afaq (Women and Horizons).

Nissa wa Afaq was founded in 2002 in Kafr Qara under the leadership of Saida Mohsen-Byadsi, a Muslim lawyer graduated from the Orthodox Jewish Bar-Ilan University. The main premiss of Nissa wa Afaq is that secular discourses are almost completely irrelevant in the Israeli Palestinian context, where Islam plays a powerful role in every aspect of life. The organization argues that in order for change to benefit women in such a society, Islam must be the vehicle for bringing public awareness of acceptable options – namely liberal and feminist interpretations of the Qur'an and Sunna. In recent years Nissa wa Afaq has become the leading organization in Israel reject-ing classical interpretations of Qur'an which subjugate women, and advocating for a feminist rereading that grants women equal status with men (Al-Tayeb 2010). The organization and its activities are inspired by not only the writings of such leading Muslim feminists as Fatima Mernissi and Farida Bennani, but also the work of Kolech, an Israeli Orthodox Jewish women's organization that has fought against discriminatory marriage and divorce laws under *halakhah*, rendering women-friendly interpretations of classical sources of Jewish law. The leading members of Nissa wa Afaq point out that the two organizations, especially early on, enjoyed close ties, as they were essentially undertaking very similar projects to advance women's rights under Islamic and Jewish laws within religious courts by rendering women-friendly interpretations of their respective traditions (Saar 2005). Nissa wa Afaq offers classes for Muslim women on the alternative liberal and feminist interpretations of Islamic law and practices relating to marriage, divorce, inheritance and maintenance. Besides its grassroots activities, Nissa wa Afaq is also working on a new code of family law to replace the 1917 Ottoman law and empower women to promote their rights as wives and mothers within the *shari'a* system.[18]

Impact litigation and the rise of Islamic feminism in India

Indian women's organizations, including mainstream Muslim women's groups, have historically adopted a secularist approach to family law reform. 'The absence of a Uniform Civil Code (UCC) in the last quarter of the twentieth century', declared the 1974 Report of the National Committee on the Status of Women, 'is an incongruity that cannot be justified with all emphasis ... placed on secularism, science and modernism. The continuation of various personal laws which accept discrimination between men and women violates the fundamental rights' (Menon 1998: 244). From the 1950s on, the general belief among Indian feminists was that improving the status of women could only be achieved through replacement of religious family laws with a UCC. However, ideological transformations since the mid-1980s, the rise of intercommunal violence, and the appropriation of the concept of a UCC by right-wing Hindu platforms (e.g. Sangh Parivar and Bharatiya Janata Party)[19] have more recently compelled women's organizations to reconsider their strategies and drop their earlier calls for a UCC (Menon 1998: 252; Agnes 2004: 5). In this new environment, a UCC has ceased to symbolize the advancement of women's rights, and instead is seen as an issue over which men appropriate women's bodies in their tribal wars.[20] As Dr Syeda Hamid, the president of the Muslim Women's Forum, put it, the monopolization of UCC debates by racist and sexist groups in the 1990s has posed difficult ideological and ethical dilemmas, particularly for Muslim feminists:

> The bottom line is that there should be a uniform law for all citizens ... But of course we changed our attitude and policy. ... We had to. ... When the community is battered, you keep your silence. How can you

talk about reform when you are being killed?... How can you use the same language [UCC] as the people who are battering you [right-wing Hindus]...? You know what happened in Ayodhya, you know about the pogroms, and genocide of Gujarat.... When the state becomes a predator ... you keep your silence, you do not talk about reforming the Islamic law, because everything is about identity and everything is about religion.[21]

Currently, Muslim women's groups pursue a combination of legislative and judicial strategies, working together with men and women from other communities (Hindu, Christian, etc.), and rely increasingly on a hermeneutic approach — like the Palestinian Muslim women in Israel — to empower themselves and challenge the gender status quo. For example, in the last two decades Muslim women's rights activists have mobilized the courts to challenge and reform gender-unequal family laws (Desai and Muralidhar 2000). In the aftermath of the infamous 1986 Muslim Women (Protection of Rights in Divorce) Act, described earlier, women's organizations launched a judicial onslaught to overturn the legislation denying Muslim women's right to maintenance beyond the *iddat* period, by invoking a seemingly innocuous clause in the law which had escaped the attention of the misogynistic promoters of the legislation. The clause stated: 'a divorced woman shall be entitled to a *reasonable and fair provision* [emphasis added] and maintenance to be made and paid her within the *iddat* period' (Agnes 2004: 8). Their campaign culminated in 2001 with the Indian Supreme Court's Danial Latifi case, in which the court overruled the minimalist interpretations of the 1986 Act, and on the grounds of this very clause decided that a Muslim husband was required to make a lump-sum payment to his ex-wife during the period of *iddat*, which would include not only maintenance (*nafaqa*), and the deferred part of her dowry (*mahr*), but also a 'reasonable and fair provision' that would financially secure her future well beyond the period of *iddat* (Subramanian 2005). Thanks to the expanded interpretation adopted by the court, Muslim women are now reported to receive some of the highest maintenance awards in the country (Menski 2006, 2007).

Like their counterparts in Israel, Indian Muslim women's groups also use reinterpretive strategies to challenge the textual authority of religious institutions and advance women's rights under Muslim family laws. In post-Shah Bano India intercommunal tensions have increased, including threats from right-wing Hindu groups, and the Muslim community has grown increasingly insular and resistant to the idea of change in its laws. The community has come increasingly under the control of conservative elements such as the AIMPLB. The Board has set up its own network of *shari'a* courts (*Dar-ul Qazas*) that apply a male-centric version of *shari'a* and has banned women from taking their cases to state courts and claiming maintenance beyond the *iddat* period (Mahmood 2001; Hussain 2007; Redding 2010). Thus, for example, the *qadi* of the Delhi Shari'a Court[22] argues that

> It is the obligation of a Muslim to live according to rules of *shariat*. When there is a *shariat* court, if one goes to civil courts and wins a case according to rules applied by non-Muslims it will be *haram* or a sin in the eyes of Allah ... Muslims have to come to *shariat* courts; even if they lose, they will still be winners in the eyes of Allah...

Against this background, it is argued that demands for change must come from within and be firmly grounded in scripture and tradition. In fact, this is what Muslim women's organizations, like the AIMWPLB and others have been doing in recent years (Vatuk 2008).

As the AIMPLB's influence over religious law and institutions has increased, many Muslim women activists have joined the organization, trying to draw attention to various discriminatory practices in family law. Women AIMPLB members' strategies have included drawing up a model *nikahnama* (marriage contract) to address the practice of triple *talaq*, wherein women stipulate conditions of the marriage contract, such as the option for delegated divorce, whereby a woman is granted the right to initiate divorce and present her petition to the AIMPLB for approval. However, the male-dominated AIMPLB rejected the document, claiming it was 'un-Islamic', working swiftly to silence reformist women's voices throughout the organization (Niaz 2004: 28). In response, in 2005 some female members, representing the major sects and schools of Islamic jurisprudence, left the organization and established the AIMWPLB, based in Lucknow. The AIMWPLB released a new *nikahnama* in 2007 consisting of a seventeen-point *hidayatnama* (marriage guidelines for brides and grooms under Islamic law), and an eight-point section on divorce process. It prohibits triple *talaq* through text messaging, email, video-conferencing or phone, and recognizes women's right to delegated divorce (*talaq-e tafwiz*), no-fault divorce (*khul'*), and details women's right to post-marital maintenance and *mahr*. Moreover, the model *nikahnama* also gives women control of their reproductive health and bodies. For example, it allows women to seek dissolution of the marriage if the husband has an illicit relationship with another woman or refuses to disclose his HIV/AIDS status before or after marriage. In order to pre-empt the possible attacks of the traditional *ulama* on the new *nikahnama*, the new marriage contract carries extensive quotations from relevant verses of the Qur'an. As Shaista Amber, the president of the AIMWPLB, reports, the new *nikahnama* continues to gain acceptance in the community and about fifty couples have so far married under the relatively gender-balanced contract.[23]

In addition, the Women's Board has also set up its own court structure (*mahila adalat*), and has begun deciding cases using women-friendly interpretation of Islamic law (Awasthi 2006). The women's court is located in Lucknow and convenes every Friday at a local mosque.[24] It currently decides about two hundred divorce cases per year. Both male and female *qadis* sit together at *mahila adalat*. While the law they apply is not substantively different from Muslim family law as applied by AIMPLB courts, the *qadis* at the *mahila adalat* implement it with an eye on universal standards of human and women's rights.[25] The Bharatiya Muslim Mahila Andolan (BMMA), another organization working to secure women's rights through feminist and humanist interpretations of Islam, has taken the cause one step further, making history by allowing a female *qadi*, Dr Syeda Hamid, for the first time ever, to solemnize a *nikah* (marriage) ceremony where all four witnesses were also women. While mainstream *ulama* were busy questioning whether a woman could solemnize marriage under Islamic law, BMMA quietly proceeded to break with tradition, opening a new chapter for Muslim women in India, who are unable to rely on either the secular state or the male-dominated communal institutions, and must therefore use their own initiative to end the discrimination they suffer under the Indian personal status system.

Conclusion

Family laws have been a significant channel through which men ensure their control over women's sexuality and autonomy. Women in many societies have struggled to change this. However, where Muslim communities are a religious minority, as is the case with many Palestinians in Israel and various Muslim ethnic groups in India, women have faced more resistance to the democratization of family laws that violate their fundamental rights and deny them control over their own sexuality. Such violations are particularly present in the realms of marriage, divorce and postnuptial maintenance. Women have responded by building cross-communal alliances, lobbying for change in family law through legislative and judicial channels, and by forming hermeneutic communities that offer women-friendly interpretations of Islam in the hope of reforming the law from within an Islamic and traditional framework. At this point, the best strategies for family law reform and the integration of international principles of gender equality into religion-based personal status systems remain to be seen. Nevertheless there are lessons to be learned from the experiences of Muslim women in Israel and India.

Laws pertaining to marriage and divorce in personal status systems are extremely difficult to reform, as they are often viewed by leaders of ethno-religious groups as the pillar of communal identity even more than in majority cultures, and the guarantor of cultural autonomy and ethno-genealogical continuity. This is especially true for Palestinians living in Israel. Muslim minorities living in non-Muslim majority states have grown increasingly defensive regarding their marital laws. And states, as evidenced by the examples of the Israeli and Indian governments, have largely refrained from directly interfering with substantive Muslim marriage and divorce laws for fear of further antagonizing patriarchal authorities and politically powerful males within minority communities. In Muslim-minority settings, where issues of marriage and divorce are intricately entangled with identity politics, women's groups have encountered similar constraints and in the past primarily addressed procedural and less controversial issues (e.g. maintenance) through legislative and judicial channels. However, they are increasingly addressing substantive issues of marriage and divorce through hermeneutic means.

It is worth noting that reforming marital laws has not been much easier for Muslim-majority governments. Even though they are in theory vested with the necessary moral and political authority and legitimacy to reform substantive family laws, their top-down secular interventions (e.g. Egypt's Law No. 44 of 1979) have often failed, sometimes ultimately harming women's cause in the long term by strengthening the hand of anti-reform conservative groups. The same can be said of judicial and legislative interventions into procedural or non-marriage or divorce-related aspects of Islamic law in non-Muslim-majority settings. For example, the Indian Supreme Courts' judgments aiming to expand Muslim women's right to maintenance have further antagonized conservative elements within the Muslim community, prompting them to boycott state courts and set up an alternative network of Islamic courts (*Dar-ul Qazas*), which in turn have prevented Muslim women from using the civil courts to claim their expanded rights to maintenance. Similarly, Law No. 5 of 2001 aiming to empower Palestinian Muslim women by granting them recourse to Israeli civil family courts in maintenance suits has largely failed, due to the inaccessibility of the courts to Arabic-speaking women, and to social pressure from within the Palestinian community condemning the use of civil courts for family matters that normally fall under the purview of *shari'a*. However, such secular interventions are not necessarily complete failures. As seen in the case of Law No. 5, the law actually induced *shari'a* courts to undertake internal reform in order to dissuade Muslim women from going to civil courts. The impact of secular interventions can thus be significant in symbolic and indirect ways, even if, in and of themselves, they fail to offer a viable option to Muslim minority women living in hostile environments.

In the final analysis the most promising approach to reform seems to be the hermeneutic approach. Muslim family laws are in fact products of human agency, which through androcentric readings of the sacred texts and tradition have denied women equal representation in the construction of religious law. As seen in the cases of Muslim women in Israel and India, by deconstructing the meaning of texts, historical narratives and tradition, hermeneutic groups are constantly altering the way we understand the legality of religious laws concerning women's rights in marriage and divorce, women's sexuality and women's status in both domestic and public spheres. The pace of reform through hermeneutic means may be criticized for being too slow. Furthermore, it may also fall short of universal and secular standards for women's rights. However, these 'limited' and 'gradual' changes are more likely to influence women's rights in the desired direction than are secular, heavy-handed legal remedies, which may cause more harm than good in the long term, in the context of patriarchal authoritative and politically volatile situations, and diminish the possibility for upholding international women's rights standards in the Muslim world. Therefore, it is our argument here that hermeneutic activity – reform from within – is an invaluable approach to expanding Muslim women's rights in the long term. And the ultimate goal of reform, whether brought about through hermeneutic, legislative or judicial means, is to dismantle long-standing, discriminatory cultural dispositions and stereotypes about women's bodily and sexual rights and their place in society.

Notes

1. The Age of Marriage Law of 1950, the Women's Equal Rights Law of 1951, and the Penal Law Amendment (Bigamy) Law of 1959.
2. Personal interview with Sheikh Ahmad Natour, Jerusalem, January 2005.
3. Personal interview with Nasreen Alemy-Kabha, the former coordinator of the Working Group for Equality in Personal Status Issues, Nazareth, January 2005.
4. For instance, under the law the minimum age for marriage is 17. According to a report prepared by the Working Group on the Status of Palestinian Women in Israel, in 2007 22 per cent of married Muslim women were under the age of 18; the figure was only 0.5 per cent among Christian Arab women (Yazbak 2007). I do not have access to information regarding how many under-age marriage cases were prosecuted by the Israeli authorities in 2007. However, we have an earlier figure from 1990–95, according to which only seven cases of underage marriages were prosecuted during the entire period, resulting in just two convictions (Working Group on the Status of Palestinian Women in Israel 1997: 63). Given that in 1995 alone nearly 1,750 under-age marriages were contracted in the Arab community, the dismal number of convictions for the period of 1990–95 demonstrates Israeli authorities' lack of interest in upholding secular family laws among its Palestinian citizens.
5. The Israeli state also tends to avoid interfering with the ultra-Orthodox

Jewish practices relating to matrimony and domestic sphere that discriminate against and oppress women (Barzilai 2003; Halperin-Kaddari 2004).

6. The Family Law Amendment (Maintenance) Law of 1959 is applicable only to individuals who do not belong to communities governed by personal status law. For further information, see Shava 1973.

7. The Supreme Court of India in 1985 ruled in the case of *Mohammed Ahmed Khan* v. *Shah Bano Begum* (popularly known as the Shah Bano case) that in accordance with Section 125 of the Criminal Procedure Code of 1973 the Muslim husband was required to provide for his divorced wife who was unable to maintain herself even after the completion of her *iddat* period. The ruling of the court created a controversy within the Muslim minority. In response to the growing threats and demands of conservative and patriarchal forces within the Muslim community, the Rajiv Gandhi government enacted the Muslim Women (Protection of Rights on Divorce) Act in 1986 in order to reverse the court's ruling, and exclude Muslim women from the purview of Section 125 of the Criminal Procedure Code of 1973.

8. Islamic law requires the husband to provide his bride with *mahr* or dowry to seal the marital contract. *Mahr* has two parts: a prompt portion is due upon signing of the contract, while a deferred part is payable upon divorce.

9. *Iddat* is the waiting period that a woman must observe following the divorce, or death, of her husband under Islamic law. During *iddat*, which lasts three months after divorce, or four months and ten days after the husband's death, the woman cannot marry another man.

10. The following organizations were members of the coalition: Women Against Violence, the Association for Citizen's Rights in Israel, Israel Women's Network, Kayan (a feminist organization), Al Tufula Pedagogical Center, the Center for Family Development, Al-Siwar, and the Arab Association for Human Rights.

11. Personal interview with Nasreen Alemy-Kabha, Nazareth, January 2005.

12. Phone interview with Heba Yazbak, April 2010.

13. Phone interview with Heba Yazbak, April 2010.

14. Personal interview with Prof. Aharon Layish, Jerusalem, June 2004.

15. For further information on *marsoum qadai*, see Reiter 1997; Abou Ramadan 2003a, 2005, 2006.

16. Phone interview with Heba Yazbak, April 2010.

17. The Palestinian government in the West Bank appointed two female *qadis*, Khuloud Faqih and Asmahan Wuheidi, to Islamic courts in February 2009.

18. Email correspondence with Nissa wa Afaq, September 2010.

19. Sangh Parivar is an umbrella organization of right-wing Hindu nationalist organizations established by followers of the Rashtriya Swayamsevak Sangh or RSS (National Volunteer Corps). The BJP (Indian People's Party), a Hindu nationalist party founded in 1980 and the second largest political party in India, belongs to Sangh Parivar. Sangh Parivar and BJP are among the strongest advocates of the Uniform Civil Code, which they consider instrumental for abolishing diverse family laws and imposing

upon religious minorities one law, the terms of which will be dictated by the Hindu majority.

20. When I asked a BJP member of the Indian parliament who introduced an unsuccessful bill to enact a UCC about his real intentions, he told me that Hindu law prohibited bigamy for Hindu men while Muslim law allowed it. He argued that if this continued, within twenty-five years Hindus would become a minority and Muslims the majority. To equalize Muslim men's status with that of Hindu men, polygynous marriage had to be outlawed through the introduction of a uniform civil code. His introduction of the UCC bill was in fact, by his own admission, primarily motivated by the political survival of a Hindu majority. Personal interview with Mr Bachi Singh Shri Rawat. New Delhi, March 2005.

21. Personal interview with Dr Syeda Hamid, New Delhi, March 2005.

22. Personal interview with Qazi Mohammad Kamil Qasmi, New Delhi, March 2005.

23. Phone interview with Shaista Amber, May 2010.

24. The mosque was founded by Shaista Amber.

25. Phone interview with Shaista Amber, May 2010.

References

Abou Ramadan, M. (2003a) 'Judicial activism of the Shari'ah Appeals Court in Israel (1994–2001): Rise and crisis', *Fordham International Law Journal* 27: 254–98.

Abou Ramadan, M. (2003b) 'The transition from tradition to reform: The Shari'a appeals court rulings on child custody (1992–2001)', *Fordham International Law Journal* 26: 595–655.

Abou Ramadan, M. (2005) 'Divorce reform in the Shari'a Court of Appeals in Israel (1992–2003)', *Islamic Law and Society* 13(2): 242–74.

Abou Ramadan, M. (2006) 'Islamic legal reform: Shari'a Court of Appeals and Maintenance for Muslim wives in Israel', *Hawwa: Journal of Women in the Middle East and the Islamic World* 4(1): 29–75.

Agnes, F. (2001) *Law and Gender Inequality: The Politics of Women's Rights in India.* New Delhi: Oxford University Press.

Agnes, F. (2004) 'Constitutional challenges, communal hues and reforms within personal laws', *Combat Law* 3(4): 4–10.

Al-Tayeb, A. (2010) 'I saw the degrading attitude shown to women, just because they were women', www.acheret.co.il/en/?cmd=articles.382&act=read&id=2240 (accessed January 2011).

An-Naim, A.A. (1992) 'Toward a cross-cultural approach to defining international standards of human rights: The meaning of cruel, inhuman or degrading treatment or punishment', in A.A. An-Naim (ed.), *Rights in Cross-Cultural Perspectives: A Quest for Consensus.* Philadelphia: University of Pennsylvania Press, 19–43.

Awasthi, P. (2006) 'Our own personal law board', *India Together*, 21 September, www.indiatogether.org/2006/sep/wom-aimwplb.htm (accessed January 2011).

Barlas, A. (2004) *'Believing Women' in Islam: Unreading Patriarchal Interpretations of the Qur'an*. Karachi: SAMA.

Barzilai, G. (2003) *Communities and Law: Politics and Cultures of Legal Identities*. Ann Arbor: University of Michigan Press.

Desai, A.H., and Muralidhar, S. (2000) 'Public interest litigation: Potential and problems', in B.N. Kirpal, A.H. Desai and G. Subramanian (eds), *Supreme but Not Infallible: Essays in Honour of the Supreme Court of India*. New Delhi, Oxford University Press, 159–92.

El-Taji, M.T (2008) 'Arab local authorities in Israel: Hamulas, nationalism and dilemmas of social change', Ph.D. thesis. University of Washington, Seattle.

Eposito, J., and Delong-Bas, N.J. (2001) *Women in Muslim Family Law*. Syracuse: Syracuse University Press.

Gaay Fortman, B.D., Martens, K., and Mohammed Sali, M.A. (2010) *Hermeneutics, Scriptural Politics, and Human Rights: Between Text and Context*. Basingstoke: Palgrave Macmillan.

Haddad, T. (1978). *Notre femme, la législation islamique, et al société*. Tunis: Maison tunisienne de l'édition.

Halperin-Kaddari, R. (2004) *Women in Israel: A State of Their Own*. Philadelphia: University of Pennsylvania Press.

Hussain, S. (2007). *Shariat Courts and Women's Rights in India*. New Delhi: Centre for Women's Development Studies.

Layish, A. (1975). *Women and Islamic Law in a Non-Muslim State: A Study Based on Decisions of the Shari'a Courts in Israel*. New York: John Wiley & Sons.

Levitt, P., and Merry, S.E. (2009) 'Vernacularization on the ground: Local uses of global women's rights in Peru, China, India and the United States', *Global Networks* 9(4): 441–61.

Mahmood, S.T. (2001) 'The shariat courts in modern India', unpublished MS, on file with author.

Mamdani, M. (1996) *Citizen and Subject: Contemporary Africa and the Legacy of Late Colonialism*. Princeton NJ: Princeton University Press.

Menon, N. (1998) 'Women and citizenship', in P. Chatterjee (ed.), *Wages of Freedom: Fifty Years of the Indian Nation-state*. Delhi, Oxford University Press, 241–66.

Menski, W. (2001) *Modern Indian Family Law*. Richmond: Curzon.

Menski, W. (2006) 'Asking for the moon: Legal uniformity in India from a Kerala perspective', *Kerala Law Times* 2: 52–78.

Menski, W. (2007) 'Double benefits and Muslim women's postnuptial rights', *Kerala Law Times* 2: 21–34.

Mernissi, F. (1991) *The Veil and the Male Elite: A Feminist Interpretation of Women's Rights in Islam*. Boston MA: Addison-Wesley.

Merry, S.E. (2006a) 'Transnational human rights and local activism: Mapping the middle', *American Anthropologist* 108(1): 38–51.

Merry, S.E (2006b) *Human Rights and Gender Violence: Translating International Law into Local Justice*. Chicago: University of Chicago Press.

Mir-Hosseini, Z. (1999) *Islam and Gender: The Religious Debate in Contemporary Iran*. Princeton NJ: Princeton University Press.

Mirow, M.C. (2004) *Latin American Law: A History of Private Law and Institutions in Spanish America*. Austin: University of Texas Press.

Niaz, N.S. (2004). 'Marriage in Islam', *Combat Law* 3(4): 25–8.

Pateman, C. (1988) *The Sexual Contract*. Stanford CA: Stanford University Press.

Rajaram, N., and Zararia, V. (2009) 'Translating women's human rights in a globalizing world: The spiral process in reducing gender injustice in Baroda, India', *Global Networks* 9(4): 462–84.

Redding, J. (2010) 'Institutional v. liberal contexts for contemporary non-state, Muslim civil dispute resolution systems', *Journal of Islamic State Practices in International Law* 6(1): 2–26.

Reiter, Y. (1997) 'Qadis and the implementation of Islamic law in present day Israel', in R. Gleave and E. Kermeli (eds), *Islamic Law: Theory and Practice*. London: I.B. Tauris, 205–31.

Saar, T. (2005) 'A feminist Koran?', www.utne.com/2005–04–01/AFeminist Koran.aspx (accessed January 2011).

Sezgin, Y. (2009) 'Legal unification and nation building in the post-colonial world: A comparison of Israel and India', *Journal of Comparative Asian Development* 8(2): 273–97.

Sezgin, Y. (2010) 'The Israeli millet system: Examining legal pluralism through lenses of nation-building and human rights', *Israel Law Review* 43(3): 631–54.

Shahar, I. (2006) *Practicing Islamic Law in a Legal Pluralistic Environment: The Changing Face of a Muslim Court in Present-day Jerusalem*. Middle East Studies. Beer-Sheva: Ben-Gurion University of the Negev.

Shahar, I. (2007) 'Legal reform, interpretive communities and the quest for legitimacy: A contextual analysis of a legal circular', in R. Shaham (ed.), *Law, Custom, and Statute in the Muslim World: Studies in Honor of Aharon Layish*, Leiden: Brill, 99–228.

Shava, M. (1973) 'Maintenance in Jewish law and in the State of Israel', *Diné Israel* 4: 181–217.

Souaiaia, A.E. (2008) *Contesting Justice: Women, Islam, Law, and Society*. Albany: State University of New York Press.

Stowasser, B.F. (1994) *Women in the Qur'an, Traditions, and Interpretation*. New York: Oxford University Press.

Subramanian, N. (2005) 'Legal pluralism, legal change and gender inequality: Changes in Muslim family law in India', paper presented at the annual meeting of the American Sociological Association, Philadelphia, 12 August.

Tucker, J. (2008) *Women, Family and Gender in Islamic Law*. Cambridge: Cambridge University Press.

Vatuk, S. (2008) 'Islamic feminism in India: Indian Muslim women activists and the reform of Muslim personal law', *Modern Asian Studies* 42(2/3): 489–518.

Wadud, A. (1999) *Qur'an and Woman: Rereading the Sacred Text from a Woman's Perspective*. New York: Oxford University Press.

Working Group on the Status of Palestinian Women in Israel (1997) 'NGO report: The status of Palestinian women citizens of Israel', www.adalah. org/eng/intladvocacy/pal_women1.pdf (accessed 26 October 2010).

Yazbak, H. (2007) 'Statistical data: The proportion of young Arab women married under 19 between years 2000 and 2007', www.pstatus.org/?todo= projects&pid=00000023&pcatid=21&sid=4 (accessed January 2011).

Zahalka, I. (2010) 'The challenge of administering justice to an Islamic minority living in a non-Moslem state: The shari'a courts in Israel', unpublished MS, on file with author.

5

Sexuality and inequality:
the marriage contract and Muslim legal tradition

Ziba Mir-Hosseini

Constructions of sexuality and gender inequality inherent in Muslim legal tradition are informed by a strong patriarchal ethos. They are based on pre-modern interpretations of the sacred textual sources, and the rulings that Muslim jurists derived from them to regulate sexuality. It is not only in Muslim contexts that such perspectives linger on and prevent women from enjoying their full equality and citizenship rights. In *The Sexual Contract*, Carole Pateman (1988) reveals how the theorists of the Western Enlightenment, whose ideas nurtured democracy and civil society, also played an important role in sustaining patriarchy. In their commentaries on the 'original contract' or 'social contract', they ignored the 'sexual contract' – by which men provide and women obey – which constitutes half the story of the 'original contract'. This to some extent accounts for the lingering of patriarchal structures, even if women in the West have won most of the legal reforms they have been asking for since the nineteenth century.

In this essay, I probe the working of the 'sexual contract' in Muslim legal tradition. My aims are more limited than Pateman's; I confine my inquiry to the rulings (*ahkam*) that Muslim jurists devised to regulate marriage and women's covering (the dress code), and the theological, legal, sexual assumptions and theories that inform them. These legal rulings are only one element in the complex set of norms, practices and structures that define and regulate sexuality in Muslim contexts and must be understood and analysed in their own proper contexts.[1] But given the intimate links between religion, law and culture, and the resurgence of Islam as both a spiritual and a political force in the last decades of the twentieth century, I maintain that, to achieve gender equality, these rulings must be debated, challenged and redressed, not just on human rights grounds, but also from within, on Islamic grounds. Otherwise, Muslim women's quest for equality will remain a hostage to the political fortunes of various political forces and tendencies, as was the case in the twentieth century. While the earlier part of the century saw a process of secularization and modernization of laws and legal systems and women's increasing presence in public space, in the large majority of Muslim states, with the rise of political Islam, there were attempts to reverse this process, and women lost some of their earlier gains.[2]

I begin by examining the link between constructions of sexuality and inequality inherent in the laws that classical Muslim jurists devised for the regulation of sexuality, and then proceed to examine twentieth-century reconstructions and modifications of this link, and its disruption by the emerging feminist scholarship in Islam. There are three elements to my argument. First, the rulings regarding marriage and women's covering are in effect two sides of the same patriarchal imperative that legitimated and institutionalized control over women in both the private space of the family and the public space of society. Second, these rulings are informed by patriarchal readings of Islam's sacred texts and premissed on a set of assumptions and theories about male and female sexuality, notably ideas of female sexuality as both property and a danger to the social order. These assumptions and theories linking sexuality and inequality are explicit and transparent in classical jurisprudential texts, but they have become implicit and obscured in modern Islamic discourses. Finally, since it is this link that sustains women's subordination in contemporary Muslim contexts, exposure of the link can contribute to breaking it, an essential step in arguing for and constructing egalitarian laws in Muslim contexts.

I start from the premiss that assumptions about sexuality and gender in Islam, as in any other religion, are necessarily social/cultural constructions, thus historically changing and subject to negotiation. There is neither a unitary nor a coherent concept of sexuality and gender rights in Islamic legal thought, but a variety of competing concepts which, in part, reflect a tension in the sacred texts between ethical egalitarianism as an essential part of their message and the patriarchal context in which this message was unfolded and implemented (Ahmed 1991: 58). This tension enables both proponents and opponents of gender equality to claim textual legitimacy for their respective positions and gender ideologies. As feminist scholarship in religion has shown, this tension, which is inherent in all scriptural religions, is productive and allows contestation from within.

There are other premises. First, I reject statements beginning 'Islam says...' or 'Islam allows...' or 'Islam forbids...'. Islam does not speak; rather, it is people who claim to speak in the name (with the authority) of Islam, selecting sacred texts (usually out of context) that appear to support their claims, and repressing other texts that oppose them.

Being concerned with Muslim legal traditions and discourses, I must also register my discomfort with the term 'Islamic law(s)', though I have used it in my own writing. 'Islamic laws', like other laws, are the product of socio-cultural assumptions and juristic reasoning about the nature of relations between men and women. In other words, they are 'man-made' juristic constructs, shaped by the social, cultural and political conditions within which Islam's sacred texts are understood and turned into law. In my view, it is more analytically fruitful and productive to speak of 'Muslim legal tradition'.

Further, it must be remembered that, as in other religious and legal traditions, notions of justice among Muslims have not until recently included gender equality in its current sense. Only around the turn of the twentieth century did the idea of gender equality become inherent to conceptions of justice, and Muslim women's demands and struggle for equality and justice present Muslim legal tradition with a challenge that it has been trying to meet.

Moreover, to understand the nature of this challenge, and map the process and dynamics of change in Muslim legal tradition, we need to recognize one of its main classical distinctions: that between *shari'a* and *fiqh*. *Shari'a*, 'the path', in Muslim belief is the totality of God's will as revealed to the Prophet Muhammad. *Fiqh*, 'understanding', denotes the process of human endeavour to discern and extract legal rulings from the sacred sources of Islam: that is, the Qur'an and the Sunna (the practice of the Prophet, as contained in Hadith, Traditions).[3] While the *shari'a* in Muslim belief embodies the revealed law, *fiqh* is the science of Muslim jurisprudence, the process of human attempts to discern and extract legal rulings from the sacred sources of Islam, as well as the 'laws' that result from this process. What we know of '*shari'a*' is only an interpretation, an understanding (i.e. *fiqh*), which like any other system of jurisprudence is human, mundane, temporal and local.

This classical distinction was central to the emergence of the various schools of law, and of a multiplicity of positions and opinions within them. But it has been distorted and obscured in modern times, when colonial authorities and nation-states created new legal systems and selectively reformed and codified elements of *fiqh*, and when a new political Islam has emerged that uses *shari'a* as an ideology. From a critical feminist perspective, it is essential to revive the distinction because it both engages with the past and enables action in the present; it empowers us to contest the patriarchal interpretations of Islam's sacred texts from within by piercing the veil of sanctity that surrounds *fiqh* and to demystify the processes of law-making.

Sexuality and inequality in classical *fiqh* texts

The classical jurists' conceptions of sexuality and gender are encapsulated in two sets of legal rulings: those that define marriage and divorce, on the one hand, and those that define women's dress code (*hijab*), on the other hand. The discussion here is confined to delineating their salient features and legal structures in classical *fiqh* texts; whether these rulings corresponded at the time to actual gender relations and marriage practices is, of course, another question, and one that recent feminist scholarship in Islam has started to address. This scholarship warns us not to take classical *fiqh* texts at face value, since there is a gap between what they prescribe and what happened in courts and in practice. Studies of medieval and Ottoman court archive materials and judgments show that *fiqh* texts should be treated as a discourse, in the sense that, rather than telling us about customary marriage and gender relations, they tell us how those who had the legitimacy and power to define the law wished them to be.[4]

Marriage: contract and domination

In classical *fiqh* texts marriage is not a sacrament, but a civil contract to render sex between a man and woman licit; sex outside this contract constitutes *zina*, which is defined as a crime subject to punishment.[5] The contract is called *'aqd al-nikah* ('contract of coitus') and is patterned after the contract of sale, which served as the model for most contracts. It has three essential elements: the offer (*ijab*), the acceptance (*qabul*), and the payment of dower (*mahr*), a sum of money or any valuable that the man pays or undertakes to pay to the woman before or after consummation.

The contract places a wife under her husband's *qiwama*, a mixture of dominion and protection, and produces a set of fixed rights and obligations for each party, some supported by legal force, others by moral sanction. Those with legal force revolve around the twin themes of sexual access and compensation, embodied in the two concepts *tamkin* (obedience; also *ta'a*) and *nafaqa* (maintenance). *Tamkin*, defined as sexual submission, is a man's right and thus a woman's duty; whereas *nafaqa*, defined as shelter, food and clothing, is a woman's right and thus a man's duty. According to some schools, a woman is entitled to *nafaqa* only after consummation of the marriage; in others this comes with the contract itself; but in all schools she loses her claim if she is in a state of *nushuz* (disobedience), which the classical jurists defined only in sexual terms. Among the default rights of the husband is his power to control his wife's movements and her 'excess piety'. She needs his permission to leave the house, to take up employment, or to engage in fasting or forms of worship other than what is obligatory (for example, the fast of Ramadan), because such acts may violate the husband's right of 'unhampered sexual access'. Likewise, a man can enter up to four marriages at a time,[6] and enjoys the exclusive right to terminate each contract at will. A woman cannot be released without her husband's consent, although she can secure her release through offering him inducements, by means of *khul'*, which is often referred to as 'divorce by mutual consent'. As defined by classical jurists, *khul'* is a separation claimed by the wife as a result of her extreme 'reluctance' (*karahiya*) towards her husband. The essential element is the payment of compensation (*'iwad*) to the husband in return for her release. This can be the return of the dower, or any other form of compensation. If she fails to secure his consent, her only recourse is the intervention of the court and the judge's power either to compel the husband to pronounce *talaq* or to pronounce it on his behalf if the wife establishes one of the recognized grounds – which again vary from school to school. Since marriage is a contract, a woman can also at time of the marriage or later acquire from the husband the right to release herself from the contract, which is referred to as *talaq al-tafwiz*, or delegated divorce.

Hijab: covering and seclusion

Classical *fiqh* texts contain little on the dress code for women. The prominence of *hijab* in Islamic discourses is a recent phenomenon, dating to the nineteenth-century Muslim encounter with colonial powers. It is then that we see the emergence of a new genre of literature in which the veil acquires a civilizational dimension and becomes both a marker of Muslim identity and an element of faith.[7]

Classical Islamic legal texts – at least the genre that sets out rulings (*ahkam*) or what we can call 'positive law' – contain no explicit rulings on women's dress, nor on how women should appear in public.[8] They do not use the term *hijab*, and they use *sitr* (covering) to discuss the issue of dress for both men and women, but only in two contexts: first, rulings for covering the body during prayers; second, rulings that govern a man's 'gaze' at a woman prior to marriage.

The rulings are minimal, but clear-cut. During prayer, both men and women must cover their *'awrah*, their private parts; for men, this is the area between knees and navel, but for women it means all parts of the body apart from hands, feet and face. As regards the 'gaze', it is forbidden for a man to look at the uncovered body of a woman to whom he is not closely related – a ban that can be removed when a man wants to contract a marriage and needs to inspect the woman he intends to marry. The rulings on covering during prayer are discussed in the Book of Prayer (*kitab al-salah*) and are among the *'ibadat* (ritual/worship acts, duties to God), while those on 'gaze' come in the Book of Marriage, and fall under *mu'amilat* (social/contractual acts, duties to people).

There is, however, another sense of *hijab* that remains implicit in these texts: 'confinement'. This rests on two interrelated juristic constructs that cut across *fiqh*'s two main divisions: *'ibadat* and *mu'amilat*. The first construct defines a woman's whole body as *'awrah*, a sexual zone, that must be covered both during prayers (before God) and in society (before men). These are found in the Book of Prayer under 'covering of private parts' (*sitr al-'awrah*), which remains the only source that requires the covering of specific parts of the body. The second construct considers a woman's sexuality to be *fitna*, a source of danger to public order, and consequently grants men the right to control women's movements. The rulings on segregation (banning interaction between unrelated men and women) have their logic in this second construct. This construct, as recent feminist scholarship in Islam has shown, was linked to political and socio-economic factors, in particular during 'Abbasid rule, such as the public presence of female slaves, who were treated as sexual commodities and forbidden to cover in order to distinguish them from free women. Significantly, classical jurists considered the *'awrah* of a female slave or servant to be different from that of a free woman; some held it to be the same as that of men, between navel and knees; others argued that it was between chest and knees.[9]

The link: women's sexuality as property

These were, in a nutshell, the rulings on marriage and *hijab* in classical *fiqh* texts. As already mentioned, they should be seen as elements in a complex system of norms and practices to regulate sexuality in ways that sanction the appropriation of women's sexual and reproductive capacity. At the core of this system is the notion of women's sexuality as property, an old patriarchal idea that, as feminist scholarship has shown, pre-dates the emergence of Abrahamic religions, including Islam.[10] There were, of course, differences between the classical schools and among jurists within each school, and there were gaps between law and practice.[11] But the fact remains that all schools shared the same inner logic and patriarchal readings of Islam's sacred texts; if they differed, it was in the manner and extent to which they translated this conception into legal rulings.

For instance, dominant opinion in the Maliki school granted women the widest grounds for divorce (the husband's absence for a year, his mistreatment, failure to provide, and failure to fulfil marital duties), but prohibits them from contracting a marriage without the presence and consent of a male guardian (*wali*). In Hanafi law, by contrast, women were not required to have a marriage guardian and may contract their own marriages, but their access to divorce was more limited: for a husband's absence to qualify as grounds for judicial divorce, it must last 99 years. These differences were of practical importance for women, who could resort to the judge whose legal school provided them with a better option in the event of marital dispute, a kind of forum shopping. These differences also remain significant for reforms and were used during the codifications of family law in the course of the twentieth century. For instance, by adopting the more liberal principles from Maliki law, governments have been able to expand women's access to divorce while staying within the bounds of *shari'a*.[12]

In revisiting these rulings we need to remember that classical jurists lived in a world in which patriarchy and slavery were part of the fabric of society; inequality and hierarchy were the natural order of things. This world and value system informed their reading and understanding of Islam's sacred texts. The jurists neither disguised nor denied the patriarchal logic of their rulings on sexual and gender relations; in their discussion, they were transparent, rational and legalistic. They alluded to parallels between the status of wives and female slaves, to whose sexual services husbands/owners were entitled, and who were deprived of freedom of movement. For instance, Al-Ghazali, the twelfth-century Muslim philosopher and jurist, in his monumental work *Revival of Religious Sciences*, devoted a book to marriage, where he echoed the prevalent views of his time. Significantly, he ends the discussion with a section on 'Rights of the Husband', in which he does not invoke any Qur'anic verses but relies on Hadith literature to enjoin women to obey their husbands and remain at home.[13] He begins:

> It is enough to say that marriage is a kind of slavery, for a wife is a slave to her husband. She owes her husband absolute obedience in whatever he may demand of her, where she herself is concerned, as long as no sin is involved. (Al-Ghazali 1998: 89)[14]

In delineating the legal structure of the marriage contract, classical jurists had no qualms in using the analogy of sale. This is how Muhaqqiq al-Hilli, the thirteenth-century Shi'a jurist, defined marriage:

> Marriage etymologically is uniting one thing with another thing; it is also said to mean coitus and to mean sexual intercourse ... it has been said that it is a contract whose object is that of dominion over the vagina (*bad'*), without the right of its possession. (Hilli 1985: 428)

Khalil ibn Ishaq, the fourteenth-century Maliki jurist, was equally explicit when it came to dower (*mahr*) and its function in marriage:

> When a woman marries, she sells a part of her person. In the market one buys merchandise, in marriage the husband buys the genital arvum mulieris. As in any other bargain and sale, only useful and ritually clean objects may be given in dower. (Ruxton 1916: 106)[15]

I am not suggesting that in classical *fiqh* marriage is on a par with a sale contract. Aware of possible misunderstandings, classical jurists were careful to stress that marriage resembles sale only in form, not in spirit, and drew a clear line between free and slave women in terms of rights and status.[16] Even statements such as those quoted above distinguish between the right of access to the woman's sexual and reproductive faculties (which her husband acquires) and the right over her person (which he does not). Certainly, there were significant differences and disagreements about this among the schools, and debates within each, with legal and practical implications. This is not the point. The point is that the notion and legal logic of 'ownership' and sale underlie their conception of marriage and define the parameters of laws and practices, where a woman's sexuality, if not her person, becomes a commodity and an object of exchange, even if it is for only one transaction.

Sexuality and inequality in contemporary Islamic discourses

During the nineteenth and twentieth centuries, the colonial rulers of Muslim countries and the subsequent new nation-states in most cases put aside classical *fiqh* in all areas of law except family and personal

status law, where they selectively reformed, codified and grafted the rulings of classical *fiqh* on to unified legal systems inspired by Western models. In codifying these rulings, the modernizers left the substance of the marriage contract as defined by classical jurists more or less intact, and instituted reforms through procedural rules, such as requiring the registration of marriage and divorce, and limiting men's rights to unilateral divorce and polygamy. There were notable exceptions: Tunisia banned polygamy altogether in 1956; the Turkish Republic abandoned *fiqh* in all spheres of law and replaced it with Western-inspired codes; while Saudi Arabia preserved classical *fiqh* as fundamental law and attempted to apply it in all spheres of law.[17]

Codification transformed the relationship between the Muslim legal tradition, the state and social practice, and had two consequences that are of relevance to our discussion. First, by limiting the flexibility and plurality that was a feature of the classical schools, when one could choose among different interpretations, codification narrowed the possibilities of substantial reform. As codes and statute books took the place of classical *fiqh* manuals, laws regulating sexuality were no longer solely a matter for Muslim scholars, the *ulama*, operating within particular *fiqh* schools, but became the concern of the legislative assembly of a particular nation-state. Deprived of the power to define and administer family law, *fiqh* and its practitioners lost touch with changing political realities and were unable to meet the epistemological challenges of modernity, including the idea of gender equality. Second, codification, which began under colonial powers and expanded in the new nation-states, gave patriarchal notions of marriage and sexuality a new lease of life: they could now be applied through the legal machinery of a modern state. These governments lacked either the legitimacy or the inclination to challenge pre-modern interpretations of the *shari'a* as embodied in *fiqh* rulings on personal status and marriage.

From the late nineteenth century, we witness the emergence of a new body of texts whose prime objective has been to shed light on 'Islamic laws of marriage' and to correct 'misunderstandings'. Published by religious houses in both Muslim and Western countries, this literature is still available (much of it on the Internet) in a variety of languages, including English.[18] Written by men, at least until recently, these texts range from sound scholarship to outright polemics; not being strictly legal in their arguments, they are accessible to the general public.

A popular genre of this literature, which can perhaps be best described as marriage manuals, has no qualms about reproducing classical *fiqh* conceptions of sexuality and gender relations. Sold at news-stands or bookshops near mosques or shrines, these texts aim to inform would-be spouses in the popular classes how to live a 'proper Islamic family life'.[19] The texts in this genre have a similar format; oral in style, they are primarily based on sayings of the Prophet or quotations from classical jurists. They contain no argument, no discussion, only commands and warnings. A woman is told that she should keep herself covered so that her beauty is not seen by anyone apart from her husband, and that she should satisfy her husband's sexual needs and his other wishes; otherwise her place will be in hell, as one Hadith has it. According to another Hadith, if she refuses her husband, she will be cursed all night by angels. A man is told to make sure that his wife observes the rule of *hijab*, and to have mercy on her. In effect, they are banal replicas, in style and world-view, of Ghazali's *Adab al-Nikah* (*Etiquette of Marriage*), which is part of his monumental *Revival of Religious Sciences*, referred to earlier. Most include chapters or sections on 'the virtues of marriage' and 'the rights and duties of each spouse in marriage'. Some also include discussions of 'sexual etiquette', covering matters such as the time, frequency and manner of sexual intercourse, permissible and non-permissible positions, states of purity and impurity and menstruation, and so on. Their language is sexually explicit, using terms such as *shahvat* (sexual desire, lust, passion), *jama'* (intercourse), etc. They reflect the concept of active female sexuality, which Mernissi (1985) observes is prevalent when women's seclusion and gender segregations are emphasized, and which she claims to be the implicit theory of sexuality in Muslim societies.[20]

The following passage from an Iranian manual illustrates the working of the theory and its key concepts:[21]

> Sexual desire [*shahvat*] is ten times greater in woman than in man. God has chained women's *shahvat* with modesty and chastity [*haya va 'iffat*]. If their modesty were taken away, it is possible that every man would be followed by ten women wanting to make love with him. In *Lali*

al-Akhbar Imam Ali is quoted as saying: what motivates the beasts of prey is their hunger, and what motivates women and draws them to men is to extinguish the fire of their desire [*shahvat*]. Modesty [*haya*] has ten parts, of which nine parts are in women and one part in men. Then, when a woman is asked for in marriage, one part of her modesty goes; when she is contracted in marriage, another part goes; when she gives birth, another part goes; when her husband has intercourse with her, another part goes; she is left with five parts, and if she commits the hideous act of *zina*, all her modesty is removed. Pity the people, when all modesty is taken from women. (Qarani and Haj 1991: 53–4)

The three concepts (*ghairat*, *haya* and *shahvat*) form a theory of sexuality according to which God gave women greater sexual *shahvat* than men, but this is mitigated by two factors, women's *haya* (modesty, shyness) and men's *ghairat* (sexual honour and jealousy). Women who show *ghairat* (when their husbands are polygynous), and do not observe the rulings on *hijab* are lacking in faith and do not believe in the *shari'a*.

These 'marriage manuals' make no mention of the issue of women's rights; they do not engage with contemporary discourses or non-religious sources; they adhere to a gender perspective that I call 'traditionalist'.

This is not the case with texts that come under the general rubric of 'women's rights in Islam', which I classify as 'neo-traditionalist'. The authors of these texts do engage with contemporary issues; their overt aim is to clarify what they see as 'misunderstandings of Islamic law'. These texts differ in style, language and sophistication, but they follow the same line of argument, based on the premises of the 'naturalness' of laws in Islam and the 'innate difference' between men and women. These two premises become the pillars of a new defence of gender inequality, as follows: men and women are created equal and are equal in the eyes of God, but the roles assigned to them in creation are different, and *fiqh* rules reflect this difference. Differences in rights and duties do not mean inequality or injustice; if correctly understood, they are the very essence of justice. This is so because these rulings not only reflect the *shari'a*, the 'divine' blueprint for society; they are also in line with 'human nature' (*fitra*) and take into consideration the biological and psychological differences between the sexes.

Aware of and sensitive to criticisms of the patriarchal bias of family law in Muslim contexts, these texts are punctuated by general and abstract statements such as 'Islam affirms the basic equality between men and women', 'Islamic law grants women all their rights', 'Islamic law honours and protects women'. They focus on the ethical and moral rules that marriage entails for each spouse, but they overlook the fact that these ethical rules, in effect, carry no legal sanction; nor do they offer comprehensive and viable arguments for translating them into imperatives. They quote Qur'anic verses and Ahadith that affirm the essential equality of the sexes in marriage, which they define using the terms 'equity' and 'complementarity'. But they keep silent on the logic that underlies the whole edifice of marriage in classical *fiqh* texts: women's sexuality as property and marriage as a form of sale.

This logic is so repugnant to modern sensibilities and values, so alien from contemporary Muslims' experience of marriage, that no author can openly admit to following it. But it comes to the surface once these texts resort to reasoning, as in Abul A'la Maududi's *Purdah and the Status of Women in Islam* and Morteza Mutahhari's *System of Women's Rights in Islam*.[22] Both authors were Islamic ideologues, and their writings, rooted in anti-colonial and anti-Western discourses, have become seminal texts for contemporary Islamist groups and movements; they offer a new defence of the classical *fiqh* rulings, and contain a new theory of sexuality.

Writing in Urdu in the 1930s, in the context of pre-partition India, Maududi appeals to radical Islamists in his adamant rejection and condemnation of modernity and liberal values. For him, the problem with Muslims is that they have abandoned the principles of Islam and its laws, which are in line with the 'Laws of Nature', and have adopted secular (i.e. Western and to some extent Hindu) values that have corrupted them and are destroying their civilization. The solution he offers is 'return to Islamic law', which recognizes the 'Law of Nature' that mandates leadership by men, and the submission of women and their exclusion from public life. 'Sexual attraction' is the force behind human civilization; 'real advancement and well-being is [geared to] the proper adjustment of the mutual relationship between husband and wife' (Maududi 1998: 1). This is the very essence of *shari'a*, as it is the 'Law of Nature', which

Maududi takes to be that defined by the jurists when it comes to gender relations. He builds his theory of sexuality and defence of classical *fiqh* notions of gender rights on a Qur'anic verse, and entitles it 'Real Significance of Sex':

> The first thing that has been stated and explained in this connection is: 'All things We made in Pairs' (41:49). This verse makes a reference to the universality of the sex-law and the Master of the Universe Himself divulges the secret of His Creation. He says that the universe has been designed on the relationship of pairs. In other words, all parts of this great machine have been created in pairs, and all that one can see in this world is indeed the result of the mutual attraction of these pairs.
>
> Now let us consider the nature of the sex-relationship. This relationship itself implies that one partner in the pair should be active and the other receptive and passive, one prompt to influence and the other ready to be influenced, one prepared to act and the other willing to be acted upon. … This is the basic relation that gives rise to all other relations functioning and operating in the world. (Maududi 1998: 134)

Having established the meaning of the verse, Maududi goes on to deduce from it three principles, which contain the gist of his theory of sexuality and offer a new rationalization of *fiqh* rulings on marriage and *hijab*. The first principle is that God as the 'Maker and Owner of the Factory cannot desire that His Factory cease to function', and that 'the existence of both the active and the passive partners is equally important for the purposes of the Factory'. From this follows the second principle, the gist of which is that if we want to keep the smooth working of the 'Factory', everything must work and be placed in the order that the 'Maker' ordained. This takes Maududi to his third principle: the superiority of men and the subordination of women:

> 'Activity' in itself is naturally superior to 'passivity' and femininity. This superiority is not due to any merit of masculinity against demerit in femininity. It is rather due to the fact of possessing natural qualities of dominance, power and authority. A thing that acts upon something else is able to do so on account of its being dominant, more powerful and impassive. On the other hand, the thing that submits and yields, behaves so simply because it is by nature passive, weak and inclined to be impressed and influenced. Just as the existence of both the active and passive partners is necessary for the act to occur, so it is also necessary

that the active partner should be dominant and able to produce the desired effect, and the passive partner yielding and inclined to be receptive ... these principles can be deduced from the basic fact of divisions into the male and female. The human male and female, being physical entities, do by their nature require that these principles should govern all their relationships. (1998: 136)

Mutahhari offers a more nuanced argument for the 'naturalness of Islamic law', and his text is more popular with moderate Islamist groups. Writing in Persian in 1960s' Iran as part of the religious opposition to the secularizing policies of the Pahlavi regime, he is less adamant in his opposition to modernity, and less overtly patriarchal, taking issue with both classical *fiqh* texts and secular discourses. He rejects one of the main assumptions of classical *fiqh* texts, that 'women are created of and for men'; and contends that, in the Islamic view, women are equal to men in creation, and do not depend on men for attaining perfection, but attain their perfection independently. At the same time, he rejects the idea of gender equality, and argues instead for the 'complementarity of rights'. Differences in rights and duties between the sexes do not mean inequality or injustice; if properly understood, they are the very essence of justice. This is so because roles assigned to men and women in creation are different; 'Islamic laws' reflect this difference.

The theory of the naturalness of 'Islamic laws' was first advanced by the most renowned twentieth-century Shi'a philosopher, Allamah Tabataba'i, in his monumental, twenty-volume Qur'anic commentary commonly known as *al-Mizan*.[23] Interestingly, Tabataba'i saw sexual desire not as fixed and innate but as malleable and social. He rejected the belief (popularly attributed, as quoted earlier, to Imam 'Ali) that women's sexual desire is nine times greater than men's; if that were so, and if *shari'a* laws work with, not against, the grain of nature, then how can they allow men but not women to contract more than one marriage at a time? Hence his advocacy of the proper Islamic education of women in society, which enhances men's sexual desire and constrains that of women.

> Women's religious education in an Islamic society teaches them chastity and modesty ['*iffat va haya*]; contrary to the common belief that women's desire [*shahvat*] is greater than men's, for which women's desire for beauty and ornaments is taken as proof, [proper religious education] makes

women's desire much less than men's, and this is what Muslim men who have Islamically trained wives know well. Therefore, a man's desire on average requires him to have more than one wife and even two and three. (Tabataba'i n.d.: 52)

While concurring with this objective, Mutahhari adds a psychological twist, contending that men and women desire in different ways:

Man is the slave of his own desire [shahvat] and woman is the prisoner of a man's love [muhabbat] ... A man wants to take possession of the woman's person and to wield power over her, a woman wants to conquer the man's heart and prevail upon him through his heart ... A man wants to embrace the woman and a woman wants to be embraced ... A woman is better able to control her desire than a man. Man's desire is primitive and aggressive, woman's desire is reactive and responsive. (Mutahhari 1991: 207)[24]

Mutahhari's language differs from that of Maududi and the classical *fiqh* texts, but his male-centred views of creation and of marriage as dominance are the same.

The association of married life rests upon the pillar of spontaneous attachment and has a unique mechanism. Creation has given the key to strengthening it, and also the key to bringing it down and shattering it, into the hand of man. Under the command of creation, every man and woman has a certain disposition and certain characteristics, when compared with each other, which cannot be exchanged and are not the same. (Mutahhari 1991: 274)

Women's sexuality, now defined as passive, is subordinated to that of men.

Nature has devised the ties of husband and wife in such a form that the part of woman is to respond to the love of man. The affection and love of a woman that is genuine and stable can only be that love which is born as a reaction to the affection and admiration of man towards her. So the attachment of the woman to the man is the result of the attachment of the man to the woman and depends upon it. Nature has given the key of love of both sides to the man, the husband. If he loves his wife and is faithful to her, the wife also loves him and remains faithful to him. It is admitted that woman is naturally more faithful than man, and that a woman's faithfulness is a reaction to the unfaithfulness of the man. (Mutahhari 1991: 274)

Mutahhari's language and arguments are less bluntly patriarchal and are more nuanced than those of Maududi; yet he too subordinates women's feelings, needs and sexuality to those of men. In this way, both authors not only justify male domination and control over women but, by resorting to notions such as 'nature' and 'essential differences', perpetuate gender stereotypes that stem from and reinforce unequal power relations in marriage.

The forming of a new discourse

In the second part of the twentieth century, with the rise of political Islam, the theory of 'the naturalness of *shari'a* law' became closely identified with Islamist political movements. Islamist forces – whether in power or in opposition – started to invoke *shari'a* as a legitimizing device. Tapping into popular demands for social justice, they presented 'Islamization' as the first step to root out corruption, to combat crime and immorality, and to bring about a moral and just society. These issues spoke to the masses, and played on the popular belief among Muslims that Islamic *shari'a* is the essence of justice; hence no law that is 'Islamic' can be unjust.

The 1980s saw the introduction of regressive gender policies in many parts of the Muslim world; for instance, gender segregation and compulsory dress codes for women in Iran and Sudan, the enforcement of Hudud Ordinances that led to the persecution of many women in Pakistan, the dismantling of family law reforms introduced earlier in the century in Iran and Egypt, and restrictions imposed on women elsewhere by state or non-state forces, as in Sudan and Algeria. But the 1980s also saw the expansion of human rights legislation, the rise of an international women's movement, and the emergence of women's NGOs in many Muslim countries. The human rights framework, instruments like CEDAW, international funds and transnational links gave women's rights activists what they needed most: a point of reference, a language and organizational tools for their struggle to resist the regressive policies of political Islam.

Like all ideologies, however, political Islam carried the seeds of its own transformation. Attempts to translate classical *fiqh* notions of gender rights into policy provoked criticism and spurred women to increased activism. The defence of pre-modern patriarchal interpretations of the *shari'a* as 'God's Law', as the authentic 'Islamic' way of life, brought the classical *fiqh* books out of the closet and exposed them to critical scrutiny and public debate. A growing number of Muslim women came to question whether there was an inherent or logical link between Islamic ideals and patriarchy. This opened a space, an arena, for an internal critique of patriarchal readings of the *shari'a* that was unprecedented in Muslim history. A new phase in the politics of gender in Islam began. One crucial element of this phase has been that it places women themselves – rather than the abstract notion of 'woman in Islam' – at the heart of the battle between forces of traditionalism and modernism.

By the early 1990s, there were clear signs of the emergence of a new consciousness, a new way of thinking, a gender discourse that is 'feminist' in its aspiration and demands, yet 'Islamic' in its language and sources of legitimacy. This discourse owes much to a new trend of reformist religious thought that is consolidating a conception of Islam and modernity as compatible, not opposed. Its advocates do not reject an idea simply because it is Western, nor do they see Islam as providing a blueprint, as having an inbuilt programme of action for the social, economic and political problems of the Muslim world. Following and building on the work of earlier reformers such as Mohammad Abduh and Muhammad Iqbal, they contend that the human understanding of Islam is flexible, that Islam's tenets can be interpreted to encourage both pluralism and democracy, and that Islam allows change in the face of time, space and experience.[25] Not only do they pose a serious challenge to legalistic and absolutist conceptions of Islam, they are carving a space within which Muslim women can achieve gender equality in law. Instead of searching for an Islamic genealogy for modern concepts like gender equality, human rights and democracy (the concern of earlier reformers), the new thinkers place the emphasis on how religion is understood and how religious knowledge is produced. Revisiting the old theological debates, they aim to revive the rationalist approach that was eclipsed when legalism took over as the dominant mode and gave precedence to the form of the law over substance and spirit. They make it possible to examine critically the older interpretations and epistemologies and to expose the contradictions inherent in earlier discourses on family and gender rights.

Yet these new religious thinkers have not addressed the issue of sexuality, as opposed to gender. In fact, while some of them are now openly advocating gender equality in society and the family, they have been silent on the issue of sexuality. The silence is significant and needs further attention. While it speaks of their ambivalence and anxiety, it has both epistemological and strategic implications that should not be overlooked: epistemological in the sense that constructing women's sexuality as defined and regulated by familial and social circumstances suggests that it is not determined by nature or the divine; that Islam as a religion has nothing to say on the subject; that what may be claimed as 'Islamic' are merely the views and perceptions of some Muslims, which are neither sacred nor immutable but human and changing – and open to challenge. Their silence is strategic because it carves out a space within Muslim legal tradition where women can be treated as social rather than merely sexual beings. In classical *fiqh* texts, gender rights and women are discussed only in terms of sexuality, and only in the context of rulings on marriage and divorce and women's covering. By diverting the focus away from women's supposed 'nature' to their 'social' experience, the debate on gender equality can be moved onto new ground, and the link (implicit in classical *fiqh* rulings) between gender inequalities and theories of sexuality can be broken.

Conclusion

The emerging gender discourse and the reformist Islam of which it is a part are still in a formative phase, and their future prospects are tied to political developments all over the Muslim world – and to global politics. Their prospects of redressing the gender inequalities in dominant interpretations of the *shari'a* rest on women's ability to organize and participate in the political process and as well as in the production of religious knowledge. Let me conclude with two comments on these prospects.

First, recent reformist and feminist scholarship in Islam heralds a new egalitarian legal paradigm that is still in the making. Feminist scholars in particular are both discovering a hidden history and rereading the textual sources to unveil an egalitarian interpretation of the *shari'a*. They contend that the classical jurists' notions of gender are not sacrosanct, nor are their rulings above critical evaluation. In contrast to scholars such as Maududi and Mutahhari, who resort to 'scientific' and 'naturalist' theories to explain and justify the disparity between men and women's rights in the *shari'a*, feminist scholars return to the textual sources and read them in light of the changed conditions of women and contemporary notions of justice in which gender equality is now inherent. In so doing they are explicitly severing the link between sexuality and inequality in Muslim legal tradition that has sustained gender inequality, despite the fact that spiritual equality of the sexes is now an undisputed element of contemporary gender discourses.

My second comment is that legal systems and jurisprudential theories must be understood in the cultural, political and social contexts in which they operate. Both the old *fiqh* paradigm, with its strong patriarchal ethos, and the emerging feminist readings of the *shari'a* should be viewed in this complex double image, as both expressing and moulding social norms and practices. Legal change often comes when theory or jurisprudence reacts to changes in social practices, to political, economic and ideological forces, and to people's experiences and expectations. Islamic legal theory is no exception – as attested to by the ways in which both legal systems and women's lives and social experiences were transformed in the course of the twentieth century, and by the feminist challenge from within that the Muslim legal tradition faces in the new century.

Notes

1. The issue of 'sexuality in Islam' has been the subject of many scholarly works, using different approaches ranging from historical to feminist. Notable among them are: Boudhiba 1975; Marsot 1979; Musallam 1983; Sabah 1984; Mernissi 1985; Yeganeh and Keddie 1986; Imam 1997; Ali 2006; Souaiaia 2007; Ilkkaracan 2008; Kugle 2010; for an insightful discussion of sexuality and women's rights, see Othman 2000.
2. For an analysis of the legal developments, see Welchman 2007; Mir-Hosseini 2009.
3. According to classical legal theory, the sources of Islamic law are four: the Qur'an, the Hadith (pl. Ahadith, 'sayings', the body of literature that recorded the sayings, decisions and actions of the Prophet), *qiyas* (reasoning by analogy) and *ijma'* (the consensus of the jurists). While the first two sources have their roots in divine revelation, the other two are the

products of human reasoning. For concise accounts, see Rahman 2002: 68–84; Bassouni and Badr 2002.

4. See, for instance, Sonbol 1996; Rapoport 2005; Tucker 2008.

5. The discussion here is intended merely to outline the salient features of the marriage contract and to give references to sources available in English. For introductions to and translations of classical texts on marriage, see Farah 1984, and Spectorsky 1993; for critical analysis of the marriage contract, see Ali 2006, 2010; and on *zina*, see Mir-Hosseini and Hamzic 2010.

6. In Shi'a law a man may contract as many temporary marriages (*mut'a*) as he desires or can afford. For this form of marriage, see Haeri 1989.

7. See, for instance, Ahmed 1992; Hoodfar 1997; El Guindi 1999.

8. Clark (2003) shows that the Hadith literature has little concern with women's covering, and does not refer explicitly to the covering of hair; there are more Ahadith on men's dress and covering their *'awrah* than on women's dress.

9. For discussion and sources, see Abou El Fadl 2001: 255–7 nn 106, 107.

10. See Lerner (1986), who argues that the establishment of patriarchy was not a single 'event' but a process developing over a period of nearly 2,500 years from approximately 3100 to 600 BCE.

11. Many legal schools emerged but few survived. Important among the surviving ones are five. The Hanafi, named after Abu Hanifa (d. 767), emerged in Baghdad and is dominant today in Turkey, Syria, Iraq, Lebanon, Jordan, Egypt, Pakistan and Afghanistan. The Maliki, named after Malik ibn Anas (d. 795), emerged in Medina and is dominant today in North and West Africa. The Shafi'i, named after Idris al-Shafi', emerged in Baghdad and is dominant today in Indonesia, Malaysia, Singapore, Philippines, Sudan, Upper Egypt and Southern Arabia. The Hanbali, named after Ahmad ibn Hanbal (d. 855), emerged in Baghdad; it was made popular by Abd al-Wahhab at the beginning of the twentieth century, and is dominant in Saudi Arabia. The Ja'fari or Twelver School, named after Ja'far, the 6th Shi'a Imam (d. 765), is dominant in Iran and Iraq. For a discussion of differences of marriage laws among schools in the formative period of *fiqh*, see Ali 2010.

12. For concise accounts of the reform methods, see Rahman 1980.

13. For critical discussion of these Ahadith, see Abou El Fadl 2001: 232–47.

14. For another rendering of this passage, see Farah 1984: 120.

15. 'Genital *arvum mulieris*' is Ruxton's prudish translation of *bad'* (vagina); Jorjani, another Maliki jurist, defines marriage as follows: 'a contract through which the husband acquires exclusive rights over the sexual organs of a woman' (quoted by Pesle 1936: 20).

16. For similarities between conceptions of slavery and marriage, see Marmon 1999; Ali 2010.

17. For codification and reforms, see Anderson 1976; Rahman 1980; Welchman 2007.

18. A sample of texts available in English include Maududi 1983, 1998; Doi 1989; Mutahhari 1991, 1992; Chaudhry 1995; Al-Sadlaan 1999. For discussion of such writings in the Arab world, see Stowasser 1993; for Iran, see

Mir-Hosseini 1999; for Muslims living in Europe and North America, see Roald 2001; for a critical engagement with them, see Shehadeh 2003.

19. Texts I have collected in Iran and Morocco since the early 1990s include titles such as: *Guide to Marital Relations from Islam's View*; *The Union of Two Flowers or the Bride and the Groom: Marriage in Islam*; *The Bride's Gift or the Happy Islamic Marriage*; *A Muslim's Conduct with his Wife*.

20. For a discussion, see Othman 2000.

21. Translations of these passages are mine.

22. Maududi 1998 (published in Urdu 1939, in pre-1947 India); Mutahhari 1991 (published in Persian 1972, in pre-revolutionary Iran); both books are available in English and Arabic and have been reprinted many times. For analysis of their gender discourse, see Shehadeh 2003.

23. The gist of this theory is found in a small pamphlet entitled *Polygamy and the Status of Women in Islam* (Tabataba'i, n.d.).

24. The published English translation renders *shahvat* variously as 'sexual drive' and 'passion'. For this passage, I supply my own translation, but later passages are taken from the published one.

25. For the textual genealogy of this thinking, see Kurzman 1998.

References

Abou El Fadl, K. (2001) *Speaking in God's Name: Islamic Law, Authority and Women*. Oxford: Oneworld Publications.

Abou-Bakr, O. (2001) 'Islamic feminism: What's in a name? Preliminary reflections', *MEWS Review* 15(4), http://amews.org/review/reviewarticles/islamicfeminism.htm.

Ahmed, L. (1991) 'Early Islam and the position of women: The problem of interpretation', in N. Keddie and B. Baron (eds), *Women in Middle Eastern History*. New Haven CT: Yale University Press, 58–73.

Ahmed, L. (1992) *Women and Gender in Islam: Historical Roots of a Modern Debate*. New Haven CT: Yale University Press.

Al-Ghazali, Imam Abu Hamid (1998) *The Proper Conduct of Marriage in Islam (Adab an-Nikah), Book Twelve of Ihya 'Ulum ad-Din (Revival of Religious Sciences)*, trans. Muhtar Holland. Hollywood FL: Al-Baz.

Ali, K. (2006) *Sexual Ethics and Islam: Feminist Reflections on Qur'an, Hadith and Jurisprudence*. Oxford: Oneworld Publications.

Ali, K. (2010) *Marriage and Slavery in Early Islam*. Cambridge MA: Harvard University Press.

Al-Sadlaan, S.G. (1999) *The Fiqh of Marriage in the Light of Quran and Sunnah: Covering the Dower, Wedding Night, Wedding Feast and Rights of Husband and Wife*, trans. Jamaal al-Din M. Zarabozo. Boulder CO: Al-Basheer.

Badran, M. (2002) 'Islamic feminism: What's in a name', *Al-Ahram Weekly Online* 569, 17–23 January, http://weekly.ahram.org.eg/2002/569/cu1.htm.

Bassiouni, C., and Badr, G. (2002) 'The Shari'ah: Sources, interpretation, and rule-making', *UCLA Journal of Islamic and Near Eastern Law* 1(2): 135–81.

Boudhiba, A. (2004) *Sexuality in Islam*. London: Saqi.

Cantwell Smith, W. (1980) 'The true meaning of scripture: An empirical historian's nonreductionist interpretation of the Qur'an', *International Journal
of Middle East Studies* 11: 486–505.

Chaudhry, M.S. (1995) *The Status of Women in Muslim Society*. Lahore:
Al-Matbaat-ul-Arabia.

Clark, L. (2003) 'Hijab according to Hadith: text and interpretation', in S. Alvi,
H. Hoodfar and S. McDonough (eds), *The Muslim Veil in North America:
Issues and Debates*. Toronto: Women's Press.

Doi, A.R. (1989) *Women in the Shari'a*. London: Ta-Ha.

El Guindi, F. (1999) *Veil: Modesty, Privacy and Resistance*. Oxford: Berg.

Farah, M. (1984) *Marriage and Sexuality in Islam: A Translation of Al-Ghazali's
Book on the Etiquette of Marriage from the Ihya*. Salt Lake City: University of
Utah Press.

Fletcher, M. (2006). 'How can we understand Islamic law today?', *Islam and
Christian–Muslim Relations* 17(2) April: 159–72.

Haeri, S. (1989) *Law of Desire: Temporary Marriage in Iran*. London: I.B.
Tauris.

Hilli, M. (1985) *Sharayi' al-Islam*, Vol. II, trans. A.A. Yazdi, compiled by Muhammad Taqi Danish-Pazhuh. Tehran: Tehran University Press.

Hoodfar, H. (1997) 'The veil in their minds and on our heads: The persistence
of colonial images of Muslim women', in D. Lloyd and L. Lowe (eds), *Other
Circuits: Intersection of Exchange in World Theory and Practice*. Durham NC:
Duke University Press, 248–79.

Ilkkaracan, P. (2008) *Deconstructing Sexuality in the Middle East*. Aldershot:
Ashgate.

Imam, A. (1997) 'The Muslim religious right ("fundamentalism") and sexuality',
Dossier: Journal of Women Living Under Muslim Laws 17: 7–26.

Khan, M.W. (1995) *Woman between Islam and Western Society*. New Delhi: Islamic
Centre.

Kugle, S.S. Al-Haqq (2010) *Homosexuality in Islam: Critical Reflections on Gay,
Lesbian, and Transgender Muslims*. Oxford: Oneworld Publications.

Kurzman, C. (ed.) (1998) *Liberal Islam: A Sourcebook*. Oxford: Oxford University Press.

Lerner, G. (1986) *The Creation of Patriarchy*. Oxford: Oxford University
Press.

Marmon, S. (1999) 'Domestic slavery in the Mamluk Empire: A preliminary
sketch', in S. Marmon (ed.), *Slavery in the Islamic Middle East*. Princeton NJ:
Markus Wiener, 1–23.

Marsot, A.L. Al-Sayyid. (1979) *Society and Sex in Medieval Islam*. Malibu: Un-
dena Publications.

Masud, M.K. (2001) 'Muslim jurists' quest for the normative basis of shari'a',
Inaugural Lecture. International Institute for the Study of Islam in the
Modern World, Leiden.

Maududi, A.A. (1983) *The Laws of Marriage and Divorce in Islam*. Kuwait: Islamic
Book Publishers.

Maududi, A.A. (1998) *Purdah and the Status of Women in Islam*, 16th edn. Lahore:
Islamic Publications.

Mernissi, F. (1985) *Beyond the Veil: Male–Female Dynamics in Muslim Society*, rev. edn. London: Saqi.

Mernissi, F. (1991) *Women and Islam: A Historical and Theological Enquiry*. Oxford: Blackwell.

Mir-Hosseini, Z. (1999) *Islam and Gender: The Religious Debate in Contemporary Iran*. Princeton NJ: Princeton University Press.

Mir-Hosseini, Z. (2003) 'The construction of gender in Islamic legal thought and strategies for reform', *Hawwa: Journal of Women in the Middle East and the Islamic World* 1(1): 1–28.

Mir-Hosseini, Z. (2004) 'Sexuality, rights and Islam: Competing gender discourses in post-revolutionary Iran', in G. Nashat and L. Beck (eds), *Women in Iran from 1800 to the Islamic Republic*. Urbana and Chicago: University of Illinois Press, 201–17.

Mir-Hosseini, Z. (2006) 'Muslim women's quest for equality: Between Islamic law and feminism', *Critical Inquiry* 32(1): 629–45.

Mir-Hosseini, Z. (2009) 'Towards gender equality: Muslim family laws and the shari'a', in Zainah Anwar (ed.), *Wanted: Equality and Justice in the Muslim Family*. Musawah: An Initiative of Sisters of Islam, www.musawah. org/background_papers.asp.

Mir-Hosseini, Z., and Hamzic, V. (2010) *Control and Sexuality: The Revival of Zina Laws in Muslim Contexts*. London: Women Living Under Muslim Laws.

Musallam, B. (1983) *Sex and Society in Islam*. Cambridge: Cambridge University Press.

Mutahhari, M. (1991) *The Rights of Women in Islam*, 4th edn. Tehran: World Organization for Islamic Services.

Mutahhari, M. (1992) *The Islamic Modest Dress*, trans. Laleh Bakhtiar, 3rd edn. Chicago: Kazi Publications.

Othman, N. (2000) 'Sexuality and gender rights: A sociological perspective', in Z. Anwar and R. Abdullah (eds), *Islam, Reproductive Heath and Women's Rights*. Kuala Lumpur: Sisters in Islam, 77–106.

Qarani, G., and Haj, S. 'Ali (1991) *The Union of Two Flowers or Bride and Groom* [*Paivand-i Du Gul ya 'Arus va Damad*]. Qum: Alhadi [1370].

Pateman, C. (1988) *The Sexual Contract*. Cambridge: Polity Press.

Pesle, O. (1936) *Le Mariage chez les Malekites de l'Afrique du Nord*. Rabat: Moncho.

Rahman, F. (1980) 'A survey of modernization of Muslim family law', *International Journal of Middle Eastern Studies* 11: 451–65.

Rahman, F. (1982) 'The status of women in Islam: A modernist interpretation', in H. Papanek and G. Minault (eds), *Separated Worlds: Studies of Purdah in South Asia*. Delhi: Chanakya Publications, 285–310.

Rahman, F. (2002). *Islam*, 2nd edn. Chicago: Chicago University Press.

Rapoport, Y. (2005) *Marriage, Money and Divorce in Medieval Islamic Society*. Cambridge: Cambridge University Press.

Roald, A.S. (2001) *Women in Islam: The Western Experience*. London: Routledge.

Ruxton, F.H. (1916) *Maliki Law: A Summary from French Translations of Mukhtasar Sidi Khalil*. London: Luzac.

Sabbah, F. (1984) *Woman in the Muslim Unconscious*. New York: Pergamon.

Shehadeh, L.R. (2003) *The Idea of Women under Fundamentalist Islam*. Gainesville: University of Florida Press.

Siddiqi, M.M. (1952) *Women in Islam*. Lahore: Institute of Islamic Culture.

Sonbol, A.A. (ed.) (1996) *Women, Family and Divorce Laws in Islamic History*. Syracuse: Syracuse University Press.

Spectorsky, S. (1993) *Chapters on Marriage and Divorce: Responses of Ibn Hanbal and Ibn Rahwayh*. Austin: Texas University Press.

Souaiaia, A. (2007) 'She is upright: Sexuality and obscenity in Islam', *Hawwa: Journal of Women in the Middle East and the Islamic World* 5(2–3): 262–88.

Stowasser, B. (1993) 'Women's issues in modern Islamic thought', in J.E. Tucker (ed.), *Arab Women: Old Boundaries, New Frontiers*. Bloomington: Indiana University Press, 3–28.

Tabataba'i, A.H. (n.d.), *Ta'addud-i Zaujat va Maqam-i Zan dar Islam* [*Polygamy and the Status of Women in Islam*]. Qom: Azadi.

Tucker, J. (2008) *Women, Family and Gender in Islamic Law*. Cambridge: Cambridge University Press.

Wadud, A. (1999) *Qur'an & Woman: Rereading the Sacred Text from a Woman's Perspective*, 2nd edn. Oxford: Oxford University Press.

Wadud, A. (2006) *Inside the Gender Jihad: Women's Reform in Islam*. Oxford: Oneworld Publications.

Welchman, L. (2007). *Women and Muslim Family Laws in Arab States: A Comparative Overview of Textual Development and Advocacy*. Amsterdam: Amsterdam University Press.

Yeganeh, N., and Keddie, N.R. (1986). 'Sexuality and Shi'i social protest in Iran', in R. Juan, R.I. Cole and N.R. Keddie (eds), *Shi'ism and Social Protest*. New Haven: Yale University Press, 109–38.

PART II

Sites of contestation:
reclaiming public spaces

6

Purity, sexuality and faith:
Chinese women *ahong* and women's mosques
as shelter and strength

Maria Jaschok with Shui Jingjun

Reducing women to their sexuality, rather than affirming that sexuality is part of the whole of women's human make up, is not going to be transformed without raising that consciousness. (Wadud 2006: 219)

A man without a wife, a home without a mistress; a woman without a husband, a body without a master. (Arab proverb, cited by Na Guangyong in a popular didactic text, 1995: 14)

The women don't acquire their knowledge from the male *ahong*,[1] or from their husbands. The men in families of Chinese Muslims don't possess religious knowledge ... actually, many men know less than women. So [the existence of] the female mosque is necessary after all. Women's mosques are needed because society needs women with superior knowledge and qualities. (Guo Dongping Ahong, interview[2])

In the first quotation above, Amina Wadud argues that the sexualization of Muslim women diminishes all other dimensions of their humanity. Characteristic of the dominant discourse on both sides of Western/Islamic exchanges, such patriarchal, reductionist treatment of women makes for complicity of secular and religious gender regimes in locking women into subjectivity and positions of perpetual dependency (Sabbah 1984; Jaschok and Shui 2000). Yet, as academics note, the construct of a homogenous 'Muslim world' – symbiotically linked with the unitary category of 'the Muslim woman' – denies the reality of a large and diverse Muslim diaspora which comprises contrasting and locally grounded traditions of being

Muslim, and of being a Muslim woman. China's long-standing and large Muslim population, estimated at between 20 and 30 million people, offers striking illustrations of this diversity, of the multitude of ways in which to negotiate the relationship of Islam to other belief systems and practices, and of the various gender regimes wherein both masculinity and femininity are informed and contested in often unique ways.

The situation of the highly diverse Muslim minority population in China and its long and troubled history under successive Imperial, Republican and Communist authoritarian regimes has created what Barbara Metcalf calls cultural 'borderlands' (Metcalf 1996) of shifting demarcations of identity and status. However, within these volatile state-controlled peripheries, women are assigned roles of central symbolic and political importance to delineate ethno-religious belonging and signify immutable identity in what is an ever-unpredictable political landscape. The continuity that women embody through conduct and appearance turns their bodies into tightly guarded and contested sites for competing claims to ownership. In Man Ke's (2010) study of closed Dongxiang Muslim communities in the borderland of Gansu province in China's northwest region, intense rivalry among local mosque- and shrine-based organizations, often living in close proximity, is conducted through the imposition of severe controls over Muslim women's physical and social mobility. Ownership of a daughter is transferred upon her marriage to her husband; a woman leaves home only when granted permission and her clothing marks her as belonging to a particular religious tradition. In contrast, in the communities of central China, the greater ease of social inter-action and thus greater openness characteristic of relations between Muslim and Han Chinese populations in the region provide women with more bargaining power. If communities are less fixated on segregational markers, women are under less pressure to represent the collective ideal, and are able to make use of social and political resources which derive from a more fluid conception of identity. Muslim women in central China see themselves as distinctively and proudly Chinese, claiming the legal and institutional entitlements which are constitutionally due to all Chinese women (Jaschok and Shui 2000).

Yet, whatever the specific geopolitical constellations of a given Muslim community, and the consequent situation of female members, all belong to what the Chinese state classifies as an 'ethnic' religion. To this day an aggressive, secular modernism of Maoist women's liberation ideology defines itself with reference to, or (during times of religio-political instability) in opposition to, religion. Muslim-minority women have ever been the eternal Other, associated by Chinese mainstream society with attributes of 'backwardness', 'feudalism' and 'past-orientation' that has marked them, until recently, as belonging to the era 'before Liberation', *jiefang yiqian* (before 1949), a temporal marker which still today assigns those who hold to religious beliefs as only tenuously, if at all, linked to progress and modernity. Only since the 1980s, in the wake of economic reforms and China's entry into global market economy, have official discourses on 'the modern Chinese woman' become less dichotomizing, and less hostile to women with religious belief.

Women are at the intersection of other inequalities as well. In her 1978 study of Muslim women in Taiwan, Barbara Pillsbury notes a double bind in relation to (non-Muslim) mainstream Han Chinese society as well as to Muslim men. Women's outsider status in relation to men's genealogy of faith is given dramatic expression in popular and widely quoted Hui folk tales, which mark religious belonging along the fault lines of gender. These are tales that speak of men's purity of origin, of descendants of unbroken patrilines of faith that bridge time and space, separating believers from a distant, sacred homeland (Li and Luckert 1994). Although not backed up by historical facts, the mythologized patriline continues to help perpetuate a belief system in which hierarchies of 'purity' and 'impurity' have created categories of spiritual insiders, men; and outsiders, women. Common sayings to this day, such as 'Hui [Arab] father, Han [Chinese] mother' (*Nanren shi alaboren, nüren shi zhongguoren*) speak to enduring beliefs that women's outsider status disqualifies them from matching men's superior level of religiosity and the male legacy of ancestral ties to the homeland of Islam, Mecca. Historically, the brides available for Muslim men were local (non-Muslim) Han Chinese women; they became Muslim wives, reproducing the faith and Muslim communities (Li and Luckert 1994). Whilst indispensable to the survival of the collective, women's rights have been closely tied to, and circumscribed by, their reproductive duties.

Our study looks at sexuality from the perspective of the unique tradition of women's mosques, which has a history of more than 300 years. It is almost exclusively concerned with women from the Hui Muslim communities in central China.[3] It is in this region that women have historically laid claim to separate, collective identities and to a negotiated sexual morality – that is, sexuality not totally within the religious or political control of a patriarchal regime. Whereas studies of Islam in China have tended to focus in particular on western and northwest borders where Muslims are most concentrated and relatively closed off from mainstream society (Gladney 1991), our interest in the mediating role played by women in the development of Islam, but also in the processes of modernization outside mosque gates, has made us turn to central China, and to local histories of prominent female presence in Islamic institutions and traditions.

Gendered constructs of women's purity, *jie*, and shame, *xiuti*

The history of women's sexuality can be traced in the changing discourses on the constructs of 'purity' (*jie/jing/qing/ganjing*) and of women's 'shame' (the parts and physical expressions of the female body to be concealed from public male gaze, *xiuti*). These have defined, circumscribed, and have come eventually to enable, women's sexuality. These discursive shifts can illuminate Muslim women's historical trajectory from outsiders (*wairen*) to claimants to their own space, to the emergence of instruction and prayer texts for women (*nürenjing*), and female congregations with their own religious leaders (*nü ahong*).

The concept of *jie* (purity) at the heart of Chinese Muslim women's traditional paradigms of the moral pious wife and mother can be found both in the Hadith (Chen 1994) and in formulations by the sixteenth- and seventeenth-century Hui scholars Wang Daiyu, Ma Zhu and Liu Zhi. Moral prescriptions transmitted from generation to generation of teachers infuse the texts taught in women's mosques even today (Jaschok and Shui 2000: 121–53). These writers sought to enunciate the faith, and the knowledge embedding the faith, in a cultural context wherein women's confined domestic lives made access to education rare, if not impossible. In the discursive context of Confucian ideals equating female ignorance with female virtue (*wuzhi cai de*), of female dependence on men (*sancong*), of essential female merits (*side*), these writers had to reconcile cultural gender prescriptions with scriptural exhortations for *all* Muslims to attain proper knowledge of God's revelations. The largely practical and ritual nature of selective texts taught to women – what has become known as *nürenjing* (women's scripture) – suggests that the emphasis of Islamic educationalists was to enlist the help of women as educators of their families; thus they focused on providing women a basic knowledge of Muslim dietary and ritual observances rather than opening their minds to a deeper understanding of the scriptures.

The concept of *jie* resounds with multiple meanings. Dress, physical mobility, social interaction with non-kin relations and with all non-Muslims, conduct and deportment, all resonate with ideas linking women's spirituality and sexuality. This essential conceptual precept is transmitted through instruction and in weekly sermons in women's mosques. As a guiding ethic, *jie* may refer to outer cleanliness but also to purity of mind. It is associated with female self-abnegation and assiduous observance of sexual strictures on the conduct of girls and women. *Jie* is also cited in support of independent, women *ahong*-led women's mosques. The safeguarding of purity has thus become a defence of a contested institution, the women's mosque, while women *ahong* also invoke *jie* to critique men's mosques, arguing that some practices are not congruent with the ideal of purity of spirit and faith. *Jie* has also been invoked in the process of redefining sexual boundaries in line with changing circumstances whereby women assume more power with regard to patriarchal claims to sexual and reproductive services. By enlarging the space for women's access to educational facilities and societal resources, the leadership of many a respected and capable *ahong* has inspired a widening spectrum of recognizably female roles.

The religious legitimization for safeguarding women's purity is expressed in the concept of *xiuti* – that which is 'shameful' and in need of concealment from the public (male) gaze. Female *ahong*-led women's mosques have historically been instrumental in reinforcing such sexual strictures, yet changes have taken place as society modernizes and women have come to reappraise this notion of 'shame' as a religious–moral straitjacket to confine female sexuality. We have argued that 'potentially far-reaching redefinitions of the religious and social implications of *xiuti* are taking place whereby women begin to separate non-negotiable affliction, ordained by God (in consequence of Eve's transgression and women's legacy of sin as daughters of Eve), from negotiable, because earthly (patriarchal), afflictions' (Jaschok and Shui 2000: 213). When women talk 'history', they organize narratives around early transgressions of God's strictures by their ancestress, Eve, and the consequences for all her female descendants when she fell from the pure state of grace. The narratives of redemption attained as 'mothers of the believers', according to both received and reinvented traditions, all are fused into a collectively shared vision of God's ordained plan for a meaningful life. In sermons and study rooms, *ahong* have reminded their congregations that the ever-present dangers and frailties facing women are a trial willed by God. But, as we have demonstrated, women's mosques over the course of time have created a space that has allowed for local dissension from received canons of morality. Social space, so Roberta Gilchrist (1994) reminds us, is a complex and active construct which changes as it is worked upon by life-experience, agency and will.

In this fluid negotiation of orthodox notions of a needful constriction of female sexuality and challenges to these from both religious and secular readings, the intervention of female *ahong* is proving decisive. Their position as authoritative interpreters of often obscure scriptural passages and their influence over independent institutions and resources, it is argued, heighten their influence over female congregations. Fatima Mernissi observes that 'Female modesty has a wider symbolic function' in that it diminishes the 'initiative and critical judgement' of a believer (1996: 113); however, *ahong* in charge of religious life in women's mosques are known for their creative strategy and authoritative interventions, balancing dutiful submission to Islamic practices with confident negotiations of ambiguities in scriptural interpretations to reflect claims for gender justice in all spheres of society. The lives of female leaders as presented in our case studies demonstrate the creative exercise of collective agency in spaces seemingly governed by inflexible norms and practices.

Nüsi women's mosque as a contested space

In our earlier work (Jaschok and Shui 2000), we trace the origin of women's mosques to a critical historical juncture which came to be known as the 'age of adversity' for China's Muslims (Bai 1983). During the sixteenth and seventeenth centuries, the very survival of the Islamic faith and of Muslim identity was threatened. Hui intellectuals responded with radical initiatives to reinvigorate faith and strengthen religious and ritual knowledge in the hope of bolstering adherence to Muslim practices, a challenge considering the overwhelmingly non-Muslim context of China. Women were both targets for educational initiatives and, in their roles as wives and mothers, also valued conduits of knowledge.

Both Confucianism and Islam required gender segregation, sheltering women from the public arena and the male gaze. Religious education for women generally took place in a secluded room or compound in a private home, to avoid any hint of impropriety concerning the mingling of the sexes (a charge levelled by Confucianist scholars at other religions also). Papanek has treated such 'sheltering' as sacrifice of women's agency (Papanek 1982); however, unlike the South Asian institution of *purdah* studied by Papanek, Chinese Muslim women have come over time to imbue their experience of seclusion with a notion of purity, which they understand not as capitulating to a dependency on men, but rather as a valuable 'complementary' (*duiying, huxiang zhichi*). This understanding of gender relations, still prevalent, actually serves to support women's claims to religious legitimacy and to women's rights and entitlements concerning human and material resources in the context of religion. With the consciousness of their place in the history of organized Islam in China, concurrent with their rights as Chinese women to social and legal equality, Muslim Chinese women have managed to expand the notion of the Muslim woman and disarm potential opposition through a discourse of complementarity.

Historically, women's religious education occurred behind the 'shelter' of a curtain, with male teachers safely instructing them from the other side. In time, the teaching role was assumed by women. Initially, *shiniang* (wives of *ahong*) were entrusted to instruct ordinary women in rudimentary religious and ritual knowledge; it was a responsibility they performed in support of their husbands' role, relying on their husbands for guidance. Over time this role was increasingly taken on by trained female teachers (*jiaoshi*) or female *ahong*.

The very architecture of women's mosques speaks to the ambiguities around women's place within institutional religion and authority (Jaschok and Shui 2000). The same religious and moral strictures on female mobility in public places have until recently meant that women's mosques did not hold daily collective worship; they lacked minarets from which to call for prayer, and female *ahong* were not expected to interact with the world outside the mosque gate. Significantly, the generally flexible prayer routine in women's mosques was such that women's religious duties did not interfere with their duties as wives and mothers.

Unforeseen, this history of segregation and the transformative power of the sacred space of women's mosques have in fact engendered the evolution of a gendered practice of collective learning and prayer, as well as of institutional organization and leadership. This in turn has created a powerful sense among women of active participation in organized Islam; women's voices represent female-centred perspectives and interests in the affairs of the Muslim community. Religious and material cultures of women's mosques are beginning to show changes as result of women's assertion that they are equal in every way (Jaschok 2012). And at the heart of this has been the all-embracing spiritual and moral leadership provided by women *ahong* as brokers of sexual morality, which has continued to mould women's lives over the centuries.

Sexual morality: Muslims, chaste wives and virtuous mothers

Sexual morality in Chinese Hui Muslim contexts is constructed at the intersection of received Confucian and Islamic norms, interpretations of Islamic scriptures transmitted in women's mosques by women *ahong*, renewed influence from Wahabbi teachings and the impact of, and reactions to, a highly visible and intrusive consumer society with its ubiquitous images of sexualized female bodies. It is arguable that women *ahong* have assumed a central and powerful position as intermediaries in the constitution of 'Islam' for ordinary Muslim women in the diasporic context of China, where Islam has been constructed through the narrating of Arabic and Farsi texts in sermons and private conversations and the images in mosques and Muslim households from holy shrines in Mecca and Medina. Until the educational projects of the 1990s, most women did not read or understand Arabic and Farsi, and thus had no direct understanding of the scriptures of their faith. Widespread female illiteracy in China generally, still common among older generations of women, has compounded dependence on the *ahong* and female religious teachers for Islamic knowledge and guidance concerning adherence to Islamic precepts. Through their perceived learnedness and their status in the wider society, female *ahong* are instrumental in shaping how ordinary Muslim women negotiate sexuality with respect to communal allegiance and identity, against the backdrop of China's rapidly developing market economy. They lead women's congregations in daily prayer, provide education on 'proper female morality' (*fudao*) and present, by virtue of lives lived under the collective gaze, ideal and idealized templates for the conduct of Muslim women.

Ideals embodied in texts taught to Muslim girls and women stem from early formulations of a sexual morality by Hui Muslim scholars, which sought to fuse Confucian and Islamic norms in order to create a viable and sustainable Muslim culture. As we have previously argued (Jaschok and Shui 2000), indigenous Yin/Yang philosophy and the positively valued, interactive complementarity of the sexes became a cornerstone of Muslim Chinese ethics.[4] Ma Mingliang has noted that historically 'Chinese Muslim scholars conscientiously combined Islamic ethics with Confucian ethics. By searching for commonalities and similarities, they developed an Islamic ethic system imbued with features of Chinese culture' (Ma 1994: 90). These indigenous cultural influences rest on a gendered moral axis of female virtues and conduct (Du and Mann 2003; Ko et al. 2003).

The codification of a traditionally gender-segregated society through observance of Confucian core precepts of sexual morality – *sancong* (obedience to father, husband and son) and *side* (characteristics of idealized feminine virtue), supports the centrality of marriage in women's lives (Rosenlee 2006). Teachings on women's moral cultivation, *fudao*, are still part of the texts taught in women's mosques today. In addition to being *xiangqi liangmu* (chaste wives and virtuous mothers), women were also to be *qiancheng* (devout in their faith); Chinese Muslim religious authorities based many of their moral instructions to women on the Confucian gender hierarchy. Though some Hui Muslim writers, such as the reformer Liu Zhi (*c.* 1655–1745), claimed that sexual instincts were constructed as natural, God-given and their satisfaction entirely proper, the dominant patriarchal and patrilineal kinship system effectively limited this understanding to male sexuality. In contrast, women's pleasure was understood to come from a willing subjection to husbands' sexual needs: 'A woman must conduct herself and win respect from others by observing the rites: say what her husband says; take what her husband allows her to take; never go out without permission; never see male strangers; and never do anything against her husband's will' (Liu Zhi, cited in Jaschok and Shui 2000: 132). Drawing from the Islamic (Arabic-language) concept of *fitna*, dangers/moral disorder arising from unrestricted social intercourse, the Hui scholar Wang Daiyu (*c.* 1548–1670) held that 'being born of a woman, a man will lose himself in the contemplation of woman … even a good man and a good woman will be overwhelmed by their sexuality if they stay near one another' (Jaschok and Shui 2000: 124).[5] Whilst it could be argued that dominant written and oral Hui Muslim traditions emphasized the natural, God-given sexuality of both women and men, its expression was granted only within marriage. Furthermore, Muslim marriage norms in conjunction with Confucian morality reinforced the virtue of submissiveness as a feminine ideal.

However, despite the persistence of faith and a great degree of prescriptive textual continuity, long traditions of gender segregation, along with twentieth-century notions of sexual equality, have given rise to a 'double reading' via the female *ahong* (Jaschok 2003: 668–9). Faithful adherence to the sacred words of the scriptures, on the one hand, and their pragmatic adaptation to the contingencies of women's changing needs, on the other, are played out daily in narratives of pious lives lived in a larger non-Muslim context. Women *ahong* adapt idealized templates of Muslim femininity to women's actual lives to ease the burden of those who regard themselves as 'deficient' Muslims. The daily conflict experienced by ordinary women in reconciling their primary duties as wife and mother with what are acutely felt pressures to attend to their spiritual life in daily ablution and prayer render the presence of a women's mosque a source of consolation, but also of perplexity. This perplexity deepens where *ahong* insist in a spirit of equality on the same discipline of prayer in their women's mosque as applies to men's mosques (Jaschok and Shui 2000). In the same way that the role and functions, as well as standing, of women's religious institutions evolved over time, becoming more diverse, organized, influential and permanent, the evolving status of female *ahong* has widened interpretations of the 'Women's Qur'an' and Hadith, reflecting the history of Chinese Muslim women as well as the charisma of individual leaders.

The educational texts that continue to be taught in women's mosques to this day, and the history of sexual norms derived from both Confucian and Islamic prescriptions, reflect the contingencies of time and place and the variety of factors, including geography and identity politics, that shape ideas and behaviours with regard to female sexuality. In view of the important historical role of educated, religiously learned women, who, supported by their male kin, provided largely illiterate women their sole access to religious knowledge and ritual, as well as alleviated their fear of *houshi* (afterlife), we turn next to an exploration of the religious, cultural and institutional resources from which they derived their authority, and the scope of their influence over women in the local community.

Women *ahong* as influential role models and exemplary leaders

Continuing the historical tradition of women's mosques and female religious leaders in central China's Hui Muslim communities, women *ahong* play vital intermediary roles in the religious, cultural and economic processes that fashion female bodies. Female morality and deportment are the more important because the influence of pilgrims and Islamic teachers from the Middle East has reintroduced debate around Arab-Muslim paradigms of female modesty and sexuality among Chinese Muslims, highlighting the tension between these and popular, secular expressions of female modernity in society at large.

Women *ahong* play a significant role in the local translations of multiple, diverse and conflicting influences on mind and body and may develop such influence that local women are inspired to make changes in their personal and communal spheres. Women *ahong* lead women's congregations in daily prayer, and provide education at the mosque on 'proper female morality', thus presenting ideal templates for the conduct of Muslim daughters, wives and mothers. They also counsel women who ask for help coping with marital tension, family conflict and intergenerational crises. Their influence depends not only on their personality and talent, but also on factors such as the presence of other, secular, women's associations. Sensitive to possible accusations by government authorities of undue interference with matters outside the religious sphere, they respond to requests for, rather than offering, advice. In the absence of secular women's organizations, as is often the case in communities that are almost entirely Muslim, *ahong* allow themselves greater flexibility in advising on such issues as family planning and use of contraceptives.[6]

Whereas historically *ahong* were confined in their duties to the guidance of women believers in facilitating understanding and application of scriptures to everyday life, contemporary *ahong* frequently occupy positions of social and political consequence in local and national bodies outside their mosque compounds. But their influence over women congregations is undiminished, as they act as often forceful intermediaries and guides in the negotiation of compromises at the most intimate level of family relations between Islamic beliefs and practices and Chinese society's secular mainstream values. Given the dependency by rural and urban Muslim women on the *ahong*, and given the trust of ordinary women in the religious authority of their leader, the strategies adopted to 'localize' or 'indigenize' Islamic religion in relation to sexuality and other aspects of life were, and still are, best illuminated by the words and life experiences of *ahong* themselves. Their interpretations and implementation of ideal Muslim conduct have wide application: influencing teaching (of women, girls and *ahong* trainees or *hailifan*), sermons, individual or collective counselling, and occasional lectures to wider audiences (see below). Their personal lives, lived in the public gaze of their congregation, are like mirrors by which ordinary women have traced, and adjusted, the moral correctness of their own action.

In Chinese cultural traditions, intergenerational learning takes place in the central relationship between *shifu* (master) and disciple, between experience tempered by knowledge and wisdom and a young mind still unformed and uninformed. Such a teacher–disciple relationship informs the concept of learning. Norms and social hierarchy place in senior positions those credited with advanced knowledge, purity of motive and incorruptible integrity exemplified through personal conduct; thus *ahong*, who stand between women's worldly life and afterlife, inspire Muslim women, such as those at a famous women's mosque in Henan province who liken their *ahong* to the 'light of the lamp' of faith, which shines all the brighter when all are in harmony with her (Jaschok 2012).

Two venerable *ahong*

Two female *ahong* embody, in their lives and careers, the multiple, at times conflicting, public expectations of religious authority and submissive femininity; they are of different generations, one aged over 80, the other in her mid-forties. The older *ahong* was born and brought up in an urban environment, and in her adult life has led a congregation in a rapidly modernizing, thriving provincial capital; the younger *ahong* was born into rural society and returned to village life when her husband took office as an *ahong*. Both *ahong* share qualities of leadership and influence which have their source as much in their learning and erudition as in the respect in which they are held for their exemplary lives, demonstrated daily in the public scrutiny of local society. As noted above, their choices and lifestyles, their relationships and balancing of family, marriage and work, offer a ready moral compass for others to apply or challenge. How do they themselves interpret and handle these changes in view of their position as leaders of Muslim female congregations?[7]

Guo Dongping Ahong: probing sexual morality in a modernizing society

Guo Dongping, born in 1967 in Haizhuang village[8] in Fengqiu county, Henan province, in central China, grew up during a time when political oppression had driven religious life underground and children were raised in contempt of all religions, including Islam.

After the late 1970s, when the Chinese government introduced less repressive religious policies, Guo Dongping's mother entrusted her to the guidance of teachers, who inspired in her strong religious fervour. Together with other girls from her village, at the age of 19 Guo took up the study of Islam at the famous Wangjia Hutong Women's Mosque in Kaifeng in Henan province.[9] In 1986, Guo and another girl from her village became the first post-Cultural Revolution (1967–77) *hailifan* to be appointed *ahong*. The admission of unmarried young girls to *hailifan* training, and eventually to the position of *ahong*, was unprecedented and highly controversial. Instead of widows and post-menopausal women, who historically were selected to *hailifan* status, authority, it seemed, could now be derived through education, transcending the life cycle limitations of gender. The resident *ahong*, Lu Ahong, who had initiated the new policy, eventually succeeded in alleviating the hostility and opposition to such innovation. She had pointed out, we were told, that the destiny of marriage awaited all, including the highly educated young *ahong*. Only their service to Allah could justify what was after all only ever a delay in entering the institution of marriage, not to be confused with its rejection. Why was there such an insistence on married *ahong*?

Women's duty to marry – and to submit to the domestication of their bodies in the service of both the secular and celestial patrilines – was enshrined in Confucian ethical codes as well as in Islamic precepts. The rigid female life cycle shaped female subjectivity and conduct; female sexuality belonged to marriage and wifely submission of the body to husband, patrilineal ancestors, and the will of Allah. Only women with experience of conjugal relations were considered suitable to the task of instructing in 'women's morality', of which the cornerstone was the husband–wife relationship. In fact, popular *jingge* (Islamic songs of moral instruction) were traditionally taught in women's mosques only by a married woman to married women. An unmarried *ahong*, by her very choice of a career over marriage, would have been considered insufficiently committed to a sexual morality that centred on marriage, enshrined in the core principle of *yicong*, obedience owed by a wife to her husband (Jaschok and Shui 2000).

It is difficult to overestimate the degree of opposition to Lu Ahong, who expanded the religious authority of women by disconnecting 'legitimate religious concerns', as they applied to conjugal and reproductive duties, from their historical source of authority, the married *ahong*. Instead, unmarried *ahong*, unburdened by marriage and motherhood, could extend the parameters of instruction to the higher aspirations for erudition and spirituality; in other words, become more akin to their male counterparts. Although, ultimately, all *ahong* were bound to marry, the extension of their formative period of education and professional experience was likely to have shaped the choices they made as married women – as happened with Guo Dongping (see below).

No doubt Lu Ahong's legendary personal characteristics of forcefulness and stubborn determination played a part in arriving at what she knew would be a controversial decision. On the other hand, women of Lu Ahong's generation were subject to both Maoist political thought reform and the dominant state-steered gender rhetoric which stressed, as we were repeatedly told by older women, 'whatever men have, women are entitled to also'. While Maoist *funü jiefang* (women's liberation) may have been forced on women, including religious women, by a state grimly determined to impose a secularist interpretation of 'socialist progress', the successful adaption of its principles and politics to the religious realm goes some way to explain the reopening of women's religious sites after the Cultural Revolution and the continuity of female *ahong*-led women's mosques in the face of accusations by male *ahong* of 'aberration' from Islamic practice (Jaschok and Shui 2000).

Guo Dongping's biography is marked by intense and personally felt tension between wifely submission (following her marriage in 1989 at age 22, see below) and a highly individualistic assertion of the right to self-determination, as practised before her by her mentor Lu Ahong. She found the traditional education under the female *ahong* of Wangjia Hutong Women's Mosque difficult. Known as *jingtangyu* (a traditional form of mosque-based Islamic education passed down over centuries), this system demands the memorization of Arabic and Farsi Qur'anic passages, selected Ahadith and popular commentaries. Guo Ahong sought to adapt this traditional method of study to her own inclinations, developing what she called the principle of 'digesting all knowledge' (or 'becoming able to relate knowledge'). In her quest to make morality an act of agency rather than obedient adherence to paradigmatic notions of *jie*, she emulated her teacher Lu Ahong.

She greatly admired Lu Ahong for the way she applied Islamic precepts in her daily life. Lu Ahong's passionate dedication to her responsibilities as *ahong*, her vocation since the age of 17, led her to take controversial measures to satisfy her husband's needs so that she could fully focus on her spiritual leadership and sustain her independence and influence. Guo Dongping recalled approvingly:

> Lu Ahong was ever a broad-minded woman. She spent a sum of 70 yuan to buy a second wife [a concubine] for her husband, letting her take care of her husband while she herself became an *ahong*. Now the second wife's children live in Kaifeng. Many people can neither understand nor accept it. She enjoys so much prestige in her local community that no one has the courage to ask her about this decision. But I consider her the most broad-minded woman. I learnt just so much from her. She is both modest and studious. She's never put on airs as an *ahong*, always humbling herself. I would say she is a real innovator.
>
> She [Lu Ahong] had glaucoma at the age of 83, yet she copied scriptures in Farsi for use at the women's mosques. There were otherwise no texts for educational use. Her man – that is, her husband – wrote large-size characters in Arabic while she wrote below in smaller characters in Farsi. The yellow, tightly written sheets of paper were then beautifully bound to be put to use during the most important religious rituals. I have learnt a lot from Lu Ahong and from her outlook and conduct. And as far as I am concerned, she has set a good example with a modest attitude towards her own learning.

Of great interest is Guo Dongping's admiration of the older *ahong*'s independent spirit and her bold courage to dare to think and act independently, as these qualities appear to violate the Confucian and Islamic feminine virtue of female submissiveness. Guo's justification for such boldly independent thinking is the higher virtue of those who enrich and guide fellow-believers by virtue of their superior knowledge. And for Guo, Lu Ahong's 'modesty', as evidenced by her lack of pride and arrogance, makes her all the more venerable, for despite her learning, and unlike her male counterparts, it is implied, she treats all around her as equals.

The time spent as a *hailifan* was initially experienced as restrictive by the forthright and independent-minded Guo Dongping. But this attitude underwent a radical change as she came under the influence of the resident *ahong*, a role model to this day. Inspired by Lu Ahong, Guo Dongping told us:

> When I was in the mosque, we were placed under a strict discipline. As I was a graduate student from school, I held an attitude typical of a student and had no intention of becoming *ahong* or *hailifan*. ... Later I got to know Lu Ahong. I learnt about what made her conduct so unique, practising religious precepts in daily life. Afterwards, I began to make a real effort to study and read, including the more obscure *Ahadith*.

Guo Dongping decided to become a teacher, her life's goal to promote Islamic knowledge. Turning her life in a new direction, she studied Arabic and Qur'an with male *ahong* in men's mosques, as well as in co-educational Arabic language schools run by the mosque, a feature of Islamic education under Communist rule. This not only enabled Guo Dongping and other Muslim women scholars to acquire knowledge beyond the confines of women's mosques; it also effected changes in the attitudes of male teachers. Guo Qingxin, famed for his scriptural knowledge, is said to have expressed high regard for Guo Dongping, acknowledging her intelligence and studious spirit. Known to be economical with praise, the old *ahong* told everyone he met that '[In the future] she [Guo Dongping] will be a rarity. As one of the most learned *ahong*, she has a bright future ahead of her.'

Conflicted subjectivity and coping strategies

Despite Guo's own talents and the respect she received from other women, and despite Lu Ahong's unconventional choice of marital abstinence and a career over motherhood, Guo Dongping bowed to pressures from family and community to subordinate her study and career to marriage. In 1989, after her marriage, the talented young Islamic scholar terminated her study in Kaifeng to follow her husband to Sangpo, a large Hui Muslim village, where he took up the position of *ahong*. It is an age-old tradition in local Muslim communities that the wife of an *ahong* supports her husband in the teaching and propagation of Islam. Indeed, this tradition pre-dates the current system of appointment of women *ahong* by a women's mosque management committee. In certain cases, where a community supports several women's mosques, traditional and contemporary appointment systems coexist (Jaschok and Shui 2000; Jaschok 2011).

Guo Dongping would have remained a *shiniang* (an *ahong*'s wife who supports her husband's religious work), had it not been for requests by women in the community that she become the leader of one of the larger women's mosques in Sangpo: the Zhang Women's Mosque. Her commanding presence and learning inspired such admiration among the women that she was appointed *ahong* by popular choice. Now she is equal in standing to her husband; the women say they seek her out for her moral authority and her familiarity with their lives. Respected for her erudition and piety, her unusual ways of teaching have aroused great interest. Never directly dismissive of what she calls 'feudal' interpretations of women's role in a rapidly changing society, she nevertheless inspires women to discuss, ask questions and consider not only the demands that family and society have on them, but the demands women must place on society. Her popularity as a teacher and religious mentor and leader help mitigate the tension between her domestic duties and her religious career. Her husband, as an *ahong*, recognizes his wife's esteem within the Muslim community, and the valuable role she plays. She is listened to when she affirms a daughter's right to full education and career before marriage, when she supports birth control and relationships of mutual respect in the family. Her openness is admired, in large part because her dedication to the public good is demonstrated constantly through her own life. She says that her life epitomizes the value of mutual understanding and compromise that respects a woman's talents and ardent yearning for self-expression.

Concerning her teaching style, Guo Ahong says: 'Reading alone would make it hard to understand things … and now things are quite different when I teach. I enable my women students to understand the meaning [rather than simply memorize incomprehensible passages].' She calls this a 'modern' approach to teaching, and it differs radically from the conventional method of learning through memorization, a method popular in secular as well as religious schools. Guo encourages discussions and questions; her reflections and responses come from her knowledge *and* life experience, and this in turn increases the esteem in which she is held and women's eagerness to emulate her values and conduct.

Although her sense of purpose has grown stronger with the confidence she has gained over the years, she is aware of the tensions generated in the contemporary context by this challenge to traditional received learning on the appropriate expression of female Muslim identity. The tensions are intergenerational and cultural; they also reveal the local impact of transnational debates. Whilst the *jingtang* education of old, which rested on Farsi texts, is rejected by younger Muslims as backward and out of touch, the 'modern', Arabic-based education is heavily shaped by what Guo Ahong refers to as 'the more simple way of interpreting the scriptures' under the growing Wahhabi influence from Saudi Arabia.[10] As this way is considered by a majority of male Islamic scholars in China as the authentic approach to revealing 'the true doctrine', she ponders: 'how dare I not follow it to the letter? There are certainly conflicts in my heart.'

Guo Ahong gives expression to some of the most fundamental challenges facing women's institutions in China's Muslim communities. Whereas Arabic-language schools are rapidly increasing in numbers and popularity, and find support among religious leaders and parents alike, they also bypass the accumulated collective experience of traditional *jingtang* education, which, Guo Ahong maintains,

> instils justice, humanity and morality as well as conduct which takes note of our [local] situation. If we truly want to develop the religion and maintain the pace of development of Islam, we need more truly learned *ahong* with a good morality, exemplary conduct and behaviour and real enthusiasm for religion. We must pass to the next generation an Islamic culture suitable to life in this country. Our religion needs people with passion. An *ahong* must ever improve herself and only thus can she persuade others. Only thus can a leader acquire prestige in the hearts of Muslims ... only when you are widely accepted by people as a person with knowledge and reputation, as a person advanced in thinking and moral cultivation, only then can you truly be called a successful woman *ahong* ... I can accept new things in all intellectual aspects. But I will never be ready to accept what I discover to be deficiency in reason in the new education [brought from the Middle East] ... from the previous generation [of Islamic scholars] we learn something about calm insistence and due caution when exercising religion ... our generation will never reach the piety and passion of past generations of believers [taught within the traditional Chinese Islamic education].

For Guo Dongping knowledge is at the heart of women's capacity to control their own lives. Women's mosques have an important role to play. She says:

The women don't acquire their knowledge from the male *ahong*, or from their husbands. The men in families of Chinese Muslim don't possess religious knowledge ... actually, many men know less than women. So [the existence of] the female mosque is necessary after all. Women's mosques are needed because society needs women with superior knowledge and qualities.

Women construct agency in sometimes surprising ways, and wherever societal crevices open up to be exploited. Unorthodox choices are clearly indicative of a wider repertoire of options which Muslim women – leading Muslim women – have created for themselves and, not infrequently, by setting examples, for women in their spiritual charge. Islam, by emphasizing the imperative for *all* Muslims to acquire knowledge, has at times been used by women to challenge, even bypass, patriarchal constructs whereby Confucian morality equated virtue with ignorance (as discussed earlier). Knowledge is the path to women's empowerment, Guo maintains, enabling women ultimately to gain control over their bodies and minds, and to defy their exclusion from the genealogy of faith. The gradual expansion of women's communal spaces has increased women's opportunity to discover that gender is not fate, that sexual identity is not fixed, and that there are other women who have successfully challenged acquiescence to the duty of female submissiveness, which is often the lot of women who live in isolation from one another. In this way, Guo Ahong continues in the proud genealogy of a long tradition of women *ahong*, including the esteemed female *ahong* we introduce here, Du Shuzhen.

Du Shuzhen Ahong:
contesting sexual morality through education

Du Shuzhen Ahong's aspiration for the deepest possible learning took her beyond the limited knowledge commonly granted to women. She equates learning with a fulfilled spiritual and social life, without overlooking the domestic focus that is the lot of the majority of women.

Du Shuzhen Ahong was born in 1924, into a family of *ahong*, and grew up in Kaifeng, renowned home to the oldest and most historically influential women's mosque. Du began her career as an *ahong* in 1948, one year prior to the establishment of the People's

Republic of China; now in her late eighties, she is an *ahong* still. One of the most influential *ahong* in Henan province and beyond, and a rare four-time Hajji, Du Ahong exemplifies the 'Four Goods' that are the criteria of worthy *ahong* of both sexes: 'Good' as expressed in religious integrity; 'Good' as a religious scholar (*erlin*); 'Good' in the mastery of the fundamentals of religion; and 'Good' at exemplifying moral quality (Yanjie 2008). Moreover, Du Ahong added the 'Good' of effective political representation.[11] Because of her great age, nowadays she confines herself to her work as *ahong* at the Beida Women's Mosque in Zhengzhou, the provincial capital of Henan province.

How do ordinary believers, *ahong* and government officials explain Du Ahong's impact? Her knowledge of Arabic and Farsi scriptures, her immersion in the teachings of the Qur'an and the broad knowledge of the world she brings to her teaching and her sermons are mentioned by local people as remarkable. But most emphatic are the references to her life history, which, so many women hold, make her uniquely qualified to understand ordinary women's lives and to mediate between universal ideals and local realities. Indeed, notwithstanding her admired erudition, she is seen as a stern but loving grandmother, a wise elder who, in the tradition of women's mosques – where congregations have always been run like extended families – settles disputes between mother-in-law and daughter-in-law, and between Han and Muslim neighbours. Older women point out that instructions from distant authorities – male *ahong* in men's mosques – are far less important than counsel from the local female *ahong*, who is always accessible to her female congregants. Only the respected and familiar authority of someone who understands the difficulties of negotiating religious ideals in the daily chaos of domestic life can help followers restore domestic harmony. As disputes are often due to intergenerational conflicts between women, such as quarrels over a daughter-in-law's reluctance to bear a child immediately after marriage, or the choice of marriage partners, it is the advice and authority of a learned and experienced woman that is sought. Du Shuzhen's biography illustrates why she is considered a revered moral arbiter.

Du Ahong grew up in an environment which allowed her to immerse herself in the study of Islam, though she was not supported in her desire to devote herself to becoming a religious educator. She was expected to marry at an early age and at 17 found herself in an unhappy marriage which brought hardships and suffering. But her marriage ended within a few months when she was widowed. Her experience of marriage forged her increased determination and spirited independence. Against her family's will, she chose the career of an *ahong* and to this end studied under Hu Ahong at the Wangjia Hutong Women's Mosque. Her mentor was influenced by the political and educational reform movements of the Republican era (1912–49) when Muslim intellectuals together with secular counterparts sought to strengthen the nation through the strengthening of education (Yanjie 2008). Du's notion of leadership has at its core the ideal of *jie* or *ganjing*, a life lived 'cleanly' and unselfishly, not to be confused with weakness or passivity. On the contrary, these concepts, which once characterized the traditionalist paradigm of Muslim femininity, should be understood as a source of strength and active engagement with society.

Du Ahong has paid close attention to societal changes and re-sponded to challenges in imaginative and innovative ways, very much in the tradition of Kaifeng's *ahong*. Having in her first years as *ahong* of the influential Beida Women's Mosque in Zhengzhou devoted much of her attention to the long-neglected restoration and expansion of the Mosque, she then turned to the needs of the congregation. Du *Ahong* and the manager of the Mosque organized excursions for their congregants. Some of these trips took them to north and northwest China, where Muslim women live under much more closed and restricted circumstances;[12] this exposure broadened participants' knowledge of the diversity of Muslim practices in China. Du Ahong has also held firm to the idea that the diverse Islamic traditions in China should not exist apart from each other; thus the Beida Women's Mosque nurtures relations with a number of male and female mosques in both the traditional and the reformist Islamic traditions in Zhengzhou and adjacent areas. In the last ten years or so, the practice of visiting other Muslim communities has become increasingly common. This has increased the prestige of the Beida Women's Mosque, and the influence of Du Ahong, far beyond the provincial capital of Zhengzhou. Ongoing exchanges and excursions allow ordinary women to understand the lives of their counterparts in the highly diverse Muslim contexts of China and to compare the different ways in which women integrate their faith and religious practices into daily life. A momentum has built such that women have frequent exchanges across traditional geographical and social boundaries, enabling networking and opportunities for mutual support. The walls, which have traditionally bounded norms and definitions of sexual identity and female purity, have become porous. Knowledge of the coexistence of other practices negotiated by women as legitimate aspects of Muslim identity has increased women's ability to challenge restrictive local practices; conversely, it has become more difficult to use local cultural traditions to legitimate the disempowerment of women.

From the first day of Du Ahong's arrival in the mosque, she and the members of her management committee cooperated, and over time a form of collaborative leadership of highly active women evolved, with Du Ahong playing a central role, wherein she is always receptive to the viewpoints of others. Legendary at handling the most complex social relations, she has won the trust of ordinary women. She has also, however, gained respect from government officials in charge of religious and ethnic affairs. This has given her role as an intermediary added political weight, which she uses to ward off encroachments on the territory of the women's mosque and to strengthen economic and legal resources. All her strategies, as she herself says, concern sustaining the future and legacy of the mosque.

Enacting purity and challenging the patriline of faith

It is not sexuality which haunts society, but society which haunts the body's sexuality. Sex-related differences between bodies are continually summoned as testimony to social relations and phenomena that have nothing to do with sexuality. Not only as testimony to, but also testimony for – in other words, as legitimation. (Maurice Godelier, cited in Scott 1988: 45)

Women *ahong* intervene in the relationship between ordinary women believers and patriarchal readings of Islamic scriptures to challenge female submission as an axiomatic marker of Muslim female identity. The important factors that have influenced and sustained the continued importance of female *ahong* include family and kin support, other female *ahong*, the collaborative nature of women's mosque leaderships, the particular traditions that have emerged in association with female congregations, evolving social trends in Chinese mainstream society, and, finally, the individual personalities of leading *ahong*.

The authority of women *ahong* is rarely exercised in a hierarchical manner but is much more akin to what Shirin Rai (2005) calls an 'associational' model of leadership. Du Ahong and Guo Ahong treat their congregants with respect and kindness. Religious knowledge, moral quality, as well as modest and egalitarian attitudes are the important qualities which account for the lasting influence of a female religious leader. But under the influence of historical and social factors, reliance on the religious knowledge of male *ahong* has traditionally been greater than for female *ahong*. Much as the typical male *ahong* in present-day China has changed the historical image of distant authority, the male *ahong* still differs from his female counterpart in many respects. Female *ahong* are expected to show patience in listening to women's views and ideas and to attend to their problems in daily life (marital issues, divorce settlements and the like). Men generally now have more education and wider social influence and networks than previously, and this has confronted male *ahong* with considerable challenges. Male *ahong* are more mobile in terms of employment, compared with the relative stability of female *ahong* (who may be under contract to the same mosque for many years). However, whereas in the past it could be argued that lower demands on a female *ahong* created greater stability, increasingly it is possible to point to other factors. Consciously nurtured collaborative leadership models, incorporating all members of the congregation into decision-making processes, and cultivation of 'family type' relations also account for the enduring contracts of many female *ahong* (Jaschok and Shui 2000; Jaschok 2011).

The authority of a female *ahong* lies in her ability to translate Islam into women's everyday existence, explaining the application of scriptural passages to a given situation. Guo Dongping Ahong observes that congregants more readily follow the recommendations of an *ahong* they trust; her authority stems in part from the long-term relationship she has built with her congregation. As for Du Shuzhen Ahong, her prestige is visible not only through her authority in religious affairs, but also in the impact she has on daily affairs in her mosque, as well as on affairs beyond the mosque gates. This stems from her religious knowledge, sexual and moral observance of prevailing norms, and her knowledge of society and of ordinary Muslims around her, as well as her egalitarian ways in her interactions with Muslims and non-Muslims alike.

Exerting tremendous effort to sustain and consolidate the existence of women's mosques, female *ahong* endeavour to adapt to changing times. How innovative they are depends on their personal abilities and on available resources. Despite this, they are daily confronted with challenges to the relevance, and thus survival, of their mosques to a modernizing Chinese society. Guo Dongping has been able to innovate, adjusting her teaching methods to the needs of young and middle-aged women who seek religious education for answers to their generations' questions and concerns. She has acquired social knowledge and supplemented the traditional curriculum of *jingtang* education with inspired pedagogy, broadening her congregants' knowledge of a diverse Muslim world. Her classes are enriched with presentations on the different cultures and traditions within which Muslim women all over the world make choices and engage in social and political life, bringing into relief the features that might be considered Chinese characteristics of the sexual morality which women's mosques have transmitted over centuries. In their negotiation of meaningful continuity, progressive secular legislation and continued state rhetoric of gender equality have proved useful for women *ahong* in legitimizing their practices vis-à-vis charges of contravening orthodox Islam. Such resort to societal resources also serves to safeguard their historical claim to public participation in matters of public interest and challenges the received patriline of faith and gendered rules of exclusion. Under growing pressures from internal and external Islamic orthodoxy, women have found legitimate channels for reclaiming 'purity' – with purity no longer something for men to protect and shelter, but rather an expression of women's own Islamic morality within their own traditions and institutions, which rival, and even surpass, the institutions created by men. Their own historical trajectory has enabled women to emerge as guardians of the true faith. Women *ahong* can be heard to lament the growing commercialization of men's mosques with their income-generating schemes. They identify *bu ganjing* (unclean) practices and critique the temptations of *jinshi* (all things connected with transitory life) and neglect of *houshi* (cultivation of spiritual life), which they associate with institutions overseen by men. The unworldly, walled-in purity of women has been replaced in recent years – as far as the more independent women's mosques are concerned – by public and competitive claims over who deserves the label of true piety. When women *ahong*, presiding over relatively small and poor mosques, claim to practise the pure, unsullied spirit of Islam, they are not easily challenged by their wealthier counterparts in the adjacent men's mosque.

China's modernization drive has effected many changes in mainstream society, but also in Muslim communities. Increased contact with the outside world, the emergence of intergenerational differences, the use of traditional educational resources in women's mosques, and young people's discontent with traditional Islamic education have all strengthened the perception of *ahong* as out of touch with modern China; this has raised fears that the tradition of *jingtang* education might soon be lost entirely. How to develop or rejuvenate the educational culture of women's mosques is a problem that will challenge what is best in the leadership provided by the current generation of female *ahong*. Guo Ahong and Du Ahong have sought active solutions, but at the same time they also endure to varying degrees a sense of helplessness in the face of an ever-changing environment, as the educational tradition associated with women's mosques was designed for a previous age. The challenge will be to change without losing what is uniquely important and empowering to women in the culture of women's mosques: the idea that talented women who excel in their conduct and in their learning must be fostered; and the idea that the quest for knowledge applies to all. For when women have a clear sense of their inherent intellectual worth and the legitimacy of their quest for knowledge, individual empowerment results, including in the arena of sexuality and life choices – as exemplified by the biographies of the *ahong* presented here, who found innovative ways to deal with restrictive gender prescriptions.

Over recent years, particularly since 1994 when registration of religious sites commenced, the trend towards women's mosques and greater autonomy – financial, religious and educational – has grown. Ironically, Chinese state mechanisms of control have, from the point of view of women, been a welcome recognition of their equal status, granting them legal and political equality. In complex negotiations of internal and external pressures to redress aberrations from Islamic orthodoxy, and in avoiding some of the negative impacts of imported orthodoxies, the authority of the *ahong* is crucial. Her reputation rests on her erudition, her integrity, her sincerity and piety, and her understanding of the needs of women in a rapidly changing society, which all inform the spirituality of the mosque over which she presides. The mosque offers shelter to worshippers who strive to reconcile religion with their social identity within the larger Chinese framework without feeling forced to privilege one identity over another or to compromise either their belief or their sense of nationhood.

Sermon of a women *ahong*: reading against the text

Weekly sermons, *woerci*, to an always crowded women's mosque prayer gathering provide Du Ahong with an important opportunity to present her thoughts on women's morality, *fudao*, in a modern world. 'The Islamic Tales of Moral Exhortations from the Scriptures'[13] is a favourite source of depictions of female sexuality and male morality used by both female and male *ahong* to embellish their moral exhortations. Not unlike Christian tales of the sinfulness of women, fatally compromised by worldly preoccupations, depictions abound in 'The Islamic Tales' of women as gullible vessels of sin, ever a source of temptation for men.

A popular tale, often cited by Du Ahong, tells of a husband who never flinches from his duty as a Muslim, and who can often be found at the mosque, praying. Yet he denies his wife the same means of spiritual salvation. One night, the husband arrived home to find his wife on the prayer mat, and no food on the table. He beat his wife most cruelly, but the next day she again did not serve him, instead succumbing to her own desire to pray. What followed was the daily infliction of physical violence, and the stubborn refusal by the wife to yield to his brutality. The tale ends with an irate husband pouring boiling water over the disobedient wife. But, as Du Ahong relates with much relish, the husband's violence did not affect his wife; her skin remained unblemished. Her faith and courage successfully challenged the wickedness of her husband. The moral of the sermon was for women to aspire to religious perfection – God was not siding, she intimated, with backward mindsets of husbands and fathers. Conversely, a too obedient wife might in fact be a disobedient Muslim.

What is remarkable is that the sermon not only counters the notion that women are spiritually deficient; it celebrates disobedience despite the concept of submission as a central pillar of female Muslim conduct. In this tale the insubordinate wife is the exemplary Muslim. Is this an act in defiance of a patriarchal gender regime? Du Ahong prefers to talk about the 'true spirit of Islam', untainted by *fengxiang sixiang*, male chauvinism. The stature of her position and her institutional authority make the reworking of a tale of domesticated sexuality not only possible, but also legitimate.

Indeed, Du Ahong's interpretation is given added strength by the very presence of women's mosques which call them to prayer, away from home. The faithful adherence to the discipline of dawn-to-dusk prayers current in many women's mosques provides us with the insistent, daily reminder of changes effected by women: that they have successfully contested women's outsider status in relation to the Islamic faith, and effectively confronted the patriarchal dictum that women's bodies need 'a master' (Na Guangyong 1995: 14) to enclose feminine purity and safeguard essential Islam. Women's allegiance to the mosque congregation to which they belong and their daily interaction with other women in the intimacy of a shared space are challenging the norms of domesticated sexuality as women's private, isolated or ordained experience.

Notes

1. The term *ahong* is used by Chinese Muslims in preference to 'imam' as a generic term for religious leaders. It is a highly contested title when applied to female religious leaders, but claimed by leaders of women's mosques in central China's Hui Muslim communities as their right and entitlement as Muslims and Chinese citizens (see Jaschok and Shui 2000). The root of *ahong* is the Persian word *akhond*, meaning preacher. In Iran, the Farsi term

only applies to men who may preach from the pulpit. Female religious leaders are called *khanom*, and they usually hold their sessions in private homes by invitation. They educate women on religious matters, but also answer their questions and concerns, which usually revolve around family matters and the rights of women within marriage and society (private communication from Anissa Hélie and Homa Hoodfar).

2. The interview with Guo Dongping was conducted in early 2010 in Sangpo village, a Hui Muslim village in Henan province, where Guo Ahong currently resides. Shui Jingjun has granted permission for interview data to be used in this chapter, and she was consulted throughout the process of writing. But responsibility for interpretation rests with Maria Jaschok.

3. Among the estimated 20 to 30 million Muslims in China, the Hui nationality is the most populous and most widely dispersed of the ten ethnic minorities classified as Muslims, amounting to more than 50 per cent of the total number. Hui Muslim Chinese live alongside other Muslim ethnic groups in greater concentration in the border provinces of Ningxia, Gansu, Qinghai, Yunnan and Xinjiang. Our study is concerned with Hui Muslims residing in central China, or Zhongyuan diqu, a region comprising the provinces of Hebei, Henan, Shandong and Shanxi. This part of Muslim China is characterized by settlement patterns of widely dispersed clusters of Hui villages, townships and suburbs. The earliest and most numerous Sunni tradition in China is the Gedimu. The Gedimu tradition came under attack when a more austere Islam, the Yihewani pai, entered central China's Muslim communities in the early twentieth century. Advocates of the Yihewani pai criticized Chinese Muslims for having made too many concessions to local Confucian norms and practices, deviating from the path of an authentic Islam as practised in Arab Muslim countries.

4. Yin (female principle) and Yang (male principle) represent dualist principles emphasizing mutuality and interdependence, but they also contain within themselves differentials of power and authority in which relationships, such as are expressed in the interaction of male and female, husband and wife, ruler and subject, are structured in terms of dominant and subordinate statuses. The principal force of Yang subordinates Yin in a hierarchical order of things which in Chinese philosophy governs both nature and human society. Islamic scholars saw many similarities in such a conceptualization of gender relations with the Islamic paradigm of a submissive Muslim woman.

5. Wang Daiyu (*c.* 1548–1670), Ma Zhu (1640–1711) and Liu Zhi (*c.* 1655–1745) may be counted among the most influential Muslim Hui scholars to have shaped an enduring construct of the ideal Chinese Muslim woman.

6. The Chinese State Council issued regulations, passed in 1994, which allow for more open religious practice, but at the same time enforced strict prohibitions on any religious activities outside particular 'religious sites'. Family planning among Muslims, as a minority not subject to the strict one-child policy that applied to Han Chinese families, would normally be guided by the state; however, in practice Muslim women in the communities we are describing often seek counsel from women *ahong*.

7. The ethnographic part of the essay forms part of the research conducted for the 'Women's Empowerment in Muslim Contexts' (WEMC) Research Programme Consortium, funded by the Department of International Development (DfID), UK Government, 2006–10.

8. Haizhuang village consists of about 300 households and has two mosques: one for women; the other for men. The village is famous among Muslims for producing erudite and influential *ahong*.

9. From the late Imperial era until well into the Republican era (late nineteenth century to the 1940s), Islam experienced a period of intellectual and educational renewal. Influenced by the new Muslim cultural movement and propelled by the innovative spirit of mainstream society, Islamic institutions in Kaifeng were active participants in social and educational reforms. Outstanding and independent-minded women *ahong* placed themselves in the vanguard of a cultural movement to popularize Islamic knowledge (Jaschok and Shui 2005).

10. Saudi Arabia's influence is mainly felt through its generous donations to educational initiatives and to (men's) mosque-based development and building projects.

11. Her public positions have been many: political adviser to the Zhengzhou city government; committee member of the Women's Federation of Zhengzhou city, Guancheng Hui district; committee member of the Henan Islamic Association; vice president and adviser of the Zhengzhou Islamic Association, among others.

12. See anthropologist Man Ke (2010) concerning Dongxiang Muslim women's lives in northwest China.

13. *Ahong Zhishi Bidu* (n.d.).

References

Ahong Zhishi Bidu (A Primary Reader for Ahong) (n.d.). Islamic Tales of Moral Exhortations from the Scriptures. Privately printed.

Bai, S. (1983) *Zhongguo Yisilanshi Cungao* [Essays on the History of Islam in China]. Yinchuan: Ningxia Renmin Chubanshe.

Chan, K.L. (2007) *Sexual Violence against Women and Children in China*. Pretoria: Sexual Violence Research Initiative.

Chen, K. (trans. and ed.) (1994) *Shengxun Jing* [Ahadith]. Privately printed.

Du, F., and Mann, S. (2003) 'Competing claims on womanly virtues in Imperial China', in D. Ko, J.K. Haboush and J.R. Piggot (eds), *Women and Confucian Cultures in Premodern China, Korea, and Japan*. Berkeley: University of California Press.

Gilchrist, R. (1994) *Gender and Material Culture: The Archaeology of Religious Women*. London: Routledge.

Gladney, D.C. (1991) *Muslim Chinese: Ethnic Nationalism in the People's Republic*. Cambridge MA: Harvard University Press.

Guo Dongping interview, February 2010, Sangpo village, Henan province, conducted by Shui Jingjun as part of a project funded by UK aid from the UK Department for International Development (DfID).

Jaschok, M. (2003) 'Violation and resistance. Women, religion, and Chinese statehood', *Violence Against Women* 9(6), June: 655–75.

Jaschok, M. (2012) 'Sources of authority: Female *ahong* and *qingzhen nüsi* (Women's Mosques) in China', in M. Bano and H. Kalmbach (eds), *Women, Leadership and Mosques: Changes in Contemporary Islamic Authority*. Leiden: Brill.

Jaschok, M., and Shui J. (2000) *The History of Women's Mosques in Chinese Islam*. Richmond: Curzon.

Ko, D., Haboush, J.K., and Piggott, J.R. (eds) (2003) *Women and Confucian Cultures in Premodern China, Korea, and Japan*. Berkeley: University of California Press.

Li, S., and Luckert, K.W. (eds) (1994) *Mythology and Folklore of the Hui, a Muslim Chinese People*. Albany: State University of New York.

Ma, M. (1994) 'Xibei musilin minzude lunli wenhua' [The Ethnic Culture of the Muslim people in Northwest China]', *Huizu Yanjiu* [Hui Nationality Research Journal] 4.

Man, K. (2010) 'Dongxiang Muslim women as "boundary subjects": Reflections on gender and identity in the borderland areas of northwest China', *Geografia* online – *Malaysian Journal of Society and Space* 6(2): 1–9.

Mernissi, F. (1996) *Women's Rebellion and Islamic Memory*. London: Zed Books.

Metcalf, B.D. (ed.) (1996) *Making Muslim Space in North America and Europe*. Berkeley: University of California Press.

Na, G. (1995) 'Yisilanjiaode hunyin zhidu' [The Islamic marriage system], *Musilin Qingnian* [Muslim Youth] 3. Kunming: Yisilanjiao Jingxueyuan Xueshenghui.

Papanek, H, (1982) 'Purdah: Separate worlds and symbolic shelter', in H. Papanek and G. Minault (eds), *Separate Worlds: Studies of Purdah in South Asia*. Delhi: Chanakya Publications.

Papanek, H., and Minault, G. (eds) (1982) *Separate Worlds: Studies of Purdah in South Asia*. Delhi: Chanakya Publications.

Pillsbury, B.L.K. (1978) 'Being female in a Muslim minority in China', in L. Beck and N. Keddie (eds), *Women in the Muslim World*. Cambridge MA: Harvard University Press.

Rai, S.M. (2005) 'Equal participation of women and men in decision-making processes, with particular emphasis on political participation and leadership', background paper prepared for the Expert Group Meeting, 24–27 October 2005, Addis Ababa, Ethiopia.

Rosenlee, L. (2006) *Confucianism and Women: A Philosophical Interpretation*. Albany: State University of New York.

Sabbah, F.A. (1984) *Woman in the Muslim Unconscious*. London: Pergamon.

Scott, J.W. (1988) *Gender and the Politics of History*. New York: Colombia University Press.

Wadud, A. (2006) *Inside the Gender Jihad. Women's Reform in Islam*. Oxford: Oneworld Publications.

Yanjie, H.Z. (2008) '*Jingtang* education in Zhengzhou North Street Female Mosque and preliminary reflections concerning the Female *Ahong* Du Shuzhen's pedagogy', http://zt.musilin.net.cn/2008/0129/article_530.html.

7

Veiled transcripts:
the private debate on public veiling in Iran

Shadi Sadr

Perhaps no other law in the Islamic Republic of Iran has faced as stiff resistance as compulsory *hijab*, which has become the regime's emblem.[1] Barely a month after the success of the revolution, on 5 March 1979, Ayatollah Khomeini announced that women must be veiled in public. Days later, International Women's Day – which was normally unmarked in Iran – witnessed the largest women's demonstration in Iranian history. Through word of mouth some 20,000 people poured into the streets, surprising the regime, which, uncharacteristically, temporarily retreated. However, manipulating the uncertainty evoked by the Iran–Iraq war (1981–88), the regime gradually reintroduced compulsory *hijab*, and by 1983 all women, regardless of their religious affiliation, faced lashes and/or imprisonment if caught unveiled in public. Women have since found many nuanced ways of expressing resistance while appearing to comply with the law (see Hoodfar and Ghoreishian, Chapter 9 in this volume) through their choice of unconventional head coverings, overalls and wearing of make-up.

To curtail these daily acts of resistance, the regime has had to devote considerable resources to the development of 'morality' police, whose numbers are estimated to be over a million and rising, to patrol public spaces. It is not clear how many members of the force are fully employed or partially rewarded for their active participation (Sadeghi 2009). The regime also invented the so-called 'bad *hijab*' offence, with legal sanctions for those who do not observe *hijab* in its officially defined form (Farahani 2007: 153). Yet thirty years after the imposition of compulsory *hijab*, its enforcement remains one of the regime's most pronounced challenges, particularly in large urban centres, where national politics for the most part play out.

One of the major unintended consequences of state interference in the private sphere has been considerable politicization of public space and mundane daily practices, such as choosing what to wear. Women who have never considered themselves the least bit political have found themselves implicated in national politics because they have reacted to the politicization of their bodies by the state. By focusing on veiling as a step towards building a gender-segregated (if not gender apartheid) society, the state has opened unconventional political pathways for women, whose scarves, attire and lipstick have become political tools (Mahmoudi 2000: 84). The fact that the state frequently launches new initiatives to improve the observance of *hijab* is an indication of its failure to do so despite three decades of forceful imposition of the law.

However, despite such a large-scale defiance on the part of the public, what is conspicuously absent is any popular oppositional discourse on *hijab*, or any public campaigns to end it. Even though women activists with diverse ideological perspectives have challenged the regime on issues of family law, discriminatory practices concerning women's higher education, and women in the labour market, few have been willing to organize around the issue of compulsory veiling. The assumption has been that the general public will not support such action, or that the cost to the development of the women's movement would be too high (Sadr 2010b: 283).

However, a few young activists organizing through the Meydaan Women's Rights website, including the author, saw daily evidence to the contrary. We were convinced that launching a public debate on compulsory *hijab* could be highly effective if timed to coincide with the run-up to the 2009 presidential election, when public discussion is typically less restricted as authorities try to put on a more democratic face. As an experienced activist, my concern was how best to start the process. Private sphere conversations were of interest to us – 'hidden transcripts', as has been so aptly analysed by Scott (1999), which under repressive situations like in Iran, where the state has almost total control of mass media discourse or 'public transcripts', are limited and distorted: the power-holders create the discourse, the powerless perform. My own experience living as a middle-class urban Iranian and interacting with low-income urban women, with whom I worked for many years as an attorney, confirmed that 'the public transcript' is at best only a partial story. The veiling question is a complex one, encompassing politics, religion and cultural practices and identity. Thus the hidden transcript – citizens' private views concerning compulsory veiling – was critical in trying to understand the absence of collective resistance to the law and to plan for future collective action.

Although to all appearances Iranians seem to have accepted, if not supported, state-regulated *hijab*, the apparent 'consent' of subordinates may simply be a tactical expression to comply with authorities' expectations, while concurrently challenging them on a more profound level. The public transcript may thus only be a 'performance', replete with pretence, deceit and lies (Scott 1999).

In urban Iran, among the allegedly 'powerless', large numbers of women have indeed found many ways of subverting the public transcript. Nevertheless, informed by Scott's methodology, accessing what people were saying 'off-stage' seemed key to understanding the dynamics around veiling. As an attorney dealing with both state and legal systems and actors, on the one hand, and subordinate citizens, on the other, I am well aware that all public 'on-stage' rhetoric is not false, while everything spoken in private is not necessarily representative or without ulterior motive. What can be said with certainty is that the hidden transcript differs from what emerges in public under oppressive political and social conditions. While there has been plenty of writing on the subject of 'veiling', especially though not exclusively on the Iranian context, in recent decades, few sources focus specifically on the free and open discourse in the public sphere between those who support or oppose the veil within the context of Iran. Evaluating the discrepancies between public and hidden transcripts can thus indicate the extent of support for the public transcript (Scott 1999: 4–5), as well as the nuances of what this support looks like from the perspective of everyday individuals – a gap in the literature this essay begins to address.

I thus designed a research project to assess the hidden transcript around *hijab* and its diversity/complexity, including the way demands for democratization and the role of religion and state feed into 'off-stage' debates around compulsory veiling. Very little data or literature exists which has examined the debates in the online sphere of blogging; under the oppressive conditions of Iranian censorship and state-owned media, the blogsphere serves as a more free and open platform for discussion and debate. With the use of pseudonym screen names and relative anonymity in online posting, there is less immediate fear of social or political ostracization, which allows many to discuss more honestly their individual opinions on a topic. Hence my project and this essay present precisely these discussions and debates which gauge the day-to-day opinions and perspectives of Iranians on compulsory veiling. The hidden transcripts are full of nuances, which tend to be lost in the binary view that people are either for or against the veil. Indeed, many women clearly view the order as a nuisance as well as an objectification of their bodies and an infringement of their basic individual rights over their body and sexuality. Yet other women believe in veiling as a personal duty, but steadfastly reject the imposition by the state of compulsory veiling as an intrusion into and denial of individual rights. Through this project I also sought to explore and gain insight into citizens' readings of the regime's constant redefinitions of veiling and morality, the impact of the politicization of women's bodies, and how seemingly mundane, insignificant choices concerning attire have transformed the political consciousness of so many millions of ordinary women.

What compels these women to set themselves apart from the policies of the Islamic Republic, and how far removed are their beliefs from those advanced by the state as the prevailing ideals of Iranian society? And, considering the ongoing atmosphere of fear and censorship, how do they express their opinions? While women are the primary agents of resistance and the performers of 'improper/bad veiling', men, as citizens and kin, are also implicated; hence their opinions were included in the analysis of the veiling situation. While I had anticipated heated debate, I was not expecting the level of enthusiastic participation, from all perspectives, which ultimately emerged.

The research

As an attorney, I began by looking at relevant laws chronologically, to illuminate not only the public transcript but also the extent to which legislators believe laws have achieved their goals of not only changing women's behaviour, but also their world-view. Despite my familiarity with veiling legislation, I was astonished by the incredible volume of laws issued, starting just days after the revolution in 1979 and spanning thirty years, to the ending of this phase of the research in January 2009. I subsequently published my findings as a book to enable others to access the data, which has important implications for understanding and negotiating political daily life in Iran (Sadr 2010a). At the very least, what became clear was that the regime feels it has not succeeded in convincing the nation of the merit of compulsory *hijab*, which is part of their strategy to control women's and men's sexuality.

The next phase of research involved my seeking unofficial discourses on *hijab*, which took me to the lively Iranian blogsphere, an arena relatively free from the censorship characteristic of formal media. Blogging has become an Iranian passion, particularly among younger generations, as it provides an anonymous venue for expression, to some extent free from fear of reprisal from the authorities, or even friends and neighbours (Alavi 2005). I delved into blogs defending veiling, some of the most popular of which are written by *basiji* (female vanguards of the revolution), female *talabehs* (seminary students) and other religious women. I decided to set up a blog entitled 'A Question Called *Hijab*' (*Mas'aleh-ee beh Nam-e Hijab*) under the pseudonym 'Bibi Monavvar', since blogging as a widely recognized secular feminist might have dissuaded some potential categories of reader from visiting the blog. Furthermore, a pseudonym allowed me to write freely without fear for my security – indeed very few people in Iran blog under their real names. I posted a March 1979 excerpt from *Ettelaat* newspaper where Ayatollah Taleghani, one of the influential revolutionary religious figures, had announced that women would not be forced to veil. In each post, I tried to recount a personal memory about veiling or an incident related to veiling in my daily life, from the point of view of a female attorney. Each post ended with a discussion topic and asked for readers' opinions. I also visited blogs by *hijab* proponents and invited them to participate in my blog discussion.

My blog readers and commenters rapidly and exponentially multiplied – evidently there is great interest in the topic of veiling; some posts received close to a thousand comments. A group of consistent commentators kept up an exchange, and, while originally I was primarily interested in religious bloggers' participation, other regular posters invited bloggers from all kinds of backgrounds to participate. The blog unexpectedly became a highly diverse forum for debating the question of veiling, providing me with an opportunity to access the hidden transcripts of a much more diverse group. The participants mostly lived in Iran. As Internet users are primarily middle-class urbanites with access to Internet cafés, if not a personal computer, this is the demographic most interested in what in Iran is termed 'social politics'. Some commentators had their own weblogs, with topics ranging from personal matters and poetry to stories and religious concepts. None of these individuals, however, was well known in Iran's mainstream blogging movement. My blog's popularity exceeded my wildest imagining. However, in April 2009 the blog was deleted by the service provider and those trying to access the website instead saw the following message:

> This weblog has been blocked for one of the following reasons:
> Order of official authorities to block the site;
> Violating the regulations of the provider;
> Publishing immoral content or content that violates the country's laws.

I was never able to find out whether the blog was removed by order of government officials or by the Internet service provider. Fortunately, aware of the possibility of this occurring, I had kept backups of almost everything from the blog. I had noticed that by the end of the blog's third month comments were becoming repetitive and no novel opinions had been posted for some time. However, over those three months I had amassed a vast amount of data concerning debates on veiling. Although the opinions posted on the blog by no means represent all of Iranian society, they nonetheless encompass very diverse views, and in fact comprise the most extensive unofficial collection of opinions on veiling – which would never have seen the light of day in the formal public sphere, the media, or any official or public forum, since expressing opposition to veiling is considered akin to heresy and subject to harsh punishment (Sadr 2010b: 186).

Arguments for and against veiling

The following draws on five hundred randomly selected comments from four broad categories of male and female blog participants:

1. those supportive of the principle of veiling;
2. those opposed to veiling;
3. those supportive of compulsory veiling;
4. those opposed to compulsory veiling regardless of whether they accepted the principle of veiling or not.

Many in favour of veiling argue that it is a religious edict and use verses from the Qur'an and Hadith (sayings of the Prophet) to support their position, without referring to the theological controversies surrounding these justifications. For example, as blogger Zamanian writes: 'Veiling is an obligatory tenet in holy Islam and didn't and still doesn't require a piece of legislation. We are either Muslims or decadent people far from Islam. There is no third option.' However, more commentators from this group simply refer to the benefits of veiling, mentioning one or two clichés, such as 'Veiling is immunity, not limitation' and 'Veiling protects women from the corrupt eyes of the men and the danger of being sexually abused.' They argue that veiling not only provides women with a sense of immunity but also immunizes society against prostitution and sexual corruption, since men are by nature more lustful than women and cannot control their sexual desires if they see unveiled women. Others in this group argued that veiling provides women with a sense of dignity: 'As a pearl inside a seashell, the beauties of a woman will be kept hidden and not exposed easily to male strangers, just as all valuable items must be kept away from the hands of a thief.'

Many of the arguments of veiling opponents are almost the mirror opposite of those used by supporters. For example, while supporters consider the veil a tool for protecting women from the uncontrollable sexual desires of men, the opposing group believes that prohibition tends to exacerbate temptation, and therefore veiling inadvertently increases the sexual desires of men, thus in practice decreasing women's safety. In response to those who present veiling as an obligatory religious duty, opponents argue that veiling as referred to in the Qur'an in no way resembles its interpretation by contemporary clerics, and that the current practice is an imposition of male jurists, not an edict issued by God. In short, both sides use religious texts to argue their position.

The large number of commentators who opposed veiling on the basis of women's personal freedom used terms and concepts such as sexual discrimination and women's rights over their bodies, and also protested veiling as a male construction – so-called women-centred arguments. The majority in this group (as opposed to the first group) were women and placed themselves as 'individuals' at the centre of the discussion, emphasizing their rights as the primary principle for opposing veiling.

The nature of arguments in response to the blog's main framework, 'A Question Called *Hijab*', were threefold. First were those focused on psychological and sociological arguments against veiling. Since these arguments directly counter the official slogans emphasizing the benefits of veiling, I have dubbed them 'counter-arguments'. Second were those I categorize as 'religion-based' arguments. Finally there are those who opposed veiling on the grounds of women's individual and citizenship rights, which I have dubbed 'citizens-rights based arguments'.

Counter-arguments

One of the Islamic Republic's main slogans is 'A woman veiled is akin to a pearl inside a shell'. This argument was repeatedly used by blog commenters supportive of veiling, who in various ways compared women's bodies with jewels to be kept out of reach, and who argue that veiling prevents men becoming attracted and excited. Those opposing veiling argued that in fact the reverse is true. Mania wrote:

> One of the most obvious and evident truths in psychology is that whatever people are prohibited from, they will desire more. From this standpoint it can be said that the reason for the insistence on the ability of female hair to attract men is only because seeing women's hair is such a novelty in our society!

She indicates that the logic behind the regime's promotion of veiling is tautological: women's hair is presented as an unruly and powerful force that must be contained; however, if veiling was not imposed to begin with, then the 'threat' of women's hair in arousing moral disorder would not exist.

Iraj, a male commentator, wrote:

> If you wrap an empty box beautifully and place it in the street you will see that many people will be tempted to pick it up. Yet if you take a valuable jewel and wrap it in normal covering that will not attract or bring any attention to its value and then place it in this manner in the street, no one will pay any attention to it. Veiling works the same way. If our women dressed normally like women everywhere else in the world, then if they were to wear hot pants and tank tops, believe me when I say no man would even bother to turn around and look at them when they pass by because it would just be normal.

Opponents of veiling refute the proposition that 'veiling brings about immunity' using sociological data alongside psychological arguments, suggesting that although veiling is compulsory in Iran the incidence of prostitution is in fact high, even in comparison to countries that 'lack a proper religious belief'. Indeed the issue of widespread prostitution has been a major preoccupation of the state in recent years and a regular subject of public discourse.

Comparing the social conditions of Iran with countries where veiling is not compulsory is the basis for the sociological arguments presented by many commentators, who noted that in Muslim countries like Turkey and Malaysia, where veiling is not compulsory, women enjoy greater safety than they do in Iran. Seyyed wrote: 'If you take a few trips to non-Muslim and even [some] Muslim countries, you will see that unveiling has no effect on men; each person is after his own business. Limitation does not provide immunity.' Increased leisure travel to neighbouring countries, in particular Turkey, the UAE and other Muslim countries like Malaysia, where it is relatively easy to obtain a tourist visa, has also significantly influenced the perspectives of blog commentators.[2] Darkoob (woodpecker) wrote:

> How come when I was in Dubai and at the beach everyone was wearing a bikini, none of the Europeans was looking at them but the Iranians

and Arabs were staring? All of this is because of what one is used to. The European guys are used to this but the Iranians and Arabs, who have always seen women in *chador* and *burqa*, naturally can't control themselves when they see an unveiled woman. Are the men in other countries not men? Or maybe your argument is that Iranians and Arabs are more lustful... Further, if Imam Ali [the fourth Muslim Caliph and grandson of the Prophet] could not control himself when faced with an unveiled woman and would shake and take refuge in God, then these Europeans and American who are dealing with women wearing tank tops and hot pants on a daily basis without losing their control must be very grand individuals.

Another comment reads

I have wished time and again that our people had the social respect and etiquette that the citizens of Ankara and Istanbul have, so that they could walk the streets without bothering women or uttering sexually suggestive comments.

Anecdotal accounts posted by Iranians who have been outside the country refute the comments by supporters of veiling who say that the absence of veiling leaves women in the West unsafe.[3] Consider the view of B. Eftekhari, who went to school in Iran, and who was veiled and living in Geneva when she posted in response to a post from Mehrdad:

How can you claim that women have safety in Iran ... or that their safety is more than that of women in Western countries? I swear I lived for thirty years in Iran, went to university and worked, and always kept my veil and was never after any fads or flashy things and yet never dared stay in the streets after dark. In the winter semester, if I had to take classes in the 5–7 p.m. time-slot, I always dragged my brother or husband to class to prevent being harassed by men. Only God knows the extent of the harassment that women deal with, yet they often keep quiet because they do not want to be blamed for it or possibly be prevented by brothers and father from going to university or working. Now, watching the safety enjoyed by women in Europe with my own eyes ... my heart aches when I remember how I was brainwashed all those years about corruption of the Western people. If a woman steps out of the house barely dressed at night, a few may steal glances here and there ... but they find it beneath them to gaze at her or make a sexual comment at her. I am not suggesting that this safety is due to lack of veiling ... there are all kinds of safety and security issues here, economic, political, job and social security ... this is a very complicated matter. Mr Mehrdad! If you want to fool yourself all your life that the Westerners are this, that and the other ... that they are corrupt ... and so our way of life is the best ... then I suggest that you never travel to Europe or a country like Switzerland ... because then a deep ache will afflict your heart when you wonder how you withered away your life by enveloping it in poisonous and false thoughts. That is of course if you are brave enough to be so honest.

Darya, another Iranian woman living abroad, also addressed the slogan 'Veiling is immunity, not limitation':

> Well, a slogan is only beautiful as a slogan. In effect, in this Islamic Iran, while wearing the veil that is supposed to keep me immune, I never felt safe; my religious brothers invaded my privacy time and again. However, in the land of apostasy, clad in what I consider revealing garments that I would never have dared to wear in Iran (or before I understood that the choice of clothing is a private matter) I didn't feel the least bit unsafe. I never saw anyone staring at me.

Shayan concurred:

> In my opinion, veiling is entirely limitation. When I lived in Iran I walked in the streets fully veiled and went to work without any make-up as I worked at a government office. However, you wouldn't believe the things that I heard on my way home. But since I have come to Europe, I leave the house even with shorts on and still no one stares at me or comments on it.

In effect, many commentators expressed the opinion that enforced veiling regulations have stripped women of their personhood and further sexualized Iranian men's view of women, and thus women's safety in public (and private) has been reduced. Bahar wrote:

> I say that the reason why they claim that veiling brings about immunity is because men, in particular those of our society (and those of any other one), have constantly been told that women are a moving sexual commodity. In place of teaching men to control their urges, they have forcefully veiled women and put them in *chador* to prevent the man from looking. Meanwhile, we all know that women (veiled or unveiled) are not safe in our society, and if this manner continues, believe me when I say that all women, *chador* wearing or not, will still encounter trouble from men in the future. You know why this happens? Because our men have been told that women are a sexual commodity or that make-up equals women sending a signal to establish sexual relations. That is it!

Along the same lines, other personal anecdotes highlight the sexual harassment encountered by veiled women:

> I have never been sexually evaluated through looks as much as where I work, a government office, where I purposefully wear a manteau that is very loose fitting and long, as well as long pants and a scarf that is closely kept and black. I even make sure to wear closed-toe shoes without heels to make no sound. I also wear no make-up and put on thick socks. And still eyes are wandering, waiting for me to lift my hand to see parts of my forearm or check out the protrusions of my breasts under my long headscarf. I can't observe myself from behind but have seen the lingering eyes of men on any woman (short, tall, fat, slim, with or without *chador* but veiled either way) who passes by.

This commentator also appears to believe that the social taboos underscored by veiling actually serve to increase predatory male sexual behaviour, making society less safe for women compared with societies where such limits are not imposed and where women's 'hair' and 'body' are seen as ordinary. Other blog posts have compared pre-revolutionary Iran (when veiling was not compulsory) with the current situation and note that not only are women not safer, but men have become more aggressive. They suggest that the state should prioritize the issue of male aggression and the sexualization and harassment of women rather than focusing on enforcing compulsory veiling, which, clearly, after thirty years has failed to be effective 'protection'. The fact that women cannot and should not have to pay the price for men's shortcomings seems to be the message of many bloggers opposed to veiling.

Another common argument in favour of veiling is predicated on Ayatollah Mutahhari's writings; he argues that veiling frees women from the binds of their sexuality and thus allows them to be viewed first and foremost as human beings rather than as sexual objects, and that veiling prevents the commercialization and objectification of women (Mutahhari 1992). Other commentators countered that veiling turns women into sexual objects by declaring individual women to be the personal sexual property of male kin, and denies women their humanity.

For example, Satin stated that 'unveiling is akin to being a human and veiling akin to being an object'. Najmeh Vahedi, who blogs on *Vahm-e Sabz* (Green Delusion), introduced herself as a feminist, and wrote that 'the essence of veiling, in fact, concurs with considering woman a sexual tool'. Bahar posted:

> As for me, I oppose compulsory veiling. More importantly, I oppose the sexual view of women that all those in favour of veiling talk about. ... all the propaganda seems to dictate that Islam does not view women as sexual objects... but as soon as one speaks of veiling, all the arguments tend to sexualize women.

Heated debate also surrounded the particular form of compulsory veiling – the black *chador* (full-length loose cape) encouraged by the government and which the regime claims creates no limitation. However, many women, both *chador*-clad and others, contested this, noting that the *chador* is especially cumbersome in a climate that is hot for most of the year in most of the country. Women who support the *chador* said they endure the hardship due to their religious beliefs.

However, Hakimeh Bahmanzadeh, a 23-year-old residing in Birjand, who writes for Southern Khorasan Radio Station, had another take on the restrictive aspect of veiling:

> I agree that observing the veil, particularly *chador*, is difficult. But I have a question: do we abandon something simply because it is difficult? *Jihad* and war are both difficult and hard, and yet necessary. I handle the difficulty of this world to be free and comfortable in the afterlife. I am a girl, a *chador*-clad girl and I consider my *chador* to be more valuable than gold and treasures.

In essence, the daily experiences of many women invalidate the transcript of power (in the public sphere) which denies that veiling causes limitations, and replace it with another logic which insists that although veiling is restrictive it is divinely ordained and necessary to prevent punishment in the afterlife.

Choosing *chador* versus overalls (or long coat) and a scarf has become a marker of group identity/ideological affiliation for many women who identify themselves as those who believe in veiling according to the regime's mandate. This perception of *chadori* women as supporters of the regime has engendered heated debates and animosity between the two groups. A commentator named Ba-hijab ('the veiled one') wrote that she does not agree that veiling is difficult and limiting. In response Darkoob posted:

Can a person go cycling, horseback riding and mountain climbing with a *chador*? If you sit at work from morning till 5–6 in the evening with a *chador*, wouldn't you get frustrated? I have no problem with it being your belief. But why aren't you logical? A group of people say that they are willing to endure the difficulty of wearing a *chador* so that they are comfortable in the afterlife. At least this group agrees that *chador* is not a comfortable garment ... and you have no problem wearing it in 40 degrees [Celsius] heat. How can you expect us to accept that?

Many of the arguments focused on veiling's impracticalities and the frequency with which it causes women to fall and injure themselves. This made many veiled blog commentators highly defensive and engendered a very heated exchange, prompting the following comment by B. Eftekhari:

Ms Ba-hijab ['the veiled one'], what denigrates *chador* is making it compulsory and then advertising it as the superior garment, as well as the feeling of superiority of the *chadori* ladies [those who wear *chador*] towards others. ... *Chador* is a garment, just like any other. Many people like it and many don't. But when it turns into an advertising tool and a thousand slogans and claims stand behind it then you should expect a few insults too.

The angry tone of the debate concerning types of adopted veiling reveals a deep chasm in Iranian society that has class elements as well, particularly between *chador*-wearing and non-*chador*-wearing women. The various blog entries claim that *chador*-wearing girls are not welcome in certain public places like coffee shops, and that they are ignored in shopping malls. On the other hand, non-*chador*-wearing women are subject to other limitations – for example, one condition of employment in many government jobs is wearing the *chador*. The analysis offered by B. Eftekhari is significant; *chador*-wearing women continually complain that society judges them based on their choice of attire and considers them to be illiterate commoners. Ley La wrote:

I wear the national *chador* because it looks good on me. For the same reason that some young women like to wear a short manteau and a shawl, I like to wear *chador*. I am not speaking as a veiled women but one who lives in this society. Many times I have gone into a boutique where, aside from me, a manteau clad girl was shopping. The salesman acted as if I didn't exist. Without paying attention to my requests as a customer, he was busy talking and explaining the goods to the manteau-clad person. I can wear a manteau too and no one would prevent me from doing so. But no one respects this choice of mine. You think that my *chador*-wearing friends and I are happy with the baton-wielding vice police and think along the same lines as them? The *chador*-clad women who think that by wearing a *chador* they have paid their Islamic dues make me want to vomit ... but I also do not want to be treated like a backwards person ... much in the same way that someone wearing a *manteau* doesn't want to be treated like an apostate or a criminal.

Darkoob believes that social judgement concerning *chador*-clad women occurs because they are viewed as a symbol of support for government oppression, writing: 'I wonder why you defend the morality police. They are doing injustice to you, the *chador*-wearing women, because people now mistrust *chador*-clad people and give themselves the right to insult them in whatever way possible.' Mandana, however, believes that *chador*-wearing women are the ones creating the divide, because 'any woman wearing a *chador* gives herself the right to tell us, "Yo girl, cover your hair!"'

The question for me and other women activists interested in launching a campaign was what strategies should we develop to bring together these women who oppose compulsory veiling, since its success would depend not just on the support of those who do not accept veiling but also of those who accept it as religious belief but oppose its compulsory nature and the state's intervention.

Religious arguments

Most women who defended veiling and its enforcement used religious arguments and claimed to be observant Muslims, although secular commentators also cited verses of the Qur'an to oppose veiling, employing the strategic use of religion to challenge religion. A religious argument that appeared regularly on the blog in various forms was that the Qur'an does not refer to veiling as it is currently defined in Iran (i.e. requiring covering the whole body) and that this form of veiling has been fabricated by clerics and government officials. Mitra wrote:

> This Muslim nation didn't even bother once to read the Qur'an properly to see where in that Qur'an, which they rely on and cite so much, is an edict about the obligatory nature of veiling, particularly in the manner

that exists today where one dresses like a black crow. In the Qur'an there is a verse – the Arabic text of which I unfortunately don't know – that says: if women wish to appear more chaste they should pull forward their veils. Nowhere does it say that it is obligatory that women, save for their faces and hands and feet, bundle their bodies up. More importantly, if the Qur'an says *la ikrah-a fi'ddin* (there is no compulsion in religion), then no one has the right to force others to perform religious orders.

Another group of commentators also attempted to interpret Qur'anic versus to argue that veiling in its present form has no roots in the Qur'an. Mania, a constant presence on the blog, who participated in all the discussions, wrote:

Another problem with veiling is how it deals with non-free women (slaves and female servants). It is well known that 'Islamic law' states that women who are not free should not be veiled! Meaning being veiled is not even optional for this group of women. Therefore the notion is introduced that there is a physiological difference between a slave woman and a free woman; that Arab men were excited at the sight of a free woman's hair but not at the sight of a female servant's hair! It is not moral to assume that because this group of women was not free, Islam made them available to all. Now if we review this reasoning, it is a collection of paradoxes: women must cover their hair to prevent men from falling into sin; women who are not free should not cover their hair to be distinguishable from free women. So if men get excited at the sight of their hair, oh well, it is their problem!

Mania also provocatively questions why women should be veiled when praying:

Women must cover their hair when praying out of respect for the creator, but men are only obligated to cover their pubic part. It appears that women have to carry more share of responsibility of respecting the creator than men. Even though men and women are said to be equal before God.

In response Atiyeh argued: 'All religious obligations have wisdom behind them that we might not understand but have to abide by nonetheless.'

Bita then asked a more fundamental question, 'Why must everyone have faith? If someone is faithless, a very personal and private matter that is none of anyone's business, how will the philosophy behind veiling be explained to her?'

Sepideh, a writer, posted that 'Islam must be updated and a few daring jurists must be found who will say that the modern meaning of Islam is not *"chador* and bondage".' Many of the faithful bloggers tried to show that true Islamic standards are not what is being promoted or executed. They often noted that though they are veiled and pious and do wear *chador*, they oppose the compulsory aspect of veiling imposed by the regime and consider it against Islamic ideals, particularly the principle of *la ikrah-a fi'ddin* ('there is no compulsion in religion'). Fariba, writer of *Hijab-e Man dar Canada* ('My Veiling in Canada'), is a young Shirazi woman who at the time of commenting was working in a government office while waiting with her physician husband to hear from the Canadian immigration office. She had started a weblog to help answer her question of how to keep her veil and still be accepted by Canadian society. She commented on a post to 'A Question Called *Hijab*':

> Nowhere in the Qur'an does it say veiling is compulsory. Furthermore, Muslims pride themselves in saying that 'There is no compulsion in the faith' – *la ikrah-a fi'ddin*, especially not for secondary concerns that are not even taken as central tenets of the religion. But what can we do when Islam has been distorted within the last 1,400 years? People and those in power have interpreted it in whatever way they wished. *There is no defect in the essence of Islam; what defect there is exists in our way of being a Muslim* ... The hearts of veiled and unveiled women bleed from these anti-women actions [emphasis in the original].

Sara posited:

> Compulsory veiling accompanies compulsory religion just because we were born to it. If we solve the issue of compulsory faith first, the problem of compulsory veiling will solve itself...

Fariba argued:

> Other edicts of Islam are not given as much weight as veiling is. I don't understand, we have all these obligatory principles in the faith: consideration for the poor, refusal to backbite or falsely accuse, refusal to steal other's property, ... but we, the religious crowd, pay no mind to any of these. But if someone came and opposed compulsory veiling, that person is the mother of all evil and a thousand and one accusations and slander are sent her way. Why are we so glued to the appearances of the faith? Why don't we observe the core of the faith, its essence?

She was not the only religious poster who passionately expressed the view that Islam should not be mixed up with the Islamic Republic. Another woman wrote:

> Myself, I am a strong proponent of veiling and would never go before strangers without my *chador* but I can't accept compulsory veiling – *la ikrah-a fi'ddin* [there is no compulsion in religion]. They can promote virtue and prohibit vice but enforcing is not acceptable under any circumstances in our beautiful and perfect faith.

Payam (male) wrote:

> Veiling is a Qur'anic recommendation and advice to the believers, not all mankind. Therefore, the Qur'an did not make veiling compulsory; people did that in the name of religion. Also, veiling can take many forms. It does not mean wearing a black *chador* from head to toe. That is an Iranian invention.

Some of the religious commentators believe that it is the compulsory aspect that has created an aversion among women to veiling specifically, and the faith generally, and that these are the grounds on which to challenge the regime:

> As important as veiling can be in Islam, it does not carry more weight than praying. Do we have the right to punish someone for not praying in Islam or force that person to pray? Even if everything the supporters of compulsory veiling say about the obligatory nature of veiling in Islam is true, ultimately what they have proved is the obligation to veil, not that it is compulsory. There is a difference between obligation to do something and that being compulsory. The Islamic government doesn't have the right to enforce this matter even if it is socially and religiously obligatory.

Ghazal, who writes *Khatkhatiha-yeh Asheghaneh* (Romantic Scratching), a weblog devoted to romantic poetry accompanied by romantic photographs of young women, argues that Iranians of other faiths should not be forced to veil:

> In my opinion veiling is every person's responsibility under *shari'a* law ... so each person should observe it and is personally responsible ... she should be dealing with God, not his subjects even if they have the seat of the state ... in my opinion prohibition of vice doesn't mean forcing people to do something ... in addition to the Muslims, there are other people in Iran who follow other faiths, and their religious edicts are

important to them and of course should be important also to Muslims, who believe that whoever believes in God is our religious brother ... and everyone should have the right to choose to sin.

The writer of *Faryad-e Roozha* (The Scream of Days), who appears from his weblog to be a *basiji* (revolutionary guard) opines:

> Veiling is obligatory for female Muslims (notwithstanding its limits). The principle of the matter is certain but whether or not the Islamic government can enforce all women, Muslim and non-Muslim, to wear the veil not only follows no reasoning, but also there are examples countering this approach from the time of the benevolent Prophet and the Caliphs.

Having read hundreds of comments, I have come to understand the main reasons for the regime's concern over debates around compulsory veiling. They know it cannot be argued for on the basis of religion, even among faithful, practising Muslims. This engenders another puzzle: why does the regime continue to insist on enforcing compulsory veiling when it has so damaged the state's legitimacy? If we are to launch a citizen campaign against it, we also should identify the regime's major reasons for its introduction and continuous imposition. We do not have a clear answer to this question; no clear reason such as economic interests, as there was behind the introduction of apartheid policies in South Africa.

Citizen-rights-based arguments

In many of the official discourses on veiling, often reflected in the comments posted to 'A Question Called *Hijab*', one of the main justifications for veiling was that the female body and hair attract men, causing sinful thoughts if not actual sins. While men are also religiously obligated to lower their gaze and refrain from looking at women, this is not a legal prohibition as is veiling. Not surprisingly many posts focused on discriminatory treatment of women and urged men to take responsibility for controlling their sexuality, while questioning why women have to shoulder the burden of veiling to prevent men from sinning. Thus Baran wrote: 'Why did God only give men the right to choose their garment? If only men could safeguard their temptations and desires so that women would not be so troubled!'

Another comment read:

In response to the Haj Agha's comments which said we should go and research *tawhid* (monotheism – the first pillar of Islam) and not veiling, has God not commanded you to shield your eyes? Why do you expect all women to be the exalted Fatemeh Zahra but you can't even be like Imam Kazem, of whom it is said he was imprisoned in the same cell with a prostitute but was able to hold himself because he willed it. Why should men be raised in a manner that things have to be kept from their line of view for them to be able to, at least in appearance, control themselves?

Some comments questioned the notion that the sight of women's hair or female bodies in Western-style clothing excite men, remarking that only men with sick minds are excited by seeing a woman without a veil and that such people should seek help:

If we are devising laws for this hand-to-hand battle, it is best to block the eyes and ears of the degenerate men for life to follow its normal course.
I think if a man's desire is awoken by a few locks of hair, it is he who should cure himself. I shouldn't have to limit myself due to his problem.

Other comments suggested that the notion that men are excited by the mere presence of an unveiled woman is an insult to men. Man Pesaram (I Am A Boy) wrote:

Males promote veiling with the slogan 'With veiling we rid you of ourselves! Because we are extremely wild, mere veiling is not enough; women shouldn't be seen, they should not have any visual or audible displays, because if they do, there is no guarantee that we male dogs will be tamed.' I ask, … don't you think this insults us a tad?

Patriarchy, discrimination, sexuality and differences between men and women are key concepts addressed by opponents to veiling. Many women place themselves at the centre of the debate, basing their arguments on personal values and beliefs. Shahrzad-e Ghesse goo (Shahrzad the Story Teller) writes:

I hate religio-centricity. The basis for my life is humanism outside of faith and … I detest all bonds and constraints. In my opinion, veiling is a form of bond and constraint, and so is despicable.

Many comments indicate that the right to choice and self-determination is paramount to the writer, including the rights to abstain from religious belief, to oppose veiling and to choose one's attire. These comments also encompass criticism of the Iranian regime for its lack of democracy. Similar to Bahar, who complains of dictatorship, B. Eftekhari wrote: 'If we had a democratic social system, maybe what one would say could be discussed. But of what importance can one's demands carry when this is the government of God!'

Shirin wrote:

> I detest veiling. However, I have many *chadori* friends who are very nice girls. I respect them and they respect me. Many people believe in veiling in our country and I think that, as they are free to choose their manner of clothing, I have the right to choose how I want to be clothed. The veiling that has become compulsory in our country is not a sign of religiosity; rather, it indicates fear, hatred and, above all, sorrow and grief.

Darkoob suggested a referendum on veiling:

> I don't accept this faith but won't insult any Muslims. Everyone should be free in their beliefs but not limit others, like have a group telling women to fix their headscarves. The same way that a group can't rape in public and then say, 'Well, this is our belief'. Also, why won't they stage a referendum about veiling? Maybe because they know what the real results of it would be!

Assal made her point with humour:

> Guys, this is Iran; everyone has go to heaven, even if by force! Everyone has to be a Muslim! Everyone has to pray! Everyone has to observe veiling! I'll see you all in heaven!!! Until then...

In fact frustration is clear in many of the opinions of those opposing veiling, which demonstrate clear understanding of the power structure and their powerlessness. Hadi discusses the matter more generally:

> We always solve problems in the direction of bottom-up, but this issue has to be solved top-down. Even if the families stop forcing their kids to wear the veil, the government's edict is still very much enforced.

However, proponents of compulsory veiling also cite rights-based arguments for choice, including democratic fundamentals and the ideal of majority rule, noting that since more Iranians are religious than not and accept veiling, the non-religious minority has either to fall in line or leave Iran. Narjes wrote:

> You forget that veiling is a matter discussed in *shari'a* that has to be observed. The number of people who don't want to observe veiling is very few and the majority wants it to be observed. How is it that in this midst you have no interest in being democratic?

Darkoob responded:

> Why does everyone insist that veiling has so many supporters. If everyone agrees with it, then the overwhelming presence of morality police is just to guide a small number of people? Please don't stick your heads in the sand. In liberal democracy, considered to be democracy today, it is not true that any demand, merely for being the demand of the majority, will be legitimized. There are principles that one cannot transgress upon. One of such principles is observing human rights and ensuring rights for the minorities ... freedom to choose clothing and freedom of opinion and religion are fundamental human rights (in a human-rights-based liberal democracy) and no law can limit them. In addition, your comment regarding those in opposition to veiling being in a minority is doubtful. I don't mean that they are in the majority, but that there is no credible evidence pointing to either group being the majority. What we witness on a daily basis establishes that neither group is small in number.

At the same time, a significant number of religious individuals defended their right to choose their manner of clothing.

> I am a 20-year-old female university student who is pursuing education in a city away from home. I chose *chador* and no one has the right to belittle me for my choice, correct? I am against compulsory *chador* and veiling because it introduces an ugly image of veiling to the society. Neither those who don't wear *chador* have the right to belittle those who do, nor do those who wear *chador* have the right to belittle those who don't.

In another blog a thread critiques the move by Western governments, especially France, to force women to take off their veils as a denial of basic human rights – that of freedom of religion or choice. Oddly they seem blind to the fact that using state power to force women to veil in Iran and other countries is exactly the same denial of rights for those who choose not to veil. This double standard, of compulsory veiling inside Iran and compulsory de-veiling in some European countries, has provided citizens with plenty of opportunity to discuss human rights, the value of democracy, and the right to choose what to wear and how to practise one's religion. Alireza wrote:

> Heads of the government say that there is no freedom in foreign countries. Why? Because Muslim women who reside there can't wear the veil. But by the blessed existence of the Islamic Republic in Iran, all women are free to have a veil. Assuming only one person (although the number is much higher than this) doesn't want to observe the veil ... over there they forcefully remove the veil, and over here they forcefully put it on. Force is force, no matter the nature of it. How is this manner of observing the veil different from their manner of banning it?

Another comment assessed the situation from the perspective of putting collective rights over individuality:

> Our regime believes that because it is a religious regime (though this is the regime's own interpretation), and because many of the Islamic regulations have roots and results in the society and community, the religious edicts must be observed. This can be logical only if our regime accepts this argument about other regimes as well and, for example, doesn't complain about other countries preventing Muslim women from veiling themselves, because otherwise this is a paradox.

Another commentator somewhat sarcastically wrote:

> I don't understand how these defenders of religious government dare hold such double standards. In the opinion of a religious regime, the major difference between a veiled German or Turkish woman and an unveiled Iranian woman is that the former chose the path to salvation and truth amidst all the difficulties of her workplace and environment, while the latter, despite all opportunities presented her, chose the path of animosity, obstinacy and ... perversion ... In this case, naturally those who have understood the truth and understand things better than her must prevent this perversion!!!

Soheila Biglarkhan wrote on the responses to the prohibition of veiling in Europe: 'This is a point that has long engaged my mind. If the freedom to choose veiling outside of Iran is so supported, then what about the freedom to choose unveiling in Iran?'

Clearly, the widespread reporting in the Iranian media about the ban on veiling in schools in France and Germany and the Islamic

Republic's stance against these bans citing human rights, freedom of religion and individual choice has inadvertently spread such principles among the Iranian public, and sparked an unwelcome comparison between the values and principles demanded from European governments by the Islamic Republic and the violation of those same values and principles by the regime.

Conclusion

The absence of open public discourse on compulsory veiling and the dominance of the official state discourse force individuals to comply and maintain a pretence of consent or acceptance regarding compulsory veiling. Although, as many of the commentators have mentioned, the presence of ever-increasing numbers of morality police indicates that large number of women are contesting compulsory veiling. Nonetheless, as the presentation of weblog debates indicates, beneath the 'public transcript' lies a multiplicity of complex views 'off the public stage' which do not concord with the official discourse, regardless of the degree of the contributors' religiosity. A review of the many comments posted on the blog I initiated on the veiling issue demonstrates that the 'public transcript' on veiling is largely invalid and dysfunctional. Some of the primary tenets of this public transcript – such as the idea that veiling provides a sense of security and impunity for women and offers women respect and dignity – has been largely undermined by everyday social reality over the last thirty years. Changes in communications technologies, globalization, increased opportunities to experience and understand other societies and cultures up close, the increasing universality of liberal democratic values, and the modern meanings of freedom and human rights have called into question many of the conventional arguments in support of compulsory veiling. Furthermore, citizen access to varying interpretations of Islam has effectively erased the theological monopoly the regime had hoped to maintain. Concurrently, the Iranian government's overzealous defence of the rights of veiled women in France, Turkey and other Western countries on grounds of freedom of religion has highlighted for Iranian citizens the regime's double standard, and in turn has also greatly weakened public transcripts concerning veiling. Ironically, this has resulted in the regime's greater insistence on the benefits of veiling for women and society at large, and the necessity of enforcing veiling on all adult female citizens. This is a rather defeatist strategy given the widespread demand for individual liberty that the preceding debates indicate.

On the other side stand the female citizens who 'perform' dress code regulations in a variety of manners, from absolute acceptance to 'improper' veiling, which on the surface appears as compliance and at the same time challenges the power structure.

The pretence of compliance with compulsory veiling is in fact increasingly disturbing to the regime. 'Improper veiling' speaks to the existence of a parallel and active hidden transcript. While no Iranian woman is seen in public without a veil, those in power are ever worried about the increasing presence of the hidden transcripts of those opposed to compulsory veiling. As Scott states, 'the idiotic game is that in return, the powerful stage a performance of leadership and superiority while they try to carefully view the image behind the masks of the subordinates in order to read their hidden intentions' (1990: 6). This constant worry and the realization by those with power of the degree to which the hidden transcripts have weakened the public transcript on veiling have engendered new state strategies over the last few years. Using new slogans and repackaging old ones, and trying to respond to arguments that are never publicly discussed, are some of the ways the state attempts to counter the hidden transcripts on compulsory veiling.

It appears that so long as unveiling is a criminal act punishable by law, and that this is sanctioned by both the religious order and cultural traditions, Iranians opposed to compulsory veiling will not be able perform on the public stage. However, it is clear that their performance, though whispered, is ever expanding 'offstage', waiting for an opportunity to come out from behind the veil and onto the public stage. Launching discourses in an informal forum such as a blog is thus perhaps a way to move towards collective articulation of demands not only to end compulsory veiling but to establish basic individual rights of women over their bodies and beliefs.

Notes

1. The question of veiling, hetero-sociability and women's right to be active in public life has been at the centre of intellectual and democratic movements since the end of the nineteenth century (Amin 2002; Afary 2009).

After several decades of public debate, the modernist regime under Pahlavi (1924–79) actually introduced compulsory de-veiling in 1936, despite strong opposition from conservative religious leaders – a move which paved the way for desegregation and the integration of women into public life (Bamdad 1978; Paidar 1995).

2. In the first four months of 2010 – not a preferred travel season due to the cold weather – around a million Iranians travelled to Turkey; these trips increase drastically during the summer holidays (Tabarestani 2010).

3. According to the latest statistics published by the National Organization for Civil Registration, around 5 million Iranians live abroad. The International Monetary Fund says that annually between 150 to 180 thousand educated Iranians emigrate (Mardomak 2010).

References

Afary, J. (2009) *Sexual Politics in Modern Iran*. Cambridge: Cambridge University Press.

Alavi, N. (2005) *We Are Iran: The Persian Blogs*. London: Portobello Books.

Amin, M.C. (2002) *The Making of the Modern Iranian Woman: Gender, State Policy*. Gainesville: University of Florida Press.

Bamdad, B.M. (1977) *From Darkness into Light: Women's Emancipation in Iran*, trans. and ed. F.R.C. Bagley. Smithtown NY: Exposition Press.

Farahani, F. (2007) *Diasporic Narratives of Sexuality: Identity Formation among Iranian-Swedish Women*. Stockholm: Acta Universitatis Stockhilmiensis.

Mahmoudi, A. (2000) *Tracks Left Behind by the Religious Traditions in the Teaching and Education of Sexual Behaviour in Iran*. Germany: Nima Publication.

Mardomak (2010) 'Deputy Interior Minister: Five million Iranians live abroad', www.mardomak.org/news/migration_from_iran_fm_report.

Mutahhari, M. (1992) *The Islamic Modest Dress*, trans. Laleh Bakhtiar, 3rd edn. Chicago: Kazi Publications.

Paidar, P. (1995) *Women and the Political Process in Twentieth-Century Iran*. Cambridge: Cambridge University Press.

Sadeghi, F. (2009) 'Foot soldiers of the Islamic Republic's "culture of modesty"', *Middle East Report* 39(250): 50–55.

Sadr, S. (2010a) *Compilation of Laws and Regulations Regarding Clothing in the Islamic Republic of Iran*. Tehran: Nili Books and Varjavand Publications.

Sadr, S. (2010b) 'Compulsory veiling and Iranian feminism: Inside and outside Iran', in G. Amin (ed.), *The Iranian Women's Studies Foundation after 20 years*. Cambridge MA: Iranian Women's Studies Foundation.

Scott, J.C. (1990) *Domination and the Arts of Resistance: Hidden Transcripts*. New Haven CT: Yale University Press.

Tabarestani, A. (2010) 'Surprise of the Turkish authorities for hosting of a million Iranian tourists', *Qods* newspaper, 28 Tir, www.qudsdaily.com/archive/1389/html/4/1389-04-28/page14.html#1.

8

Kicking back: the sports arena
and sexual politics in Iran

Homa Hoodfar

Iranian women, particularly in urban settings, have learnt through centuries of exclusion from public space – due to both cultural norms and state authority since the sixteenth century – that public space access is pivotal to autonomy, especially with regard to equality, full citizenship and control over their sexuality.[1] Challenges to exclusion and strategies to assert women's public presence have become a constant feature of Iranian social politics, particularly since the establishment of the Islamic Republic in 1979 and the state's attempt to build a society largely predicated on gender segregation. This attempt has included framing women's bodies as both obscene and erotic, in the process of asserting control over women's sexuality, which ideologues in power have viewed as a source of public disorder (*fitna*). In response women have sought avenues and strategies to resist, nullify and dislodge the regime's efforts to control their sexuality and exclude them from public life. Evidently, women have understood that visibility is power, a rather inverted understanding of Michel de Certeau's assertion 'power is bound by its visibility' (1984: 97).

However, the authoritarian and repressive nature of the regime has precluded conventional oppositional organizing, and thus women have largely engaged in 'non-organized resistance movements' – that is, multitudes of individual women and small groups have engaged in similar actions, including small acts of resistance in various venues, such as parading in the streets in attire not completely compliant with officially prescribed *hijab* (see Sadr, Chapter 7 in this volume). The nature of 'non-organized' resistance has effectively transformed various arenas previously considered 'frivolous' or non-political into locales of subversive political action that have engendered social change. In the context of extreme state oppression of civil society, 'politicizing' spheres previously considered outside the realm of 'politics' – for example, the quiet refusal to withdraw from public spaces or to comply perfectly with dress codes – contest the regime's interpretations, religious justifications, and imposed sexual norms and policies. Through seemingly non-political avenues, women have achieved some degree of political, social and structural transforma-tion, even at the level of state power structures, concerning gender and sexual norms (Hoodfar 1999, 2010; Bayat 2010). In this context, sport, and in particular women's sport, has emerged as an important site of women's (and youth) activism, and as such is important to look at in order to understand the nature of public politics and, especially, gender politics in Iran.

The Iranian government's moves to 'Islamicize' women's sport by imposing restrictive dress requirements and segregated facilities has been regarded by many women's sport proponents not as a practical move to comply with religious requirements, but rather as a means of pushing women out of public space. Gender equality and female sport advocates in Iran have continued to challenge this and other policies which effectively work to exclude women from public space, using various strategies to resist the myriad rules directed towards controlling women's bodies, their expressions of sexuality, their mobility and their civic rights. Sport has emerged as an important arena where women of all ages, classes, religious and political backgrounds challenge the regime's gender ideology and reiterate their claim to public space. Especially in recent decades public football matches are increasingly sites for political contestation pitting the public against the regime. In this context, the issues of women's sport and women as football spectators have gained new significance for women's rights proponents.

Based on data collected during two research projects, one under-taken from 1991 to 2001 and the other from 2005 to 2009, this chapter presents the various ways that women of diverse backgrounds and political persuasions have made sport a vibrant venue of heightened public discourse over the last three decades, challenging the regime's gender ideology at considerable cost to its legitimacy.[2]

Women's sport, modernity and social change in Iran

Degrees of veiling and gender segregation have persisted in Iran and some other Middle Eastern societies, where in some contexts 'ideally' women remain largely within the private sphere and away from public life. However, in Iran proponents of modernization and particularly the Pahlavi dynasty (1924–79) viewed public gender equality and hetero-sociability as integral to modernity and thus adopted various strategies, including the expansion of female education and the promotion of de-veiling, to encourage women's public presence. It was in this context that social policymakers in Iran (and in other countries of the region) in the latter part of the twentieth century turned to sport as a means of integrating young women into public life (Squires 1982; Sfeir 1985; Schayegh 2002; Yurdadön 2004). Thus, for example, national celebrations frequently included parades of schoolgirls marching and performing in Western clothing (Woodsmall 1975). This affronted many religious leaders opposed to modernity and its emphasis on democracy and equality, as well as its promotion of de-veiling and gender desegregation (Paidar 1995). Although the religious forces' hostility extended far beyond the expansion of women's roles, given that democratization greatly threatened their power and influence (Paidar 1995; Afary 1996, 2009) they found it easier to galvanize support when they focused on women, and morality and sexuality issues. Indeed many Iranian religious leaders continue to equate women's participation in sport with immorality and a European conspiracy to destroy Islamic mores.

With the establishment of the 'Islamic' Republic in 1979 the new regime instituted policies attempting to establish gender apartheid. Within weeks of coming to power, Ayatollah Khomeini cancelled family law reform (so that once again men had total legal power over their wives), encouraged polygamous as well as temporary marriages, announced women could not be judges, segregated sport facilities and beaches, and attempted to introduce compulsory *hijab* and segregated public transport. No sphere was left untouched. Along with family and personal status law, public mobility, rules regulating music, dancing and socializing, the Islamic revolution's impact on sport was particularly notable. The religious leaders of the revolution considered international sports competitions a corrupting European influence and a luxury Iran could do without. The regime refused to send teams to the Asian and Olympic Games during the 1980s, to the great detriment of sport culture in Iran. In response to critics, they argued it was unjustifiable to invest in the training of an elite group of athletes when the 'Islamic' ideal of sport was to promote public health, not to produce a handful of champions.

In their move to 'Islamicize' sport, the regime instituted policies which effectively diminished the ranks of female athletes and coaches under various pretexts; the imposition of complete gender segregation of sport facilities meant they were only available to women for a few hours a week, if at all, and women's sports had to be played in enclosed venues where they could not be seen by men. Women were banned from wrestling, boxing and soccer, which the regime deemed 'unfeminine'. The prohibition of any contact between unrelated men and women, combined with the lack of female coaches, presented a strong obstacle to the development of women's sport. It also meant that international games were off-limits to Iranian women, since men were present as coaches, referees and spectators.

In the general chaos and insecurity following the revolution, there was little public resistance to the new regulations concerning sports. Other concerns took priority, such as the cancellation of the Family Protection Act (1967), which had moderately improved their legal position within marriage, as well as the introduction of compulsory *hijab* (Paidar 1995; Hoodfar 1999; Yaghoobi, Chapter 2 in this volume). This situation, along with the beginning of the eight-year Iran–Iraq war (1981–88), allowed the regime to implement their anti-sport policies with relative ease. Nevertheless, women's and citizens' rights advocates have reacted to restrictions on women's bodily autonomy and public mobility. In so doing, issues concerning sexuality and women's right to public discourse have emerged in ways not always anticipated by either proponents or adversaries of women's sport.

Daily discipline and early resistance

Revolutions are not only about political change; they also lend themselves to rapid social and cultural transformation. Such changes can be introduced by new regimes; they can also result from resistance or innovation by the general public to impositions from new rulers. One widespread phenomenon in the early months after the 1979 revolution, at least in Tehran, was women exercising in public parks. This was a particularly popular pursuit, especially among married women from less wealthy neighbourhoods, who normally wake very early to pray and buy fresh bread for their family's breakfast, and take the opportunity to go to the park, exercise and chat with other neighbourhood women.

A few months into the revolution some conservative religious leaders began objecting to women exercising in the open where men could see them. Though *hijab* was not yet compulsory, women from less wealthy neighbourhoods generally tended to dress conservatively, often wearing a *chador* that covered them head to toe. The religious leaders argued that regardless of modest clothing, exercising in view of men was 'un-Islamic' as it encouraged men to have immoral thoughts; thus, they argued, Islam prohibits women from sport. Along with their speeches they dispatched vigilantes to the parks to dissuade women from exercising, sometimes using force. The situation, in the context of yet another restriction on women's access to public space and the ongoing process of objectifying women as generically problematic temptresses, became a topic of public discussion.

The increasing restrictions on women's public presence galvanized even more women to join in morning exercise gatherings in protest, especially middle-class women, who joined in the discourse and who loudly demanded proof that Islam prohibits sport for women. They used Qur'anic verses and Ahadith[3] to support their position, including a saying where the Prophet encouraged sport for his own wife, Aisha. The phrase 'a healthy mind dwells in a healthy body' became commonplace, and female religious preachers[4] and their congregants popularized the notion that Islam commands Muslim men and women alike to take care of their health and bodies, since the body is a gift from God; therefore it is the duty of an Islamic government to assist its citizens in this.

Religious leaders were taken aback by the unprecedented heated and pervasive public debate challenging their position. Top religious leaders publicly reversed their stance, co-opting women's opposition by concurring that Islam does encourage sport (specifically riding and fencing, according to the Prophet's sayings); however, they continued to insist that women's sport could only take place away from the gaze of any unrelated male.

Women's response was to demand that the government fulfil its Islamic duty to provide secure and protected environments for women's sport. The pressure was such that, with some fanfare, one of the major sport centres in Tehran was allocated to women and renamed 'The House of Hijab'.[5] The government also promised more protected areas in public parks designated for women only, as well as trained instructors for women who organized themselves into exercise groups. The government began walling off designated women's section in parks and installing simple exercise equipment. While walling off sections of parks has ceased, all parks now have sports equipment, and many municipalities continue to provide instructors for women's aerobic exercise classes. This was one of the first occasions where religious leaders were forced to compromise with women's demands, and to justify publicly and defend their position to female constituents, a trend which has continued ever since.

From the Olympics
to Muslim women's solidarity games

The Iran–Iraq war saw debate over sports fade; however, after the war, pressure from the athletics community saw the regime send a small male team to compete in wrestling, cycling and taekwondo at the 1988 Seoul Olympics. As such, the ban on Iranian women competing internationally increasingly drew heated debate. Conservatives argued that the Olympic atmosphere compromised Muslim women's dignity; women's rights proponents argued this was simply an extension of the regime's manipulation of Islam to justify excluding women from public life. A group of secular women wrote to the International Olympic Committee (IOC) linking Iranian women's exclusion from sport and the Olympics to South Africa's apartheid exclusion of blacks from international competition (Hain 1982). This caused alarm among more politically shrewd Iranian leaders, who responded that their position was in fact 'anti-imperialist', opposed to modernist Western hegemonic ideals of sport and women's rights. They argued that their goal was to develop Islamic women's rights and social and political agency, and women's participation in sport, without the 'sexualization' and 'objectification' of women in Western societies.

Some women publicly responded that compulsory veiling and obscenification of women's bodies, justified by the need to prevent men from lustful thoughts, was the ultimate sexualization of women. Others, including former top female athletes and women's rights advocates, working within an Islamic framework (including the then president's daughter, Faezeh Hashemi), lobbied for women's sport to fulfil Islamic ideals of health and participation, demanding that Iran create and host an international 'Muslim Women's Olympics', which could promote solidarity among, and provide an international arena for, Muslim women athletes. While this initiative lacked input from secular perspectives and thus endorsed the regime's perspective on women's bodies and sexuality (as will be discussed later), proponents were able to push their agenda by arguing that such an event would send a positive message to counter the image of women in Iran as excluded and oppressed due to Islamic ideology.

The idea was initially dismissed by authorities, and some proponents of women's sport were also sceptical. However, supporters of a Muslim Women's Olympics lobbied nationally and regionally, using Qur'anic texts and Hadith, the physical and mental health sciences, and the constitution (which enshrines the right of women to health and education). Prominent Islamic women used their influence to voice their support through national broadcast and print media. In the context of an oppressive regime and the absence of democracy, sport – initially seen as outside the political arena – was reframed as an issue of public participation and attracted much attention as an avenue for expressing opposition to the regime's gender ideology and policies.

Once activists had secured support from other nations, an advisory council was formed to lobby the IOC for formal recognition, which was granted on condition that the games be named the 'Islamic Countries' Solidarity Games for Women'.[6] Given broad public support for the Games, conservative leaders avoided publicly opposing the initiative, but insisted on strict adherence to *hijab*, which they hoped would halt the Games' implementation.

Despite many obstacles, Faezeh Hashemi and her collaborators organized the first games in Tehran in 1993, hosting forty-six teams from eleven countries competing in eight events. The numbers have grown each time the Games are held. The initiative parallels that of European women, who held the International Women's Games (1920s–1930s) before winning their battle to include women in the Olympics (Pfister 2000; Kluka 2001). Ironically our subsequent interviews made it clear that the women involved in the Iranian campaign had no knowledge of their European predecessors.

At the first Games, the 190 referees and all the trainers and technicians were women; men were barred from the site. Despite this, all present were required to observe *hijab*. The media, under the control of conservatives, made only a cursory announcement on the radio; the Games were not televised – justified by the claim that to show women in sport (even wearing *hijab*) would be erotic and un-Islamic. Such statements and the level of eroticization inherent in this perspective suggest that the intent was to render women invisible under the guise of religion, a point not missed by the public, including numbers of observant Muslims. To counteract the lack of media coverage, the coordinating committee organized a spectacular opening ceremony featuring women athletes in regional 'Islamic' garb, who carried torches several kilometres past cheering crowds lining Tehran's busiest street to the sports stadium. This infuriated opponents in the government, who denounced the spectacle as erotic, un-Islamic and an affront to the martyrs of the revolution.[7] As one of the event volunteers told us, 'their denouncement was the best advertisement … more people, even those not interested in sport, came in our support'. The result was a great deal of public discussion on women's public access and their right to sport – precisely what conservative leaders had been trying to avoid.

Although the idea of Islamic Games for women emerged as a strategy to address Iranian women's exclusion from international sporting competition and public space, the need for such Games was clearly felt beyond Iran's borders. As the Games became known internationally, Muslim women from non-Muslim countries became

interested in participating, and concern grew that the Games were inadvertently reinforcing conservative ideologues' attempts to exclude
Muslim women from the global community. The Games' advisory
council thus revised its constitution, opening them to other women
and changing the event's name from 'Islamic Countries' Solidarity
Games for Women' to 'Muslim Women's Games'. The event continued to take place in Iran (1993, 1997, 2001 and 2005), which has
the facilities and expertise for segregated sports tournaments that
satisfy even the most conservative clerics, and hundreds of women
from across the world have participated. However, the regime
cancelled the 2009 Games using political upheaval over the disputed
presidential election results as pretext, and the Games' coordinating
committee offices were subsequently shut down.[8]

Yet, in challenging their forced exclusion from public space,
Iranian women have successfully brought religious arguments, scientific findings and legal frameworks together to lobby both the
authorities and the public at large in support of women's sporting
rights. They have found new avenues for political resistance and in
the process built a global network and their own capacity to engage
on the issue of women's bodily rights at the national level. This
has set a precedent for women in other Muslim societies as well.
Proponents of women's sport were able to establish the legitimacy of
their claim and start to dislodge the patriarchal control of women's
lives. They have kept women's sport on the public agenda and
challenged religious justifications with religious justifications. They
have invented 'appropriate Islamic' sports uniforms so that dress code
violation cannot be used an excuse for exclusion, forcing the Iranian
government, however reluctantly, to send women to international
and regional competitions.[9]

Yet the use of Islam to support the fight for women's right to
sport has, in a way, made it harder to fight gender segregation and
dress codes, and to tackle issues of women's sexualization from a
secular perspective. Religious arguments were used by conservative leaders to keep the Solidarity Games from being televised or
photographed, for all practical purposes rendering invisible these
moments in history. Unlike the European International Women's
Games, which garnered huge media attention and led to the change
in IOC policy (Pfister 2000; Kluka 2001), Iranian women's defeat of

the conservative intention to remove women's bodies from public space, though significant, was only partial. However, the transformation of sport into a channel for political resistance and change through which Muslim women can challenge their exclusion from public life remains a significant achievement.

Football and Freedom Stadium: struggling for space and a public presence

As mentioned, until 1988 the regime cancelled all international games, and the nation's largest stadium (built by the Shah, primarily for football) was renamed 'Freedom Stadium' and used almost exclusively for government rallies. Especially during the Iran–Iraq war, the regime justified its suppression of civil society and all critical perspectives as necessary to national security. However, following the war football emerged as a national passion and a major preoccupation of Iranian youth. By 1989 the national Iranian football team reformed and went on to participate in several Asian games.[10] Each of its wins inspired nationwide celebration, and catalysed an expression of nationalism and pride decidedly different from that which the regime was promoting.

Attending or watching national and international football games in Freedom Stadium in huge numbers, Iranians reclaimed the stadium as a public space. While the regime reluctantly approved the stadium for sporting events, women have not been able to breach the unofficial ban against female attendance at matches.[11] The ban was originally 'justified' as a religious necessity; the regime claimed that it was un-Islamic and immoral for women to look at men who were not 'fully dressed', presumably because it might stimulate women's sexual desire. This was ridiculous in any case since all games were televised and widely watched by Iranians of both sexes at home. Indeed the name 'Freedom Stadium' became synonymous with the regime's obsession with eroticism and its absurd notion of freedom, which seemingly applied exclusively to men; the stadium's name became the butt of many jokes referencing mullahs' alleged homoerotic fantasies.[12] The efforts to keep women from attending games at the stadium were seen by many as yet another attempt to exert control over women and keep them out of sight. Some women started dressing as men to attend games; increasingly this has become a strategy for protesting the ban. Azar, a 25-year-old Arabic teacher, who has done this herself, said:

> How would you feel if you saw no woman minister or president or judge or political leader and not even any women in the football stadium where tens of thousands of men go for a few hours, feeling good about themselves and their national teams, yet there is no woman there? These games are televised and yet you see no woman there? What does that tell you if you are a 16- and 17-year-old girl and you know your brothers go there with no problem? It tells you that women have no rights; they have to be covered in public and exist only at the service of men. That is how I and many other women felt, and we were angry about it, so I made sure at least once or twice I would go there, even if I had to dress as a man.

Jaleh, a 22-year-old student, observed:

> What makes me angry is to know that my mother had the right to go the stadium forty years ago and now I have to fight for the same right. The younger generation is expected to have more rights, not to have to fight for those their mothers enjoyed. Everywhere in the world women are advancing and claiming more rights; here we are regressing. This is what makes the ban even more intolerable.

When Iran beat the USA in a World Cup football match in 1998, Iranians burst into the streets in numbers reminiscent of the 1979 revolution; to the great annoyance of the authorities, women removed their scarves to wave them in the air, and men and women danced together in celebration, in deliberate defiance of both compulsory veiling and public gender segregation. While the pretext of the celebration was the Iranian team's victory, the subtext was a clearly and deliberately engaged public choosing to politicize a sporting event to challenge the regime's control, reclaiming public space and movement. The impromptu football victory celebration, on the heels of the landslide election of reformist President Khatami (1997–2005), was a landmark in domestic politics, greatly unsettling conservative forces. At the time many observers believed the street celebrations marked the beginning of a new public politics and the rebirth of civil society after almost two decades of suffocation (Chehabi 2001, 2002, 2006; Gerhardt 2002).

Unable to check the throngs pouring into the streets, and concerned the celebration might erupt into an anti-regime demonstration, political leaders ordered moral police and other security forces to co-opt the situation by joining the public dancing and distributing sweets. Many Iranians, weary of the regime's ceaseless control of public spaces, saw the event not only as a victory for the Iranian football team, but for public resistance against the regime's oppression. The moment marked a turning point as football, and Freedom Stadium, became symbolic of citizens' contestation of the boundaries of state control.

Particularly for many youth who came of age under the regime, the event demonstrated their determination to find a voice. Reflecting on the day some two years later, Jairan, a 20-year-old student, who filmed a video of the celebration, commented: 'until then I just loved football as a game, but that day I realized football is a political space and scene for us as young people and women, to push for our rights without ever talking about politics'. In response to my query as to how such an event could avoid referencing politics, she noted:

> Yes ... but the beauty of this politics is that neither the government nor our parents who worry about us being arrested and jailed want to or can afford to call it politics. This gives us, the young women, a lot of space to act. Don't you believe me? Watch it, I am sure the future will prove me right. Politics in Iran has a different face. In fact public politics in Iran is veiled, just like its women! (laughter)

The ban on women entering the stadium took on new meaning as a political struggle for collective space, and women's visibility and public legitimacy. The homecoming of the team, which coincided with an Islamic government summit in Tehran, saw a huge crowd of men and women at the airport waiting to greet the players. Hoping to regain some control over the situation, the regime invited the public to come instead to Freedom Stadium where the team would be brought from airport. Thousands of women powered past security forces and were among the first to enter the stadium (Minouie 1998), at some cost to President Khatami, who refused to have the women removed from the stadium despite intense pressure from the Office of the Supreme Leader and the conservative ayatollahs of the Qom seminary.[13]

Despite periodic discussion, the ban on women spectators at the stadium remains, as conservatives continue to argue that women observing men in shorts playing football is sexually provocative and counter to Islamic morality.[14] Women continue to pressure the government to lift the ban, especially during games which draw international media attention, including a 2002 match against Ireland in Tehran, when approximately 300 Irish women intended to come to Tehran to cheer for their team. News of their presence generated national and international controversy; the Iranian news agencies reported that the women were refused visas, but the Irish embassy bussed 25 Irish women to the stadium to watch the game, when the threat of cancellation was imminent due to the Irish women's protests.[15] Iranian women, who remained unable to enter the stadium during the game, facetiously noted that apparently the eroticism and morality of non-Iranian women did not require government control! Many activists saw the Irish women's presence as an act of solidarity with Iranian women, with potential political implications for the regime and for their struggle to get access to the stadium.[16]

During the sixth parliament (2000–2004), the ban was reportedly debated on various occasions. At least one female MP, Tahereh Rezazadeh, used her parliamentary privilege to attend a football match, and said in an interview that there are no grounds in Islam for such a ban (Afzali 2008). While she drew some criticism, various women's magazines and blogs strongly supported her action and urged other MPs and prominent female officials to follow her example in support of women's civic rights and access to public space.

Debates on the issue continue on websites and blogs and on the pages of sports and women's magazines.[17] Female reporters are occasionally able to access games, and increasing numbers of women disguise themselves as males, often with support from male colleagues, to gain entrance. Those who are caught are generally subject to harsh treatment by security forces, and yet many treat it as a winning situation because it gives them and others the opportunity to discuss their event in virtual and traditional media accessed by thousands, with hundreds leaving comments.[18]

Football and the ban on women attending games have remained common topics of conversation. At a family gathering Parvin, a 22-year-old student aware of my interest in the debate, told me:

Because they [mullahs] have dirty minds and they cannot control them-selves [her mother interrupts, saying the mullahs think with the little head between their legs], ... they think that seeing a few hairy naked legs in such a large crowd would sexually excite women to the extent that they lose themselves and commit sins!

Her 20-year-old brother, who had just come into the room, com-mented: 'I wish! We men have to work so hard just to get girls to look at us', at which point everyone laughed loudly. The father, an observant Muslim who had been sitting quietly, said: 'It is so sad that this regime has made our religion subject to such daily ridicules. I do not dare to talk about religion and morality to my children any more. The regime has truly ruined Islam forever.'

On another occasion 15-year-old Susan seemed angry as she commented:

They think if men see women, they would get sexually excited, so they force us to wear this nasty *chador*. Well, now, if women see hairy legs and get sexually excited then it is only fair that men should wear long pants to play, and not prohibit women from going to the stadium for that reason.... Shouldn't this be part of the Islamic justice they talk so much about? ... I think they just think of women for sex and not as human beings. I hate them all.

Her mother added: 'They have forgotten the power of logic. How can they expect citizens to respect these laws?' Sitting in on family gatherings and informal meetings over the years I have heard similar sentiments expressed in many ways, even by observant Muslims who lament that the regime has reduced Islam almost to pornography with its emphasis on sexual rules, *hijab* and the segregation of men and women, and in the process true Islamic spirituality has been forgotten.

Collective action: the Open Stadiums Campaign

Despite widespread views on the hollowness of religious arguments concerning the ban on women at Freedom Stadium, the position of the regime's conservative ideologues has grown more extreme, making the targeting of women in public space ever more evident and undermining their own religious justifications. The regime's underlying goal of minimizing potential collective challenges from women has become more and more obvious as it has worked to minimize public contact and networking between women. For years no organization was able to form to contest the ban; however, several years ago a group of young women, who later became involved with the website *Meydaan*, decided to take up the cause.[19]

Their campaign was launched during the 2005 presidential election, taking advantage of the diminishment in police harassment that accompanies election campaigns. An open letter signed by 120 prominent activists was sent to officials, including several women politicians, demanding their safety be assured as they planned to enter Freedom Stadium to watch a match between Iran and Bahrain.[20] This pre-qualifier match for the 2006 World Cup was scheduled for 8 June. The letter garnered much attention due to the unprecedented involvement of female politicians and prominent women from all backgrounds. It revived widespread public discussion and drew extensive coverage by the international media. The broad general support for the removal of the ban in turn prompted support from reformist political parties and some liberal candidates.

As the stadium opened for the game, thirty-plus women in white scarves (symbolizing the trademark non-violent feminist strategy) waved placards demanding their right to access the stadium. Not surprisingly the women were confronted by security forces. One woman was injured; she was picked up by an ambulance. The rest of the women were permitted inside to watch the game (without their placards) for the first time in twenty-six years. While foreign media and blogs widely reported this event as a success, none of the major Iranian newspapers (all of which are state-controlled) was allowed to carry the story.

The women's attendance at the game signalled to Iranian activists that concerted action against the ban was possible, and the 'Open Stadiums Campaign' was set in action. However, not all women's rights activists supported a formal initiative challenging the stadium ban; some women's groups feared the campaign might divert support from priorities such as family law reform. But many saw challenging the ban as a winnable goal which could be strategic in fostering gender awareness – especially among younger women less concerned with or aware of family law issues. The fact that sports-related issues were not considered political also meant campaigners and supporters would not be putting themselves in danger; the campaign was launched.

Apart from online arenas, the campaign had no access to local media, so the organizers gave interviews to foreign media, where many Iranians get their news. Many of those interviewed stated that while they did enjoy football their primary interest was in the fight for basic citizen's rights regardless of biological sex.

The first organized collective action of the Open Stadiums campaigners, by then known as the 'women with white scarves', was to try to enter the stadium during the match between Iran and Costa Rica in March 2006. This time a crowd of much younger women, many of them high-school students in uniform, also participated in the hope of entering the stadium. The post-election atmosphere was very tense and security forces threatened the women. The women remained outside the stadium waylaying male spectators as they approached and explaining their demand. The protest drew considerable attention, and photographs of the slogans as well as of security forces roughing up schoolgirls were widely circulated. One appeared on the cover of *Zanan* (2005, issue 131), the most popular Iranian feminist magazine, which in turn drew international attention in print and online, to the annoyance of the regime.[21]

As Iranian women reached out to international organizations for support in their efforts against gender discrimination, the newly installed conservative Ahmadinejad regime was trying to establish itself as a regional power and role model for Islamic states. However, as it grew increasingly evident that the issue of women's public access was not going away, shrewder politicians knew they would have to find a way to address the issue of the ban without directly confronting the conservative *ulama* with its removal.

President Ahmadinejad's controversial move

Two months after the Iran–Costa Rica football game, as Open Stadiums campaigners were strategizing for the World Cup play-offs, President Ahmadinejad unexpectedly ordered the sectioning off of an area for women in the stadium for international matches, announcing that the presence of women and families at the matches would encourage 'good' behaviour. The conservative *ulama* of the Qom seminary, who although not formally part of the state structure exert considerable influence on Iranian politics, were furious and publicly criticized the president as going beyond his role as an elected leader in issuing an order requiring religious authority and knowledge. An open letter from several conservative parliamentarians advised the new president to, at the very least, consult with parliament and *ulama* before dealing with matters beyond his authority,[22] and to be wary of creating moral chaos by promoting public mixing of the sexes.

There was a wave of public outrage in response to the letter and the criticisms of the *ulama*, asking where religious authorities were drawing the line, in light of the daily (non-problematic) interaction of the sexes on buses, in shops and at work and universities, and questioning whether, twenty-five years after the revolution, the regime did not trust that it had managed to instil a deep Islamic morality in the people. How could the *ulama* condemn women spectators in the stadium when millions of women watch the matches on television? More and more Iranians began to question the agenda underlying the ban, and public debate on the topic in the media, on buses, in taxis and grocery stores was unprecedented as it became more and more obvious that the issue at hand went far beyond sports and was really about the 'acceptable' public role of women, and the implications of this for women's physical autonomy and presence.

For the Open Stadiums campaigners the whole incident represented a major victory; it not only brought the issue of women in public space to the forefront of political debate, it also made it very clear that many conservative leaders do not actually support the ban. This encouraged even more people to express their support for its removal.

Ahmadinejad's conservative critics suggested the move was a tactic to reach the youth and middle class he had neglected during his electoral campaign; in fact his support did increase among women, many of whom had been sceptical of his position on gender issues, and yet other observers credited him with showing more courage than Khatami had during his eight years in office (1997–2005). However, not everyone was persuaded; sceptics noted that renowned director Jafar Panahi's (2006) acclaimed film *Offside* (banned in Iran but seen by most Iranians anyway), showcasing the stories of young women arrested and detained for dressing as males and sneaking into football matches, had won several international prizes and nominations.[23] If Iran qualified for the World Cup, the film would no doubt gain even wider international attention, bringing more international scrutiny on the regime's treatment of women. In fact the president, never expecting the wave of internal opposition, had followed the suggestion of some key advisers in issuing the order for a women's section to try to pre-empt international criticism.

The most heated discourse, however, was among feminists and women's rights activists familiar with Ahmadinejad's well-established positions opposing gender equality. Some argued he was trying to gain legitimacy by riding the wave of interest generated by the Open Stadiums Campaign. Others analysed the move as a statement to ultra-conservatives opposed to any extension of women's rights and of his alignment with his 'new populist conservative' constituency. Shadi Sadr (2006), a prominent feminist leader involved with the campaign, pointed out that while social movements can more easily realize their goals when they strategically formulate demands that coincide with politicians' political motives, activists must be vigilant to ensure the benefits do outweigh the potential risks of aligning interests with the powers that be. The Iranian government, facing sanctions over its nuclear programme, needs to cultivate a popular base in the country and the region. As Sadr notes, Ahmadinejad issued an order he assumed would cost him and the regime little but would pacify women and broaden his support.

Regardless of Ahmadinejad's intentions, extremists from parliament and the Qom Seminary started to attack him. The pressure was such that the Supreme Leader instructed Ahmadinejad to withdraw the order.[24] The conservative *ulama* of Qom issued more verdicts stating that having women spectators at football games is *haram* (not religiously permitted). In response, campaigners organized interviews with a variety of national and international figures, stating:

- Social consensus and mutual respect should rule a society, not an imposed segregation of women and men.
- Women cheering and encouraging the Iranian team does not breach any moral values, only a historical taboo wrongly erected to keep women out of public life.

- The senseless exclusion of women from the stadium has resulted in many young women disguising themselves as males to attend the matches; citizens are becoming convinced the only way to obtain legitimate rights guaranteed by the constitution and supported by collective cultural values is to break the law.
- Implementation of oppressive policies and indifference to citizens' demands are detrimental to society's health and to peoples' trust in laws and the state.

The press release asked the public to support them by making their opposition to the exclusion of women known.[25]

Campaigners also petitioned the Fédération Internationale de Football Association (FIFA) and the Asian Football Confederation (AFC), documenting how over the campaign's two-year existence Open Stadiums participants had been met with arrests and verbal and physical assaults by authorities, and that while the Iranian government justifies women's exclusion as being for 'women's own protection', expatriate women have been allowed to enter the stadium. Campaigners requested that FIFA take action as per Article 3 of its constitution and Article 6 of its ethical guide: 'We are asking you to use your organizational influence to demand the end to this discrimination.'[26] Ultimately the petition garnered 160,000 signatures. Although it did create some pressure, the government took no action once it was clear Iran was in no danger of being banned from FIFA for gender discrimination.[27] FIFA, not known as a particularly democratic organization (see Darby 2002), is unlikely to take any serious action without pressure from the wider world community.

Despite potential security risks to those publicly associated with Open Stadiums, the campaigners turned to international women's rights and sports organizations for support. The campaign received a major boost when director Panahi dedicated his 2006 Berlin International Film Festival Grand Jury Prize for *Offside* to the 'White Scarf Women' in his acceptance speech and wished them success. In 2007 campaign supporters made the short documentary *90 Minutes of Equality*[28] about defying the ban and smuggling a girl into Freedom Stadium. The film was screened at many international venues, as well as all over Iran (through underground channels) as a discussion-opener on women in the public sphere; the implications of eroticizing women through the imposition of *hijab* and segregation; and the real reasons why conservatives want to exclude women as spectators at football games. Iranian activists continue to invite foreign women to attend international football matches in Iran, highlighting the ridiculousness of the ban and at the same time increasing international support for their cause.

This campaign (as well as 'One Million Signatures' for family law reform and 'Stop Stoning Forever' in objection to stoning for adultery) has galvanized public awareness of women's citizenry rights and how the law and the state objectify women's bodies.[29] Activists believe that the campaigns have led to growing general displeasure with the regime's gender ideology, and to the mass presence of women at the protest rallies over the disputed June 2009 presidential election. As one of our interviewees observed:

> They wanted to push us out of public space and back home under the thumbs of our husbands. But we refused and found ways of being in public and in their faces. The campaigns have done their jobs by raising consciousness among women, as well as changing our society and social norms... We have learnt to be vigilant and ready to protect what we have gained as well as mobilize to demand what is ours by right.

Indeed, a regime-supported website posted an analysis piece inadvertently crediting the Open Stadiums Campaign and other women's rights initiatives with mobilizing women who then joined election protest rallies which evolved into the 'Green movement' in support of a democratic society.[30] This generated much commentary on opposition and women's websites; shortly thereafter the text noting the influence of women's rights campaigns was removed.

Conclusion

Although women's sport was used by the Pahlavi regime to promote its vision of modernity and to support the public presence of women, it was not until the government of the Islamic Republic of Iran began instituting gender segregation and reversing previously secured women's rights that sport caught women's attention as an arena in which to oppose gender discrimination and assert women's public presence. Centuries of formal and informal exclusion from public space have left women in no doubt that their full citizenry rights are contingent upon their equal access to public space and their freedom to move autonomously. Iranian women have thus devised various strategies to dislodge the regime's attempts to limit women's public presence under the guise of religion and moral order by character-izing women's bodies and minds as obscene.

Questioning the regime's characterization of sport for women as un-Islamic using their own religious knowledge, and decrying their exclusion from international sport in the name of religion, Iranian women lobbied inside and outside the country to create space for Muslim women's sport. Their establishment of the International Muslim Women's Solidarity Games opened the way for women in other Muslim contexts to challenge their exclusion from sport and, by extension, from other aspects of public life. Recognizing the increasing importance of the global arena, Iranian women have strategically forged solidarity with transnational movements promot-ing gender equality.

The use of an Islamic framework helped legitimize the cause of women and sport in Iran and justified the training of hundreds of women as coaches, referees and technicians in Iran and in other Muslim contexts. However, rooting support for their cause in Islam has limitations. Conservative opponents continue to apply the concept of 'Islamic modesty' selectively and to prevent the broadcasting of Muslim women's international sporting events, despite all the athletes' compliance with 'Islamic' dress code. Thus while the strategy has made sport legitimate for women, it has had less success in engendering more room for women's visibility in public space generally, or challenging gendered notions of modesty and morality.

Despite (or perhaps in reaction to) the regime's hostility to football and other games, football has emerged as a national passion in Iran. Watching football and celebrating the team's victories have become a form of non-organized contestation between civil society and the regime. The ban on women spectators, justified by the regime's stance that it is erotic for women to see male players in shorts, is widely understood as a flimsy excuse for women's exclusion from one of the most visible public spaces in contemporary Iran. This has led to public campaigns of various sorts and the documenting of strategies such as women disguising themselves as men to attend games in protest at the ban. This has led to increasing non-organized forms of resistance and ultimately to the Open Stadiums Campaign. To their great credit, Iranian women have made their exclusion from Iran's most popular public space a sticking point between the various political factions of the regime, thus undermining its stability and legitimacy. They have managed to present their challenge in a socially and legally valid way, keeping the issue of women's citizenry rights and the state's objectionable eroticization of women's bodies on the public agenda.

Notes

1. While gender segregation has been practised in Iran for centuries, it was with the establishment of the Safavid dynasty (1501–1722) that the state tried to regulate formally women's public presence (Szuppe 2003).
2. The 1991–2001 Women and Law project examined how customary, religious and codified laws shape women's lives and autonomy, and the 2005–09 research explored women's empowerment in Muslim contexts. Both were multi-country projects coordinated by Women Living Under Muslim Laws. The research on sport looked at policy documents and newspaper articles, and included interviews with women athletes and physical education officials, as well as with non-governmental organizations dealing with women's sport. There were also extensive interviews with activists involved in various campaigns concerning women and sport. Other data were gathered through informal conversations with people primarily in Tehran, Mashhad and Kermanshah.
3. Sayings ascribed to the Prophet.
4. Female religious preachers play a very prominent role in shaping women's general understanding of Islam and religion in Iran (Betteridge 1980; Hoodfar 2001).
5. The renaming took place in 1980, and the symbolic significance of this has not been lost on the general public.
6. The Iranian public and media often continue to refer to them as the Muslim Women's Olympics.
7. Referring to those who died during the uprising against the Shah (1979).
8. See www.fararu.com/vdcaimnm.49neu15kk4.html (accessed 22 July 2011) and http://muslimwomeninsports.blogspot.com/2010/08/islamic-federation-of-women-sport-ifws.html (accessed 4 July 2011).
9. Iran still does not permit women to compete in swimming or gymnastics at the international level.
10. Although Iran played in several Asian and Premier League World Cup qualifying matches, it was not until 1998 that the team made it to the final rounds of the World Cup, held that year in France.

11. The ban was introduced in the early days of the revolution as part of a segregation policy, but it attracted little attention initially, as no major games were played until after 1988.

12. 'Mullah' is the common title given to lay and lower-rank religious leaders. Given long years of trainings in all-male dormitory settings during their youth, mullahs are reputed to engage in homosexual conduct almost as a rite of passage. Indeed male homoeroticism has been part of many Sufi traditions and has been notably practised, at least in urban settings (Najmabadi 2005; Afary 2009).

13. Mohammad Abtahi, Khatami's parliamentary adviser, explained this in his blog, in response to many who asked why Khatami did not simply remove the ban against women watching football matches (24 April 2005, quoted in Afzali 2010).

14. More liberal ayatollahs have argued that there is no moral issue given the distance between the spectators and the players.

15. *Qods* newspaper, no. 3998, 2002: 12.

16. There are no statements or documents to support or reject this claim of solidarity.

17. Virtual media provide unprecedented space for public debate in Iran, and Farsi language blogs are the third most numerous in the world (Rahimi 2003; Hendelman-Baavur 2007).

18. The most popular youth magazine in Iran, *Chel-chragh*, was actually charged with inciting people to break the law. The charges were dropped but the magazine was forced to stop publishing articles on the ban.

19. See http://meydaan.com/campaign.aspx?cid=44 (accessed 9 June 2011).

20. See www.radiofarda.com/content/article/302629.html (accessed 7 June 2011).

21. The picture showed two young women with the Iranian flag painted on their faces holding a placard that read '100,000 boys stadium' rather than '100,000 person stadium'.

22. Iran has a dual political structure. The president is popularly elected but the Supreme Leader, a religious figure appointed by an assembly of religious experts, oversees the work of government with the help of other religious leaders to ensure that Iranian laws do not contradict (their version of) Islam.

23. The film also appeared on several critics' top-ten lists of the best films of 2007 and was an official selection for the 2006 New York and Toronto film festivals.

24. *Iran* newspaper, 1 May 2006.

25. This summary is based on an interview on 5 May 2006 with Shadi Sadr and Mahbobeh Abassgholizadeh, two of the major proponents of the campaign, outlining various points they had highlighted in media interviews and public talks to various women's groups and women's magazines.

26. According to Article 3 of the FIFA Statutes, the imposition of any kind of discrimination on the basis of race, gender or religion is not permitted. Article 6 of its ethical guide strongly recommends that member countries have to work to eliminate any kind of discrimination. See FIFA

Statutes, www.fifa.com/mm/document/affederation/generic/01/48/60/05/
fifastatuten2011%5fe.pdf.

27. According to Mahbobeh Abassgholizadeh, who had gone to meet with FIFA
and AFC authorities in Malaysia on behalf of the campaign, the Iranian
authorities and FIFA organizers had several meetings after the submission
of the letter, but there is little knowledge of what discussion went on in
these meetings. See also http://isna.ir/ISNA/NewsView.aspx?ID=News-
1206346&Lang=P for an AFC meeting report ensuring Iran would not
be excluded despite its discrimination against women.

28. The ten-minute short film was produced as part of the Women's Empowerment in Muslim Contexts research programme 2006–10; www.wemc.
com.hk.

29. For more on these campaigns, see www.meydaan.net/english/campaign.
aspx?cid=0; and www.we-change.org/english. See also Hoodfar and Sadeghi
2009.

30. Hoda Fatemi is the editor of the conservative site *Bohran*, who inadvertently
credited the campaigners and feminists for their role in mobilizing women
in support of the oppositional demonstration and the Green Movement in
June 2009; see www.borhan.ir/NSite/FullStory/News/?Id=778. See also
her article entitled 'Women with unlimited demands', where she criticizes
feminist campaigners, http://borhan.ir/NSite/FullStory/News/?Id=784 (accessed 4 July 2011).

References

Afary, J. (1996) *The Iranian Constitutional Revolution 1906–1911: Grassroots Democracy and the Origins of Feminism*. New York: Columbia University Press.

Afary, J. (2009) *Sexual Politics in Modern Iran*. Cambridge: Cambridge University Press.

Afzali, N. (2008) 'Enghalb-efarhigi va baghi ghazaya' [The cultural revolution and other stories], *Meydaan-e-Zanan*, http://meydaan.net/aboutcamp.
aspx?cid=44.

Afzali, N. (2010) 'Sociological analysis of Iran's policies on women's sport',
M.A. thesis. Department of Women's Studies, Tehran University.

Bayat, A. (2010) *Life As Politics: How Ordinary People Change the Middle East*.
Stanford CA: Stanford University Press.

Betteridge, A.H. (1980) 'The controversial vows of urban women in Iran',
in N. Falk and R. Gross (eds), *Unspoken Worlds: Women's Religious Lives in
Non-Western Cultures*. Harper & Row, New York, 141–55.

Chehabi, H.E. (2001) 'Sport diplomacy between the United States and Iran',
Diplomacy and Statecraft 12(1): 89–106.

Chehabi, H.E. (2002) 'A political history of football in Iran', *Iranian Studies*
35(4), Fall: 371–402.

Chehabi, H.E. (2006) 'The juggernaut of globalization: Sport and modernization in Iran', *International Journal of the History of Sport* 19(2–3): 275–94.

Darby, P. (2002) *Africa, Football and FIFA: Politics, Colonialism and Resistance.* London: Routledge.

de Certeau, M. (1984) *The Practice of Everyday Life*, trans. Steven Rendall. Berkely: University of California Press.

Gerhardt, M. (2002) 'Sport and civil society in Iran', in E. Hooglund (ed.), *Twenty Years of Islamic Revolution.* New York, Syracuse University Press: 36–55.

Hain, P. (1982) 'The politics of sport and apartheid', in J. Hargreaves (ed.), *Sport, Culture and Ideology.* London: Routledge & Kegan Paul.

Hendelman-Baavur, L. (2007) 'Promises and perils of Weblogistan: Online personal journals and the Islamic Republic of Iran', *Middle East Review of International Affairs* 11(2), June: 77.

Hoodfar H. (1999) *The Women's Movement in Iran: Women at the Crossroad of Secularization and Islamization.* Montpellier: Women Living Under Muslim Laws.

Hoodfar, H. (2001) 'Muslim women mullahs as volunteer reproductive health workers', in C.M. Obermeyer (ed.), *Cultural Perspectives on Reproductive Health.* New York: Oxford University Press.

Hoodfar, H. (2010) 'Health as a context for social and gender activism: Female volunteer health workers in Iran', *Population and Development Review* 36(3) September: 487–510.

Hoodfar, H., and Sadeghi, F. (2009) 'Against all odds: The building of a women's movement in the Islamic Republic of Iran 1979–2007', *Development* 52(8): 1–11.

Kluka, D.A. (2001) 'The Olympic Games and the Olympic Movement: Toward global understanding and acceptance', in G.L. Cohen (ed.), *Women in Sport: Issues and Controversies.* Oxon Hill: AAHPERD Publications, 255–78.

Minouie, D. (1998) 'The victory of the audience of Freedom', *Zanan* 82: 11.

Najmabadi, A. (2005) *Women with Mustaches and Men without Beards.* Berkeley: University of California Press.

Paidar, P. (1995) *Women and the Political Process in Twentieth-Century Iran.* Cambridge: Cambridge University Press.

Pfister, G. (2000) 'History, women and the Olympic Games', in B.L. Drinkwater (ed.), *Women in Sport.* Oxford: Blackwell.

Rahimi, B. (2003) 'Cyberdissent: The Internet in revolutionary Iran', *Middle East Review of International Affairs* 7(3), September: 101–15.

Sadr, S. (2006) 'The winning game', *Meydaan*, http://meydaan.org (accessed July 2009).

Schayegh, C. (2002) 'Sport, health, and the Iranian Middle Classes in the 1920s and 1930s', *Iranian Studies* 35(4), Fall: 1–30.

Sfeir, L. (1985) 'The status of Muslim women in sport: Conflict between cultural tradition and modernization', *International Review for the Sociology of Sport* 20(4): 283–306.

Squires, M.L. (1982) 'Competitive sport and the "cult of true womanhood": A paradox at the turn of the century', in R. Howell (ed.), *Her Story in Sport: A Historical Anthology of Women in Sports.* New York: Leisure Press.

Woodsmall, R.F. (1975) *Moslem Women Entering a New World*. New York: AMS Press

Yurdadön, E. (2004) 'Sport in Turkey: the post-Islamic Republican period', *The Sport Journal* 7(1), www.thesportjournal.org/article/sport-turkey-post-islamic-republican-period (accessed 6 June 2010).

9

Morality policing and the public sphere: women reclaiming their bodies and their rights

Homa Hoodfar and Ana Ghoreishian

West Java, Indonesia: Lilis Lindawati, the pregnant wife of a local teacher, was arrested around 8 pm as she boarded local transport on her way home from her waitressing job. She was subsequently charged with being a prostitute (the clinching evidence being that she was carrying lipstick in her handbag), fined Rp 300,000 (about US$50) and detained for four days. (Noerdin 2002: 179)

Hamedan, Iran: Zahra Bani Yaghob, a 27-year-old Iranian volunteer doctor, was arrested on 29 November 2007 while walking in a public park with her fiancé, on the charge of being accompanied by a 'non-related male'. The morality police took both into custody. While her fiancé was released an hour later, she was kept in jail and her bruised and bloody body was returned to her family the next day. The morality police told her father: 'Iran does not need such medical doctors.' No authority has been questioned on her death.[1]

Since the early 1980s women in many Middle Eastern and Asian nations have been struggling against a rising tide of religious fundamentalist pressures to restrict their presence and participation in public life.[2] A wealth of research indicates that religious fundamentalist movements, regardless of their complex and diverse socio-political roots, seem to share a commitment to reinvigorate a patriarchal family structure, and impose greater control over women's bodies (Freedman 1996; Sahgal and Yuval-Davis 2002; Bennoune 2007; Derichs and Fleschenberg 2010; Razavi and Jenichen 2010). In Muslim contexts, religious fundamentalist movements tend to utilize a particular discourse to impose state control over women, as well as guardianship by male kin, in order to limit women's access to public life. Although Islamist fundamentalists (and most religious conservatives) have incorporated many aspects of 'modernity', including scientific inventions and knowledge, into their policies and socio-economic platforms, they have never accepted the idea of equality between men and women (or between Muslims and non-Muslims). They insist that God has ordained men to be in control of their womenfolk and that women's place is in the domestic sphere. They thus advocate for a social system where women's mobility is very restricted and women do not come into contact with non-kin male individuals, except when supervised by their male kin.

Where religious fundamentalists have control of state machinery such as in Saudi Arabia and Iran (or even provincial state machinery, such as in Aceh) they have reinvented the institution of 'morality police' (Commission for the Promotion of Virtue and the Prevention of Vice) as a vehicle for operationalizing their visions of gender-apartheid societies. In other contexts, such as Indonesia, Egypt and Algeria, Islamist fundamentalists have adopted a combination of indirect control of state structures as well as mobilization of non-state actors (local mullahs and vigilantes), using a method of persuasion and violence to ensure women (and men) conform to their strict visions of dress code and social mingling. While attempts to exclude women from public space are not new, the systematic crackdown on women's citizenry rights within the modern state structure through the revival – or rather reinvention – of 'morality police' across Asia and the Middle East invest these attacks with significant meaning for proponents of gender equality and participatory democracy. This is especially so, given that the rise of morality police institutions has been concurrent with the spread of human rights and social justice discourses across the region.

In response, women activists across various Muslim contexts have organized and strategized to defy the restrictions imposed on them and to (re-)expand their shrinking civil rights. They have been particularly creative in contexts where non-democratic conditions prohibit women from overtly and publicly organizing. Alongside conventional modes of resistance, women fight back in the context of their everyday lives and by engaging in 'non-organized movements' where large numbers of individuals and small groups engage in common but decentralized actions (Bayat 2010). Thus women taking strolls on the sidewalk, sitting in parks or otherwise intentionally claiming a public presence in defiance of ideology which confines them to the home are engaging in acts of resistance (Loukaitous-Sideris and Ehrenfeught 2009). In doing so, individual women thus transform ordinary public spaces into arenas of contestation against oppressive state or state-supported as well as non-state actors' restrictions.

This chapter will briefly review the historical evolution of the institution of morality police as a background to the different ways that 'moral policing' is being conducted in various social and political contexts by fundamentalist forces. We trace examples of moral policing both within and outside official state structures across Algeria, Iran, Malaysia and Saudi Arabia, in an effort to begin a discussion of moral policing as a transnational phenomenon that requires a much more systematic analysis and response across contexts. However, our major focus is on the strategies that considerable segments of women have often innovatively adopted in order to resist or subvert the curtailing of their rights by religious fundamentalists. We focus on Saudi Arabia, Iran, Malaysia and Algeria as key contexts where the dynamics and complexity of fundamentalisms are on full display. In these contexts fundamentalist forces play a major role in shaping public discourse and policy, particularly around issues of gender presentation, roles and identity.[3] Moreover, women's incorporation into many fundamentalist projects, whether as political supporters or as paid morality police agents, adds complexity to the picture and demonstrates the need for much more nuanced attention and response to countering fundamentalist projects. The question is whether such developments, particularly women's active participation in fundamentalist projects, can be considered a subversion of the fundamentalists' proclivity towards creating gender-apartheid societies, or rather a temporary compromise on the part of fundamentalists in their process of institutionalizing secondary citizenship rights for women on a systemic level. Despite varying political regimes and socio-economic conditions, examining the trends in these four countries in recent decades stresses the common political struggles that women who insist on the realization of citizenry and human rights for all continue to face. The emphasis on resistance strategies highlights some of the unique, significant and innovative forms of resistance that have often been overlooked in women's rights literature as apolitical or non-strategic.

The political evolution of morality police

To understand the reinvention of the institution of 'morality police' it is necessary to revisit briefly its historical roots. Contemporary institutions (such as the 'Commission for the Promotion of Virtue and the Prevention of Vice' in Iran and Afghanistan, as well as the *Mutawwa'in* in Saudi Arabia) function to impose and enforce a far-reaching and singular moral code on the entire population. This rather new institution is often presented as the successor to the office of *Muhtaseb*. Yet the office of *Muhtaseb*, a historical Muslim institution, which itself derived from the pre-Islamic Agoronomies, was mainly responsible for overseeing market transactions and taxation, ensuring that the guilds did not rise against the state and that market practices were in line with state regulations. This institution existed in various kingdoms, including pre-Islamic Iran, Babylon and Roman Palestine (Floor 1985: 54–7). During the Abbasid dynasty (750–1258) the *Muhtaseb* developed various formats across Muslim centres, and rulers incorporated it into their administrative structures up until the rise of the Ottoman Empire around 1299. The responsibilities of this office consisted primarily of checking scales and prices, ensuring that business carried on in an orderly and upright manner, and at times monitoring and inhibiting political foment against rulers, as well as overseeing the conduct of religious minorities (Floor 1985: 62). Thus the main duties of the *Muhtaseb* were non-religious. Further, after 950 CE the office of *Muhtaseb* actually leased out its responsibilities to the highest bidders, who in turn could auction the work in whole or part to other contractors, clearly underlining the material rather than moral nature of the undertaking (Floor 1985: 61–2).[4]

Yet the current versions of these institutions and the expansion of their reach to policing Muslim's public morality have been justified with reference to the religious obligation of Muslims to 'command the right and forbid the wrong'.[5] In the Qur'an, other than the charge 'let there be one community of you, calling to good and commanding right and forbidding wrong', there are no guidelines suggesting who performs such duties, nor a definition of what constitutes the 'right conduct' (Cook 2000: 13–17).[6] Even in the accounts of the Prophet's life, there are few references to the Prophet Muhammad playing this role. Thus, although the 'duty' was not expressly rejected, scholarship suggests that during early Muslim history it was neither required nor encouraged (Cook 2000: 57). In fact there is record that in Medina a prominent and pious man named Ibn-al Munkadir (d. 747 CE) reproved another man in the bathhouse for 'immoral behaviour', who then complained to the city's *qadi* (judge). The *qadi* ordered Ibn-al Munkadir flogged for his moral overzealousness (Cook 2000: 70).

Historically, many religious thinkers discouraged rulers and political authorities from becoming involved in issues of individual morality. Some accounts, such as that of Ibn Hanbal (780–855 CE), the founder of the Hanbali school of Muslim jurisprudence, reports that authorities were not to perform the 'morality duty' given the absence of checks and balances to prevent rulers from unjustly enforcing punishment (Cook 2000: 103).[7] Rather, the Hanbali school stressed the public nature of this institution, to be carried out by way of example and encouragement and not by physical force.

A significant shift occurred in the thirteenth century when the prominent Hanbalite scholar Ibn Taymiya (1263–1328) explained the duty of 'commanding the right and forbidding the wrong' in terms of cooperation with the state, characterizing it as akin to a holy war and first and foremost the responsibility of the authorities. His writings were the first step towards legitimizing state authority to regulate public behaviour and morality in the name of religious duty. This opened possibilities for political authorities (and/or contenders for political power) in Muslim societies to appropriate the institution to support various agendas, including justification for legitimately expanding control over economic and commercial centres (*bazaars*), preventing the development of other public institutions with oppositional political potential, as well as closer monitoring of public morality and practices. In contexts where the authorities took advantage of these possibilities, their moves were facilitated by investing religious authorities with the responsibility to carry out the duty. However, these developments were few and far between, and practically speaking materialized only in major urban centres given the limited reach of state authorities over the rural majority.

During this time period, the Turkish Ottoman Empire (1299–1923) was establishing itself as a stronghold in the region. Through its gradual expansion across many Muslim regions, including Arabia, the Empire increasingly projected a 'Muslim' character. It developed an encompassing and intricate state-controlled policing and legal system that allowed for diverse Islamic legal schools and separate courts for religious minorities (van den Boogert 2005). This vast apparatus effectively annulled the office of *Muhtaseb*. However, despite the Empire's vast reach, the ability to exercise direct control in many areas, including Arabia, remained limited. It was in such regions that *Muhtaseb* either continued, or was resurrected in some form by local political leaders to deal with specific local needs (Commins 2006).

In Najd, a desolate region in the northeast of the Arabian peninsula overridden by constant raiding and conflict between its various tribes over the limited resources for subsistence, the institution of *Muhtaseb* was promoted by Muhammad ibn 'Abd al-Wahhab (d. 1792), as a means to legitimize his attempts to bring different tribes under his rule and influence (Uwaidah 2002). 'Abd al-Wahab argued that most of 'the neighbouring tribal Muslims' were in reality polytheistic (*shirk*) and non-believers and thus appropriate targets for holy war under the edict of 'forbidding the wrong'. What he lacked was a strong military force to realize his plan. He formed an alliance with the military–political arm of ibn Saud's tribe, which led to the conquering and control of the peninsula. With the other tribes under their rule, ibn Saud and 'Adb al-Wahab established the Saudi state around 1823 and set up a state Commission for the Promotion of Virtue and the Prevention of Vice (commonly known as the office of *Muhtaseb*) to legitimate state control over public life and to promote a Wahhabi interpretation of Islam.[8] Thus the use of the office of *Muhtaseb* in Arabia began as a political strategy for control, rather than stemming solely from non-political religious ideals or morals. Indeed the development of this rather new religio-political line of Islam was not without its local adversaries, given that by the fifteenth century Hanabalite religious schools of thought were well established in the Arabian peninsula.[9]

Once in power, to ensure support of Wahhabi leaders, the Saudi rulers agreed to emphasize the duty of forbidding the wrong as official policy, requiring their emirs (local representative rulers) to support those who performed the duty (Cook 2000: 165–77; Uwaidah 2002; Bowen 2008). In 1932, Wahhabi religious leaders renewed their full support to the modern kingdom in return for recognition of their interpretation of *shari'a* law as the official law of the land. Given that women who lived in accordance with conventional gender and social roles were not a central concern of this agreement at the time, it was not anticipated that the agreement would have profound negative consequences on women's lives in Saudi Arabia (Yamani 1996). Nor was it expected that this agreement would have repurcussions on women's lives in other Muslim contexts during subsequent economic and political developments, which we discuss below.

Several historical conjunctures in the second half of the twentieth century contributed to the evolution and spread of the Wahhabi school and in particular their gender vision for their 'ideal Muslim society'. With the rise of oil prices in the 1970s Saudi Arabia was transformed into one of the richest states in the region. As part of its foreign policy it moved to provide financial support to help poorer Muslim states struggling with debt crises and a reduction of economic aid from international donor agencies due to widespread neoliberal economic reform. In particular Saudi Arabia helped to set up schools and mosques that propagated their interpretation of Islam – an interpretation which increasingly focused on creating and enforcing rigid gender segregation through regulating dress codes and public mobility (Neumayer 2003; Abouharb and Cingranelli 2007).

During the same period, an alliance was formed between the Reagan administration in the USA (1981–89) and their allies, notably Britain under Prime Minister Thatcher (1979–90), as well as Saudi Arabia against the Soviet Union's attempted expansion into Afghanistan. Seeking to oust the Soviet Union from Afghanistan without committing their own troops, the allied governments adopted a policy of using radical Islamists to fight 'infidel Russia' (Maley 1998; Rashid 2001). The assumption was that religious fanaticism among the fighters would spur their efforts to defeat the 'Godless Communists' and non-believers. In this unholy alliance, America in support of its geopolitical interests poured money and weaponry as well as military and guerrilla training into the most radical Afghan and other Islamist political organizations. Meanwhile, Saudi Arabia, the major US ally, flush with oil revenues, poured money into promoting its version of restrictive Wahhabi Islam as the 'truest and purest Islam' to the hundreds of thousands of Afghan refugees and Muslim radicals from various nations who had joined the fight against the Soviets in Afghanistan (Rashid 2001; Commins 2006). The *mujahideen* (Islamic warriors), then commonly referred to as freedom fighters in the American and British media (though today referred to as terrorists and warlords), were praised openly. Their atrocities in the war and their appalling treatment of women, particularly in refugee camps, were viewed as a small price to pay to defeat the USSR (Moghadam 2002).[10] Added to this geopolitical context was the success of the popular Iranian Revolution of 1979, spurred by anti-imperialist sentiments that toppled one of the stronger US-supported states in the region. The revolution led to the creation of the Islamic Republic, demonstrating once more the political potential of Islamism as a tool for nation-building and hence attracting the keen interest of political Islamist groups in other Muslim contexts.

Having defeated the Soviet Union in Afghanistan in 1989, the West had no further use for the Islamist freedom fighters from Afghanistan and other Muslim nations that they had trained and supported. While the radicalized militants thus dropped from the Western radar, by this point they had become a powerful social and military force. Flush with victory and a newly won legitimacy, the fighters returned to their own countries and joined radical Islamist organizations in Pakistan, India, Malaysia, Sudan, Egypt, Yemen, Algeria and elsewhere (Rashid 2001; Wright 2006). In turn, they revitalized local radical Islamist organizations and propagated an ideology that claimed their path of 'pure Islam' to be the only way to salvation for their nations.

Their 'pure Islam' called for a return to an (imagined) 'glorious past', but the details of how to re-create the 'glorious past' in modern societies which for the most part were quite integrated into the world economy was left conveniently vague. However, the most common aspect among the diverse fundamentalist forces was eminently clear:

the question of women and gender roles was central to the 'return to Islam'. Women's public presence was posited as a major source of social disorder, and the creation of an Islamic society was argued to be predicated on the use of archaic religious laws, several of which had never even been practised in many Muslim communities. Relegating women to the domestic sphere, requiring strict *hijab* and limiting women's political and economic opportunities were propagated as the social norm. The imposition of this vision required mass public persuasion, the fastest route to which was the creation of formal and informal institutions for policing morality. In short, though perhaps unforeseen and unintended, a major consequence of geopolitical developments during the 1970s and 1980s has been the bolstering of militant social forces whose core ideology hovers around exclusionary practices against the rights of women and minorities.

Examining how such forces have tried to operationalize their socio-political vision in several different contexts underlines three broad and overlapping strategic configurations. The first, exemplified by Iran, Saudi Arabia, Afghanistan under the Taliban, and Sudan highlights fundamentalists' successful ascendance to state power and their use of state machinery to reverse women's legal gains and create morality police forces to block women's advancement. The second common strategy, exemplified in contexts such as Malaysia, Egypt and Indonesia, is to infiltrate in large numbers key state ministries, such as justice and education, in order to promote fundamentalist social ideology among the youth and within law-making institutions (Starrett 1998; Abdul Aziz 2010). Third, in the case of weak states, such as Bangladesh or Algeria during the 1980s and 1990s, religious fundamentalists organized as non-state actors to enforce their vision of Islamic society through the creation of extrajudicial measures imposed though public harassment, intimidation and sanctions. Across the three configurations, 'moral policing', either state-sanctioned or by vigilante groups, emerges as an important means by which to impose and uphold social capitulation to the social goals sought by fundamentalist forces. The institutions charged with 'commanding the right and forbidding the wrong' or 'Promoting Virtue and Preventing Vice' are used to create and enforce policies which regulate and control public and private dress codes, gender roles, sexual activity, and public mobility and visibility. Developing a comparative analysis of the tactical strategies used by fundamentalists is very important for those who intend to form sustainable resistance, as is learning from the various ways that, against all odds and often at great cost to themselves, women have continued to resist this policing and to promote gender justice.

Reaching out: women and public space in Saudi Arabia

Religious fundamentalists have been an integral part of the modern state structure in Saudi Arabia, and as such have a strong hand in blocking women's access to public life and public space. However, although many of the restrictions placed on Saudi women are justified in the name of religion and 'tradition', the extent to which such constraints on women's public presence and participation existed or were enforced in the early stages of Wahhabism is unknown. Though there is a lack of historical sources on Saudi Arabian women of that era, some records, such as those of Ghaluyya al-Wahhabiyya, an eighteenth-century woman who led an Arab military resistance against the Ottoman recapture of Mecca, indicate that at least some women in the Gulf region participated in the political public sphere (Mernissi 1993). Other records indicate that women went about their daily chores in public spaces quite freely, in order to provide for their families. Furthermore, though women similar to men wore a *jalabia* and a headscarf, they did not usually cover their faces. Until 1940, Saudi Arabia remained one of the poorest and least politically and economically developed states of the Gulf region. There was no centralized legal system; instead people lived according to tribal traditions, where women played a pivotal role in the household economy. In this context, the regulation of public order by a morality police force operating under the state had little to do with women.

The situation changed post-World War II, as a result of rapid urbanization, the development of the oil industry, and the widespread immigration of male non-nationals fuelling xenophobia. While the Saudi state sought to industrialize and modernize to reap the benefits of economic expansion, democracy and citizens rights were not on the agenda. The state remained a strict Wahhabi Islamic society based on religious hierarchy, gender segregation and rigid sexual morality laws. Fearful of the implications of rapid social and economic changes on gender ideology, conservative religious authorities pushed for a significantly larger moral police force, primarily charged with the duty to ensure women's obedience to the Wahhabi moral code. In particular, morality police were to restrict women's mobility and ensure women were accompanied by their male kin in public spaces. In this moral framework women of any age are legally forced to obtain permission from their male guardian (husband, father, son or brother) to leave the house, marry, divorce, travel, study, work, or even to have surgery. In essence Saudi women are treated as legal minors in need of supervision and control. Consistent with this mentality, the Saudi religious authority has pushed to exclude women from education, political participation, public life, and banned them from driving. Last but not least, women must observe strict veiling requirements and wear a head-to-toe black cover called *abaya*. Ideally veiling includes a *niqab* (face mask), which leaves only the eyes visible.

Yet Saudi women are not simply capitulating to such regressive laws and policies; it is important to recognize that the growth of morality police forces is a significant indication that women have consistently found ways to resist restriction of their rights. Women's strategies include appropriating religious rhetoric and using Islamic arguments to counter claims by conservative religious leaders that educating women engenders female immorality and is un-Islamic. As part of these efforts, following much heated public debate, Saudi women have won the right to education at every level, though the system remains gender-segregated. They have also drawn on their Islamic right to stipulate conditions such as the right to work and to education in their marriage contracts. In the highly non-democratic Saudi context women clearly view their participation and success in education, as well as in the commerce sector, as part of their struggle against exclusion.

A major obstacle to women's public participation that has come under international scrutiny recently is the allegedly Islamic-based ban on women driving; a ban which serves only to keep women at home and male-dependent. According to Saudi women's rights activists, this unjust and discriminatory law continues to be exploited by abusive fathers, brothers, husbands and even hired drivers, and has made women more vulnerable to violence. The impracticality of this ban is especially evident in the busy urban centres where women require a male driver and an escort to accomplish simple daily domestic tasks such as food shopping, taking their children to school, or going to various appointments and activities, not to mention commuting between home and work. While oil income means many urban families can afford a driver, most ordinary middle-class and low-income families cannot do so, which places extra hardship on women from lower socio-economic classes. In response, women's challenge to the driving ban[11] has emerged as the symbol of women's struggle against subordination and exclusion from public space.

One of the most prominent strategies has been the launching of public campaigns to debate and denounce the un-Islamic nature of the restrictions placed on women. In this way women have galvanized considerable support among the more liberal-minded population. Given the lack of democracy and the disregard for public opinion in the kingdom, Saudi women have also utilized the relationship between Saudi Arabia and the West, particularly the United States, to muster external support for their struggles. To this end Saudi women have connected with the transnational women's movement and used its reach to ensure the resonance of Saudi women's demands across the international public sphere. In 1991 during the first Gulf War, when female US military personnel in Saudi Arabia were driving military vehicles to protect one Muslim state from another, Saudi women revived the debates around their right to drive. Subsequently, forty-seven women from influential Saudi families organized a fifteen-vehicle convoy driven by Saudi women in Riyadh.[12] They were successful in ensuring the presence of journalists and spreading the news worldwide (Mallick 2011). While the participants were arrested, jailed for several days and their male guardians admonished, the issue of banning Saudi women from driving became the subject of international discussion and a major source of embarrassment for the country's close ally, the United States. Especially since at the time the USA was condemning Saddam Hussein for being a dictator while Iraqi women had more rights than their Saudi counterparts (Wynn 1994).

Women's civil disobedience angered state authorities and religious leaders, who were already under public pressure from Muslim communities worldwide to refuse to allow the American government to launch attacks on Muslim nations from the home of Islam's most holy sites. In an attempt to assuage the incensed conservative religious leaders, Saudi authorities charged the women drivers with 'defacing the country in the eyes of the international community', an invented crime. Nonetheless, since most Saudis have access to international radio and television, particularly CNN, news of the 'Women's Driving Convoy' continued to be hotly debated across the kingdom. Since this first convoy in 1991, there have been isolated instances of individual women deliberately driving in Riyadh conveying their rejection of the ban. Regardless of rising public support for women's right to drive and the approval of the more liberal religious leaders and some government officials, the religious authorities continue to insist that allowing women to drive would lead to immorality.[13]

Seeking opportune moments to push for their rights, during the 2011 political uprisings of the Middle East region Saudi women renewed their campaign to drive, calling for democracy, human rights and social justice. With the eyes of the world watching the 'Arab Spring', on 19 May 2011 a Saudi technology consultant, Manal al-Sharif, posted a YouTube video of herself driving and describing the problems created by women's lack of the right to drive. She invited women throughout Saudi Arabia to drive their cars in protest on 17 June. Within hours news of the video had spread across the kingdom and by 23 May some 500,000 people had accessed the video clip. The morality police promptly arrested al-Sharif and charged her with breach of public order and security, 'deliberately inciting civil disobedience', and 'inciting other Saudi women to drive cars'. After al-Sharif's arrest, Maha Taher, another activist who had launched her own campaign for women's driving rights four months earlier, along with a coalition of leading Saudi women's rights activists, bloggers and academics, all pulled together to publicize her case, share details of her arrest, and mobilize the public to organize for her release. More than 4,500 Saudis signed an online petition to the king requesting her freedom (Murphy 2011). Within hours, action alerts and petitions were issued by various women's rights and human rights organizations, including WLUML, Amnesty International and Human Rights Watch, and within a couple of days more than 50,000 people had signed petitions to free al-Sharif and drop the charges. Before being released, Manal al-Sharif was forced to sign a statement agreeing not to speak further on the issue; although her supporters were harassed, this has not discouraged them from continuing critical resistance. Many have sporadically driven cars in protest since.

Despite a backlash which saw conservative forces harnessing social media to set up their own sites and blogs encouraging men to beat up women they saw driving (Sidiya and Hawari 2011), on 17 June a group of women did follow al-Sharif's call to action, and drove their cars in protest. The morality police, aware of international scrutiny, chose to ignore the action since further arrests would have led to more international pressure. This indicates that the core of the issue is not religion, but rather a power struggle between Saudi citizens demanding full rights and conservative forces. As in 1991, supporters of the driving campaign once again engaged international attention, issuing a public letter demanding that the European Union step beyond quiet diplomacy and instead publicly hold Saudi Arabia accountable. Women from various EU countries lobbied their representatives in support of Saudi women and demanded more forceful criticism of the kingdom's discriminatory policies. Saudi women wrote to US Secretary of State Hillary Clinton demanding her public support. The gradual emergence of international public support has led to a growing urgency among Saudi rulers to remove the ban; however, religious conservatives continue to block such a move. In the fall of 2011 King Abdullah, whose legitimacy rests on the approval of conservative forces, attempted to pre-empt international criticism and announced that women would be allowed to vote in municipal elections in 2015 – ignoring the upcoming elections in October 2011. While municipal councils are merely advisory and have no real political clout, the symbolic value of women participating in 2011 would have been significant.[14]

Although women have yet to gain the right to drive, the latest protest has shaken the conservatives, and it is clear that the ever-expanding morality police force and the lack of democracy have not broken women's resistance to their exclusion from public life. Throughout 2011 women launched numerous campaigns demanding an end to their exclusion and legal reforms,[15] using their rights to education and economic participation as well as regional and transnational networks to continue publicizing their demands for full citizenship rights.

Everyday action as street politics: Iranian women facing morality police[16]

Since its establishment in 1979, the Islamic Republic of Iran has focused on building an 'Islamic' society which at its core rests on gender segregation and the obscenification of women's bodies – which the regime's ideologues view as a source of public disorder (*fitna*), rather similar to their Saudi counterparts. To this end the state has limited women's access to the formal labour market, segregated sport facilities, beaches and public transit, banned unrelated women and men from mingling, and imposed compulsory *hijab* – initially even prescribing what colour (black, brown, navy or grey) women's veils should be.[17] To enforce these regulations, the regime created a new moral police force (For the Promotion of Virtue and Prevention of Vice) based on the Saudi Arabian model. While the size of this ever-expanding force is not clear, in 1995, excluding thousands of volunteers, there were 230,000 employees (*basiji*) (*Kehan*, 25 November 1995); and in 1997 the government announced it would train more than 3.5 million youth to join the force (*Ettelaat*, 2 May 1997). These numbers have increased drastically since the 2005 elections that brought neo-conservatives into power.[18] Since its inception the morality police forces (and the pro-regime vigilantes) have rigorously policed not only veiling but also the presence of women in public. They have continually disrupted the lives of millions in their attempt to limit women's presence to spaces that the regime deems legitimate, such as hospitals, mosques and pro-regime demonstrations.

Increasing numbers of Iranian women from diverse cultural and economic backgrounds are highly dissatisfied with the situation, including many who were initially supporters of the revolution and the regime. Post-1979 women quickly formed organizations to resist the new gender policies, but the regime used extreme violence to attack all organized opposition (Paidar 1995); thus women activists had to find other ways of challenging their exclusion.

Religious pro-revolution women activists declared their support for the Islamic regime in principle, but presented woman-centred readings of Islamic texts and objected to the injustices imposed in the name of Islam. They demanded that their leaders address their concerns. Working within an Islamic framework, creating much public debate and awareness, they pressured the regime to introduce reforms to re-establish rights, including a national marriage contract specifying women's right to divorce and the removal of a ban on women studying disciplines that the ideologues had deemed masculine (such as geology and agriculture). Women were also reinstated as judges in family courts (Paidar 1995; Hoodfar 1999). While these were important improvements, they fell a long way short of what women's movements across ideological tendencies were demanding, and women's rights remained more restricted than they had been prior to the revolution. In the absence of democracy and freedom of expression, it also became clear that women needed alternative ways of organizing and demonstrating. However, since the regime was not concerned with its international relations or reputation, Iranian women did not have the option of mobilizing transnationally to place direct pressure on the regime, as did women in Saudi Arabia. Hence they embarked on the occupation of public spaces and engaged in small acts of civil disobedience as a popular strategy of resistance.

Indeed many Iranian women, particularly in urban settings, where the majority of the population lives, have recognized that access to public space is pivotal to claiming autonomy, controlling their sexuality, and fully exercising their rights to citizenship (Bamdad 1977; Paidar 1995; Amin 2002). They have understood that visibility is power. Given the extremely repressive nature of the regime, which precludes the formation of oppositional organizations, women have engaged in 'non-organized' movements, where large numbers of individuals and small groups engage in common actions in a decentralized manner. These include small acts of resistance in their daily lives. The extent of these actions has often resulted in compromises by the regime, and also created shifts in public opinion, which increasingly accepts such actions as legitimate (Bayat 2007; Loukaitous-Sideris and Ehrenfeught 2009; see also Hoodfar (Chapter 8) and Sadr (Chapter 7), in this volume).

A common and widespread form of action within this framework is apparently 'frivolous' street parades, which in fact are thinly veiled demonstrations of resistance and contestation. Women marchers challenge the dress code by showing varying degrees of hair, wearing non-approved colours, talking loudly, and conversing with non-related males. Reflecting on the early post-revolution years, an interviewee explained that 'parading in the street was no longer a way of killing extra time or leisure but a political vehicle for us, then young women in our twenties. We were aware that as women, we had lost a lot and we were determined to protect the little that was left for us.' Large numbers of women in small groups adopted parading as a strategy to assert their right to be in public, to walk the main streets and to be equals alongside their male counterparts. The regime ideologues grew increasingly uneasy with the large number of women parading in the street for 'frivolous' reasons. Because they viewed women primarily as wards and chattels of their male kin and the vessels of male honour, women parading in public under men's gaze was deemed an affront to their ideal of an Islamic society.

The sheer extent of resistance by large segments of urban women forced the revolutionary regime to orchestrate pro-regime rallies and mobilize tens of thousands of women from conservative backgrounds to participate. They also increased the size of the *basij* forces, instructing them to 'clean up the city' so that women's presence in the streets would not 'tempt moral Muslim men'. This led to widespread harassment of women, particularly young women. Yet, contrary to conservatives' goals, the increased presence of morality policing engendered ever more creative strategies through which women expressed their resistance. For example, in 1993 on a cool autumn morning, a 40-year-old woman was stopped by a young morality police officer for wearing sandals and having painted toenails. She took his hand and in a loud voice began addressing him endearingly, noting that for a young man such as himself to notice her painted toenails (which by implication erotically excited him) to the degree that he felt compelled to warn her, she would 'gladly bear [his] sin for these immoral thoughts. If only [her] husband would notice these as well!' The woman held tight to the young man, and asked him to come home and counsel her husband on how to pay better attention to his wife. The surrounding crowd was laughing and growing larger by the moment, making the morality police officer increasingly embarrassed and uncomfortable. When the woman finally released his hand, he hurried away and the crowd applauded the woman. Generally, such actions and stories would travel quickly and widely and encourage similar acts among other women. Indeed the sheer number of women engaging in these types of action has often paralysed morality police in their attempts to enforce control.

As indicated, a uniquely complicating factor in the Iranian context has been the regime's mobilization of thousands of women from conservative backgrounds to support the regime's gender vision. Although initially these women were volunteers, gradually the regime had to create a formal paid staff for a women's wing of the morality police forces, in response to public criticism that, according to the regime's own moral code, male morality police should not be publicly engaging with or monitoring women who are not their close kin. Some women saw this as an ironic 'victory', since the formal employment of women as morality police is already a defeat for the regime, which continues to try to restrict women's public roles and limit mingling between unrelated men and women. Indeed, women morality police have often had to work alongside their male colleagues in pairs. Some feel that since this has created new economic opportunities as well as a source of formal power for some women, the move has made it more difficult to mobilize women as a collective against the regime. However, others believe that the mobilization of women under the fundamentalist banner, paid or unpaid, will likely lead to a questioning and reformulation of fundamentalists' gender ideology 'from within'. Indeed many of the aforementioned progressive reforms took place with the support of and activism by women who were regime supporters (Hoodfar 1999). There is also research from various contexts which documents how women working with Islamist parties has lead to a modification of their gender vision (White 2003; Iqtidar 2008).

Yet, while women are incessantly harangued, fined and even jailed for 'hanging out', for wearing veils that are not perfectly in line with the requirements, for wearing make-up, for speaking with unrelated males, and more, resistance continues. The number of paraders has been increasing and women have managed to expand their occupation of public spaces.[19] The huge participation of women in the protest rallies of June 2009, which was reminiscent of their participation in the 1979 revolution, is an indication of their refusal to be made invisible (Mir-Hosseini 2009). Indeed, even in the face of brute force women have refused to act repentant even though it has cost them dearly, as evidenced by the murder of Zahra Bani-Yaghob, described at the beginning of the chapter. In the words of a female ex-morality police officer, 'there were so many of [these daily contestations] that we simply could not take everyone to the *setaad* (morality police station). [The actions] particularly by older women, were quite clever and often made us the subject of public amusement.' For many young women, and among the urban population, arrest by the morality police is practically a badge of honour, which brings public recognition.

Malaysian women's struggle against religious *fatwas*

Multi-ethnic, multi-religious Malaysia gained independence from Britain in 1957 fairly peacefully and adopted a democratic constitution similar to that of Britain (Andaya and Andaya 2001). Although initially a democratic, self-professed moderate Muslim nation with a successful economy, since the late 1980s Malaysian society has radically transformed through the revival of Islamism in politics. Similar to many other contexts, international developments including the 1970s' oil boom, the Iranian Revolution, and Western countries' support of *mujahideen* in the Afghan war have fostered a legitimacy and vigour to the proponents of Islamism in Malaysia (Abu Bakar 1991; Noor 2003; Abbott and Gregorios-Pippas 2010: 127).

During Mahathir's government (1981–2003), in an effort to maintain popularity in the face of rising support for Islamism, the ruling political parties formed coalitions with Islamists. Some secular parties also made overtures to Islamist groups in order to expand their support base (Abbott and Gregorios-Pippas 2010). Indeed one of the most influential factors contributing to a loss in the secular nature of the Malaysian state has been capitulation by public officials to the insistence of the orthodox *ulama* that the public is not qualified to express opinion on *shari'a* and religion (Abdul Aziz 2010). This has been used as a platform to silence opposition; in response to objections by lay intellectuals and women rights activists to *shari'a* rulings on the grounds that they are unconstitutional, the Ulama Association of Malaysia has charged them with the crime of insulting Islam and warned all violators of harsh consequences (Anwar 2004).

Though they openly intimidate public intellectuals, no public authority has challenged the threats of the *ulama* to freedom of expression. In fact, the *fatwas* (religious pronouncements) of the National Fatwa Council, which exclusively comprises members of the Ulama Association of Malaysia, have now gained the force of law and so any transgressions are legally punishable. Intellectuals, MPs and government officials have grown fearful of making public objections; furthermore, citizens are often unaware of the nature of these *fatwas* which affect various aspects of their lives until after the implementation of *shari'a* laws. Although there are no formal morality police in Malaysia, when morality laws are passed the regular police, many of whom are sympathizers of the conservative religious leaders, act to enforce these laws. The legitimization of restrictive morality discourse also encourages the enforcement of morality norms by non-state actors. Such developments increasingly render religion a powerful political ideology, with serious implications for women, as well as religious and sexual minorities (Abdul Aziz 2010).

Another strategy by Islamist parties has been to participate in local electoral processes to take advantage of local governments' relative autonomy to facilitate the introduction of ultra-orthodox *shari'a* laws at the municipal level. This practice has also been adopted by fundamentalist forces in Indonesia. Over the past two decades, multiple laws which erode women's rights have been introduced at both local and federal levels. In the 1990s, the Malaysian government amended family laws to facilitate polygamy and to limit women's rights regarding marriage, divorce, custody and inheritance (Foley 2004: 58; Anwar 2004; Abdul Aziz 2010). In addition, since the 1990s laws have been passed concerning morality, dress code, and control of women's behaviour and sexuality, particularly at the local level. These laws have increased gender segregation, limited women's public participation and hampered male–female social and economic interaction, particularly outside the major cities (Foley 2004: 58).

In concrete terms this has meant that consensual behaviour associated with women's sexuality has increasingly been targeted for control and repression. For example, in June 1997 under the Islamic Criminal Law Enactment, three Malay women were arrested in Selangor for participating in a beauty contest. Other regions subsequently arrested women under similar legislation (Liow 2009: 59). In the effort to push for further segregation of the sexes, in March 2003 in the state of Kota Bharu a male and a female secondary school student were publicly lashed for conversing in the school canteen. Several local governments have passed laws to segregate sport facilities and ban women's participation in sports that are deemed 'non-feminine'. In 2007 state authorities ruled that under local bylaws Kuala Lumpur could prosecute a Chinese couple for 'indecent activity' in a public park. The argument was that 'kissing and hugging' were not the 'norm' in Malaysia (Liow 2009). Notably non-Muslims and Muslims are treated identically under such policies.

Intermingling between men and women is not the only target; the dress codes and gender presentation of women and men are also being regulated. Perhaps the most notorious recent code is the National Fatwa Council's 2008 ruling that 'tomboyism' – women dressing or behaving 'like men' – is un-Islamic.[20] The *mufti* of northern Perak state, Harussani Idris Zakaria, condemned these women as disrespectful to the faith and claimed that such behaviour leads to homosexuality. Clearly *ulama* hold enough political power to issue 'Islamic' rulings even if there are no precedents within religious practices, and the state seems unwilling to check their power. Intellectuals are intimidated. Thus women are left on their own to contest these breaches of their basic rights.

Another recent attempt to control public expression of 'sexuality' is the attack on Valentine's Day. This day has gained popularity among Muslim youth from Iran to Egypt and Malaysia, in part as a reaction to religious and state authorities' attempts to curb their expression of sexuality. In February 2011 several Malaysian states launched the 'Mind the Valentine Day Trap' campaign, drawing on a 2005 *fatwa* stating that 'the spirit of Valentine's Day celebrations is associated with elements of Christianity and vice activities that are prohibited in Islam'. The *fatwa* has remained on the books, in spite of the Council of Churches of Malaysia's request for its withdrawal (*The Star* online 2011). Despite morality police warnings, hundreds of youth celebrated on 14 February 2011, resulting in many arrests, which could lead to jail terms of up to two years and/or a fine of up to US$280.[21] 'Happy V-Day. Am so grateful for a government that micro-manages my life and does all my thinking', renowned human rights lawyer Malik Imtiaz Sarwar sarcastically tweeted (Looi 2011).

In response, civil society and women's organizations have joined forces and mobilized on multiple levels. A notable example, and particular target of Islamist criticism, is the organization Sisters in Islam (SIS), which has been active since 1988 working on women's rights from within an Islamic framework. They question the authority of *ulama* by using the very same Islamic texts from which *ulama* purport to draw their authority. SIS studies the impact of the morality laws on the lives of women and children and organizes conferences and training sessions presenting woman-centred readings of Islam. They challenge the *fatwas* of the *ulama* and their outdated views as irrelevant to citizens whose complex lives are integrated into the global world. They promote a rights-based approach to women's rights in Islam in conjunction with women in other Muslim contexts and the transnational women's movement. In February 2009, SIS hosted and launched the international campaign *Musawah* (equality), where over 350 women from forty-eight countries visited Kuala Lumpur to build on more than half a century of national women's movements towards the development of an international democratic framework for Muslim family law.[22]

Since their establishment SIS activists have been outspoken against the mobilization of Islam to violate women's rights. SIS integrates human rights and Islamic principles of social justice to argue that all sources of law and public policies including religion and Islam should be subject to extensive public debate. They have been highly vocal against the conservative religious forces that have limited the ability to publically write, speak and debate on Islam to the *ulama* and other supposed Islamic authorities. SIS has argued that such a state of affairs is tantamount to a theocratic dictatorship. They ask, if citizens have the right to speak on political, economic and social issues that shape their lives and rights, then why must they stay silent on matters of religion in deference to the *ulama*? (Anwar 2004: 73).

Algerian women's struggle against
fundamentalists within and without the state

Algerian women's story of struggle against the imposition of fundamentalist gender ideology is a long one. While Islamists initially
tried to impose their vision through the state structure, by the
late 1980s self-proclaimed moral police organized outside the state
and began terrorizing women and liberal forces. During the 1980s
and 1990s, thousands of women were raped, subjected to sexual
slavery, forcibly impregnated and murdered by the fundamentalists
simply for opposing the imposition of the Islamists' morality codes.
Algerian women had precious little support from the Algerian
state, which was preoccupied with ensuring its own survival. The
international community also failed to extend its support, at least
in part because the Islamists were held in high regard as 'freedom
fighters' during the Afghan war with the Soviet Union. Even
organizations such as Amnesty International and Human Rights
Watch were reluctant to bring the plight of Algerian women
to the attention of the international community.[23] Naziha, an
Algerian activist who suffered at the hands of fundamentalists,
reflects: 'principles, freedom, and human rights mean nothing to
Western liberal states when their interests are at risk'.[24] Indeed the
collective consciousness of Algerian women has been coloured by
their realization of how little women's human rights mean when
the national interests of powerful forces are at play. Nonetheless
Algerian women have continued to stand their ground and push
for their rights, then and now. Indeed their struggle has become
even more urgent since the launch of the 2005 'National Reconciliation' policy, which has granted amnesty to many individuals who
have committed atrocities against women and democratic forces.
Furthermore, several known Islamists who have never declared
a change in their gender perspectives now hold ministerial and
other influential posts. To women who have suffered so heavily,
this state of affairs has been unacceptable and a recipe for further
loss of their citizenry rights.

A million Algerian and French citizens died in a bloody anti-
colonial struggle before Algeria won independence in 1962. Women
were pivotal to the success of this struggle. Their bravery was
mythologized across the Middle East and beyond, yet after the

liberation war they were once again relegated to subordinate citizens (Hélie-Lucas 1987). After independence Algerians adopted a welfare state, but, despite the country being a republic, the leaders of the National Liberation Front (FLN) opted for a one-party system, allowing little room for democracy to flourish. With the exception of groups organized around religion, civil society was stifled. Initially petroleum exports fuelled the economy, but debt combined with a lack of sustained economic growth undermined the state's ability to deliver social services. Unemployment rose to unprecedented levels. Political leaders turned to the World Bank and accepted severe austerity measures, cutting government services and increasing disparities; poverty and political unrest followed, some of which was directed against women (Dillman 2000). In 1988, thousands of youth took to the streets protesting inequitable social and economic policies, state corruption and the lack of civil liberties; many died in the ensuing crackdown. Ultimately these events forced the state to amend the constitution, allowing a multiparty parliamentary system. Although religion-based parties were in theory not permitted, several such parties were formed, including the currently outlawed Islamic Salvation Front (FIS). Given the new global legitimacy of Islamic 'freedom fighters' and Islam's revival as a political ideology, the liberal voices that objected were ignored.

In the 1989 local elections FIS and other Islamist parties won over half of the elected seats by promising to fight corruption and to create jobs and affordable housing. Many citizens voted for the Islamic parties in protest against the existing government and the twenty-five-year one-party rule, thus making the Islamist victory inevitable. Where they were elected the Islamists sought to impose *hijab* on female employees and gender segregation throughout the workplace. They banned satellite dishes as a Western source of evil influence and depravity. The vice president of FIS, Ali Belhadj declared that he 'didn't believe in democracy because the only source of power is God – through the Qur'an and not the people; people voting against God's law must be punished since their authority cannot be substituted for that of God' (IWHRLC and WLUML 1999). The hypocrisy of using the elections and a democratic structure to gain access to positions of power was conveniently unaddressed and ignored by Belhadj and other leaders.[25]

It was due to these developments that in 1991, faced with the possibility of FIS winning the national election, the government declared FIS illegal and cancelled the election to protect its hold on power; large segments of women and liberal civil society movements supported the government despite their reservations. They viewed the move, regardless of its initiators' intentions, as a counter-theocracy measure, a yardstick absent from the perspectives of many international observers who criticized the move. Women and girls suffered due to FIS and other fundamentalists' extrajudicial action through the 1980s, while the government and international community stood by. The government had tried to appease Islamists early on by compromising women's rights, and, despite women's vigorous opposition, passed an extremely regressive family law in 1984 which essentially reduced them to subjects of their fathers and husbands. The government also issued a decree that allowed male heads of household to vote on behalf of their wives and daughters (IWHRLC and WLUML 1999). It also gave free rein to conservative Islamists in the Ministry of Education to design the national school curriculum. During the 1980s the government approved an education bill strengthening the Islamic Studies curriculum's emphasis on women's domestic role and female obedience, and removed girls' sports as a required class (Ait-Hamou 2004).

After being declared illegal, FIS and its military wing, which had trained and fought in the Afghan war against Russia in the 1980s, went underground and began a new war against the Algerian state. Civilians at large, women and liberal intellectuals who opposed FIS's vision of an Islamic state were also all targeted. The Islamist Armed Group, working closely with FIS, sent letters to prominent women demanding that they veil and refrain from appearing alone in public; they also proclaimed Western women's clothing and lipstick corrupt. Rather than demanding state accountability for increased unemployment, Islamists blamed women for stealing men's jobs, arousing hostility towards working women and increasing the harassment of women on university campuses. In some towns, Islamists imposed segregation in public spaces, buses and schools, and forced women to wear a black *hijab* or full *abaya*, as in Saudi Arabia (Ait-Hamou 2004).

The state, by not stepping in to protect women, tacitly approved these actions. Non-compliant women were physically attacked, kidnapped and killed, or their families were targeted in retaliation (Bennoune 1997). News of such attacks was publicized as a warning to other women. These self-appointed morality police were responsible for at least 30,000 out of 150,000 estimated civilian deaths, many of whom were women. Among them were teachers, journalists, activists and traditional workers, including Turkish bath attendants, hairdressers, those who refused to veil and women living without an adult male guardian (Bennoune 1997; Ait-Hamou 2004). There were hundreds of cases where young women who refused to veil or appeared unaccompanied were kidnapped into sexual slavery by Islamist soldiers. Escapees who were recaptured were killed as a warning to other captives. Others were left to escape when they were pregnant, knowing this would bring shame on their families. Yet throughout, the Islamist perpetrators claimed their moral vision was a divine 'Islamic' system, superior to democracy.

Having learned that women's rights do not appear on the priority list of most human rights organizations, the Algerian women's movement, with support from the transnational women's movement, has worked tirelessly to draw international attention to the horrific abuses suffered by Algerian women. The words of Tahr Djaout, a journalist who was eventually murdered by fundamentalists, became Algerian women's resistance anthem and motto: 'Silence means death. If you speak out, they will kill you. If you keep silent, they will kill you. So, speak out and die' (cited in Ait-Hamou 2004: 123).

In this context, the most powerful form of resistance for women was to live their everyday lives despite the horrifying violence, and not to allow the Islamists to break their spirit. Women hid their school books in shopping bags, carried a scarf they wryly referred to as 'a convertible *hijab*', and simply refused to stay home and give up the liberties won by previous generations (Lazreg 1994: 195–226; Ait-Hamou 2004). Women also organized nationally, holding public meetings and demonstrations displaying pictures of murdered or abducted women. They warned the nation of the dangers of fundamentalism, provided support for families of murdered and kidnapped women, and aired televised interviews with women who had escaped captivity and who, despite social stigma, told of their sexual slavery, warning Algerians not to be deceived by slogans of 'Islamic social and economic justice'.

Despite death threats, representatives of women activists spoke at the 1993 Vienna tribunal on women's rights abuses.[26] Through their advocacy Algerian women have played a major role in bringing the fundamentalist attacks on women to the attention of conventional human rights organizations and making women's human rights an international concern. The harsh realities of living under fundamentalists' oppression has eroded youth support for political Islamists, although some fundamentalists, with the support of a global Islamist network including al-Qaeda in the Maghreb, continue their acts of violence. Nonetheless, Algerian women have managed to create a public wariness of fundamentalism and public support for the idea of a collectively built democratic system protecting the well-being of all citizens. They decry having to choose between a corrupt government and fundamentalists; a task that has become even more difficult since the creation of the 'national reconciliation' based on a large-scale amnesty for many who were involved in violence against citizens in 2005. In response Algerian women's groups have instigated the annual 'Day Against Forgetting' to remember the women who paid with their lives for refusing to be forced to wear *hijab* or give up their citizenry rights. The women's movement remains vigilant and continues its gender activism and work for democratic reform even as Islamists change tactics and search for other ways to impose their gender vision on society.

Conclusion

Contemporary religious fundamentalism has focused on reviving patriarchal hierarchy; in various Muslim contexts, this has meant attempts to create gender-segregated societies where women are subjects of men. Fundamentalists' rhetoric states that male supremacy is ordained by God, and further that women's bodies are sinful and their public presence a threat to social order, morality and societal well-being. They have thus tried to impose veiling, to limit women's public mobility, and at times women's access to the labour market and even education. Across contexts, they have heralded their singular interpretations of Islam as the only version of Islam

– a version which must remain the purview of religious scholars to discuss and debate, but which must be respected by all. The public has been conspicuously silenced, through harassment, intimidation, detention or physical violence – all justified in the name of 'Islamic justice'. The tools they use are diverse: legislative bodies, formal commissions, police forces, curriculum design and more. This cursory tracing of strategies and institutions used by fundamentalists to enact their vision, as well as of the different ways in which women have resisted, is the first step towards challenging the spread of Islamist fundamentalisms and particularly the institution and practice of moral policing.

Where fundamentalists have either fully or partially become state players, measures to enforce this ideology, including laws and the implementation or expansion of moral policing, have been detrimental to women (and minorities) on many levels. In contexts where a degree of democracy exists, such as in Malaysia and Indonesia, women activists have worked from both secular and religious perspectives on women's rights. While secular women have used international conventions and the discourse of human rights, those working from within a religious framework have used the same religious texts to challenge fundamentalist interpretations. They have also created strong national and transnational networks, within Muslim contexts and globally, to publicize the misogyny and violence of religio-political fundamentalist gender ideology.

Facing stiff resistance and accusations of misogyny, in contexts like Iran or Malaysia where a degree of state legitimacy in the public eye is required, fundamentalists have mobilized segments of women as their political supporters and/or paid employees to assist them in achieving their goals. While the inclusion of women in public life can be read as a small compromise on the part of fundamentalist forces, the long-term consequences of these developments is yet to be determined.

In contexts with little democracy, such as Iran and Saudi Arabia, or where fundamentalist forces are powerful non-state actors, in the name of religion they have forced women to submit to a morality code that violates women's basic human rights. For a host of complex reasons, including limited definitions of political abuse and political action, international human rights organizations have been slow in taking up these abuses. Thus women activists have built and strengthened their connections with transnational women's rights movements to reach out for support, as well as sharing and learning their strategies of resistance, especially where local options for collective actions are limited due to lack of democracy.

In the meantime, well aware of fundamentalists' efforts to impose their gender ideology in the context of everyday life, women activists have turned their mundane routines into arenas of resistance. Using ordinary spaces such as the workplace, sidewalks and parks, and everyday items such as clothing, they challenge the fundamentalist attempts to control their bodies, their behaviour and their public presence. Through small actions, numerous individual women are transforming ordinary public spaces and daily choices into direct points of contestation against often state-supported fundamentalist oppression, cultivating the seeds of change and civil rights in their societies:

> They [the Iranian state] can win the war against the USA and Iraq, but they cannot win the war against women. Our battles for equality over centuries have made us as hard as iron, yet we are as gentle as clouds; we are collective and yet individuals. We find gentle ways to resist, ways they could not have dreamed of. We will win sooner or later. This is not a struggle we can afford to lose, for our sakes, for our daughters' sakes but also for our sons to whom we have given life. (Pouran 47, mother of three, Tehran 2007)

Notes

1. See http://aftabnews.ir/vdca0in49onii.html (accessed 3 October 2011).
2. We are aware of the major controversy on the usefulness of the term 'fundamentalism' and in particular Muslim fundamentalism (Afary 1991; Freedman 1996; Ter Haar and Busattil 2003; Told 2004). Here we are focusing on 'Muslim fundamentalism', which refers to a political perspective that appropriates a rigidly defined religious 'identity' as the basis for overall social organization. Such fundamentalists declare their ideology in accordance with 'divine laws' based on their particular readings of religious texts, and deny the diversity of lived Islam over time and space. Their ideological perspective rejects gender equality and demands a gender-apartheid social system. Proponents of Muslim fundamentalism are dogmatic and intolerant of 'the Other', especially non-Muslims, and notoriously reject principles of universal human rights.
3. Saudi Arabia and Iran are taken as examples of countries where fundamentalist forces are in control of the state. Malaysia is an example

of how attempts to court religious leaders has led to the undue influence of fundamentalists and religious conservatives over legislation and state machinery. Algeria is explored as one example of non-state actors taking it upon themselves to impose their moral code on women through vigilante policing and violence.

4. The office of *Muhtaseb* had to be bought. For example, in 961 CE Qadi al-Shawarib bought the office of al-*Muhtaseb* for 200,000 dirhams per year. He then leased it out at 20,000 dirham per month to make a profit (Floor 1985).

5. This is apparently a pre-Islamic precept that is referred to in the Qur'an (3:114) as a requirement of the 'people of the book', referring to adherents of all the Abrahamic religions: Judaism, Christianity and Islam.

6. Apart from a few Qur'anic references concerning individuals advising their sons, there is no indication of enforcement of this duty.

7. There are four formal legal schools in Muslim jurisprudence. Ibn Hanbal was the founder of one of these schools.

8. Some people, including scholars, prefer to use the term 'Saudi-Wahhabism' to indicate that it was this alliance that led to the establishment and spread of Wahhabism.

9. Indeed Ibn 'Abd al-Wahhab's own father (Salman) – who was a *qadi* – was the first to oppose Wahhabism and criticize his son, in a book entitled *Al-Sawa`iq al-Ilahiyya fi Madhhab al-Wahhabiyya* (The Divine Thunderbolts Concerning the Wahhabi School). Islamic scholars of the time almost unanimously considered Wahhabism as *khawarij* (against Ottoman rule) and they fought against its spread. Egypt, under Ottoman order, invaded Saudi Arabia and conquered Mecca and Medina for a while in an attempt to subdue the Saudi-Wahhabis. In fact it was not until some decades later in the twentieth century that Al-Azhar (a leading scholarly institute in Egypt) accepted Wahhabism as 'legitimately' Islamic, though many theologians have continued their reservations (a point brought to our attention by Dina Jadallah). For a well-grounded overview of these discussions and the position of the Ottoman rulers, see http://benaraby. net/2010/03/10/وثيقة-توضح-تكفير-الخلافة-العثمانية-لل/.

10. Unfortunately the regional voices of feminists in Afghanistan and Pakistan, and organizations such as Shirkat Gah and Women Living Under Muslim Laws (WLUML), who called attention to these atrocities being committed under the guise of 'liberating Muslims and Islam', were dismissed as Westernized and thus inauthentic (Moghadam 2002). This lent even more legitimacy to violent and rigid Islamism on the world stage, and further silenced women who were already resisting the increasing fundamentalism, war and militarism on the ground.

11. Saudi women have launched public campaigns to muster support for challenging the ban as un-Islamic. There is no written Saudi law barring women from driving, but rather many *fatwas* issued by Wahhabi clerics. For more details on the driving protest, see http://yallafinance. com/2011/06/20/the-economic-aspects-of-saudi-women-driving-ban.

12. It was agreed that women from less influential families should not participate

since in the event of arrest that they would likely be treated more harshly than women from elite families. See http://americanbedu.com/2008/06/24/saudi arabia-the-women-who-dared-to-drive (accessed 26 July 2011).

13. See www.wluml.org/node/5920 (accessed 21 July 2011).

14. See www.thenational.ae/news/worldwide/middle-east/women-remain-barred-from-voting-as-saudi-arabia-announces-elections (accessed 3 October 2011).

15. Women have particularly targeted European institutions that claim to support gender equality to recognize their demands for driving rights. Another example is a petition on Change.org (www.change.org/petitions/subaru-stop-selling-cars-where-women-cant-drive) demanding that companies like Subaru stop selling cars to Saudi Arabia until women can drive.

16. The following data are based on two studies on women's public sphere access: 'Women and the law – Iran' (1992–99), and 'Women's empowerment in Muslim contexts' (2006–10). Both studies were carried out by Women Living Under Muslim Laws and compared data on women's social and legal rights across several countries.

17. The regime attempted to introduce mandatory veiling in 1979, but protests by thousands of women forced them to withdraw the initial regulation. It was reintroduced in 1981 (Paidar 1995). See also: www.youtube.com/watch?v=pxGYLk92edY.

18. Ahmadinejad's election in 2005 brought a new faction of extreme religious conservatives to power who have placed *hijab* and gender segregation at the centre of their political ideology (Khatam 2009; Sadeghi 2009).

19. The new commercialized economy that targets women home-makers as primary shoppers has also helped women increase their public presence. See Rendell 1998 for further discussion of this point.

20. See www.wluml.org/node/4844 (accessed 23 August 2011).

21. See www.wluml.org/node/5081 (accessed 22 October 2011).

22. *Musawah*: www.musawah.org. For a brief conference review, see www.youtube.com/watch?v=6fSrxo-9AtE.

23. Yet these same groups had no qualms about denouncing Iran's mistreatment of women, given that Iran was a key Western adversary (Bennoune 1995; Hélie-Lucas 2005).

24. Personal communication with Caroline, an Algerian women's right activist, Montreal, 2007.

25. Not surprisingly, by the 1991 parliamentary election FIS's appeal had fallen to 24 per cent of those who actually participated in the election, yet due to the electoral system they managed to gain 43 per cent of the seats.

26. The transnational women's movement organized a parallel people's tribunal, 'Women's Rights Are Human Rights', in Vienna in 1993. Through this campaign the activists collected hundreds of thousands of signatures in support of women's rights and a considerable number of testimonies on violence against women from sexual abuse to economic violence. This very high-profile campaign increased the formal recognition of women's rights as human rights by the UN (Keck and Sikkink 1998).

References

Abbott, J.P., and Gregorios-Pippas, S. (2010) 'Islamization in Malaysia: Processes and dynamics', *Contemporary Politics* 16(2): 135–51.

Abdul Aziz, Z. (2010) 'Malaysia – trajectory towards secularism or Islamism?', in C. Derichs and A. Fleschenberg (eds), *Fundamentalisms and Their Gendered Impacts in Asia*. Berlin: Friedrich-Ebert-Stiftung, 44–67.

Abu Bakar, M. (1991) 'External influences on contemporary Islamic resurgence in Malaysia', *Contemporary Southeast Asia* 13(2): 220–28.

Abouharb, M.R., and Cingranelli, D. (2007) *Human Rights and Structural Adjustment*. Cambridge: Cambridge University Press.

Afary, J. (1991) 'War against Feminism in the name of the Almighty: Making sense of gender and Muslim fundamentalism', *Dossier: Journal of Women Living Under Muslim Laws* 21: 7–31.

Ait-Hamou, L. (2004) 'Women's struggle against Muslim fundamentalist in Algeria: Strategies or a lesson for survival', in A. Imam, J. Morgan and N. Yuval-Davis (eds), *Warning Signs of Fundamentalisms*. London: Women Living Under Muslim Laws.

Amin, C.M. (2002). *The Making of the Modern Iranian Woman: Gender, State Policy, and Popular Culture, 1865–1946*. Gainesville: University Press of Florida.

Andaya, L.Y., and Andaya, B.W. (2001). *A History of Malaysia*, 2nd edn. Basingstoke: Palgrave Macmillan.

Anwar, Z. (2004) 'Islamisation and its impact on laws and the law making process in Malaysia', in A. Imam, J. Morgan and N. Yuval-Davis (eds), *Warning Signs of Fundamentalisms*. London: Women Living Under Muslim Laws.

Bamdad, B. (1977). *From Darkness into Light: Women's Emancipation in Iran*. Hicksville: Exposition Press.

Bayat, A. (1997) *Street Politics: Poor People's Movements in Iran*. New York: Columbia University Press.

Bayat, A. (2010) *Life as Politics: How Ordinary People Change the Middle East*. Stanford CA: Stanford University Press.

Bennoune, K. (1997) 'SOS Algeria: Women's human rights under siege in faith and freedom: Women's human rights in the Muslim world', in M. Afkhami (ed.), *Faith and Freedom: Women's Human Rights in the Muslim World*. London: I.B. Tauris, 161–74.

Bennoune, K. (2007) 'Secularism and human rights: A contextual analysis of headscarves, religious expression, and women's equality under international law', *Columbia Journal of Transnational Law* 45(2): 367–426.

Bowen, W. (2008) *The History of Saudi Arabia*. Westport CT: Greenwood Press.

Commins, D. (2006) *The Wahabi Mission and Saudi Arabia*. London: I.B. Tauris.

Cook, M. (2000) *Commanding Right and Forbidding Wrong in Islamic Thought*. Cambridge: Cambridge University Press.

Derichs, C., and Fleschenberg, F. (eds) (2010) *Religious Fundamentalisms and Their Gendered Impacts in Asia*. Berlin: Friedrich-Ebert-Stiftung. http://library.fes.de/pdf-files/iez/07061.pdf.

Dillman, B. (2000) *State and Private Sector in Algeria: The Politics of Rent-seeking and Failed Development*. Boulder CO: Westview Press.

Floor, W. (1985) 'The office of *Muhtasib* in Iran', *Iranian Studies* 18(1): 53–74.

Foley, R. (2004) 'Muslim women's challenges to Islamic law: The case of Malaysia', *International Feminist Journal of Politics* 6: 53–84.

Freedman, L. (1996) 'The challenge of fundamentalisms', *Reproductive Health Matters* 4(8): 55–69.

Hélie-Lucas, M. (1987) 'Women, nationalism and religion in the Algerian struggle', in M. Badran and M. Cook (eds), *Opening the Gate: A Century of Arab Feminist Writings*. Bloomington: Indiana University Press.

Hélie-Lucas, M. (2005) 'International: When women's human rights defenders face political non-state actors', www.wluml.org/node/2944 (accessed 11 January 2012).

Hoodfar, H. (1999). *The Women's Movement in Iran: Women at the Crossroad of Secularisation and Islamisation*. London: Women Living Under Muslim Laws.

IWHRLC (International Women's Human Rights Legal Clinic) and WLUML (Women Living Under Muslim Laws) (1999). *CEDAW Shadow Report on Algeria*, www.wluml.org/node/416.

Iqtidar, H. (2008) *Secularizing Islam: Jana'at-e-Islami and Jama'at-ud-dawa in Urban Pakistan*. Illinois: University of Chicago Press.

Keck, M.E., and Sikkink, K. (1998) *Activists beyond Borders*. Ithaca NY: Cornell University Press.

Khatam, A. (2009) 'The Islamic Republic's failed quest for the spotless city', *Middle East Report* 39(250): 44–9.

Lazreg, M. (1994) *The Eloquence of Silence: Algerian Women in Question*. New York: Routledge.

Liow, J. (2009) *Piety and Politics: Islamism in Contemporary Malaysia*. New York: Oxford University Press.

Loukaitous-Sideris, A., and Ehrenfeught, R. (2009) *Sidewalks: Conflict and Negotiation over Public Space*. Cambridge MA: MIT Press.

Maley, W. (ed.) (1998) *Fundamentalism Reborn? Afghanistan and the Taliban*. London: C. Hurst.

Mallick, M. (2011) 'Why aren't Saudi women allowed to drive?' *International Business Times*, www.ibtimes.com/articles/169621/20110626/twitter-facebook-saudi-women-hillary-clinton-drive-youtube-islam-council-petition-legal-freedom-law.htm (accessed 12 January 2012).

Mernissi, F. (1993). *The Forgotten Queens of Islam*. Cambridge: Polity Press.

Mir-Hosseini, Z. (2009). 'Broken taboos in post election Iran', *MERIP Online*, 17 December, www.merip.org/mero/mero121709.

Moghadam, V.M. (2002) 'Patriarchy, the Taleban, and politics of public space in Afghanistan', *Women's International Forum* 25(1): 19–31.

Murphy, C. (2011) 'Saudi driving ban challenge revs up as women take the wheel', *The Star*, 18 June, http://arabawakenings.thestar.com/article/1011185-saudi-driving-ban-challenge-revs-up-as-women-take-the-wheel (accessed 7 July 2011).

Neumayer, E. (2003) 'What factors determine the allocation of aid by Arab countries and multilateral agencies?', *Journal of Development Studies* 39(4): 134–47.

Noerdin, E. (2002) 'Customary institutions, Syariah law, and the marginalisation of Indonesian women', in K. Robinson and S. Bessel (eds), *Women in Indonesia – Gender, Equity and Development*. Singapore: Institute of South East Asian Studies, 179–86.

Noor, F. (2003) 'Blood, sweat and jihad: The radicalization of the political discourse of the Pan-Malaysian Islamic Party (PAS) from 1982 onwards', *Peace Research Abstracts* 41(4): 200–232.

Paidar, P. (1995) *Women and the Political Process in Twentieth-Century Iran*. Cambridge: Cambridge University Press.

Penketh, A. (2008) 'Iran's brutal morality police are growing in power warns nobel prize winner', *Independent*, 7 June, www.independent.co.uk/news/world/middle-east/irans-brutal-morality-police-are-growing-in-power-warns-nobel-izewinner842090.html (accessed 3 October 2011).

Rashid, A. (2001) *Taliban: Militant Islam, Oil and Fundamentalism in Central Asia*. New Haven CT: Yale University Press.

Razavi, S., and Jenichen, A. (2010) 'The unhappy marriage of religion and politics: Problems and pitfalls for gender equality', *Third World Quarterly* 31(6): 833–50.

Rendell, J. (1998) 'Displaying sexuality: Gendered identities and the early nineteenth century street', in N. Fyfe (ed.), *Images of the Street: Planning, Identity and Control in Public Space*. London: Routledge.

Sadeghi, F. (2009) 'Foot soldiers of the Islamic Republic's "culture of modesty"', *Middle East Report* 39(250): 50–55.

Sahgal, G., and Yuval-Davis, N. (eds) (2002) *Refusing Holy Orders: Women and Fundamentalism in Britain*. London: Women Living Under Muslim Laws.

Sidiya, F., and Harawi, W. (2011) 'Adventure behind wheel lands al-Sharif in custody again', *Arab News*, 24 May, http://arabnews.com/saudiarabia/article422616.ece (accessed 20 October 2011).

Starrett, G. (1998) *Putting Islam to Work: Education, Politics, and Religious Transformation in Egypt*. Berkeley: University of California Press.

Ter Haar, G., and Busuttil, J.J (2003) 'Religious fundamentalism and social change. A comparative inquiry', in G. Ter Haar and J.J. Busuttil (eds), *The Freedom to Do God's Will: Religious Fundamentalism and Social Change*. New York: Routledge, 1–24.

Told, M. (2004) 'Catholic fundamentalism, right-wing politics and the construction of womanhood', in A. Imam, J. Morgan and N. Yuval-Davis (eds), *Warning Signs of Fundamentalisms*. London: Women Living Under Muslim Laws. www.wluml.org/sites/wluml.org/files/import/english/pubs/pdf/wsf/05.pdf.

Uwaidah, A.J. (2002) *Najad before Salafi Reform*. Reading: Ithaca Press.

van den Boogert, M.H. (2005) *The Capitulations and the Ottoman Legal System: Qadis, Consuls and Beratlis in the 18th Century*. Leiden: Brill.

White, J.B. (2003) *Islamist Mobilization in Turkey: A Study in Vernacular Politics*. Seattle: University of Washington Press.

Wright, L. (2006) *Looming Tower: Al Qaeda and the Road to 9/11*. New York: Knopf.

Wynn L. (1994) 'Saudi Arabian driving protest in 1991 and its aftermath', Honours thesis, Department of Anthropology, McGill University.

Yamani, M. (1996) *Feminism and Islam: Legal and Literary Perspectives*. New York: NYU Press.

10

'Living sexualities': non-hetero female sexuality in urban middle-class Bangladesh

Shuchi Karim

This chapter explores non-heteronormative sexualities of women in urban middle-class Bangladesh. The title connotes the possibility and realities of multiple sexualities, as desired and/or practised by women at various stages of their lives. My interest lies in exploring sexuality within Bengali society, taking into account cultural norms, values and moralities, in order to assess whether and to what extent non-normative sexualities can/do exist. I concentrate mainly on non-heterosexuality among women in Dhaka and a few other major cities, focusing on lived experiences in the 'private' spaces of family life. As I will describe below, my broader research shows that within the Bengali hetero-patriarchal family-household structure, there are spaces and scope for ambiguity, plural identities and varied performances of gender and sexuality. I argue that there is no simplistic/straightforward mapping of 'queer' versus 'straight',[1] but rather interconnected factors at play – including dynamics of age, class, economic independence and distance from parental family households – which create spaces for women to negotiate their respective life choices, including sexualities.

Bangladesh is a highly patriarchal society in both private and public spheres: women's access to social, economic, political and legal institutions is mostly mediated by men. If women transgress dominant norms for reasons other than economic, they are assumed to be of questionable character and morality, and may face hostile and/or violent consequences (Baden et al. 1994; Muna 2005; Mohsin 2007; Siddiqi 2007; Haq 2008; Azim and Sultan 2010; Mahmud 2010). Rapid urbanization and the rising middle class in major cities such as Dhaka also contribute to a context where maintaining the reputation of families, lineage and *samaj*[2] is paramount, and is significantly predicated on the conduct of female members. Here, the norms upheld by the *samaj* are often at odds with the laws of the country (Blanchet 1996: 31).

The necessity to focus on women from the urban middle class, especially within the framework of the household, has been brought to light by researchers in recent years. The nitty-gritty of family life, of intra-household and intergenerational relations, and the practices surrounding marriage and motherhood within the middle class lifestyle can help us understand new dynamics of intimate relations, sexualities and gender relations in the ever-transforming middle classes (Donner 2008).

Thus the 'inside' or 'private' space of the family household, a unit that still represents the base and core of Bengali society, is an appropriate focus for exploring female sexualities, as one significant location among the 'multiple sites where sexuality has been embedded' (Nair and John 1998: 1).

Using 'snowball' sampling[3] to select interviewees, I documented the life stories of twenty-six women aged between 20 and 61.[4] Sixteen of the women were non-heterosexual; ten were unmarried heterosexual women (aged 25 plus).[5] While the focus of this chapter is on non-heterosexual women, single heterosexual women's voices offer vital reference points for understanding normative female sexuality within the Bengali socio-cultural context – primarily because of their defiance of norms concerning marriage. The inform- ants in this category were middle- to upper-middle-class women, with higher education and white-collar jobs. The non-heterosexual women included three distinct groups based on how they labelled or identified themselves: (1) *shomo-premi* (love for the same) women; (2) lesbians (who identified themselves using the English term); and (3) women who do not claim any non-heterosexual identity label. The *shomo-premi* group (four interviewees) comprised educated, middle-class women with white-collar jobs, familiar with global sexuality rights politics, discourses and activism. All are members of a same-sex-oriented women's support group that rejects sexual-identity labels such as lesbian. The 'lesbian' group (five interviewees) comprised commercial sex workers (somewhat less educated)[6] who identify using the English term 'lesbian' as a strategic activist move in the hope of being able to access sexual-rights-related development programmes in Bangladesh. The third group of women (seven interviewees) is not affiliated with any group, either because they are uncomfortable with aspects of their sexuality and with labelling themselves, and/or because they are not aware of sexual identity discourses, due to lack of exposure and/or language.

While using 'middle class' as a generic term is problematic given the varied, non-economic cultural specifics that characterize the actual components of this group, in the South Asian/Bangladeshi context, the middle-class stratum is not delineated solely by income level but also through values, cultural affinities, educational achievements, aspirations, and so on. The commercial sex worker informants we worked with have monthly incomes from 10,000 taka (approximately US$120) upwards, and live in comfortable households located in Dhaka's suburbs; most importantly, they maintain and aspire to a 'respectable middle-class social image' for themselves as well as for their children.

The chapter is divided into three main sections. The first briefly looks at women's gender and sexuality as constructed through Bengali middle-class cultural norms and practices. The second section explores how individual women accommodate and perform their non-heteronormative lives within the domestic/family sphere, especially considering the prevailing norms around marriage for women. The third section examines the social constraints faced by women with non-normative sexualities and the strategies they adopt in order to assert their agency.

Construction of Bengali women's sexuality

What constitutes 'acceptable' female sexuality in Bangladesh? The code of conduct that shapes female sexuality is based on concepts of shame and modesty, and defines marriage as the normative path of female adulthood. While the myth of a 'liberal, modern, progressive' Bengali identity has taken hold among the burgeoning urban middle class (Kamruzzaman and Ogura 2008), in practice specific restrictions on female sexuality continue to prevail in this population. It is uncommon to see pubescent and post-pubescent urban middle- class girls playing and moving about in public, and their physical activities are often restricted to walks in groups or pairs within a designated area. The works of White (1992), Blanchet (1996) and Karim (2007) on women and households show that girls' mobility is not only restricted, monitored and chaperoned by family members, but also that they enjoy fewer homo-social activities compared to boys of similar age and background. Girls have very limited access to sport, are less involved in independent outdoor activities and are constantly being 'groomed' into femininity, in sharp contrast to norms of masculinity, which characteristically include the acceptance of restlessness and unruly public behaviour. This is even more so for urban locales such as Dhaka, where open space is scarce and the threat of violence against women is real (Blanchet 1996; Karim 2007).

Lady Bug (aged 26)[7] illustrates the restrictions imposed in such a context. She is a single, heterosexual woman from a modern, urban, upper-middle-class background who struggled against dominant expectations within her family and household concerning what constitutes a 'good, normal, moral, feminine girl'.

> I played with male cousins, and loved playing outside with them most of the time. My female cousin was more feminine, and into girlie games like doll's house, etc. One time I was playing outside with my other cousins when my cousin wanted me to play with her inside, which I refused. When she complained about me to her mum, my *khala* [aunt] came and scolded me, and I asked why couldn't my cousin come out and play with us. In reply she told me 'because my daughter is a normal girl, unlike you, who are a *hijra*'. I was 7 and had no idea what the word *hijra* meant ... so I asked my mum, and she answered that it is something in between male and female ... and almost for a year I had this fear of waking up to a growing penis.

The use of the term *hijra* here is significant, indicating the possibility of sexual 'abnormality' for a girl who is not conforming to feminine norms; however, it is also a mechanism of intimidation used by an authority figure to discipline the respondent, placing her in a marginalized position within the gendered structure of the household.

Whatever physical space is available to girls is further limited in the urban context. Most of the interviewees confirmed that efforts are always made to keep young girls as non-sexual or as asexual as possible, through monitoring of their activities, their mobility and the spaces they may access; restricting knowledge of sex/sexuality; and minimizing interaction with the opposite sex. Mechanisms include denial of information (or providing false information), fear, intimidation and coercion. The 'pure' versus 'whore' duality is internalized by young girls through this process; they are continually warned of the possible loss of respectability and the threat of being perceived and labelled as a *bajaar er meye* (market girl) – prostitute. Social class is very much at play and gendered notions of piety, sobriety and modesty are emphasized for all female family members.

In the strict heteronormative structure of middle-class Bengali households, the concept of privacy and private space is highly gendered, with most privileges afforded to men. Women's sexuality is disciplined, controlled and monitored from within the family, because it is viewed with suspicion, mistrust and as inherently problematic. Women's sexual desires, needs and assertion are negated outside the heteronormative framework: women are defined by their family relationships, with marriage playing a key role (White 1992). As Blanchet (1996), Gulrukh and Chowdhury (2000), and Muna (2001) have shown, the Bangladeshi middle class tends to uphold its moral norms and control its members within the 'protective' realm of the household. It is within this space that gender normativity and sexual practices are given primary meanings, with marriage being central to expressions of sexual desire.

While marriage is the preferred option by far, celibacy, and preferably asexuality, is expected of unmarried women in a context where cultural norms dictate that daughters remain under parental supervision, living within the parental household until they start their own *shongshar* (family household). Irrespective of the age of a single woman (but especially if she is within the age bracket of what is socially perceived as 'marriageable' and reproductive) or of her income capacity, 'character' (i.e. socio-sexual reputation) is to be protected. Unless parents are affluent enough to provide a semi-detached living space, a single woman cannot negotiate much private space where she can be an autonomous sexual individual.

Kamrun (single, heterosexual, aged 33) notes her frustration with her unsuccessful negotiation for a personal space:

> I did indeed want to have a place of my own and I discovered that (a) people consider you to have loose morals if you want to live on your own, and (b) no one wants to rent out to a single woman. Even in university (where I teach), I can't apply for a flat unless I have a husband.

The family household is at the core of both class and gender relations. It is the basic unit through which family members enter into society, and performs several, perhaps somewhat contradictory, functions: 'it gives people a common identity, but not necessarily common interests, and it also divides them into specific roles and places within the hierarchy' (White 1992: 120). Kamrun (and a few other single heterosexual informants) failed in her negotiations to try to live more independently, and soon went abroad to pursue higher education, which allowed her to live autonomously for a time. Her example illustrates the dilemma and tension between women's desires for independence in terms of space and lifestyle choices, on the one hand, and the fear of losing the benefits of 'membership' within the *samaj* and social class, on the other.

Sexuality and non-hetero sociality

Bengali culture has a history of *sakhi* (intra-female friendship), and *shakha* (intra-male friendship) – intense homo-social bonds are socially legitimate.[8] This social acceptance of strong same-sex friendship bonds also suggests that homosexual desire is not excluded from societal consciousness (Connell 1992). However, male and female homosexuality[9] is preferably ignored, and remains legally punishable by the Sodomy Law (Penal Code section 377).[10] Interestingly Law 377 is not generally seen as problematic by the LGBTQ community, or among my interviewees, as only one case has been brought under this law.[11] The combination of social tolerance of close same-sex bonds and denial of non-normative sexualities allows their existence, as long as they do not openly surface and individuals live according to the dominant markers of social morality, and remain respectable members of their *samaj*.

That being said, social reactions to non-normative sexuality are highly gendered. An example of the 'accommodation' of male homosexuality can be drawn from my conversation with peri-urban brothel sex workers in Faridpur,[12] who discussed male homosexual practices within the brothel community[13] matter-of-factly, with no ridicule, shock or concern. The multiplicity of male sexuality was apparently accepted, and did not seem to involve any reductionism of male social identity (unlike, for example, 'businessman' or 'shopkeeper'). Same-sex male sexual behaviour was simply termed *obbhyash* (a 'tendency' or practice). In contrast, when female homosexuality was mentioned, it raised eyebrows, and also generated ridicule, contempt and a questioning of religious morality (as well as hint of perversion on my part for even asking such a question). Further discussion revealed that among these brothel workers female homosexuality is recognized but not tolerated (female couples had in fact been banished from the brothel). A few of the brothel workers to whom I spoke admitted having intimate partnerships of 'love' with female colleagues, involving *ador* (caresses), the sharing of everything from food to clothing, feeding each other with their own hands (a sign of extreme care and motherly affection), dependency, and heartbreak when the intimate friend left the brothel. But I was told categorically that it couldn't be sexual, because that would be dirty and perverted. Nevertheless, within the broader sex industry female same-sex relations are believed to be widely practised (according to the sex workers interviewed for this essay), even though they are condemned, especially if they become public. Commercial sex worker lesbians who took part in this research shared their experiences of violence, discrimination and sanctions from within the sex worker community[14] for attempting to organize themselves as 'lesbian' women within the sex industry in Dhaka.

Interviewees employed various strategies in their expression of non-heteronormative sexuality. These include identifying as gay/*shomo-premi*/lesbian; defying marriage norms within the parameters of 'straight' sexuality; refusing to categorize themselves through sexual identification while claiming to be 'just sexual'; and by maintaining an asexual image that is simultaneously respected and suspected. Whatever the strategy, non-normative life choices are in fact a commentary on the normative model as it deconstructs heterosexual dominance and its conceptual stability. The following section looks into the real lives of a sample group of non-heterosexual women in urban middle-class Bangladesh.

Living non-heterosexualities in the household

From isolation to negotiation to independence

Our interviewees related the discovery of their sexualities and at-traction to other women as encounters with the self, which brought awareness of particular desires but also marked the recognition of difference in the context of a powerfully dominant model of compulsory heterosexuality. The process engendered dilemmas and internal conflict for many of the women to whom we spoke, as they struggle to come to terms with their feelings, erotic desires and sexual behaviours. Below are three testimonies that highlight the challenges faced by women who struggle against a backdrop of social constructions that demonize, or at least stigmatize, non-heterosexual identity.

Flora: 'All my life I felt that I was the only woman here'

Flora's story is a revealing example of a woman's sexual discov-ery through different phases of her life – from inner conflict to heterosexualization to the ultimate acceptance of her non-heterosexual identity. Her exposure to alternative identities and options for non-normative lifestyles, as well as the acquiring of new language tools and the ability to access information readily, appear to have been crucial to the process. Now 60 years old, Flora is a self-identified *nari shomo-premi* (women-loving woman). She is an activist and the founder of a support group for women in same-sex relationships, and is a deeply religious/spiritual follower of Islam. She has had a successful professional career in the development sector. She leads an independent life and enjoys her own apartment. Brought up in a rather conservative family in the southern part of Bangladesh, a region which was and is quite conservative (for example, in her village in the 1960s girls did not continue schooling post-puberty), she proved to be a rebel. At the age of 14, Flora was married off to a poorly educated man ten years her senior, very different from herself. After the wedding the couple moved to another small town and she enrolled in a girls' school, where Flora became involved in a love relationship with a schoolmate. In her words, a classmate 'knocked'[15] at her, and she responded. Though there was nothing sexual between them, it was nevertheless a very close, affectionate relationship: they exchanged secret love letters, shared snacks, held hands and relished each other's company. Only once did her 'friend' kiss her.

Flora soon left her husband and small-town life to pursue higher education in Dhaka. As an undergraduate she fell in love with a female friend and they shared a committed relationship – to the degree that they planned to live together after graduation, and started collecting household items for their future together. Flora's girlfriend proved to be bisexual and she began dating a man, whom she subsequently married and left the country with in her early thirties. At this time, Flora won a scholarship to study in Europe, where she encountered people who were open about sexuality and who introduced her to the international sexual rights movements. She became friends with another female student, who took her to conferences on sexuality and helped her learn more about the issues. They also had a sexual relationship, 'my first proper sexual relation with any woman'.

> I never thought my interest in women was something exceptional, abnormal or extra-ordinary – I have understood this as spontaneous and natural and right because it felt right to me. What other people were/are doing, is never my concern, but I do what I think is right! All my life I felt that I was the only woman here, in this country, who was like this.... I would look for others, but could not find ... but again, I used to think, there must be other women like me, because I have had women who were attracted to me, I had girlfriends who loved me as well ... where are these people, who are these women ... where do I find them? How does one find them?

This quest for similar 'others', a reference point of normalcy or a search for community, was commonly expressed by my interviewees. Such a quest is filled with dilemmas that derive from social constructions and an internalized notion of 'normal' desire as heterosexual. But the women also expressed experiencing conflict as to whether their sexual orientation is essentialist or a later-life development stemming out of other experiences (for example, sexual violence or other negative heterosexual experiences). Some of the women I interviewed appeared to believe that sexual orientation can be compromised, and reoriented or negotiated – that if enough effort is made and one 'gives it a chance' desire can be heterosexualized. Much of this inner conflict no doubt stems from living in a very restrictive, heterosexual, male-dominated and highly religious society wherein women have no point of reference, in discourse or in practice, pointing towards possibilities for non-heterosexual identity. Because of the prevailing rule of absolute marriage-normativity, most Bangladeshi women, whatever their sexual orientation, will marry and practise heterosexuality.

Mukta: 'loving the wrong person – a woman'

The narrative of Mukta, a 32-year-old woman, highlights the heterosexualization process and marriage-normativity as active mechanisms of denial of one's sexual subjectivity. Mukta's lack of language skills and ability for self-expression, as well as the absence of any reference point for non-normative identities, illustrates why many non-heterosexual women remain invisible and closeted in Bangladesh. Mukta is a divorced[16] woman from Sylhet, one of the most conservative districts of Bangladesh. She is a middle-class college dropout and lives with her conservative, religious family. She had been in love with her friend's elder sister (a married woman with adult children, referred to here as B) for over twelve years at the time of our interview. She sees herself as 'unnatural'; since her formal Bengali language skills are limited and she has no knowledge of English, she doesn't know where to look for information on her – as she puts it – 'type' of desire, nor how to articulate it. Mukta says that she has never had sexual relations with B, who doesn't approve of 'unnatural' sex or sexual desires, which she considers sinful. Mukta doesn't know how two women can have a sexual relationship, but she feels that the desire in her body for B can find a way to express itself.

> I am a very sexy woman, I have a lot of sexual desire, and I know this about me. I want to have sex and I want to satisfy my sexual needs … but I love this 'wrong' person – a woman – and I don't know how two women can have sex with each other. I know that I want B and I want to have sex with her. I sometimes joke with B that, 'if I was a man, I would have raped you!'

Mukta's association of sexual desire with sexual violence is interesting for several reasons: first, it is a cue to broader social acceptance of male sexual violence as an expression of masculine 'uncontrollable' sexual desire. Second, it expresses heterosexualization of desire and the notion that penetrative sex is the primary if not sole form of sexual expression, thus constructing women's same-sex desire as 'non-sexual' and/or non-threatening. Third, it signals suppression of female same-sex erotic love because it cannot seem to find 'acceptable' or understandable expression in the heteronormative framework of sexuality.

Age, education and urbanization influence the assertion of sexual desires and identities, as can be seen through Bani's story. Bani is in her early thirties, living outside her hometown in Dhaka with a respectable job and financial independence that affords her a safe, independent living space to share with same-sex partners. The difference between Bani and Mukta, who are of the same age group, lies in their respective educational backgrounds, economic situations and location. Unlike Bani, Mukta is constrained by her lack of education and economic independence: she has no job, lives with her parental family, and relies on financial support from brothers – all of which is seen as 'normal' for unmarried middle-class women in conservative Bengali society. These circumstances do not avail her of opportunities that a bigger city, like Dhaka, or the connectedness that jobs, supportive social circles and education can offer.

Lesbian sex workers have very different narratives concerning sexuality and sexual identity formation. All five interviewees in this group said they had experienced strong female friendships since childhood or adolescence but were not aware at that point of any 'telltale' signs of homoerotic desire. Most of the women had either married at an early age or went to Dhaka and became commercial sex workers for socio-economic reasons. Common to all these is that each spent at least a few years in state-sponsored 'vagabond' or 'correction' centres (now known as 'rehabilitation centres', where street children sex workers are sent to be 'reformed'). While strong friendships and partnerships are forged in these all-female units, the interviewees said their experiences in the centres did not explain their 'lesbian' identity, noting that they in fact had access to men within the premises, and had heterosexual encounters prior to and after their time in these facilities. However, interviewees did recognize that during their years in the correctional system – an environment devoid of resources, compassion and support – inmates had only each other for comfort and forged deep bonds which offered more than sex. Though they all had their first same-sex erotic encounters in this context, it was the female camaraderie and love that endured after they were released from the institutions. And, though sexual relations between inmates were commonplace in the correctional centres, they had to be hidden from the authorities, who addressed such 'deviant acts' and 'abnormalities' with strict discipline – for example, interviewees described punishments such as being tied up across balcony grilles, or being suspended from a tree branch and flogged until 'guilt' was admitted.

The narration of the abuse, trauma and humiliation of being imprisoned as a 'vagabond' or a sex worker, and punished for one's sexual choices, was matter-of-fact and resigned, often accompanied by a sad smile. But it was also evident that this period in their lives shaped these women's resolution to stick to what felt 'right' to them, and once free they all set up homes with female partners and continued as heterosexual sex workers. Most of these interviewees share the desire of most Bangladeshi women for motherhood and either already have biological and/or adopted children or plan to do so someday. Interviewees who had children at the time of the research did not see the absence of a father or the all-women set-up as problematic, but at the same time said they did not expose the sexual aspect of their relationships to their children, describing this as something children do not need to know – similar to mainstream heterosexual middle-class families. However, perhaps somewhat contradictorily, the sexual nature of the women's profession is not necessarily kept secret (these households are actually located in areas dedicated primarily to the sex industry), though they make efforts to conceal their conjugal same-sex relationships.

Despite their marginalized status on three fronts – as women, sex workers and lesbians – these women appear extremely reso-lute, strategic and pragmatic, especially in their networking and organizational skills. In their private lives, the couples enacted a heterosexual structural model of 'husband and wife', though all the women maintained conventionally feminine appearances and attire, in part a function of their roles as heterosexual commercial sex workers. Though none of the interviewees articulated any desire to express a more masculine physical persona, several mentioned the desire to 'live like a man', perhaps a reflection of a yearning for the power that men hold in hetero-patriarchal societies.

Class differences certainly affect interviewees' awareness of their sexual subjectivities. While female-headed households are not uncommon in Bangladesh, especially due to economic migration (both internal and external), they are less common among the educated middle class. While our data suggest sex worker lesbians maintain female-couple headed households, other *shomo-premi* women with children are more appropriately termed 'single mothers', as they do not share households with female partners. However, all the mothers we interviewed have their respective parental families involved in their everyday household affairs to some degree. While the concepts of same-sex marriage, cohabitation and same-sex co-parenting do not readily translate into the Bangladeshi social-legal context, clearly the sex workers who participated in our study most closely resemble models for these practices.

'Private social lives': creating space for the socio-sexual self

Social networks and safe social environments are crucial to any marginalized group; for non-normative/non-heterosexual women these provide contexts for organizing, for debating the politics of sexual rights and identities, and for extending mutual support. The following section explores how the women in our study strategically manipulate heterosexual norms such as sex segregation/homosociality to create such shared spaces for negotiating sexual identity and building lives that reflect their own choices.

Problematics of sexual identity

Identity is fluid and the narratives of the women in this study suggest that they make strategic decisions to move in and out of different sexual identities (Holiday 1999; Eves 2004). The *shomo-premi* women – the most visible, educated and professional among my interviewees – debate the label 'lesbian' in terms of political correctness and its political usefulness in the broader sexuality rights movement/framework. They prefer to describe themselves as *shomo-premi* ('love for the same') – emphasizing 'love'. While a few interviewees used the term 'lesbian' to describe their sexual identities, they refused the notion of restricting themselves to one fixed identity. The issue of labelling was debated during a workshop entitled 'Gay Women: Issues and Concerns – Perspectives from Bangladesh'.[17] The discussion, which ranged from lesbian identity to invisibility to survival mechanisms, was summed up this way:[18]

- 'Lesbians in Bangladesh prefer the term *nari shomo-premi*' (women-loving women).
- 'The relationship between two women is spiritual, mental, and social. Sex is just a part of it.'
- 'Image also depends on the term that we use' (i.e. terms used for sexual identities need to have less of a sexual connotation).
- 'Female homosexuality issue is silent, invisible' (i.e. it is not talked about and is not on the social radar).
- The term 'lesbian' is used in international communication (i.e. they reject the English term, but its practical use in international level communication and participation is recognized).
- 'Same-sex love does not occur due to lack of interest from the opposite gender. This is something which is built in the heart.'
- 'Female sexuality is more fluid. So the lesbian identity is also fluid.'

Our interviews clearly show that the interviewees' conceptions of gender roles and of their own femininity have been moulded by the traditional role of women in Bengali society – where women's projection of overt sexuality, or any emphasis on female sexual desire, is not welcome. Thus women as the epitome of love, affection, loyalty and sacrifice laced with patience dominate their notions of female sexualities and how these can be asserted. The recognition that women are sexual – and in this case sexual in a way that is deemed 'deviant' – is understood to undermine the mainstream notion of 'respectable female sexuality', which is seen to transcend the sexual and align more with the spiritual. Thus *shomo-premi* women want to distinguish themselves from the overtly sexual *shomo-kaami* (gay) culture (*shomo*, same; *kaami*, desiring/lustful/lover). They shun the *shomo-kaami* label, used commonly as a generic term for homosexuality (and implying male homosexuality) precisely because they do not want their sexual lives to be seen as the main marker of their identity. Their approach is a holistic one wherein sexual identity is one aspect of their life choices within the mainstream framework of femininity and within the Bengali cultural context that constructs women as caring, loving, soft, home-bound, home-makers and as not overtly sexual. However, and very significantly, they expand their push against the boundaries of this framework by asserting sexual agency, which is not an aspect of the mainstream construction of Bengali femaleness. *Shomo-premi* women thus struggle for the right to choose their partners and to live with respect and dignity without facing sanctions.

The sex workers usually use Bangla terms such as *nari-premi* (love for women) or *bon* (sister) to describe themselves, but have more recently learned the term 'lesbian' through various intervention programmes designed for sex workers (for example, HIV/AIDs prevention initiatives). Their move towards affiliation with a broader platform of sexual rights activities has engendered their use of the English label 'lesbian' due to its universal currency. The third group of interviewees, the so-called 'non-heterosexual women without any label', are women who either have no term in their vocabulary for their situation (because in Bangla there is no popular term expressing women's same-sex desire and because their knowledge of English is limited), or feel they are in sexual transition and do not conform to one single sexual identity, as expressed by the following two women:

> I would like to know if I am lesbian or not – so that I could get out of my dual life – this sense of guilt and shame. But whatever might be the interpretation or identity or even the opinion of the society regarding my sex life, I know this is what gives me joy. (Rima, aged 25)

> Nowadays, they have so many names for this … homosexual, girl-on-girl, etc. … but I cannot think of myself in those terms, or categorize myself by those names. (Tamanna, aged 29)

Because the rigid construction of femininity in Bangladesh defines marriage and motherhood as intrinsic to achieving womanhood, women with non-heterosexual or non-heteronormative identities express discomfort in labelling themselves outside the normative framework of sexual identity.

Agency, strategy, negotiation and resistance:
reworking social norms

In the Bengali context, women with non-heterosexual desires often suppress, delay or never fulfil them, allowing prescribed gender ideology to take precedence (a marked difference to men in similar situations, if we can extrapolate from the Indian context (Nayar 2007). This derives from the expectations related to gender roles and performativity within the heteronormative structures of sex, sexualities and genders. It often took years for the women we interviewed to recognize and come to terms with their sexual desires, and a great deal of internal debate and negotiation to accept their sexual identities. It is arguable that men in South Asian contexts have an easier time negotiating non-normative sexualities (Nayar 2007; also see quotation from interviewee Nahar below) than women. For example, it took Flora, Parveen and Nahar each almost forty years to arrive at a point where they could simultaneously juggle gender roles and duties while achieving satisfaction in their personal lives. These women long denied their needs for fulfilling intimate relationships before achieving economic independence, a degree of privacy, and respect from their families. In part this is because women in Bangladesh face intense pressure to conform to heteronormative roles early on, but this pressure decreases as they age. After the age of 30 a woman's chances of marriage are slimmer; expectations of motherhood decrease as a woman reaches her forties. By middle age, if women have managed a career and achieved some economic independence, even though they continue to be perceived as awkward and strange, they are also left alone. It was at this point in their lives that some of the interviewees found ways to live their sexualities.

The following section looks at how these women strategize and negotiate the difference phases of their lives, making use of existing gender norms. Two prevailing norms in Bangladesh society are especially salient in the processes of women's experiences of non-normative sexualities: sex segregation and family/household structure. The prevailing homo-sociability engendered by sex segregation can offer opportunities and arenas for women in same-sex relationships to be together while keeping up the appearance of an asexual performative femininity, though surveillance and control over women by family, especially non-normative women (both heterosexual and non-heterosexual) and those who remain unmarried, is marked. The non-heterosexual women we interviewed for the most part accept the centrality of family and the strategic importance of incorporating their families into their lives in order to maintain social reputation, order and respectability.

Keeping it 'under the radar': making use of homo-sociability

Nahar, a lawyer and feminist activist in her late forties, lives independently in Dhaka. Originally from a smaller town, she spent her high school and university life in female student residences. She exemplifies how education, relative economic independence and increasing age allow women to assert sexual agency, and also how homo-sociability (combined here with class) allows women to maintain same-sex relations without overtly challenging prevailing norms which prescribe asexuality to unmarried women:

> Girls' hostels and having a room of one's own (as a senior student) made it easier to meet friends. Being in university gave a lot of opportunities: to study, play together, go to sports complexes … etc., but once university was over, there was no reason or opportunity to stay together, or sleep over, etc. In Bangladesh, lesbians have no 'date life', there is no opportunity to date or to meet others … maybe the players[19] have a group, where they can spend time together, or sleep with each other – that is all. There is no security for our kind of relations. It would be easier to be a gay man in Bangladesh to get sex or even a long-term relationship – I would not have to care much about who thinks about what!

The question of security is a crucial one; though homo-sociability provides women opportunities to be together, it by no means guarantees that women can enjoy safe intimacy. Nahar's reference to 'security for our kind of relations' points to how insecure same-sex relationships are under the pressure of heterosexual norms in Bangladesh. While a gay man may more easily combine heterosexual marriage with homosexuality, this is much harder to do for women with same-sex desires or relationships, who often bow to marriage pressure. For example, while Nahar has always been self-assured and assertive in terms of her sexual identity, she is nevertheless challenged by the pressures of prevailing gender norms, and her relationships have all ended with her female partners leaving her for a heterosexual life: a male lover or marriage:

> They all told me in the end that 'I find our relationship abnormal, unnatural, tasteless – it feels repulsive… I don't know why I got involved in this relationship and/or you, and it is sinful, I feel like I have sinned' – and none of these women was religious, or at least practising, but in the end they always referred to religion to prove that it was all wrong and that it was a sin.

Religion is central in many Bangladeshi women's lives, and there are ways that individual woman have negotiated with religious norms and rules that conflict with sexual desires and identities. Mukta, for example, wanted to be part of this research in order to 'talk out' her secrets, and find out whether she was 'satanic and unnatural'. But in fact she had already resolved this tension by herself:

> I never turned out to be that religious. *Mullahs'* children don't need to be *mullahs* and I don't think I had to be like my father – I am a human being and I have my limitations, and I do commit occasional sins – but I do say my prayers; for the rest, I am fine with myself!… I might look like an old-fashioned, backdated woman from outside, but I know how 'fast'[20] I am from inside. I have a very different sense of 'sin' in me; I don't consider myself as a sinner – maybe mad – but not a sinner.

Bani, born into a Buddhist family, believes that because her religion has relatively less rigid socio-sexual norms she has escaped many disciplinarian aspects of familial life regarding gender and sexuality. Bani, who is not from Dhaka but studied and has a job in the city, lives outside the more usual family supervision and close proximity of relatives that is normally almost mandatory for single women. She has had live-in relationships with other women, an arrangement that made use of homo-sociability to camouflage the intimate sexual nature of these relationships. She also credits her higher education and choice of a 'respectable' career in teaching, which has made relatives and family more cautious about interfering with her personal life.

Achieving a life outside of conventional sexual norms does not seem possible for women without a renegotiation of gender roles and family structures, yet striking a balance is difficult since 'family support, acceptance and love are central to a happy life with self-made choices' (Flora). For 60-year-old Flora, staying under the public radar is her strategy for living on her own terms. 'In Bangladesh you can be yourself. As long as you don't stir the system they will let you be.' Flora has had intimate relationships, and lived with a former partner in her own apartment. She recognizes that her personality, professional career and education make her appear respectable and allow the acceptability of her current status. At this point in her life she feels her family and others no longer intrude into her life. Her front door sports a 'women in same-sex relationship' sticker; this is in fact a statement she also makes without words. Flora underlines that personal relationships with families is crucial to bring about more acceptance. Her own solid relations with her parents and siblings, and the fact that they value her as a person and love her unconditionally, has made it easier for them to accept her life choices.

The potential advantages afforded by homo-sociability are evident in the case of Parveen (aged 51), who is currently in a relationship in which her female partner is somewhat part of her household's everyday life (her partner is married with children, living in a heterosexual family household). Parveen is divorced with a teenage daughter, and her household includes her mother. Since she is not romantically involved with any man, her sexuality is assumed to be non-existent, as is expected of single women. Parveen 'came out' to her mother and daughter last year; their initial shock gradually diminished. The couple's separate households do not overtly challenge heteronormative appearances, and Parveen's mother's presence in her house actually makes it easier for her to maintain an unquestioned reputation.

While female sex workers in same-sex relationships are embedded in the same hetero-patriarchal social context, their interpretations and performances of gender and heteronormativity reflect their marginalized position as sex workers. Their status at the bottom of the hetero-patriarchal hierarchy shapes their household arrangements and relationships within a broader societal/familial context that highly values kin and community networks. These women and their households form a very close-knit community of 'sister' (lesbian) sex workers, which functions as an extended family that helps them maintain multiple social–sexual identities. The support derived from these networks helps them cope with a variety of demanding roles, which include: keeping the appearance of 'respect-able' working women when visiting the village family home;[21] acting as responsible mothers; being involved in a sex workers' network (providing safety in instances ranging from client violence to police cases); and maintaining a couple relationship with another woman within the home. Living with another woman is compliant with homo-sociability, but it is the immediate community of sex workers, who prefer to live in clusters, that provides for a sense of space and freedom. This contrasts with mainstream 'respectable' middle-class existence that requires supervision and surveillance of women living outside matrimonial arrangements. If family support is crucial to many educated, middle-class non-heterosexual women, for 'lesbian' sex workers it is their immediate community that forms a 'family' safety net and supports the maintenance of same-sex family households.

Conclusion

This chapter has attempted to explore the creation, dynamics and operation of private 'spaces' created by non-heteronormative/non-heterosexual women from their own perspectives – investigating the boundaries of gender and sexual spatiality in urban, middle-class Bangladesh. As the narratives show, erotic desires can find multiple expressions, especially in urban locations. Based on my interviews, I argue that multiple, ambiguous and paradoxical 'sexual spaces' exist within middle-class family households. These settings constitute socio-symbolic worlds within which diverse sexual desires, identi-ties and practices can be/are accommodated. The assumption that dominant heterosexuality implies absolute power over the Other – in this case non-heterosexual/non-normative women in Bangladesh – is challenged by the everyday lives of my respondents. While hetero-normativity certainly dominates social space and produces/maintains control over power/spatial structures, this power is not absolute. Interviewees repeatedly demonstrate that their skills – associated with a thorough knowledge of the norms governing their situations relative to age, class, location and gender – are effective in navigating the demands of a hetero-patriarchal framework. Their flexibility in accommodating normative categories when required (through dress,

mannerism, marriage, child-rearing and fulfilling gender expectations and responsibilities) allows them to live their sexuality more
or less successfully. Homo-sociability and gender segregation offer
a protective cover to both men and women involved in same-sex
relations, as long as they conform on the surface to heteronormative
roles.

Women's same-sex desires are not only ignored or denied in
Bangladesh generally; mainstream society seems unable to recognize
such desires or practices. And, regardless of sexual orientation,
women of childbearing age who resist predominant gender ideals
(especially marriage) are seen as social anomalies. However, respectability and socio-familial acceptance can be acquired through
maintaining the appearance of asexuality and through achieving
middle-class markers of success (such as higher education, social
status, economic independence). Also, alternative strategies for asserting non-heteronormative identities exist beyond the achievement
of public acceptability. Thus some women more boldly assert their
socio-sexual identities through public self-labelling, the creation
of safe social spaces and networks, and organizing more broadly
around sexual rights. Especially for those who cannot easily access
the relative securities of middle-class lifestyles, alternative strategies
are necessary to effect positive change in societal perceptions over
the longer term, enabling women and men of all classes to define
and enjoy their sexualities as they see fit.

Notes

1. 'Queer' is used here as an umbrella term to include all sexual minorities, and
   any sexuality that rejects the absolutist framework opposing homosexual-
   ity/heterosexuality (see Andermahr et al. 1997), especially with reference
   to the commonly used term 'straight' for heterosexuality, against which,
   in Bangla, the term *banka* – bent/crooked/twisted – is used.
2. According to the *Samsad Bengali Dictionary*: '[samāja] (n.) human society,
   society; any one of the divisions of biological history; a community; a
   nation or race; a collective body of people having something in common,
   a class, a community an association; a gathering esp. a social one. (v.) to
   allot a lowly place in the society (to somebody).' See http://dsal.uchicago.
   edu/cgi-bin/romadict.pl?query=samaj&table=biswas-bengali.

   Blanchet (1996: 31) explains the concept of *samaj* in the Bangladeshi
   context: '*Samaj* has shifting meanings, both contextually and historically.
   For most Bangladeshis, far more important than being citizens of a nation

state, is to be a member of a *samaj*. The *samaj* upholds a moral order which is far more compelling on its members. It is associated with proper living as Bengali, as Muslims, as Hindus, as a civilized people.'

3. Snowball sampling (also called referral sampling) is a technique where initial study interviewees recruit other subjects from among their acquaintances to participate in the study. Hence the sample group grows like a rolling snowball. This technique is often used for research populations that might be hard to access for various reasons, sometimes connected to their marginal or stigmatized status – for example, drug users or sex workers. Snowball sampling can also allow researchers gain insights into the social networks connecting the population being researched.

4. The narratives were collected over an eighteen-month period in 2009–10. Because of the sensitivity of the topic and fear of backlash, pseudonyms are used.

5. Remaining single after the age of 25 is seen as non-normative, hence the inclusion of such participants in this category. In Bangladesh the median age at marriage for women currently aged 20–49 is 14.8 years. The median age at first marriage among women 20–24 years old in the lowest wealth quintile is 14.6 years; girls in the highest quintile marry at a median age of 18.3 years (Burket et al. 2006).

6. Up to 10th standard education.

7. October 2009, Dhaka. This is the interviewee's choice of pseudonym.

8. Bird (1996) refers to a generic understanding of these relations as non-sexual and states: 'it promotes clear distinctions between women and men through segregation in social institutions; and also promotes clear distinctions between hegemonic masculinities and non-hegemonic masculinities by the segregation of social groups'. Also see Connell 1992.

9. *Shomokamita* is actually the legal term for homosexuality.

10. South Asian legal frameworks derive from British colonization, but have seen recent amendments. One significant change occurred in India when Section 377 of the Indian Penal Code (which criminalized sexual activity 'against the order of nature') was repealed by the High Court of Delhi on 2 July 2009 (except for cases involving minors and coercive sex). The movement to repeal Section 377 was led by the Naz Foundation (India) Trust, an activist group. The law remains operative in Bangladesh.

11. This information was provided by the Sexuality Coalition Convener and the leader of the *shomo-premi* women's support group. In other interviews from my Ph.D. research, ten urban gay men reported that they all engage or have engaged in sexual acts with other men in public spaces (roadside, bushes, parks, lake-side pathways, the grounds of parliament, etc.) in Dhaka, and have never been caught or harassed by police. Female and transgender sex workers face harassment from police, but mainly for the purpose of extorting money, a common practice in Bangladesh. A report by Ain-O-Salish Kendra (2008) states: 'Although there has been only one reported case involving Section 377 in the four decades since the independence of Bangladesh, the existence of this offence is reportedly used by law enforcing agencies and others to threaten and harass individuals, and thus

inhibit their free exercise of expression and behaviour. ... More significant is the abuse of Section 54 of Criminal Procedure Code and Section 86 of the Dhaka Metropolitan Police Ordinance (and related provisions in the police ordinances applicable to other Metropolitan cities), which are commonly used to harass persons using public spaces.'

12. Brothel sex workers were not part of my three interview groups for this study; they were informants for other research and are distinct from the cohort of sex workers in same-sex relations in Dhaka that were interviewed for this essay.

13. For more information on Bangladeshi brothel structures and spatiality, see Blanchet 1996; Karim 2004; Tahmina 2004; Haq 2008.

14. The commercial sex worker lesbian interviewees showed me documents issued by the Sex Workers' Samiti (Organization), of which they all are members, stating that there should be no further reports on female-intimate 'friendship' and relations, and that any future reports would result in harsh punishments.

15. Flora used the English term 'knocked' in her interview to describe how other women wordlessly or otherwise conveyed to her their desire for her. Flora and several of the other interviewees used the term 'knock' frequently – it connotes 'knocking at the (closed) door'.

16. She left the marriage after seventeen days, as it took her away from her village and she could not bear to be separated from the 'love of her life' Ms B. The interview with Mukta took place in November 2009, in Sylhet, Bangladesh.

17. The workshop was part of a forum on 'Sexual Diversity and Coalition Building', 6–7 February 2009, in Cox's Bazaar, Bangladesh, with financial support from LLH Norway (www.llh.no/eng). A total of thirty-four participants from various NGOs, women's organizations and member groups of the LGBTQ Coalition took part, including many of my interviewees who self-identify as *shomo-premi*.

18. Statements in quotations are the exact words of the *shomo-premi* women, as documented in the final report of the workshop (unpublished, on file with author).

19. 'Players' here refers to the female athletes who are part of different national teams and live in residential training facilities in Dhaka and other large cities.

20. In Bangladesh, 'fast' is a commonly used English term to describe individuals (especially women) perceived as non-traditional, non-conservative, 'modern', 'Western' in lifestyle, and often to indicate loose sexual moral character.

21. All sex workers in this research are migrants who maintain one household in Dhaka while supporting their parental families back in the villages. Thus their image has to be managed at two levels to cover up both their professional and their sexual identity.

References

Ain-O-Salish Kendra. (2008). *Kendra Report on Violation of Human Rights on Sexual Minorities*, https://lgbtbangladesh.wordpress.com/2009/07/03/624 (accessed 12 September 2011).

Andermahr, S., Lovell, T., and Wolkowitz, C. (eds) (1997) *A Glossary of Feminist Theory*. London: Arnold.

Azim, F., and Sultan, M. (eds) (2010) *Mapping Women's Empowerment: Experiences from Bangladesh, India and Pakistan*. Dhaka: University Press.

Baden, S., Green, C., Goetz, A.M., and Guhathakurta, M. (1994) 'Background report on gender issues in Bangladesh', *BRIDGE* 26, www.bridge.ids.ac.uk/reports/re26c.pdf (accessed 25 August 2011).

Bird, S.R. (1996) 'Welcome to the men's club: Homosociality and the maintenance of hegemonic masculinity', *Gender and Society* 10(2): 120–32.

Blanchet, T. (1996) *Lost Innocence, Stolen Childhoods*. Dhaka: University Press.

Burket, M.K., Alauddin, M., Malek, A. and Rahman, M. (2006) *Raising the Age of Marriage for Young Girls in Bangladesh*. Pathfinders International. www.pathfind.org/site/DocServer/PF_Bangladesh_FINAL.pdf?docID=6601 (accessed 25 August 2011).

Connell, R.W. (1992) 'A very straight gay: Masculinity, homosexual experiences and the dynamics of gender', *American Sociological Review* 57(6), December: 735–51.

Donner, H. (2008) *Domestic Goddesses: Maternity, Globalization and Middle Class Identity in Contemporary India*. Farnham: Ashgate.

Eves, A. (2004) 'Queer theory, butch/femme identities and lesbian space', *Sexualities* 7(4): 480–96.

Gulrukh, S., and Chowdhury, M. (eds). (2000) *Kortar Shongshar: Naribadee Rochona Songkolon* [*Master's House: Collection of Feminist Writings*]. Dhaka: Rupantor.

Haq, S. (2006) 'Sex-workers's struggles in Bangladesh: Learning for the women's movement', in A. Cornwall and S. Jolly (eds), *IDS Bulletin: Sexuality Matters*, 37(5), October: 134–7.

Holliday, R. (1999) 'The comfort of identity', *Sexuality* 2(4): 475–92.

John, M.E., and Nair, J. (1998) *A Question of Silence: The Sexual Economies of Modern India*. Delhi: Kali for Women.

Kamaruzzaman, M., and Ogura, N. (2008). 'Housing for the middle income group in Dhaka, Bangladesh', *Journal of Architecture and Planning* 73(627): 947–54.

Karim, S. (2004) 'Exploring the household compositions of female sex-workers in brothels: Daulatdia, a case study', *BRAC University Journal* I(2): 33–48.

Karim, S. (2007) 'Gendered violence in education: Realities for adolescent girls in Bangladesh', Action Aid International Bangladesh, www.actionaid.org/docs/aa%20bangladesh%20vags%20research%20report.pdf (acccessed 25 August 2011).

Mahmud, S. (2010) 'Our bodies, our selves: The Bangladesh perspective', in F. Azim and M. Sultan (eds), *Mapping Women's Empowerment: Experiences from Bangladesh, India and Pakistan*. Dhaka: University Press.

Meem (2009) *Bareed Mista3jil: True Stories*. Beirut: Meem.

Mohsin, A. (1997) *Politics of Nationalism: The Case of the Chittagong Hill Tracts, Bangladesh*. Ann Arbor: University of Michigan Press.

Muna, L. (2005) *Romance and Pleasure: Understanding the Sexual Conduct of Young People in Dhaka in the Era of HIV and AIDS*. Dhaka: University Press.

National Coalition of Anti-Violence Programs (2008) *NCAVP National Hate Violence Report*, www.avp.org/publications/reports/reports.htm (accessed 10 December 2011).

Nayar, P.K. (2007) 'Queering cultural studies: Notes towards a framework', in B. Bose and S. Bhattacharyya (eds), *The Phobic and the Erotic: The Politics of Sexualities in Contemporary India*. Kolkata: Seagull, 117–48.

Siddiqi, D. (2007) 'Heteronormativity and its implications', Monograph Series 15, *International Gender and Sexuality Workshop Papers*, James P. Grant School of Public Health, BRAC University, Dhaka, Bangladesh.

Tahmina, Q.A (2004) *Sex workers in Bangladesh – Livelihood: At What Price?* Dhaka: SEHD.

White, S. (1992) *Arguing with the Crocodile: Gender and Class in Bangladesh*. London: Zed Books.

11

Risky rights? Gender equality and sexual diversity in Muslim contexts

Anissa Hélie

A multiplicity of discourses – present in the Western media, but also in academic writing and political commentaries – fail to recognize the diversity that exists across and within Muslim societies. In particular Western neoconservative discourses, along with some misguided human rights and sexual rights advocates, characterize both 'Muslim women' and 'gay Muslims' as uniformly oppressed categories. However, the status of women and of lesbian, gay, bisexual, transgender, transsexual and intersex people (LGBTTI[1]), their social realities, and the legal frameworks that guarantee or deny them rights, are much more varied than is usually portrayed. If we are to recognize the agency of those struggling for gender equality in Muslim contexts, prevalent constructions of 'Muslim women' and 'gay Muslims' must be questioned. For a start, the fact that 'Muslim women' are generally assumed to be heterosexual and 'gay Muslims' are generally assumed to be male[2] points at the reductionist perspectives that often underscore such labels.

My goal is not to deny the serious challenges that obstruct sexual rights for all in Muslim contexts; indeed, conservative Muslims also capitalize on the myth of a homogenous 'Muslim world' to advance a restrictive agenda, and human rights defenders – whether women or LGBTTI people – are often targets of violence and discrimination. Rather, this chapter intends to contrast Western homogenizing views with the vibrant strategies developed by advocates in diverse

Muslim societies. However, my perspective is informed by a critique of discourses of power in both 'the West' and the 'Muslim world'. I have written elsewhere (Hélie 2004) about the need to challenge monolithic representations on all fronts, recognizing that, on the one hand, sexism, homophobia or transphobia are defined as inherently linked to 'Islam' and, on the other hand, sexual and gender diversity is constructed as inherently linked to a Western model. While I mostly address here some of the biased views produced in Western contexts, it remains essential to analyse both these discourses in order to expose their impact on people's lives as well as their broader geopolitical implications.

And, while I am keenly aware that these do not always overlap, I intentionally weave through spaces of resistance carved by feminists and sexual rights activists. This approach derives from an analytical premiss which broadens the understanding of 'sexual rights' beyond issues of sexual orientation or gender identity. A coherent analysis of sexual rights needs to encompass heterosexuals as well as LGBTTI people, because governments and non-state actors regulate both sexuality and reproduction, and sanction those whose sexual conduct (real or perceived[3]) defies normative frameworks. Although the scope of this chapter only allows for an emphasis on LGBTT people, highlighting these connections is crucial given the strong resistance to a sexual rights agenda for all.

The first part of the chapter explores whether mainstream assertions of sexual diversity and gender equality as intrinsically Western derive from (post)colonial constructions of race, religion, gender and sexuality. It discusses the implications of such assumptions for debates related to the politics of sexuality. Section two demonstrates that the insistence on victimhood – of both 'Muslim women' and of 'gay Muslims' – renders invisible three sets of realities. First, gender equality is lacking throughout the world, including in countries that claim to champion women's and sexual rights. Second, (in)equality is articulated in multiple ways, and gender and sexuality ought to be examined in connection with a variety of factors. Third, social movements advocating for sexual and gender equality are increasingly vocal in Muslim contexts – a trend examined in section three. Section three shows that the policing of sexuality affects both heterosexuals (women in particular) and LGBTT people but insists primarily on the vibrancy of LGBTT activism. Disputing the denial of agency implicit in the portrayal of women and gays as victims only, section three considers concrete instances of collective organizing at local, national and international levels, and highlights a range of efforts geared towards asserting sexual diversity in diaspora settings and Muslim-majority countries.

Representations: The politicization of 'gay Muslims' and 'Muslim women'

Historical perspectives on contemporary debates

The ways mainstream discourses framed gender and sexuality in the past have been closely connected to political interests and mechanisms of control. While Western views of 'indigenous' sexual conduct supported imperial agendas, they can serve a similar purpose in the postcolonial era. Both colonial and neocolonial ideologies rely heavily on sexuality and gender discourses, the crafting of which varies according to evolving notions of morality, modernity and geopolitics. Although they are not our focus here, it is worth noting also that today's opponents of gender and sexual equality in Muslim societies legitimize their views by emphasizing national sovereignty and cultural or religious specificity. Recent declarations by Iranian and Israeli leaders illustrate below how LGBTT people's status often provides fodder to assert different political agendas. Drawing the links between Western colonial and contemporary constructions of both 'gay Muslims' and 'Muslim women', this section also considers the current political implications of such depictions, especially the collusion of some sexual rights groups with neoconservative forces.

In 2007, during a speech at Columbia University, Iranian president Mahmoud Ahmadinejad made a statement which was translated as: 'In Iran, we don't have homosexuals. In Iran we don't have this phenomenon. I don't know who told you we have it' (Borger and MacAskill 2007). This led to an outcry – but also to misguided declarations in the Western media[4] and among sexual rights groups. Earlier controversies had already produced widespread assertions that 'Iran enforces Islamic *shari'a* law, which dictates the death penalty for gay sex.'[5] Whether politically motivated or the result of ignorance, such a claim displays a misconception regarding *shari'a* on at least two counts. First, there is no single interpretation of Muslim laws that applies uniformly across Muslim-majority nations. Second, while Iran does prescribe extreme penalties for adults involved in same-sex acts,[6] there is nevertheless no consensus among religious scholars regarding sexual orientation or gender identity: as a result, religious prescriptions vary according to context, as do legal and cultural norms.

This reality did not prevent Israeli prime minister Benjamin Netanyahu, in his May 2011 address before the United States Congress, from defining the Middle East as 'a region where women are stoned, gays are hanged, Christians are persecuted'.[7] Presenting the Middle East as a homogenous entity is at best misleading[8] – particularly at a time when LGBTTI activism is increasingly visible in Muslim contexts; particularly also when some Muslim-majority states in the region are showing a willingness to engage more positively with issues of gender equality and sexuality. For example, Tunisia has recently established gender parity for electoral candidates (Al Jazeera 2011), while other nations craft policies seeking to lessen violence and discrimination against LGBTTI people – including attempts in Lebanon and Jordan to accommodate LGBTTI people seeking refuge (Duncan 2011).[9]

But, interestingly, the depiction of an entire region – or of Muslim societies generally – as inherently anti-gay is antithetical to earlier discourses: nineteenth-century Europeans commonly referred to (male) same-sex acts as the 'Persian disease', the 'Turkish disease' or the 'Egyptian vice'. This identification of 'Islam with corrupt sexuality and especially degenerate sodomy' (Ben-Naeh 2005: 85) had been long established: in the 1660s the British Consul to the Ottoman Empire referred to men 'burn[ing] in lust one towards another' and emphasized the 'deformity of their depraved inclinations' (Rycaut 1668: 63–4, cited in Ben-Naeh 2005: 85).

In terms of women's status, Western historical and contemporary assumptions show little variation. Nineteenth- and early-twentieth-century Europeans consistently asserted that, 'compared to the condition of women of other religions, [the Muslim woman] is a slave. A luxurious animal to the rich; a beast of burden to the poor; she is nothing more than a poor creature sacrificed to the pleasure of the male' (Servier 1923: 3095, cited in Mabro 1996: 174). As colonial imagery carefully staged visuals emphasizing seclusion or idleness (Alloula 1986; Graham-Brown 1988), scholars and travellers disseminated depictions of women 'who seemed already half buried from life and clothed in the garments of the grave' (Macdonald 1864, cited in Mabro 1996: 52). Indeed, the subjugation of 'Oriental' women long provided a core argument against aspirations of self-rule. For example, Lord Cromer, British Consul General in Egypt (1883–1907), asserted that 'The position of women in Egypt, and in Mohammedan countries generally, is a fatal obstacle to the attainment of that elevation of thought and character which should accompany the introduction of European civilization' (Mitchell 1991: 111).

These quotes illustrate that Western colonial and contemporary mainstream discourses remain centred on demonizing the Other, and on positing Western and Muslim societies as oppositional. (Ahmadinejad's 2007 comments remind us that Muslim ultra-conservatives resort to similar tactics.) Whether emphasizing a lack of sexual morality or systematic sexism, Western stereotypes appear designed to promote politically or economically motivated agendas, as the current construction of 'Muslim homophobia' also suggests, below.

Centre and periphery: stereotyping and a new queer order

While the colonial project sought justification for imperialist expansion in women's subjugation and natives' perversions, contemporary discourses (in both Western and non-Western contexts) often associate gender equality and sexual diversity with 'the West', displaying a striking example of amnesia regarding the criminalization of homosexual conduct introduced during colonial times,[10] and generally in the name of Christian values (Bleys 1996; Kirby 2011). When articulated by Western actors (ranging from progressive to conservative), these discourses seem to engender a theoretical confusion, with many voices conflating sexual freedom, 'modernity' and claims of secularism.[11] Such confusion is no less politically motivated than the colonial agenda was, and carries its own 'civilizing mission'. As shown below, it can serve a neoconservative project spearheaded by the 'clash of civilizations' theory, popularized by Huntington (1996) and Lewis (1990), which predicted an increase in conflicts linked to 'competing cultural identities'; and attributed diminishing Western political control over the world, during the twentieth century, to the rise of Islam.

Endorsing the vision of a Western civilization under assault from Muslim forces,[12] some writers denounce a gender order inculcated, they argue, in order to achieve the 'supremacy of Islam'. Harris, for example, warns that Muslim 'boys, in particular, are taught to be dominating' as he contrasts the upbringing of American teens and future 'holy warriors': 'While we in America are drugging our alpha boys with Ritalin, the Muslims are doing everything in their power to encourage their alpha boys to be tough, aggressive and ruthless' (Harris 2008: 303, 331).

And how do LGBTTI people fare in such threatening contexts? A typical response can be found in a multi-country survey, the Gallup Coexist Index (Gallup Center 2009), which claims that the level of acceptance of homosexuality among British Muslims is ... 0% and, predictably, concludes 'the Muslim–West gap rests on differences in attitudes toward sexual liberalization and gender issues'.[13] The widespread emphasis on irreconcilable differences between East and West constructs all 'Muslims' as essentially sexist and homophobic, and relies on gender stereotyping of Muslim men as aggressive machos, and of Muslim women and LGBTTI people as victimized by oppressive traditions. Again, this echoes colonial constructs in that it depicts 'Muslim cultures' as backward, in contrast with an enlightened and 'modern' West.

Such a dichotomized world-view produces problematic responses with regard to 'gay Muslims' – leaving little room for nuances and allowing no space for local resistance. A similar mechanism applies to 'Muslim women': casting non-systematic practices as the norm allows emphasis on the 'backwardness' that supposedly characterizes their plight. Western media and many scholarly works on women display a selective interest in oppressive customs such as forced marriage, honour killing, imposed veiling, and so on. Where indicators do provide a more positive picture (for example, regarding female access to education and employment, or – God forbid? – involvement in feminist activism) they tend to be ignored.

This wilful selectiveness is matched, in relation to homosexual conduct, by biased representations of Muslim men's sexual encounters:

all 'gay sex' is reduced to anal sex, which itself is supposedly characterized by asymmetric patterns of relations. Apparently, in the
seemingly unavoidable scenario of who-penetrates-whom, sexual
partners have no choice but to follow the roles predetermined by
their respective position of power (with individuals' age and social
status playing a key function). As Hayes observes, recent publications
often associate 'gay Muslims' with European 'pre- or early modern
sexualities' – that is, patterns 'associated with the ancient world'. In
other words, today's 'gay Muslims' simply cannot quite shake off the
legacy of the Ancient Greek model of pederasty. Noting the 'medieval tone of modern descriptions', Hayes points at the 'narratives of
progress towards the Western model of homosexuality' contained in
various Western studies devoted to Muslim men's sexuality (Hayes
2000: 4). Once again, an idealized 'Western civilization' – complete
with its promise of egalitarian gay relationships – is pitted against
the hierarchical sexual practices and overall oppressive traditions
allegedly prevailing in Muslim contexts. Such narratives lend cred-
ibility to the belief that 'the West, once the bearer of civilizational
morality (monogamy, heterosexual marriage, sexual control), has
reassumed its rightful place, but now in the name of a sexual liberation' (Haritaworn 2008).

The framing of LGBTT Muslims as uniformly victimized – with
no analysis of the privileges afforded by class, marital status, gender
expression or mobility within public space – leads to denying the
reality of local resistance and advocacy efforts. It also allows some
Western sexual rights advocates to portray themselves as liberators.
This trap (into which some feminist groups keen to 'save' powerless
'Muslim women' have also fallen[14]) reduces the scope for true solidarity across regions and substitutes a pervasive rhetoric of 'saviourship'.
Scholars have denounced the trend towards homonationalism[15] (Puar
and Rai 2002; Puar 2007), but I specifically draw here from Haritaworn, Tauqir and Erdem (2008), critical of the support that some
European gay groups lend to the discourse of the war on terror in
the name of supporting 'gay Muslims'. The political deployment of a
threatening, homophobic Islam has implications for Muslim societies
at large, especially given that 'the construct of "Muslim homophobia"
is central to the debates around security and "core values" in the
new Europe' (Haritaworn et al. 2008: 78). Indeed this analysis can be

applied to North America as well, particularly as conservative gay voices in the USA debate whether to support a military strike against Iran, a development that would have life-threatening consequences for civilians (LGBTTI people included).

Stereotyping also directly impacts on diaspora Muslims, and especially migrant populations in the West. The prevalent discourse that 'equates "gay" with white and "ethnic minority" with heterosexual' while defining 'people of colour only as perpetrators of homophobia' leads to a false dichotomy: 'sexual rights and migrant rights have become constructed as mutually contradictory' (Haritaworn et al. 2008: 72, 74, 2). Whether consciously or unconsciously, some Western gay advocates and feminists are 'deeply implicated in this racialised project' (Haritaworn et al. 2008: 86). By propagating essentialist stereotypes about 'Muslims' and downplaying resistance from within Muslim communities, they contribute to the legitimization of exclusionary discourses and policies directed towards both Muslim migrants and European/North American citizens with Muslim ancestry. As some have argued, endorsing a national discourse of exclusion may offer political benefits to these sexual rights and feminist activists, who no longer appear as marginal Others but rather as mainstream participants in Western societies that are increasingly marked by racism against 'foreigners'.

The West and the Rest: a broad spectrum of discrimination

As seen above, a selective insistence on the victimization of 'Muslim women' and of 'gay Muslims' leads to defining both feminist aspirations and sexual agency as primarily Western. Most European and North American nations posit themselves as champions of women's rights and, increasingly, as global advocates of LGBTT people's rights. But are these claims reflected on the ground? Assertions of gender equality should be matched by reality, both on the home front and on the international scene. As I briefly show in the first subsection, violence and discrimination – against both women and LGBTTI people – remain pervasive in Western contexts. The second subsection raises two issues relevant to the international level: the question of aid conditionality, which arose in recent debates on sexual orientation and gender identity; and the contrast between pro-LGBTT rights statements by Western world leaders and state practices (particularly regarding asylum proceedings). Finally, in the last section, I highlight the need to go beyond West/Islam dichotomies, and to take into account a broad range of variables that affect individuals' ability to access and enjoy their sexual rights. Indeed, an intersectional analysis is key, as sexual rights cannot be achieved in isolation but are closely connected to, and need to be guaranteed by, a broader set of human rights.

West is best, white is right?
Looking at one's own back yard

Before briefly considering the status of LGBTT people in 'the West', I rely on a few facts to show that a majority of Northern women remain impacted by deeply entrenched gender-related discrimination. This brief focus may appear to detract from my main argument, but we must challenge the framing of most Western nations as deeply concerned about sexism. I am not suggesting that all Western states' public endorsement of women's equality is empty rhetoric: while some leaders and governments do manipulate issues of women's rights to implement their political and economic agendas abroad, others appear genuinely concerned. However, Western states' moral authority to carry out an oft-stated objective – that is, 'exporting' women's rights to Muslim countries (or African ones for that matter) – requires a factual assessment of their own records; especially as gender parity and sexual freedom are defined as the new 'objective' indicators for modernity and/or democracy.

From domestic violence to economic disparity to sexual harassment and political leadership, personal stories as well as tangible parameters indicate that Western contexts continue to be affected by systemic gender inequalities. If economic achievement is any indication of one's position in society, recent statistics regarding the status of women in the USA offer little to boast about. Economic discrimination starts early (the gender pay gap reaches 20 per cent within a year of graduation and increases afterwards) and never seems to end (in 2000, the poverty rate among older women was twice that among the general elderly population). Further, these facts provide an incomplete picture in so far as disparities linked to factors other than sex are not accounted for – women of colour, for example, earn significantly less than their white counterparts.

The sexual liberation project does not fare as well as advertised either. For example, in the Netherlands, a self-professed sexually inclusive society, an anti-bullying website received over 200 reports of homophobic abuse within less than a month of its launching (Radio Netherlands Worldwide 2011). In various European countries and the United States, alarming suicide rates among LGBTTI youth, and hate crimes (including murders, targeting transgender people especially) raise concerns. States also still uphold discriminatory policies: almost two dozen European countries require sterilization for transgender people seeking legal gender change on official documents (European Union Agency 2010: 17–18). In the USA, the Employment Non-Discrimination Act, which would outlaw firing, refusal to hire or failure to promote an employee on the basis of sexual orientation and gender identity, has been debated in Congress for over a decade and is still not ratified.[16]

My intention is not to undermine the significant advances made by women and sexual rights advocates in Europe and North America. Rather, it is to highlight the false basis of a discourse of difference which underplays discrimination 'at home'[17] while ignoring achievements in other regions.[18] The political implications of this discourse of difference are worth examining, particularly as it impacts on foreign relations, as seen below with regard to the issue of aid conditionality. Further, the treatment of LGBTT asylum-seekers provides an example (among many possible others) that illustrates the gap between Western leaders' statements and realities on the ground.

Foreign policy: loving you from afar?

Significant affirmations of LGBTT people's right to equality made the news recently. In December 2011, US president Barack Obama and secretary of state Hillary Clinton asserted that LGBTT rights are a 'key element' of US foreign policy. More controversially, in November, British prime minister David Cameron appeared to have linked development aid to human rights, and LGBTT rights in particular. He has since said this was misconstrued, but widespread perceptions that his government did threaten to withhold aid from countries with a homophobic record have stiffened national pride in many countries. I explore below some of the reactions to Cameron's statement by both advocates and opponents of LGBTTI rights.

Because Cameron's remarks were unanticipated, with no prior consultation of LGBTTI advocates in Southern countries, an immediate concern was that it showed a disregard for local movements' role and agency. Various activists, from Africa and the Caribbean particularly, felt their leadership was being undermined – a typical 'West knows best' approach, which veteran Trinidad and Tobago LGBTTI activist Colin Robinson rightly criticizes: 'Those of us who live in, understand and engage daily with the states and the localities we wish to change must form the pivot around which any international advocacy strategy or emancipator movement is built' (Robinson 2012). Various human rights defenders were also alarmed that the spotlight on LGBTT rights could obscure other widespread abuses and pointed at the fact that the threat of donor sanctions would likely reinforce unequal power dynamics between Northern and Southern countries. Furthermore, they warned that Cameron's speech could well strengthen the backlash against local organizing – that is, themselves.

Indeed, Cameron's statement on aid conditionality sounds like a windfall for conservatives and fundamentalists, providing them with ready-made anti-imperialist arguments and reinforcing their motto that homosexuality is a Western imposition. For example, a typical homophobic response to perceived Western pressures came from Gambian president Yahya Jammeh, who stated in April 2012 that his country has no 'room for gays and lesbians'. Drawing from anti-imperialist rhetoric, he relied on assertions of self-sovereignty and religious rightfulness, adding:

> If you want us to be ungodly for you to give us aid, take your aid away, we will survive. We will rather eat grass than accept this ungodly evil attitude that is anti-God, anti-human and anti-creation … There are certain things that are ungodly, evil, and a challenge to the Almighty Allah's wisdom in creating a man and a woman. Let me make it very clear that if you want me to offend God for you to give me aid, you are making a great mistake. You will not bribe me.

The Gambian leader concluded by further emphasizing (selective) notions of religious and cultural specificities: 'We will not compromise our dignity, we will not insult our religion, and we will not insult God by doing something in the name of human rights' (Hatab 2012). It is worth noting that, even where not linked to this particular controversy, assertions of LGBTT rights by Western leaders would likely be manipulated by religious fundamentalists of various creeds.[19]

Overall, raising the issue of aid conditionality in such a unilateral manner was rather counterproductive: local sexual rights advocates resented not having been consulted on how to promote LGBTTI rights in contexts about which they can claim far more expertise than British politicians. On the other hand, opponents of LGBTTI rights saw the threat (real or perceived) as another tool used by Western powers to assert political, cultural and economic control.

Importantly, this episode suggests that well-intentioned Western leaders – that is, those who do not simply use the rhetoric of sexuality to further their own agendas – must cautiously assess their ability to promote gender equality norms abroad, and the potentially negative impact of their strategies. The best way to encourage a true culture of inclusiveness is to acknowledge local leadership and to collaborate with interested constituencies. If truly concerned, Western nations should consider supporting LGBTTI people on their own terms, including for example through increased funding of sexual rights groups. In the same vein, they should also stop sacrificing women's rights when economic interests are at stake – and yet admission of secret US talks with the Taliban does not bode well for the future of Afghan women (Ryan et al. 2011). The case of LGBTTI asylum-seekers, considered below, offers one example among others of a terrain which could benefit from a commitment by Western leaders to curb discrimination and improve existing policies.

The Obama administration, to its credit, has pledged to 'enhance [its] ongoing efforts to ensure that LGBT refugees and asylum seekers have equal access to protection and assistance' (White House 2011).[20] This issue is a broad one: with 10 to 12 million refugees worldwide, only an estimated 100,000 are resettled each year (Newland 2002). But European Union-wide data on LGBTTI asylum applications (roughly 10,000 annually) reveals 'worrying trends' of discrimination: in a nutshell, 'European State practice is below the standards required by international and European human rights and refugee law' (Jansen and Spijkerboer 2011). Officials often deny international protection to 'persecuted bisexuals [and] other LGBTI people who do not behave in accordance with the stereotypes used by decision makers: lesbians who do not behave in a masculine way, non-effeminate gays, and LGBTI applicants who have been married or who have children' (Jansen and Spijkerboer 2011). Overall, assessments made by officials appear arbitrary and discriminatory, although it is difficult to determine whether decision-makers are well-intentioned but uninformed and poorly trained, or motivated by their own homophobia or transphobia.

Jansen and Spijkerboer (2011) also point to a hierarchy that privileges some categories of identity, noting that 'patterns of persecution of lesbian, transgender and intersex people are less highlighted than those of gay men'. Furthermore, they deplore that 'LGB asylum applicants are regularly returned to countries where they have a well-founded fear of being imprisoned or sentenced to death', and express concern that 'serious human rights violations against trans people often do not lead to asylum'. The European data presented here corroborate other reports that highlight the worldwide discrimination of LGBTTI refugees, including the fact that they face 'persecution in the countries *to which they flee*, in addition to in the countries *from which they fled*' (Human Rights First 2010).

LGBTTI refugees constitute a distinct subset of people, but their treatment in asylum proceedings can be linked to wide-ranging patterns of discrimination. In fact, stigmatization and violence affect all regions,[21] even countries where LGBTTI people are not criminalized. As documented by the first ever United Nations report on sexual orientation and gender identity, LGBTTI people – or anyone perceived to be non-normative – face a broad 'pattern of human rights violations ... that demands a response' (High Commissioner for Human Rights 2011).

Hence, the dichotomization between a sexually liberal West and a sexually oppressive Muslim world does not reflect the full extent of discrimination that exists throughout the world. This construct also ignores the fact that overlapping factors intersect in an individual's life, with issues such as class, caste, ethnicity, education, legal or marital status, and so on, playing a crucial role in terms of how women and LGBTTI people are able to negotiate their lives and rights. The notion of intersectionality is crucial, and is addressed specifically in the following section.

Intersectionality matters

At a 2010 symposium, feminist theorist Ros Petchesky remarked that 'Yes, women's bodies are sexualized – but not only. And there is an interrelation that we need not forget: women's bodies are also hungry bodies, homeless bodies, racialized bodies, militarized bodies...' This observation can be extended to people whose gender identities, sexualities or non-conforming bodies are stigmatized. People's specific circumstances have an undeniable impact on their respective (in)ability to access a whole range of rights – from the right to live free of coercion and violence, to the right to privacy, to the right to freedom of movement, and so forth. Blanket statements related to the plight of 'Muslim women' or 'gay Muslims' wilfully ignore to what extent one's position in society affects one's claim to equality.

A couple of examples show how just three elements – class, ethnicity and the aftermath of natural disaster – intersect with sexuality and gender identity. (Of course, a more comprehensive approach ought to consider other parameters, including health status, physical and mental ability, access to food or education, income, bio-body, etc.) The first example relates to the United States, debunking the myth that 'Western societies' offer a safe haven to people with alternative sexualities. In autumn 2011, a violent death occurred in New York: was this just another 'unfortunate incident' in a city with a high homicide rate? In fact the gunning down of 57-year-old Yvonne McNeal, a disabled lesbian of colour and homeless shelter resident, was the result of police shooting. The Queers for Economic Justice (QEJ, a New-York-based NGO) press statement highlights the price paid by those who are at once impoverished, non-white and sexually non-conforming. Citing data documenting an increase in reporting of hate crimes against LGBTTI people across the nation,[22] QEJ denounces specifically the threat posed by police forces:

> Yvonne's killing underscores the reality that the police cannot be relied on to respond compassionately to low-income LGBTQ people. QEJ has seen this repeated pattern of racism and disregard for human life ...

because we are poor, from communities of color and may also be lesbian, gay, bisexual and transgender or perceived as such. (QEJ 2011)

While studies rarely document the links between poverty and denial of sexual rights, economic realities need to be considered; especially given the impact of transnational economic policies imposed by the International Monetary Fund or the World Bank, and their disproportionate effect on vulnerable populations, including in Muslim countries. Indeed, emerging research shows that 'in many cases, poor people are more vulnerable to abuses of sexual rights, and that such abuses can entrench poverty'. For example, 'under *shari'a* law in Northern Nigeria, poor people are more likely to be charged with and convicted of sodomy and illicit sex, as well as other crimes, than more middle-class people' (Jolly 2010).[23] However, the issue also plays out in more complex ways, as Jolly points out:

> Some richer people are more constrained in terms of expressing their sexuality for fear of jeopardising their inheritance or reputation. And some people who break rules around sexuality may gain in material terms – for example a girl who stays in school instead of marrying young, or … some *kothis* (a feminine male identity in South Asia) [who] report that their gender identity can have a positive impact on their economic status due to opportunities to sell sex.

The second example centres on the massive floods that occurred in Pakistan in 2010, and their impact on *hijras* – a disenfranchised community who often combine non-conforming gender identity and low economic status. The crisis affected up to 20 million people and left 1.5 to 2 million in relief camps or temporary settlements. According to local reporting, the most marginalized were systematically denied assistance: 'the *hijras* in all of the camps complain[ed] about discrimination'. In various instances, administrators were to blame: '*Hijras* [were] refused food, medicine and other relief goods', including tents – not a light punishment during the monsoon season. In other cases, other refugees rejected them: 'in Multan, a group of 33 *hijras* were forced out of the camp by other residents who said they did not want "sinners" living amongst them' (Red Ribbon Initiative 2010). Such reactions by 'ordinary people' derive from deep-seated cultural prejudice – but they are also fuelled by religious fundamentalists, whose propaganda often exploits natural disasters to further their ideology (as Vivienne Wee relates in Chapter 1 of this book with regard to Islamist groups blaming unveiled women for the tsunami in Aceh).[24]

An intersectional approach offers broad rewards – as Petchesky asserts: it 'incites us to conceptualize every domain or issue of political economy ... as profoundly gendered and sexualized from the start. Conversely, every arena of sexual, gender and reproductive health has its deeply macroeconomic and development-related dimensions' (Petchesky 2011: 1). Further, the above examples provide a lesson for every researcher on sexuality or intersectionality: the context in which people experience their overlapping sexual, ethnic, social, cultural, religious or economic realities define their everyday lives as well as the scope of their possibilities for action. The following section explores avenues of resistance in Muslim societies: I envisage first some of the main challenges at stake, then instances of collective organizing developed in response, with a focus on sexual rights advocacy.

Rights, restrictions and resistance in Muslim contexts

In her 2010 report, the UN Special Rapporteur on the Situation of Human Rights Defenders stated that those 'work[ing] on sexual and reproductive rights face risks including harassment, discrimination, stigma, criminalization and physical violence'. Such risks do not only affect activists: this section demonstrates that LGBTT people in Muslim communities are particularly targeted by conservative forces, which also generally endeavour to limit women's rights (a dual trend by no means specific to the 'Muslim world'). But, for the sake of building stronger constituencies in support of sexual rights for all, I preface my review of the main obstacles facing 'gay Muslims' with a reminder that the sexual rights of heterosexual people are also regulated and curtailed. A few examples from within Muslim contexts will make this clear (however, this focus is determined by the limited length of this chapter, and does not suggest that such rights are only restricted in Muslim societies).[25] Finally, I explore a range of strategies devised by LGBT activists to address ongoing challenges and to assert their right to participate in, and shape, Muslim cultures.

Heterosexuals and queers unite?

Selected examples (related to dress codes, virginity testing and alleged sexual offences) show that heterosexual women – and some men – do face restrictions, from both state and non-state actors. Most societies are deeply invested in maintaining a strict gender order and in upholding normative 'feminine' or 'masculine' attributes. In conservative Muslim contexts – and especially with the rise of fundamentalist politics – this has increasingly taken the form of a focus on dress codes. State-imposed regulations in Iran, Saudi Arabia and Sudan require veiling for women, and are severely enforced. In one tragic case in 2002, fifteen Saudi schoolgirls died in their burning school: the Saudi religious police[26] prevented them from fleeing because they were not adhering to the required dress code. More recently, in 2009, in Sudan, Lubna Ahmed al-Hussein was sentenced to forty lashes for wearing trousers. The basis of her conviction was Article 152 of the Sudanese Criminal Code, which prohibits 'dressing indecently' in public. She is far from being an exception: 'According to the director of police, in 2008 in Khartoum State alone, 43,000 women were arrested for clothing offences' (Hussein 2009).

In recent years, countless women have been subjected to local, regional or national veiling regulations – from Aceh in Indonesia to the Malaysian state of Terengganu to Chechnya and beyond. In some contexts, such as Northern Sri Lanka, conservative community members are implicated in enforcing dress codes. However, in most places religious fundamentalists are the most vocal and aggressive proponents of veiling. In the new 'democratic Tunisia',[27] several schools and major universities are targeted by large groups of Salafists[28] who violently demand gender-segregated classes and attack both faculty and administration, including female professors, for their 'un-Islamic' dress or teachings (Human Rights Watch 2011; Mellakh 2012). While arguments justifying veiling generally cite 'tradition' – a notion that ought to be scrutinized (Hélie 2012) – the link with sectarian politics and the imposition of a theocratic project is clear. The link with sexuality is equally evident: women's bodies ought to be covered, or they will provoke male lust. However, male cross-dressers may also face prosecution. Thus, for example, in Kuwait in 2007 an amendment to the Criminal Code criminalizes people who 'imitate the appearance of the opposite sex'.[29] This law has been used primarily to discipline male-to-female transgender people (Human Rights Watch 2008a), but it can potentially affect a broader constituency (since many cross-dressers are heterosexuals who maintain a mainstream gender identity in public). Furthermore, this limitation on gender expression reinforces prevailing notions of masculinity, to which all men are expected to conform.

In many Muslim communities, prevailing notions of femininity contribute to defining public space as primarily male. The imperative of maintaining gender segregation has led governments and non-state actors (particularly religious extremists) to curtail women's freedom of movement. In various instances, women visible in the public arena (such as students, professional women or human rights defenders) have had their 'sexual purity' questioned: for example, several Muslim states have resorted to 'virginity tests', including Turkey up until 2002 (BBC News 2002). Most recently, in March 2011, the Egyptian army attempted to discredit Tahrir Square women human rights defenders by forcing almost two dozen female demonstrators to undergo 'virginity checks'. While the women faced potential accusations of prostitution, an Egyptian general justified detaining them, stating 'these girls were not like your daughter or mine. ... These were girls who had camped out in tents with male protesters' (Amin 2011). (Meanwhile, the Egyptian Muslim Brotherhood uses the same issue – preserving women's chastity – to promote female genital mutilation.[30]) Of course, the exclusion of women, and even of little girls, from public space is by no mean the prerogative of 'Muslims', as recent trends of policing women in Jewish Orthodox communities can attest: as fundamentalist ideology gains ground in all religions, some feel entitled to claim that 'to spit on a girl who isn't behaving according to the law of the Torah is justified'.[31]

Other examples show that heterosexual people who transgress sexual boundaries can face strict penalties. In various Muslim contexts, accusations of adultery may lead to sanctions, ranging from stigmatization to arrest or worse, with women (rather than their male partners) being the primary targets of punishment: in 2006, in Chechnya a 23-year-old pregnant woman was tortured by police (Chivers 2006); over the years, up to a dozen Iranian women have been sentenced to stoning for the same alleged offence,[32] and there has been at least one recent such case in Sudan. From Iran to Pakistan to Nigeria, 'honour crimes' also target heterosexual couples who chose the 'wrong' partner – in terms of caste, ethnicity or economic status. The notion of sexual morality remains a powerful tool, used by both conservative Muslims and currents within Islam seeking to further a theocratic social project. As examined below, these forces promote a patriarchal and homophobic agenda and specifically target LGBTTI people.

The politics of homophobia: culture, religion and the law

In Muslim communities where public space is seen as a male domain, women are generally unwelcome – but those perceived to be lesbians face even harsher discrimination. The following is not atypical: the day after the October 2011 elections in Tunis – the capital of a country with an assertive feminist movement and where women tend to be visible and vocal – a group of Islamists told a young butch lesbian: 'You are the devil and we'll make sure you end up in hell.'[33] Likely empowered by the electoral success of Ennahda,[34] these men nevertheless expressed a prejudice still enshrined in numerous legal systems.[35] I briefly highlight below recent developments at the United Nations, and the impact of fundamentalist politics at the national level, with a focus on Malaysia.

The policing of sexuality engenders debate at multiple levels – from the streets to the UN. In 2008, a Statement on Human Rights, Sexual Orientation and Gender Identity was the first attempt to condemn sexuality/gender-related violations since the founding of the institution in 1945. As the USA abstained from voting (the only Western country to do so), the Organization of the Islamic Conference (OIC) responded by circulating a statement condemning homosexuality.[36] Meanwhile, the then president of the UN General Assembly (2009–10), M. Treki from Libya, stated that homosexuality was 'very sensitive, very touchy. As a Muslim, I am not in favor of it. I think it's not really acceptable by our religion, our tradition. It is not acceptable in the majority of the world' (Santoscoy 2009). On the other hand, since 2010 UN chief Ban Ki-moon has repeatedly called for the repeal of all laws that criminalize homosexuality, and so has the High Commissioner for Human Rights Navi Pillay (most recently by commissioning a ground-breaking report, discussed at the Human Rights Council in March 2012). This is just one example of the heated debates at the UN level; another is evidenced by the General Assembly's deletion in November 2010 of the mention of sexual orientation from a UN Resolution on Extrajudicial, Summary or Arbitrary Executions (even though it had been listed for almost a decade as one of the grounds on which killings are often based). Following international outcry, this reference was reinstated a month later, but this testifies to how contentious the issue remains.

In fact, sexuality is a key point of alliance between ultra-conservatives and representatives of the religious right. 'Fundamentalists' from different religions are often portrayed as sworn enemies of each other – but the politics of sexuality provides them with a shared political agenda. Examples of transnational collaboration across religious lines often involve North American fundamentalist Christians and evangelists, who gladly share their strategies regarding criminalizing abortion or same-sex conduct with opponents of sexual rights in Southern contexts.

As in M. Treki's statement above, 'religion and tradition' – that is, religious and cultural beliefs – are also regularly conflated at the national level. In the seventy-plus countries imposing criminal sanctions on consensual same-sex relations,[37] laws are often justified with reference to religion or culture. A law-in-the-making provides a relevant example: in November 2011, the Nigerian Senate approved a draconian 'Same-Sex Marriage Prohibition Bill' – a proposal which has been debated for years. Back in 2006, Justice Minister Bayo Ojo invoked both religion and 'indigenous values' to justify criminalization: he claimed that homosexual conduct was 'un-African and, if you look at the Holy books, the Bible and the Qur'an, it is prohibited' (IRIN 2006).

How severely discriminatory legal provisions are enforced depends on various factors, including whether governments wish to divert public attention from other issues,[38] or whether fundamentalists are able to affect national agendas. Malaysia – where homosexual conduct is illegal – provides a striking example of the latter: documented attacks on LGBTTIs' and women's rights abound. The past three years witnessed: a *fatwa* against women who behave or dress 'like men' (2008, issued by the National Fatwa Council to prevent the spread of lesbianism); a young woman sentenced to caning for drinking beer

(2009, ultimately commuted to community service); three women caned for 'illicit sex' (2010); the establishment of 'Obedient Wives Clubs' (2011, promoting polygyny, obedience and sexual skills to retain one's husband). On the sexual orientation front, the past year included: a 'reminder' by a high-ranking politician that 'homosexuality goes against Islam and its practice in the country is therefore unconstitutional' (2011, M. Nazri, a minister in the prime minister's department); a ban on an annual sexuality rights festival, the *Seksualiti Merdeka* (2011); attempts to 're-educate' teenagers deemed effeminate (2011, 66 boys sent to special camp for religious education and counselling on masculine behaviour). These examples constitute a worrying trend in a specific Muslim-majority context. They also confirm a fact evident in all regions: where religious extremism becomes powerful, discrimination against women and LGBTTI people becomes legitimized – by both states and non-state actors. In such contexts, lesbians and trans people are especially at risk (along with others perceived as deviant).[39] The key question is: how do people resist?

Gay Muslims organizing: resistance

The cultural and political diversity among and within Muslim contexts is reflected in the varied assertions of sexual rights found in different societies. I highlight several significant cross-regional trends (based on several years of monitoring activities and my own involvement in advocacy), specifically: efforts geared towards 'reclaiming culture', interpreting religious texts, and increased visibility of LGBTT people. One cautionary note: strategies operate at many levels – individual, local, national, regional or international. The initiatives easiest to document tend to be those that are less grassroots, more urban/middle class, and connected to national or international efforts. Less visible but equally relevant are strategies designed by individuals not linked to groups, and by rural and poor people. However, this section cannot do justice to the range of efforts advocates in Muslim societies are engaged in, especially given that ever-increasing numbers of informal affinity groups as well as established NGOs have sprouted in all regions over the past fifteen years.

A few examples attest to the vibrancy of sexual rights organizing in Muslim contexts. Numerous groups in both urban and rural settings aim at breaking the isolation that LGBTTI people face, and coalition-building (including with non-Muslim members of society) is often a priority. NGOs also engage in collective initiatives, such as joint advocacy trainings or lobbying at both national and international levels. Sharing expertise within and across regions allows both the identification of worrying trends and the formulation of political claims: for example, the Lebanese gay group Helem launched its 'Homophobia Monitor', a web-based tool which 'collects information and resources related to the conditions and situation of the homosexual community in the Arab World'. Further, various NGOs focus on asserting a range of human rights – including the right to life and security of the person, to equality, to non-discrimination, to privacy, to freedom of assembly and association, and so on – devoting much effort to the crucial but painstaking work of documenting human rights violations and to circulating information in international forums.

In addition, many groups participate in annual events of global or regional magnitude, such as IDAHO (the International Day Against Homophobia and Transphobia, celebrated since 2005) and 'One Day, One Struggle', a broad campaign launched by the now decade-old Coalition for Sexual and Bodily Rights in Muslim Societies to 'promote sexual autonomy, privacy, pleasure, equity, sex education and health care'. Coming together on a regular basis helps LGBTT people support one another – an approach spearheaded by the Al-Fatiha network as early as 1997. The recent MantiQitna Qamb (QamB) initiative follows a similar model, although there is an added emphasis on articulating common strategies. First held in 2010, QamB brought 'queer Arab activists' from Egypt, Lebanon, Jordan, Syria, Palestine, Iraq, Morocco, Tunisia, Algeria, Yemen, Kuwait, the Emirates, Qatar and Sudan, with an aim to 'grow and nurture each other as activists for social justice and [increase] the connectivity between us outside the confines of ethnic identities and arbitrary borders'.

Among these initiatives, 'reclaiming' both culture and religion is a key strategy pursued by activists and scholars across Muslim communities. I now concentrate on concrete efforts linked to revisiting the past – in order to reveal historical instances of gender and sexual 'nonconformity' – and on gay-friendly interpretations of Muslim religious texts (in South Africa and Indonesia). Finally, I refer to the increased visibility of LGBTT people – both in their communities and in cultural production (in Lebanon, Turkey, Morocco) – before briefly evoking the backlash currently under way in Egypt.

Reclaiming cultural diversity

Chiang (2008: 51) points at a 'shift in queer theory', which now privileges 'a mode of inquiry that does not posit heterosexuality as the privileged cultural paradigm of human intimacy' in past societies, and which evaluates the 'significance of erotic desire in different times and places'. While we should remain alert to the potential romanticizing (and the political reconstruction) of history to 'imagine communities', identifying one's own 'roots' does strengthen collective identities. Furthermore, asserting historical legitimacy is a legitimate response to religious and cultural claims that exclude LGBTTI people – on the basis that they do not belong to the nation, or have no place among 'Muslims'.

While female same-sex relations have been mostly disregarded in previous publications (Murray and Roscoe 1997; Wright and Rowson 1997), scholars have recently offered well-grounded research using Arabic medieval and modern primary sources focusing on women (Habib 2007, 2009; Amer 2008).[40] Documenting a time when 'religiosity was not so punitive', Habib points at the destruction of sources in the post-medieval period. Shaheed and Lee-Shaheed (whose book provides numerous examples of 'Muslim women' asserting their rights from the eighth century to the 1950s) refer to a surviving source from the twelfth century: a male scholar who notes in his medical treatise, published in Baghdad, that

> There are also women who are more intelligent than the others. They possess many of the ways of men, so they resemble them even in their movements, the manner in which they talk, and their voice ... This makes it difficult for her to submit to the wishes of men and bring her to lesbian love. Most of the women with these characteristics are to be found among the educated and the elegant women, the scribes, Koran readers and female scholars.[41] (Shaheed and Lee-Shaheed 2005: 17)

Non-scholars also rely on historical sources to emphasize the indigenous character of same-sex relations and distinguish themselves from the notion of 'importing from the West'. Walid Diamond, a Beirut-based writer, asserts that 'What Lebanon needs in order to genuinely advance gay rights is a leap into modernity. Not an imported ready-made idea of modernity. But, instead, one that reclaims the past and reinterprets local culture' (2010). The ultimate goal of the Algerian LGBT group Abu Nawas, set up five years ago, is the 'decriminalization of homosexuality'. But it also aims at reclaiming local cultures: in a 2010 statement celebrating the annual 'Algerian LGBT Day', the group commemorates Ottoman sultan Selim I (1470–1520) as a 'fierce warrior who [when] near his beloved found himself a poet', and quotes one of his verses: 'I, who make the Lions of Europe shake under my powerful claws, become a soft lamb when near this beardless youth with the eyes of a doe'. The rationale for selecting Selim I is clearly stated. Linking its current struggle to 'historical and religious symbolism', the group reasserts its motto: 'We want to maintain our membership in the Arab world. We do not follow a fashion, a Western model. We are not in a logic of mimicry' (Abu Nawas 2010). Indeed, by naming itself after the famous classical author of male erotic poetry, Abu Nawas (756–810), the group sought a historical foundation for same-sex relations. While it remains problematic that a self-professed 'LGBT' group chose a poet who ridiculed female same-sex sexuality, Abu Nawas did celebrate his young male lovers:

> I die of love for him, perfect in every way,
> Lost in the strains of wafting music.
> My eyes are fixed upon his delightful body
> And I do not wonder at his beauty.
> His waist is a sapling, his face a moon,
> And loveliness rolls off his rosy cheek.
> I die of love for you, but keep this secret:
> The tie that binds us is an unbreakable rope.
> How much time did your creation take, O angel?
> So what! All I want is to sing your praises.[42]

Overall, initiatives to 'reclaim history' stem from the need to challenge conservative and fundamentalist forces which take ownership of the past in order to deny LGBTTI people their human rights.

These attempts to make 'gay Muslims' visible also support political claims, validating resistance to an imposed narrative. As seen below, similar goals inform ongoing efforts towards reinterpreting religious scriptures.

Reclaiming religious texts

Theologians and scholars, aiming to break the monopoly of male conservative interpretation, re-examine religious texts to promote a less homophobic[43] and sexist[44] lens. Following the tradition of *ijtihad* (independent reasoning), they argue that the Qur'an and Hadith ought to be analysed from the perspective of the current context. Among them, Imam Hendricks, director of the South African queer Muslim organization the Inner Circle, challenges the condemnation of homosexuality by various Islamic scholars and, more broadly, 'patriarchal views on gender and masculinity'. Relying primarily on Qur'anic sources, he intends to 'provide uncomplicated answers to the ordinary Muslim' by making them aware that 'Islam, at its very core, does not condemn non-heterosexual intimacy. Instead it is embraced as part of a divine plan'. He stresses the core message of the Qur'an as promoting 'equality, freedom of choice and expression' and seeks to demonstrate that 'the *Shari'ah* law which criminalises homosexuality is inconsistent with the Qur'an' (Hendricks 2010: 31–2, 35). Useful in its accessibility to a large constituency, Hendricks's research also provides specific guidance, including for example through a deconstruction of the Story of Lot (or Luth), and Sodom and Gomorrah. This latter parable is used to stigmatize non-normative sexualities, but, in common with other progressive theologians, Hendricks says it has been misinterpreted over the centuries.

Theologian Musdah Mulia, of the Indonesia Conference of Religions and Peace, also asserts that consensual homosexual relationships among adults were and are permissible in Islam. Her analysis is solidly anchored in Islamic texts, yet her framing of sexual rights is broader than most:

> We must be uncompromising and passionate in our efforts to decrease stigma and improve access to service, to increase recognition of sexuality as a positive aspect of human life. Marginalized groups such as young people, transgender people, sex workers, people who are gay, lesbian or bisexual, child brides and girl mothers particularly need our compassion.

Too often denied, and too long neglected, sexual rights deserve our attention and priority. (Musdah Mulia 2009: 1)

Denouncing both patriarchal views and heteronormativity, she develops her argument drawing from a range of sources – including the Qur'an, *fiqh*, the human rights framework, historical facts and local customs (for example, the normalized status of transgender people in South Sulawesi or East Java). This allows her to stress that,

As a Muslim woman I do believe that the Holy Qur'an has a universal meaning that should be in continuous dialogue with Muslims according to different times and temporal settings. The universal values and truths of the Holy Qur'an are absolute. While the particular values and truths obtained historically via the interpretations of the text of the Qur'an are relative. (Musdah Mulia 2009: 6)

Thanks to the work of theologians, human rights defenders, feminists and legal practitioners, alternative sexualities and gender expressions have become increasingly visible in various Muslim countries and communities. However, along with visibility come challenges.

Visibility: reclaiming public space or public discourse

Visibility often carries consequences, whether people are visible to antagonistic relatives, to hostile community members, or to an oppressive state. These consequences vary, in part, according to the status of the perpetrators (as non-state or state actors), and can include humiliation and violence, forced medical examination or HIV testing, rape, and even murder. Lesbian and trans activism is commonly more risky, likely because it challenges gender norms that are more strictly enforced within families and homes (compared to boys and men, whose lives tend to be less policed). But some groups are paving the way, such as the Palestinian lesbian group Aswat in Israel, or Meem in Lebanon, which includes self-identified women of various sexual orientations and gender identities.

One Meem activist raises a pertinent issue, questioning the 'international understanding of "visibility" and "coming out" as signs of progress in LGBT movements across the world'. She challenges 'a foreign framework that links visibility closely to pride', asking: 'Had we tagged our foreheads with the words "lesbian", "queer" or "transgender" and went on national TV shows ... would we have been able to be as effective in our community and movement building as we have been so far?' This perspective was articulated after a few years 'trying to organize alongside a majority of gay men within the framework of LGBT public advocacy', when Meem activists realized they had to prioritize creating 'a safe space for ourselves as women first'. Confidentiality and anonymity were subsequently defined as 'key elements in our organizing'. But the emphasis on confidentiality certainly does not translate into Meem activists being voiceless, as they make their presence felt in Lebanese society and continue to interact with various constituencies within their communities, including religious leaders. The group also maintains a strong online presence with its weekly Arabic magazine *Bekhsoos* (Meem 2010). Further, aware of the power of telling people's stories, Meem published *Bareed Mista3jil: True Stories* in 2009, a collection of forty-one short testimonies. While authors remain anonymous, their personal messages resonate powerfully, including through staged readings of the book in queer and transgender circles in the region and beyond.

In other regions, visibility takes more traditional forms. For example, although the gay group Lambda Istanbul, established in 1993, waited almost a decade before holding its first Pride March, and only fifty pioneers dared to join, by 2010 the Gay Pride event counted between 3,000 and 5,000 participants. The same year Trans Pride Istanbul started with a few hundred members; estimates are that by 2011 (i.e. within just a year) the Trans parade included almost a thousand transgender people.

Public visibility also manifests in literature, films and comics.[45] Increasingly, cultural productions raise issues of sexuality, especially in connection with gay men (in this field as elsewhere, lesbian, bisexual, transgender and intersex people remain comparatively sidelined). The Moroccan novelist Abdellah Taia's public coming out in 2007 in a Moroccan French-language magazine has had significant impact in the Maghreb and beyond. Explains Taia in a 2009 interview:

> As a homosexual I knew that Moroccan society would only destroy me. I had already talked about [homosexuality] in my books. I didn't want to keep up the hypocrisy and schizophrenia like other Moroccans and

Arabs. I had to go along with my own truth. ... I did it because it was necessary to speak out. Just to name things, for some people, is dangerous – it's revolutionary. That's why I continue to write: to be part of this revolution with literary arms.

Taia paid a personal price for his openness, especially following an interview in an Arabic-language magazine:

'My mother said: "What did you say? We are not like this. ... We are good people."' But Taia believes he did the right thing, in part because his class-background (he comes from a very poor family) does not support the usual stereotypes: his gayness cannot be constructed as typically middle-class or Westernized. He declares 'I feel Muslim', adding 'There is no incompatibility between Islam and choices of sexual identity. I understood somehow that all those rules were invented by humans, but not by me. I'm not obliged to respect them – traditions, religion.' (Whitaker 2009)

While Taia breaks ground in Moroccan literature, documentary films also started exploring the issue of homosexuality in Muslim communities.[46] The widely promoted *A Jihad for Love*, filmed in twelve countries on four continents, features Maha, an Egyptian woman, who in the film expresses another perspective on Islam and sexuality: 'If asked of my sin on Judgment Day, I will stand before God and say that my sin is that I loved and Allah is merciful and forgiving.' Indian film-maker Sharma notes: 'All the people in my film are coming out as Muslims. Islam is the heart of this film. They are proud to be gay, but fundamentally they're coming out as Muslims and saying they're as Muslim as anybody else, and their Islam is as true and fundamental as anybody else's' (Kay 2007). He adds: 'Not everyone who has seen the film is smiling. In South Africa, the Muslim Judicial Council issued a *hukum* (judgment), similar to a *fatwa*, calling homosexuals *murtads*, apostates' (El-Katatney 2008) – an accusation that carries a most severe penalty in Islamic jurisprudence.

In the Egyptian context, attempts to mute the visibility of gay themes include political pressure. Referring in 2008 – pre-Tahrir Square – to 'the wave of conservatism in Egypt and the Arab world in recent years', the Egyptian Underground Film Society (EUFS, the team behind the first Egyptian movie centred on gay characters, *All*

My Life, 2008) deplored the fact that 'artists have become increasingly unable to tackle a number of subjects that were dealt with in Egyptian cinema in the past'. They cite the 2007 controversy provoked by *The Yacoubian Building*, by renowned Egyptian film-maker Youssef Chahine, when '112 members of the Egyptian Parliament – one-quarter of the total – signed a petition demanding the removal of the scenes portraying the only homosexual character in the film' (EUFS 2008).[47] Meanwhile, there is no indication that the post-Mubarak era will ensure freedom of expression and creativity: echoing the South African clerics' Islamist ideology, Salafi lawyers accused several prominent artists (writers, actors and film directors) of 'defaming Islam' (Metwaly 2012). There have been previous attempts to impose religiously justified censorship in Egypt[48] (including repeated efforts to ban *One Thousand and One Nights*), and one can expect artists and democrats to fight back. But these recent legal proceedings – a sure sign of the creation of a 'culture' in line with fundamentalist Islam – do not bode well for the visibility of sexual rights or for the future of democracy or secularism in general.

Conclusion

Sexuality remains a contested and highly patrolled terrain in all societies. It is also a strongly politicized arena, and has been for a long time: a glimpse at colonial and contemporary discourses reminds us about the ongoing use of gender and sexuality as tools to assert and reinforce asymmetrical power relations. Recognizing the political dimension implicit in mainstream Western portrayal of 'Muslim women' as victims only highlights the fact that, to borrow Shaheed's words, 'the notion that all men in Muslim societies are misogynistic is as much a myth as the notion that women are only silent victims' (Shaheed and Lee-Shaheed 2005: xvii). The same remark is eminently applicable to the monolithic notions that all 'Muslims' are homophobic, and all 'gay Muslims' are passive and oppressed, as the examination of LGBTT organizing trends has demonstrated.

The diversity and vibrancy of locally grounded movements in favour of LGBTTI people's rights in effect challenge mainstream discourses, which in various regions continue to deny the reality of sexual rights advocacy in Muslim communities. This chapter has also stressed some of the challenges faced by those who appear not to conform to dominant sexual and gender norms, particularly violence and discrimination justified in the name of both culture and religion. Nevertheless, by engaging in numerous initiatives to advance sexual and gender diversity, from the local to the international level, LGBTTI activists are far from fitting stereotypes propagated in both Western and Southern contexts: they are not 'exceptions' that need disciplining (as Muslim conservatives and fundamentalists would have it), nor a voiceless constituency that needs saving (as many Westerners pretend).

Overall, my discussion attempts to raise conceptual possibilities, especially regarding intersectionality as it plays out in the lives of racialized, ethnicized, gendered 'gay Muslims', and as it relates to our analysis of sexuality. Including intersectionality as an analytic tool is key: we must recognize that numerous factors affect the experience of sexuality, as well as access to leadership within sexual rights movements. We also need an intersectional analysis of sexuality to account for the role played by religion – as it operates at personal, local, national and international levels – through its diverse practices, and through its diverse normative and ideological frameworks. While a great deal of attention has been paid to the intersection of gender, class, race and sexuality, religion appears to be mostly (if not exclusively) framed as a domain of dominant heterosexual norms, values and practices. The examples provided in this chapter established that religion is practised by people with highly varied sexual and gender practices and identities. In fact, social actors shape and reshape what it means to be 'Muslim' and queer on an ongoing basis.

Finally, research on sexuality remains dominated by women's and gender studies; while these perspectives are crucial, they need to be enriched by histories of culture and regions – the relevance of multidisciplinarity cannot be overemphasized.[49] As culture and religion influence people in different ways, this influence needs to be analysed more closely, not least to take into account the fact that various actors are engaged in remodelling Muslim societies from within, and to look at how these processes find public expression.

Notes

1. Throughout this chapter, I use the LGBTTI acronym, or LGBTT in instances where intersex people are not addressed (sadly, the status and advocacy of intersex people is often not included in non-specialized literature). This term remains politically useful because it provides a common umbrella for coalition-building, lobbying and organizing purposes, but I have noted elsewhere that it ought to be problematized for multiple reasons (Hélie 2006). First, LGBTTI categories exclude a number of social actors, including those who engage in homoeroticism yet do not identify as LGBTTI people; or celibates, who also challenge both heteronormativity and compulsory sexuality. Second, the LGBTTI label renders invisible other conceptions of sexual/gender nonconformism and erases a variety of culturally specific terms and identities (see Fabeni and Fried 2007 for a glossary of selected terminologies). Finally, it also blurs existing power dynamics within sexual rights movements.

2. In this chapter, 'gay Muslims' includes women; but see also note 3 below.

3. I am grateful to Cynthia Rothschild for highlighting the need to acknowledge that individuals face discrimination and violence on the basis of their alleged or perceived sexual orientation and gender expression, rather than simply on the basis of their actual gender and sexual preferences. This fact, documented throughout the world (see in particular the report by the High Commissioner for Human Rights 2011), also points at the inherent weakness of formulas such as 'gay Muslims'. References to 'gay Muslims' are intentionally kept in quotation marks throughout this chapter because the formula's essentialist bent does not take into account how deeply others' perceptions of one's sexuality impact the treatment one faces; and because it assumes that all LGBTTI people from Muslim origin are believers in Islam, while rendering invisible broad cultural differences (when expressions of sexuality and gender vary greatly depending on many social factors, including whether individuals are part of, for example, South African, Indonesian, Sudanese, or French Muslim communities).

4. Highlighting the political manipulation of these issues in conservative Muslim contexts as well, the question of mistranslation has been raised repeatedly in Iranian media close to the regime. The quotation below (from original sources in Farsi) claims that Ahmadinejad's comments were misquoted. On 23 October 2010, Ahmadinejad's chief of staff, Mr Mashaei, told an international scientific festival in Tehran that

> At Columbia University, Mr. President had a long discussion. Someone asked him, 'Why don't you allow homosexuals to legally engage in activism in your country?' In response, President Ahmadinejad said that unlike your country [i.e. United States], in our country homosexuals do not have a set of articulated demands. Mr. President's comments were mistranslated, and it was understood as if he was saying there are no homosexuals in Iran, which caused the audience to laugh and be shocked to hear that there are no gays in Iran.

www.tabnak.ir/fa/pages/?cid=126874.

5. Linked to the 2005 execution of two Iranian teenagers in Mashhad, this mantra was repeated in over a dozen online publications and forums, including ILGA, *UK Gay News*, *OutRage!*, *Seattle Gay News*, etc. For a critique, see Long 2009.

6. Penalties apply to *mosaheqeh* (female same-sex, liable to 100 lashes) and to *lavat* (male same-sex, liable to capital punishment; note that this term is also spelled *liwat* in other Muslim contexts). See relevant Iranian law: http://irqr.net/islamicpunishment-e.htm (accessed 30 November 2011).

7. 'Speech by PM Netanyahu to Joint Meeting of the US Congress', Israel Ministry of Foreign Affairs, 24 May 2011, www.mfa.gov.il/MFA/Government/Speeches+by+Israeli+leaders/2011/Speech_PM_Netanyahu_US_Congress_24–May-2011.htm (accessed 30 November 2011).

8. For years, Palestinian LGBTTI activists (including Al-Qaws, Aswat, Pinkwatching Israel, PQBDS (Palestinian Queers for Boycott, Divestment and Sanctions) and Helem in Lebanon) have denounced similar stands as illustrations of 'pinkwashing', a policy pursued by Israel to distract from its systematic discrimination against Palestinian Israelis and from the ongoing violence of occupation.

9. Recognizing that would-be refugees face a variety of obstacles (not least the fact that Lebanon did not ratify the 1951 Refugee Convention), Duncan nevertheless documents numerous cases of sexuality- or gender-related asylum-seekers.

10. It is worth remembering the 'brutal history of European homophobia[,] its continuing legacy of violence, pathologisation and criminalization' of LGBTTI people (Haritaworn 2008: 88), and its impact on postcolonial contexts. See also Human Rights Watch (2008b), which documents 'how laws in over three dozen countries, from India to Uganda and from Nigeria to Papua New Guinea, derive from a single law on homosexual conduct that British colonial rulers imposed on India in 1860'.

11. I intentionally refer to 'claims' to emphasize that Western 'secular democracies' are in fact more entangled with religion, and with conservative religious actors, than they wish to admit.

12. While neoconservatives insist on 'Western civilization' being threatened by Muslim extremists, it is worth pausing to consider the facts. As Bennoune (2011) reminds us, casualties inflicted by a fundamentalist networks such as al-Qaeda disproportionately strike at civilians or dissenters within Muslim countries themselves. Bennoune quotes from a '2009 study of Arabic media sources by the Combating Terrorism Centre at West Point [which] found that only 15% of all of the casualties of al-Qaida between 2004 and 2008 were Westerners. Between 2006–2008, fully 98% of al-Qaida's victims were inhabitants of Muslim majority countries.' The full report is available at www.ctc.usma.edu/posts/deadly-vanguards-a-study-of-al-qaidas-violence-against-muslims (accessed 15 January 2012).

13. British media coverage of the Gallup poll centred on sensationalist headlines about British Muslims' 'zero tolerance of homosexuality' (Butt 2009). Note that contradictory findings, in a survey conducted by the British think-tank Demos in 2011, are nevertheless presented with a highly paternalistic

tone by some British journalists, who qualify British Muslims' views on gay rights as 'startlingly liberal' (Dunt 2011).

14. The Feminist Majority Foundation-led Campaign to Stop Gender Apartheid in Afghanistan provides an example of misguided efforts, with its insistence on women's victimization – rather than resistance – and its lack of analysis of the role played by Western Coalition members in supporting misogynist warlords, or of the links between violence against women and increased militarization in the region. As a result, it has been accused of 'collu[ding] with the hegemonic projects of the US state' (Russo 2006).

15. Popularized by queer theorists such as Butler, the term 'homonationalism' refers to the tendency among some LGBTTI organizations and individuals to, unwillingly or purposefully, condone and perpetuate ideas of white superiority, thereby marginalizing non-whites.

16. In April 2012, President Obama declined to sign an Executive Order to expand protection against discrimination for federal LGBTT workers. The Human Rights Campaign notes that 'In 29 [US] states, it's still legal to fire someone solely because they're lesbian, gay, or bisexual; in 34 states it is legal to fire someone solely for being transgender.' See http://sites.hrc.org/sites/passendanow/index.asp (accessed 1 May 2012).

17. In light of the recent statements made by the US political leadership, it is worth remembering that legal discrimination against homosexual conduct has only been tackled recently: for example, only in 2003 did the Supreme Court overturn a previous ruling (related to Georgia's anti-sodomy statute, *Bowers* v. *Hardwick*, 1986) and establish that consensual sexual conduct between adults was protected under the Fourteenth Amendment of the US Constitution (in *Lawrence* v. *Texas*, 2003). More recently, the 'Don't Ask, Don't Tell' policy, which banned openly gay and lesbian people from serving in the US military, was only overturned in 2011.

18. For example, references to legal achievements could include South Africa and Ecuador, which were among the first countries to expand the basis for discrimination to include sexual orientation, and to incorporate anti-discrimination provisions in their constitutions; or the gender identity law passed by the Argentinian Senate on 9 May 2012, which includes the most progressive disposition on transgender rights in the world. Some regional human rights bodies have also taken a stand recently in favour of non-discrimination of LGBTTI people, as happened in March 2012 with the Inter-American Commission on Human Rights' condemnation of the State of Chile in the groundbreaking case of Karen Atala Riffo.

19. For example, when the US embassy in Islamabad held its first ever LGBT 'pride celebration' in June 2011, the Jamaat-e-Islami immediately organized protest rallies in Islamabad, Karachi and Lahore. A representative stated: 'They have destroyed us physically, imposed the so-called war on terrorism on us and now they have unleashed cultural terrorism on us' (Goodenough 2011). Opposition to the US stand did not stem only from Muslim countries: in El Savador, over forty Latin American organizations reacted to a pro-sexual diversity article by the US ambassador, accusing her of 'disregarding our profound Christian values, rooted in natural

law', by trying to 'impose ... a new vision of foreign and bizarre values, completely alien to our moral fiber, intending to disguise this as "human rights" ... [with] "an air of superiority"' (Contrapunto 2011).

20. Human rights officials have only recently paid attention to LGBTTI asy-lum-seekers. In 2008, UNHCR published its 'Guidance Note on Refugee Claims relating to Sexual Orientation and Gender Identity'. In 2011 the Commissioner for Human Rights of the Council of Europe published its report on 'Discrimination on Grounds of Sexual Orientation and Gender Identity', covering all forty-seven member states.

21. The recognition of this fact prompted the publication *Protection for LGBTI Defenders* (which contains examples from Muslim contexts), available online at www.protectionline.org/Protection-Manual-For-LGBTI.htm (accessed 15 August 2011).

22. National Coalition of Anti-Violence Programs (2008) 'NCAVP National Hate Violence Report'. See the press release at: www.ncavp.org/media/ MediaReleaseDetail.aspx?p=2313&d=2440, and the full report at: www. avp.org/publications/reports/reports.htm (accessed 10 December 2011).

23. See also Sharma 2006.

24. The Aceh example is reminiscent of other religious fundamentalists and of their manipulation of disasters, natural or otherwise. Following the 9/11 attacks, Pat Robertson, a widely popular Christian evangelical, denounced 'the pagans, and the abortionists, and the feminists, and the gays and the lesbians [and] all of them who have tried to secularize America – I point the finger in their face and say "you helped this happen"'. See www. actupny.org/YELL/falwell.html (accessed 15 November 2011).

25. Indeed, numerous examples – ranging from imposed sterilization of trans people to the curtailing of sex education in favour of abstinence-only programmes, to efforts to ban abortion – could illustrate the fact that sexual rights are also threatened in Western contexts.

26. I.e. the 'Committee for the Promotion of Virtue and the Prevention of Vice', or *mutawwa'in*. For more details, see Hoodfar and Ghoreishian, Chapter 9 in this volume.

27. The quotation marks here are meant to remind readers that electoral pro-cesses are not the most salient, or the unique, mark of 'democracy' – as many would like us to believe following the uprisings in the Middle East and North Africa. In Tunisia (as in Egypt), elections have consolidated the power of fundamentalist parties. Despite opportunistic assurances to the contrary, these parties only pay lip service to 'democracy': they do not support equality of all citizens, nor gender equality – tenets which should continue to be seen as hallmarks of democracy.

28. Among the various strains of political Islam, contemporary Salafists are deeply sectarian movements 'often indistinguishable from Wahhabism' (which originated in eighteenth-century Saudi Arabia) but have a broader reach. For an excellent summary, see Awaaz – South Asia Watch 2006: 3–5.

29. 10 December 2007, Art. 199 bis, Criminal Code.

30. The Freedom and Justice Party (the Muslim Brotherhood's political wing) offers 'free circumcision', flaunting the legal ban on female genital

mutilation (Abdel Salam 2012), and highlighting the emphasis placed by Muslim fundamentalists on controlling women's sexuality.

31. Segregated buses in Orthodox neighbourhoods in New York City and worse discriminatory trends in Jerusalem have recently shown that women and young girls are unwelcome in the public arena unless they conform to strict gender rules. For New York, see Chavkin and Nathan-Kazis 2011. For the Jerusalem case, see Sommer 2011.

32. For a documentation of past and ongoing cases, see WLUML (www.wluml. org) and the Violence Is Not Our Culture Campaign (www.violenceisnot-ourculture.org).

33. Personal communication, 26 October 2011.

34. A Tunisian Islamist group that was granted permission to form a political party shortly after the fall of Ben Ali's regime in the spring of 2011, Ennahda has since obtained over 40 per cent of the votes in the October 2011 Constituent Assembly election.

35. See note 37.

36. The OIC-backed statement (which attracted 57 signatures) criticized the initial statement (endorsed by 66 states), arguing it could lead to 'the social normalization, and possibly the legitimization, of many deplorable acts including pedophilia' (Farrior 2009).

37. Legal sanctions even prescribe the death penalty in at least Iran, Mauritania, Saudi Arabia, Southern parts of Somalia, Sudan, Yemen, Afghanistan and twelve states in Nigeria. There is dispute as to whether 'sodomy' is punishable by death in the United Arab Emirates (ILGA 2011).

38. Including economic crises and poverty, corruption or electoral politics.

39. Including sex workers or divorced women but also religious minorities.

40. Persian scholars (Afary 2009; Najmabadi 2005, 2012) also greatly contributed to the field of sexuality and gender relations, examining in particular the rise of heteronormativity in the Iranian context. See Yaghoobi, Chapter 2 in this volume.

41. T. Haddad [aka Abu Nasr al Isra'ili], *Ktab nuzhat al-ashab fi mu'asarat al-ahbab fi'ilm albah*, Part 1, paras 6–8; cited in Walther 1981.

42. Queers in History 2011.

43. See Kuggle 2010.

44. For a feminist reinterpretation, see for example the work by Ali Kecia, Hassan Riffat and Shaikh Shamima.

45. See the reference to the Yogyakarta Principles in comic form, in Vivienne Wee, Chapter 1 in this book.

46. Recent films focusing on sexual identity include, for example: *I Exist – Voices from the Lesbian and Gay Middle Eastern Community*, USA (Barbosa and Lenoir, 2002); *Mijn zus Zahra/My Sister Zahra*, Belgium (Choua 2006); *Gay Muslims*, UK (Channel Four 2006); *A Jihad for Love*, USA (Sharma 2007); *Toum Omry/All My Life*, Egypt (Sabry 2008). Films on gender/trans identity include *Just a Woman*, France/Iran (Farahani 2001); *Be Like Others*, UK (Eshaghian 2008), which focuses on the systematic gender-reassignment surgeries in Iran as 'a cure for homosexuality'.

47. On *The Yacoubian Building* controversy, see also BBC News 2006.

48. Apart from efforts by proponents of political Islam to target LGBTTI people, we should remember that one of the most brutal instances of repression against 'gay Muslims', the Queen Boat case in 2001, was carried out under Mubarak. This is not, however, unrelated to the rise of fundamentalist ideology, as the Mubarak regime attempted to project itself 'as the guardian of public virtue, to deflate an Islamist opposition movement' (Baghat 2001). On this case, see also Long 2004.

49. Najmabadi's latest book (2012) is precisely an effort in this direction, with a deliberate effort to combine historical and ethnographic approaches.

References

Abdel Salam, M. (2012) 'Egypt Brotherhood organize mobile FGM convoys', *BikyaMasr*, 14 May, http://bikyamasr.com/68750/egypts-brotherhood-mobile-fgm-convoys-condemned-by-womens-group (accessed 5 May 2012).

Abu Nawas (2010) 'Journée Nationale des LGBT Algériens – Un mouvement est né', press release, 10 October, www.wluml.org/fr/node/6664 (accessed 11 December 2011).

Afary, J. (2009) *Sexual Politics in Modern Iran*. Cambridge: Cambridge University Press.

Al Jazeera (2011) 'Tunisian gender-parity "revolution" hailed', 21 April, http://english.aljazeera.net/news/africa/2011/04/2011421161714335465.html (accessed 10 December 2011).

Alloula, M. (1986) *The Colonial Harem*. Minneapolis: University of Minnesota Press.

Amer, S. (2008) *Crossing Borders: Love between Women in Medieval French and Arabic Literatures*. Philadelphia: University of Pennsylvania Press.

Amin, S. (2011) 'Egyptian general admits "virginity checks" conducted on protesters', *CNN*, 30 May, http://articles.cnn.com/2011–05–30/world/egypt.virginity.tests_1_virginity-tests-female-demonstrators-amnesty-report?_s=PM:WORLD (accessed 5 December 2011).

Awaaz – South Asia Watch (2006) 'The Islamic right – Key tendencies', June, www.centreforsecularspace.org/sites/default/files/AWAAZ,%20Islamic%20Right%20Key%20Tendencies%281%29.pdf (accessed 1 January 2012).

Baghat, H. (2001) 'Explaining Egypt's targeting of gays', *Middle East Report and Information Project*, Press Information Note 64, 23 July.

BBC News (2002) 'Turkey scraps virginity tests', 28 February, http://news.bbc.co.uk/2/hi/europe/1845784.stm (accessed 1 January 2012).

BBC News (2006) 'Egypt debates controversial film', 5 July, http://news.bbc.co.uk/2/hi/entertainment/5150718.stm (accessed 15 December 2011).

Ben-Naeh, Y. (2005) 'Moskho the Jew and his gay friends: Same-sex sexual relations in Ottoman Jewish society', *Journal of Early Modern History* 9(1–2): 79–105.

Bennoune, K. (2011) 'Remembering all al-Qaida's victims', *Guardian*, 3 May, www.guardian.co.uk/commentisfree/cifamerica/2011/may/03/osamabin-laden-al-qaida (accessed 15 December 2011).

Bleys, R. (1996) *The Geography of Perversion: Male-to-Male Sexual Behavior Outside the West and the Ethnographic Imagination, 1750–1918*. New York: New York University Press.

Borger, J., and MacAskill, E. (2007) 'As protesters jeer, Ahmadinejad denies Iran wants nuclear weapons', *Guardian*, 25 September, www.guardian.co.uk/iran/story/0,,2176530,00.html (accessed 1 December 2011).

Butt, R. (2009) 'Muslims in Britain have zero tolerance of homosexuality, says poll', *Guardian*, 7 May, www.guardian.co.uk/uk/2009/may/07/muslims-britain-france-germany-homosexuality (accessed 25 November 2011).

Chavkin, S., and Nathan-Kazis, J. (2011) 'Riding together on sex-segregated bus: Men and women divided by curtain on ultra-Orthodox routes', *Jewish Daily Forward*, www.irac.org/NewsDetailes.aspx?ID=1278 (accessed 5 November 2011).

Chiang, H. (2008) 'Empires of desires: History and queer theory in an age of global affect', *Critical Studies in History* 1: 50–71.

Chivers, C.J. (2006) 'In Chechen's humiliation, questions on rule of law', *New York Times*, 30 August, www.nytimes.com/2006/08/30/world/europe/30chechnya.html?_r=1&oref=slogin (accessed 15 January 2012).

Contrapunto (2011) 'Ultraconservadores se enojan con la embajadora estadounidense', *Contrapunto*, 7 July, www.contrapunto.com.sv/sociedadcivil/ultraconservadores-se-enojan-con-la-embajadora-estadounidense (accessed 30 December 2011).

Diamond, W. (2010) 'Gay, straight, or just Lebanese?', *Guardian*, 28 August, www.guardian.co.uk/commentisfree/2010/aug/28/lebanon-gay-pride-boy-george (accessed 30 November 2011).

Duncan, D. (2011) 'LGBTI refugees seek haven in Lebanon', 16 November, *Global Post*, www.globalpost.com/dispatch/news/regions/middle-east/lebanon/111115/lgbti-refugees-seek-haven-lebanon (accessed 18 November 2011).

Dunt, I. (2011) 'Surprise poll shows widespread Muslim support for gay rights', *Politics*, 2 June, www.politics.co.uk/news/2011/06/27/surprise-poll-shows-widespread-muslim-support (accessed 25 November 2011).

El-Katatney, E. (2008) 'Out of the closet and onto the screen – A controversial film breaks open the taboo topic of homosexuality and Islam', *Egypt Today*, 15 February, http://etharelkatatney.wordpress.com/2008/02/15/out-of-the-closet-and-onto-the-screen-2 (accessed 28 November 2010).

EUFS (Egyptian Underground Film Society) (2008) 'Press Release', 20 May, http://maraiafilm.com/eufs/prelease.html (accessed 10 January 2012).

European Union Agency for Fundamental Rights (2010) 'Homophobia, transphobia and discrimination on grounds of sexual orientation and gender identity – Comparative legal analysis', http://fra.europa.eu/fraWebsite/attachments/FRA-2011–Homophobia-Update-Report_EN.pdf (accessed 1 May 2012).

Fabeni, S., and Fried, S.T. (2007) *Manual on Sexuality-Based Advocacy*. Washington DC: Global Rights.

Farrior, S. (2009) 'Human rights advocacy on gender issues: Challenges and opportunities', *Journal of Human Rights Practice* 1(1): 83–100.

Gallup Center for Muslim Studies and Coexist Foundation (2009) *The Gallup Coexist Index 2009: A Global Study of Interfaith Relations*, www.euro-islam. info/wp-content/uploads/pdfs/gallup_coexist_2009_interfaith_relations_uk_france_germany.pdf (accessed 10 January 2012).

Goodenough, P. (2011) 'Pakistani Islamists protest U.S. embassy's "Gay Pride" event', *CNS*, 5 July, http://cnsnews.com/news/article/pakistani-islamists-protest-us-embassy-s-gay-pride-event (accessed 5 January 2011).

Graham-Brown, S. (1988) *Images of Women: The Portrayal of Women in Photography of the Middle East 1860–1950*. New York: Columbia University Press.

Habib, S. (2007) *Female Homosexuality in the Middle East: History and Representations*. New York: Routledge.

Habib, S. (2009) *Arabo-Islamic Texts on Female Homosexuality, 850–1780 A.D.* Amherst: Teneo Press.

Haritaworn, J. (2008) 'Loyal repetitions of the nation: Gay assimilation and the "War on Terror"', *Dark Matter*, 2 March, www.darkmatter101.org/site/2008/05/02/loyal-repetitions-of-the-nation-gay-assimilation-and-the-war-on-terror (accessed 1 December 2011).

Haritaworn, J., Tauqir, T., and Erdem, E. (2008) 'Gay imperialism: Gender and sexuality discourse in the "War on Terror"', in E. Miyake and A. Kuntsman (eds), *Out of Place: Interrogating Silences in Queerness/Raciality*. York: Raw Nerve Books, 72–95.

Harris, L. (2008) *The Suicide of Reason: Radical Islam's Threat to the Enlightenment*. Philadelphia: Basic Books.

Hatab F. (2012) 'Gambia: No room for gays, lesbians – President Jammeh', *Daily Observer* (Banjul), 23 April, http://allafrica.com/stories/201204230896. html (accessed 24 April 2012).

Hayes, J. (2000) *Queer Nations: Marginal Sexualities in the Maghreb*. Chicago: University of Chicago Press.

Hélie, A. (2004) 'Holy Hatred', *Reproductive Health Matters: Sexuality, Rights and Social Justice* 12(23): 120–24.

Hélie, A. (2006) 'Threats and Survival: The Religious Right and LGBT Strategies in Muslim Contexts', *Women in Action – Queering: Social Movements and Feminist Theories*, 1:19–31, Manila: ISIS.

Hélie, A. (2012) 'Problematizing "autonomy" and "tradition" with regard to veiling – A Response to Seval Yildirim', *Journal of International Law* X(1).

Hendricks, M. (2010) 'Islamic texts: A source of acceptance of queer individuals into mainstream Muslim society', *Equal Rights Review* 5: 31–51, www. equalrightstrust.org/ertdocumentbank/muhsin.pdf (accessed 10 November 2011).

High Commissioner for Human Rights (2011) 'Discriminatory laws and practices and acts of violence against individuals based on their sexual orientation and gender identity', 17 November, www2.ohchr.org/english/bodies/hr-council/docs/19session/A.HRC.19.41_English.pdf (accessed 2 December 2011).

Human Rights First (2010) Persistent needs and gaps: The protection of LGBTI Refugees, 30 September, www.humanrightsfirst.org/wp-content/uploads/

pdf/Persistent-Needs_LGBTI_Refugees_FINAL.pdf (accessed 7 November 2011).

Human Rights Watch (2011), 'Tunisia: Fundamentalists disrupting college campuses', 9 December, www.hrw.org/news/2011/12/09/tunisia-fundamentalists-disrupting-college-campuses (accessed 15 January 2012).

Human Rights Watch (2008a) 'Kuwait: Repressive dress-code law encourages police abuse', 16 January, www.hrw.org/en/news/2008/01/16/kuwait-repressive-dress-code-law-encourages-police-abuse (accessed 18 November 2011).

Human Rights Watch (2008b) 'This alien legacy – The origins of "sodomy" laws in British colonialism', 17 December, www.hrw.org/en/reports/2008/12/17/alien-legacy-0 (accessed 5 December 2011).

Huntington, S. (1996) *The Clash of Civilizations and the Remaking of World Order.* New York: Simon & Schuster.

Hussein, L. (2009) 'When I think of my trial, I pray my fight won't be in vain', *Guardian*, 4 September, www.guardian.co.uk/commentisfree/2009/sep/04/sudan-woman-trousers-trial (accessed 20 October 2011).

ILGA (International Lesbian and Gay Alliance) (2011) 'State sponsored homophobia', May, http://old.ilga.org/Statehomophobia/ILGA_State_Sponsored_Homophobia_2010.pdf (accessed 6 December 2011).

IRIN (Integrated Regional Information Networks) (2006) 'Nigeria: Government proposes law to ban same-sex marriage', UN Office for the Coordination of Humanitarian Affairs, 20 January, www.irinnews.org/printreport.aspx?reportid=57879 (accessed 15 November 2011).

Jansen, S., and Spijkerboer, T. (2011) 'Fleeing homophobia', COC Netherland/ Vrije Universiteit Amsterdam, September, www.rechten.vu.nl/nl/Images/Fleeing%20Homophobia%20report%20EN_tcm22–232205.pdf (accessed 15 January 2012).

Jolly, S. (2010) 'Poverty and sexuality: What are the connections? Overview and literature review', *SIDA*, September, www.sxpolitics.org/wp-content/uploads/2011/05/sida-study-of-poverty-and-sexuality1.pdf (accessed 15 November 2011).

Kay, J. (2007) 'Hearts and minds', *Guardian*, 5 September, www.guardian.co.uk/film/2007/sep/06/gayrights.religion (accessed 10 December 2011).

Kirby, M. (2011) 'Sodomy offense: England's least lovely criminal law export?', *Journal of Commonwealth Criminal Lawyers* (1): 22–43.

Kuggle, S.S. (2010) *Homosexuality in Islam: Critical Reflection on Gay, Lesbian, and Transgender Muslims.* London: Oneworld Publications.

Lewis, B. (1990) 'The Roots of Muslim Rage', *The Atlantic* 266(3): 47–60.

Long, S. (2004) 'The trials of culture: Sex and security in Egypt', *Middle East Report Online*, 34(230) Spring.

Long, S. (2009) 'Unbearable witness: How Western activists (mis)recognize sexuality in Iran', *Contemporary Politics* 15(1): 119–36.

Mabro, J. (1996) *Veiled Half-Truths: Western Travelers' Perception of Middle Eastern Women.* London: I.B. Tauris.

MacDonald, G. (1864) *An Invalid's Winter in Algeria.* London: Alexander Strahan.

Meem. (2010) 'Framing visibility: Coming out and the international LGBT spectrum of progress', December, www.bekhsoos.com/web/2010/12/framing-visibility-coming-out-and-the-international-lgbt-spectrum-of-progress-2 (accessed 2 December 2011).

Meem. (2009) *Bareed Mista3jil: True Stories*. Beirut: Meem.

Mellakh, H. (2012) 'L'Intelligentsia Tunisienne dans la Tourmente de la Nouvelle Inquisition', *Algérie Patriotique*, 15 May, http://algeriepatriotique.com/article/l-intelligentsia-tunisienne-dans-la-tourmente-de-la-nouvelle-inquisition (accessed 15 May 2012).

Metwaly, A. (2012) 'Islamists on art', *Majalla Magazine*, 26 April, www.majalla.com/eng/2012/04/article55231343 (accessed 10 May 2012).

Mitchell, T. (1991) *Colonizing Egypt*. Berkeley: University of California Press.

Murray, R. (1997) *Islamic Homosexualities: Culture, History, and Literature*. New York: New York University Press.

Musdah Mulia, S. (2009) 'Understanding sexuality in Islam – Promoting the Appreciation of Human Dignity', September, www.bekhsoos.com/web/wp-content/uploads/2009/09/Homosexuality-and-Islam.pdf (accessed 5 December 2011).

Najmabadi, A. (2012) *Sex-in-Change: Configurations of Gender and Sexuality in Contemporary Iran*. Durham NC: Duke University Press.

Najmabadi, A. (2005) *Women with Mustaches and Men without Beards: Gender and Sexual Anxieties of Iranian Modernity*. Berkeley: University of California Press.

Newland, K. (2002) 'Refugee resettlement in transition', Migration Policy Institute, September, www.migrationinformation.org/Feature/display.cfm?ID=52 (accessed 15 November 2011).

Petchesky, R. (2010) 'Body', panel presentation at the Center for Women's Global Leadership Twentieth Anniversary Symposium, Hunter College, New York, 6 March.

Petchesky, R. (2011) 'Biopolitics at the crossroads of sexuality and disaster: The case of Haiti', February, www.sxpolitics.org/wp-content/uploads/2009/02/petchesky-biopolitics-paper-2011–revised-final.pdf (accessed 7 December 2011).

Puar, J. (2007) *Terrorist Assemblages: Homonationalism in Queer Times*. Durham NC: Duke University Press.

Puar, J., and Rai, A.S. (2002) 'Monster, terrorist, fag: The war on terrorism and the production of docile patriots', *Social Text* 20(3): 117–48.

QEJ (Queers for Economic Justice) (2011) 'QEJ condemns the killing of a new providence shelter resident', 5 October, http://q4ej.org/qej-condemns-the-killing-of-a-new-providence-shelter-resident (accessed 30 November 2011).

Queers in History (2011) 'Abu Nuwas, Islamic poet of male love', http://queer-history.blogspot.com/2011/09/abu-nuwas-islamic-poet-of-male-love.html (accessed 29 November 2011).

Radio Netherlands Worldwide (2011) 'Anti-gay bullying reports flood in', 21 November, www.rnw.nl/english/bulletin/anti-gay-bullying-reports-flood (accessed 30 November 2011).

Red Ribbon Initiative (2010) 'Help flood-affected hijra, trans and sex worker communities in Pakistan', http://gaya-nusantara.blogspot.com/2010/09/help-flood-affected-hijra-trans-and-sex.html (accessed 15 November 2011).

Robinson, C. (2012) 'Decolonizing sexual citizenship: Who will effect change in the south of the Commonwealth?', London: Commonwealth Advisory Bureau, www.commonwealthadvisorybureau.org/fileadmin/CPSU/documents/Publications/April_Opinion.pdf (accessed 3 May 2012).

Russo, A. (2006) 'The Feminist Majority Foundation's campaign to stop gender apartheid – The intersections of feminism and imperialism in the United States', *International Feminist Journal of Politics* 8:4: 557–80.

Ryan, M., Strobel, W., and Hosenball M. (2011) 'Exclusive: Secret US, Taliban talks reach turning point', *Reuters*, 19 December, www.reuters.com/article/2011/12/19/us-usa-afghanistan-idUSTRE7BI03I20111219 (accessed 19 December 2011).

Rycaut, P. (1668) *The Present State of the Ottoman Empire*. London.

Santoscoy, C. (2009) 'New UN president says being gay "not acceptable"', *On Top Magazine*, 23 September, www.ontopmag.com/article.aspx?id=4582&MediaType=1&Category=26 (accessed 1 August 2011).

Servier, A. (1923) *L'Islam et la psychologie du musulman*. Paris: Challamel.

Shaheed, F., and Lee-Shaheed, A. (2005) *Great Ancestors: Women Asserting Rights in Muslim Contexts*. London: Women Living Under Muslim Laws/Lahore: Shirkat Gah.

Sharma, M. (2006) *Loving Women: Being Lesbian in Underprivileged India*. New Delhi: Yoda Press.

Sommer, A.K. (2011) 'The 8-year-old girl who woke up Israel', *Jewish Daily Forward*, http://blogs.forward.com/sisterhood-blog/148571 (accessed 26 December 2011).

Walther, W. (1981) *Women in Islam*. Montelair: Abner Schram.

Whitaker, B. (2009) 'Interview with Abdellah Taia', *Al-bab*, January, www.al-bab.com/arab/articles/abdellah_taia_salvation_army.htm (accessed 5 August 2011).

White House (2011) 'Presidential Memorandum – International initiatives to advance the human rights of lesbian, gay, bisexual, and transgender persons', 6 December, www.whitehouse.gov/the-press-office/2011/12/06/presidential-memorandum-international-initiatives-advance-human-rights-l (accessed 8 December 2011).

Wright, J.W., and Rowson, E.K. (1997) *Homoeroticism in Classical Arabic Literature*. New York: Columbia University Press.

About the authors

Ana Ghoreishian is an Iranian American educator/activist/scholar who obtained her JD from CUNY School of Law with a focus on international women's human rights. In her work at the New Orleans Public Defender's office she advocated for indigent clients in the criminal law system. She has also advocated for human rights through her work with organizations like Human Rights Watch, the Center for Constitutional Rights and CONNECT. She has also supported various projects at the international solidarity network Women Living Under Muslim Laws. Currently, Ana teaches courses in race and gender in the Middle East at the University of Arizona while studying the connected histories of gender and sexuality in Turkey and Iran.

Maria Jaschok is the Director of the International Gender Studies Centre and a Senior Research Scholar at the Institute for Chinese Studies, University of Oxford. Through her collaborative research on women's interests with Shui Jingjun, she has catalysed direct and indirect local developments for change, including the reinvigoration of the Henan Research Centre of Islamic Cultures (RCIC). Her research interests include the problematic politics of representation, the women's movement in China, and the state-steered 'development' agendas in China. She is particularly interested in how Muslim women have evolved, protected and transmitted their identity, which is both similar and yet distinct from that of non-Muslim Chinese women around them. Her work examines the growing impact of international fundamentalist Islam in China on attitudes to, and practices within, women's traditions of their own religious sphere, on women's strategies for addressing the changing circumstances, and the implications for grounded development policies.

Shuchi Karim is a final year Ph.D. candidate at the International Institute of Social Studies (ISS), The Hague. She studied for her first M.A. in English Literature and Language at Jawaharlal Nehru University (Delhi, India), and her second M.A. in Gender and International Development at the University of Warwick. Ms Karim taught at the Women and Gender Studies department, University of Dhaka, as an Assistant Professor, and also has worked at BRAC University and on the BRAC Education programme. Her research interest includes sexuality, gender, disability and identity. Shuchi Karim is from Bangladesh.

Hooria Hayat Khan is a research associate with Shirkat Gah Women's Resource Centre in Pakistan. She has a background in law with a specialized LLM in Public International Law. Prior to joining Shirkat Gah, she worked at the International Criminal Court at The Hague as a legal intern in the Victims and Witnesses Unit. Alongside working at Shirkat Gah, she has also taught two components of the LLB Programme at the University of London. Her current research examines issues surrounding women's sexuality from the perspective of culture, religion and the Pakistan legal system.

Ziba Mir-Hosseini is an independent consultant, researcher and writer on Middle Eastern issues, based at the London Middle East Institute and the Centre for Middle Eastern and Islamic Law at University of London, SOAS. She holds a Ph.D. in Social Anthropology from the University of Cambridge (1980). She has held numerous research fellowships and visiting professorships, including at Wissenschaftskolleg zu Berlin (2004–05) and NYU (2002–08). She is a founding member of Musawah Global Movement for Equality and Justice in the Muslim Family, and a council member of Women Living Under Muslim Laws. Her publications include *Marriage on Trial: A Study of Islamic Family Law in Iran and Morocco* (1993, 2002) and *Islam and Gender: The Religious Debate in Contemporary Iran* (1999), among others. She has directed (with Kim Longinotto) two award-winning feature-length documentary films on contemporary issues in Iran: *Divorce Iranian Style* (1998) and *Runaway* (2001).

Shadi Sadr is a human rights lawyer and an independent researcher, journalist and activist. She has published extensively on the impact of legal inequality in Iranian Family Law on women's lives. She is one of the key leaders of the 'Stop Stoning Forever' campaign in Iran. She is the Director of Justice Iran, an organization that researches and documents human rights abuses in Iranian prisons. She has been awarded several human rights prizes for her work, including the Special Prize founded by Lech Walesa, and the Tulip Prize (2009). Her most recent book is *Thirty Years of Dress Code in the Islamic Republic of Iran* (2010).

Yüksel Sezgin is an Assistant Professor of Political Science at John Jay College, City University of New York. He earned a Ph.D. in political science and public law from the University of Washington, and holds M.A.s in Near and Middle Eastern Studies from SOAS, University of London, and the Hebrew University of Jerusalem. He has held research positions at the American University in Cairo and the University of Delhi, and has published on issues of legal pluralism, informal justice systems, religious law, state–society relations, and human and women's rights in the context of the Middle East, South Asia and sub-Saharan Africa. He is currently working on the book *Women's Rights in the Triangle of State, Law, and Religion*, which explores the impact of polycentric personal status systems on human rights, and individuals' responses to rights violations under religious institutions in Israel, Palestine, Egypt, India and Sierra Leone.

Vivienne Wee is an anthropologist who has done extensive research and published on issues of gender, power, religion and ethno-nationalism, especially in Indonesia. She has taught at the National University of Singapore, the Chinese University of Hong Kong and City University of Hong Kong. She was Director of the Research Programme Consortium on Women's Empowerment in Muslim Contexts (2006–09). She is currently a research consultant with Women

Reclaiming and Re-defining Culture, a programme coordinated by Women Living Under Muslim Laws and the Institute for Women's Empowerment. As a public intellectual, she has worked to enhance a more participatory and holistic understanding of development issues and processes, through collaboration with other academic researchers, civil society organizations and local communities, as well as with various UN and development agencies.

Claudia Yaghoobi holds a Bachelor's and a Master's degree in English Language and Literature from Islamic Azad University in Iran. She received her second M.A. degree in English Literature at California State University of Los Angeles. She is currently a Ph.D. candidate at UC Santa Barbara, studying comparative literature, with an emphasis on feminist and gender/sexuality studies. Her research interests include the influences of Western and Sufi mysticism on English and Persian medieval literature respectively, as well as Iranian women's movements and sexuality. She has presented at various symposia on these topics, and has also taught courses on Western Literature, Feminism and Modern Iran at the University of California Santa Barbara.

Index

Abassgholizadeh, Mahbobeh, 230 n25, 231 n27
Abbasid dynasty: *Muhtaseb*, 237
'Abd al-Wahab, Muhammad ibn, 239, 263 n9
abortion, 29
Abu Nawas (poet), 317
Aceh tsunami, 37
adultery, 311–12; Stop Stoning Forever campaign, 73; *see also zina*
Afary, J., 61
Afghanistan: Campaign to Stop Gender Apartheid, 326 n14; fundamentalism, 240–41, 242; Soviet invasion of, 240–41; US and women's rights, 305
ahkam rulings, 124–5, 129–30
Ahmadinejad, Mahmoud, 223–5, 296–7, 324 n4
ahong (female mosque leaders): advice to congregants, 171; appointments system, 167; collaborative leadership models, 174–5; description of, 178 n1; difference from male *ahong*, 174; Du Shuzhen Ahong, 170–73, 174, 175, 177–8, 180 n11; education of, 164, 165, 172; family planning advice, 162, 179 n6; 'Four Goods', 171; Guo Dongping Ahong, 151, 163–70, 174, 175, 179 n2; and illiterate women, 159; introduction of unmarried *ahong*, 164–5; links with other Muslim communities, 172–3; Lu Ahong,

164–5, 166; modernization challenge, 176; origins, 157–8; pressure from Islamic orthodoxy, 175–6, 177; and renewal of Islamic knowledge, 180 n9; role as educators, 151, 154–6, 157–8, 168–70, 175; as role models, 161–3, 168; Saudi Arabian influence, 169, 180 n10; sermon on domesticated sexuality, 177–8; and wifely duties, 166, 167
aid conditionality: and LGBT rights, 303–5
AIMPLB (All India Muslim Personal Law Board), 106, 114
AIMWPLB (All India Muslim Women Personal Law Board), 106, 114–15
Al-e Ahmad, Jalal, 68–9
al-Qaeda: Muslim casualties, 325 n12
Alatas, A., 34
Alemy-Kabha, Nasreen, 108
Algeria, 256–60; Abu Nawas LGBT group, 317; fundamentalism, 242, 260; ignored by international community, 256; Islamic Salvation Front (FIS), 257–8; National Reconciliation Policy, 256; vigilante policing and violence, 235, 256, 258–9, 263 n3; women's resistance, 259–60, 264 n26
Amber, Shaista, 115
Argentina: transgender rights, 326 n18
arranged marriage: pre-modern Iran, 55, 56

asylum-seekers, 297, 305–6, 325 n9, 327 n20
aurat/'awrah (private parts), 34–5, 36, 129–30

Babayan, Kathryn, 59
Balochistan province: honour killings, 79–81
Bamdad, Badr ol-Moluk, 65–6
Ban Ki-moon, 312
Bangladesh, 269–93; fundamentalism, 242; gender segregation, 284–5; gendered attitude to homosexuality, 275; girls' upbringing, 272–3; importance of family and marriage, 273, 285; middle-class expectations and upbringing, 271, 272–3; patriarchy, 269–70; Sodomy Law, 274; street children sex workers, 279–80; unmarried women, 273–4; women's traditional role, 282
Beida Women's Mosque, 172–3
Ben-Yehuda, N., 25
Bennett, L.R., 30
Bennoune, K., 325 n12
bisexuality, 4; see also lesbian, gay, bisexual, transgender, transsexual and intersex people (LGBTTI)
Blanchet, T., 272
boxing: women's boxing, 41
Brenner, S., 35, 36
Britain: aid conditionality and LGBT rights, 303–5; support for Islamists in Afghanistan, 240–41

Cameron, David, 303–5
CEDAW (Convention on the Elimination of All Forms of Discrimination Against Women), 28–9
China: borderlands, 152; Confucianism and Islam, 155, 157, 158, 159–60; female illiteracy, 159, 161; Gedimu Muslim tradition, 179 n3; gender segregation, 157; Haizhuang village, 163, 180 n8; Hui Muslims, 154, 179 n3; Muslim population, 152; teacher–disciple relationships, 163; Yihewani pai, 179 n3; Yin/Yang philosophy, 159, 179 n4
Chinese Muslim women, 151–81; conflict between family duties and spiritual life, 160–61; hailifan religious trainees, 164, 165; Hui scholars,

154–5, 160, 179 n5; knowledge of scriptures, 155–6; outsider status, 153; purity (jie) and shame (xiuti), 154–6; religious education, 157–8; sexual morality within marriage, 159–61; see also ahong (female mosque leaders)
clash of civilizations, 298–9, 325 n12
colonialism, 297–8, 325 n10
comics, 41
communism: and sexual immorality, 24–6
Confucianism: and Islam, 155, 157, 158, 159–60
Cromer, Lord, 298
customary laws: Pakistani case, 12 n8

diaspora Muslims, 301
divorce: by mutual consent (khul), 115, 128–9; classical fiqh, 131; and customary law, 12 n8; iddat period, 105, 113–14, 119 n9; in India, 104–5, 113–15; in Iran, 56, 67, 249; in Israel, 102–4, 108; maintenance awards, 103–4, 104–5, 108, 109–10, 113–14; talaq al-tafwiz (delegated), 114, 129; talaq unilateral divorce, 102; triple talaq, 104, 114–15; zina as reason for, 30
Donner, H., 270
dower payment (mahr), 119 n8, 128, 132
dress codes, 33–7, 129–30; see also veiling
Du Shuzhen Ahong, 170–73, 174, 175, 177–8, 180 n11

Ebadi, Shirin, 72
Egypt: family law, 140; female genital mutilation (FGM), 311, 328 n30; fundamentalism, 242; homosexual repression, 321–2, 329 n48; virginity tests, 311

family law: colonial codification, 132–3; discrimination against women, 101–2; India, 98–9, 104–5, 112–14; Iran, 67, 71, 140, 211, 249; Israel, 98–9, 102–4, 107–111; personal status systems, 99–101; resistance to reform, 98; see also divorce; marriage
Farrokhzad, Forough, 67, 76 n7
female genital mutilation (FGM), 29, 31–3, 311, 328 n30
female imams, 9, 12 n10, 13 n11, 31; see also ahong (female mosque leaders)
films: and homosexuality, 321–2, 328 n46

fiqh (jurisprudence): classical, 130–32, 142; distinct from *shari'a*, 126–7; on dress codes, 129–30; and gender inequality, 30–31; marriage a civil contract, 128–9; women's sexuality as property, 130–32

fitna (social disorder), 31, 33, 36, 56, 82

football: *90 Minutes of Equality* (film), 226–7; Ahmadinejad's placatory move, 223–5; Asian and World Cup games, 217, 218, 223, 229 n10; ban on female attendance, 217, 220–21, 230 n11; and FIFA, 226, 230 n26, 231 n27; media coverage, 220, 222, 223, 225–6, 230 n17–18; *Offside* (Panahi film), 224–5, 226, 230 n23; Open Stadiums campaign, 221–7; *ulama* (Qom Seminary) views on, 219, 224, 225; women in public celebrations, 218–19

football supporters: foreign female, 220; Tahereh Rezazadeh (MP), 220; women attending dressed as men, 218, 220

fundamentalism *see* Muslim fundamentalism

Gambia: and LGBT rights, 304–5

Garland, D., 25

'gay Muslims', 299–300, 324 n2–3

Gedimu Muslim tradition, 179 n3

Gellner, E., 41–2

gender in/equality, 1–2, 135–40, 142–3

gender segregation: between unrelated men and women, 23, 129–30, 157; protective cover for women in same-sex relationships, 284–5; in sport, 211

Gerwani (Indonesian Women's Movement), 24–6

Al-Ghazali, Abu Hamid Muhammad, 131–2, 134

Gilchrist, Roberta, 156

Goode, E., 25

guardianship, 86–7, 93–4, 96 n6, 131, 244

Guo Dongping Ahong, 151, 163–70, 174, 175, 179 n2

Habib, S., 316

hailifan religious trainees, 164, 165

Hanafi school of law, 131, 144 n11

Hanbali school of law, 144 n11, 238

harems, 60

Harris, L., 299

Hashemi, Faezeh, 214, 215

Hayes, J., 300

headscarves *see* veiling

Henricks, M., 318

hermeneutic approach, 105–6, 111–12, 113–14, 115, 116–17

hetero-sociability: Iran, 62–3

hijab see veiling

al-Hilli, Muhaqqiq, 132

historical scholars, 55–62, 237–9, 316–17

homonationalism, 300, 326 n15

homosexuality: Bangladesh Sodomy Law, 274; British Muslim opinion, 299, 325 n13; considered God-given, 41; films, 321–2, 328 n46; gendered acceptance in Bangladesh, 274–5; in Indonesia, 40–41; Iran, 60–61, 62, 73, 74; in literature and film, 320–21; and sacred texts, 318–19; *shomo-kaami* (gay) culture, 282

honour crimes, 79–81, 82, 84, 88–94, 95 n3, 312

Hui Muslims, 154, 179 n3

human rights, 140

Hussain, Neelum, 87

Ibn Abdul-Wahhab, Muhammad, 19

Ibn Hanbal, 238

Ibn Taymiya, 238

Ibn-al Munkadir, 238

imams *see ahong* (female mosque leaders); female imams

India: All India Muslim Personal Law Board (AIMPLB), 106, 114; All India Muslim Women Personal Law Board (AIMWPLB), 106, 114–15; Bharatiya Muslim Mahila Andolan (BMMA), 115; BJP (Bharatiya Janata Party), 112, 119 n19, 120 n20; civil marriage law, 99; and divorce, 104–5, 113–15; family law, 98–9, 104–5; family law reform, 112–15; hermeneutic approach to reform, 113–14, 115, 116–17; maintenance awards, 104–5, 113–14; marriage ceremonies, 115; marriage contract reform, 114–15; Sangh Parivar, 112, 119 n19; Shah Bano case, 104, 119 n7; Uniform Civil code (UCC), 112–13, 120 n20; women's court (*mahila adalat*), 106

Indonesia, 17–51; Aceh tsunami, 37; anti-communism, 24–6; CEDAW Convention, 28–9; Compilation of Islamic Laws (1991), 30; contraception and family planning, 29; Dharma

Wanita (Women's Duty), 27; diverse tribal societies, 18–19; dress codes, 33–7; Dutch colonialism, 20–21; early acceptance of women's sexual autonomy, 17–18; female genital mutilation (FGM), 29, 31–3; fundamentalism, 242; gender segregation, curtain (*tabir*), 23; Gerwani (Women's Movement), 24–6; LGBT groups attacked, 40–41; Marriage Law (1974), 26–7, 29, 30–31; morality police, 36, 234; Muslim villages, 42; New Year dance show, 39–40; polygyny, 22–4, 31; Pornography Law (2008), 37–40; Q! Film Festival, 40–41; religious diversity, 18; *Three Women* sculpture, 40; Wahhabism, 19–21; women's boxing, 41

Indonesian Council of Ulama, 32, 38, 40

Indonesia Pornography Law (2008), 37–40, 44 n32–33

International Lesbian and Gay Association Asia Conference, 40

Internet access, 9, 13 n12

Internet activism, 74, 230 n17, 246–7, 320; *see also* veiling bloggers

Iran: Constitutional Revolution, 63–4; divorce, 56, 67, 249; European contact, 62–3; family law, 67, 71, 140, 211, 249; fundamentalism, 235, 242, 263 n3; hetero-sociability, 62–3; homosexuality, 60–61, 62, 73, 74; Internet access, 9, 13 n12; Internet activism, 74, 230 n17; Iran–Iraq War, 72, 182, 211, 217; Iranian Revolution, 70; marriage practices, 55–6; morality policing (*basij*), 234, 248, 250–52; One Million Signatures campaign, 73–4; penalties for same-sex acts, 296–7, 325 n6; penalties for sexual offences, 53, 71, 73; polygyny, 55–6, 62, 65, 67, 71; population statistics, 76 n1; pre-modern era, 52, 55–62, 74; prostitution, 190; public civil disobedience acts, 249–52; resistance strategies, 53–4, 56–60, 73–4, 208–9, 227, 231 n29, 249–52; sexuality and modernity, 62–70, 74–5; young people's opposition to Islamic Republic, 53–4, 72–3, 75, 76 n1; *see also* sport; veiling

Iranian women, 52–78; economic independence, 68; education, 62–3, 65–6, 249; employed as morality police, 251; female identity and Islam, 68–9; Islamic Republic regulations, 53–4, 70–74, 75, 210–11, 249; marriage expectations, 74; morality police (*basij*), 234, 248, 250–52; openings under Islamic Republic, 71–2; Pahlavi regime modernization, 54, 64–5, 74, 210; poets, 67, 76 n7; political activism, 63–4; political rights, 66–7; pre-modern era same-sex relations, 60, 61; pre-modern sisterhood bonds, 57–60; and religious texts, 72; resistance strategies, 53–4, 56–60, 182, 183; right to sexual pleasure, 67; sexual agency, 56–60; sexual frustration, 57; and women's rights, 71–2, 76 n10; *see also* same-sex sexuality; veiling; veiling bloggers

Islam: Islamization, 89, 140; and politics of gender, 140–42; and polygyny, 23–4; and veiling, 196–200; *see also ahong* (female mosque leaders); Qur'an; sacred texts

Islamic fundamentalism *see* Muslim fundamentalism

Islamic jurisprudence *see fiqh* (jurisprudence)

Islamic laws *see* Muslim legal tradition

Israel: divorce, 102–4, 108; failure to enforce civil laws, 102–3; family law, 98–9, 102–4; family law reform, 107–11, 117; Islamic texts and women's rights, 111–12, 117–18; maintenance awards, 103–4, 108, 109–10; and Palestinian LGBTTI activism, 319, 325 n8; *shari'a* courts, 102–3, 109–10; under-age marriage, 118 n4; Working Group for Equality in Personal Status Issues, 107–8, 109, 119 n10

Jammeh, Yahya, 304–5

Java: polygyny, 27–8

Jewish Orthodox communities, 111–12, 311, 328 n31

jurisprudence *see fiqh* (jurisprudence)

Kar, Mehrangiz, 72

Karim, S., 272

Katjasungkana, Nursyahbani, 34

Khalil ibn Ishaq, 132

Khansari, Molla Aqa Jamal: *Kolsum Naneh*, 58–9
Khatami, Mohammad, 218, 219
khul (divorce by mutual consent), 128–9
Kuwait: criminal code, 310–11

LBH APIK (Indonesian Women's Association for Justice), 27, 39
Lebanon, 297, 315, 317, 319–20, 325 n9
Lee-Shaheed, A., 316
legal schools, 130–31, 144 n11
lesbian, gay, bisexual, transgender, transsexual and intersex people (LGBTTI): activism and resistance strategies, 314–16, 325 n8; Ahmadinejad's comment, 296, 324 n4; and aid conditionality, 303–5; asylum-seekers, 297, 303, 305–6, 325 n9; colonial perceptions, 297, 297–8, 325 n10; comics, 41; and criminal sanctions, 313–14, 328 n37; 'gay Muslims', 299–300, 324 n2–3; hate crimes, 303; *hijra* treatment after Pakistan floods, 308; historical legitimacy for, 316–17; homonationalism, 300, 326 n15; in Indonesia, 40–41; lesbianism, 271, 275, 279–81, 283; in Middle East, 297; Netanyahu's comments, 297, 325 n7; and sacred texts, 318–19; transgender people, 303, 310–11, 326 n18; use of term, 324 n1; visibility, 319–22; Western stereotyping as victims, 299–301; Western and US discrimination, 303, 326 nn16–17; Yogyakarta Principles, 41, 44 n35; *see also* homosexuality; same-sex sexuality
Liu Zhi, 154–5, 160, 179 n5

Ma Minglian, 159
Ma Zhu, 154–5, 179 n5
Mahdavi, Pardis: *Passionate Uprisings*, 73
maintenance awards, 103–4, 104–5, 108, 109–10, 113–14
Malaysia, 252–6; criminal sanctions for LGBTTI behaviour, 313–14; fundamentalism, 235, 242, 263 n3; sexual control, 254; *shari'a* laws, 253; Sisters in Islam (SIS), 255–6; tomboyism, 254; *ulama*, demands of, 252–3; Valentine's Day arrests, 254–5
Maliki school, 131, 144 n11
Man, Ke, 152

marriage: age of, 55, 67, 118 n4, 290 n5; annulment, 12 n8; arranged marriage in pre-modern Iran, 55, 56; Bangladesh, 273, 285, 290 n5; ceremony conducted by female *qadi*, 115; and Chinese Muslim women, 159–61; classical *fiqh*, 130–32; compensation (*'iwad*) for release from, 129; dower payment (*mahr*), 119 n8, 128, 132; *fiqh* contracts, 128–9; and guardianship, 86–7, 96 n6, 131; India, 99, 114–15; Indonesia, 26–7, 30–31; Iran, 55–6, 67, 74; Israel, 118 n4; maintenance obligations (*nafaqa*), 103–4, 128; marriage manuals, 133–5; neo-traditionalist texts, 135–40; Pakistan, 86–8, 94–5, 96 n8; same-sex, 41; sexual intercourse within, 26–7, 30; *see also* divorce; honour crimes; polygyny
Masalha, Nawwaf, 108
Maududi, Abul A'la: *Purdah and the Status of Women in Islam*, 136–8
Meem LGBT activism, 320
men: cross-dressers, 310–311; mullahs' homoeroticism, 217, 230 n12; and sexual desire, 31, 134–5, 138–9, 200–201; *see also* homosexuality
Mernissi, Fatima, 156
Metcalf, Barbara, 152
modesty (*haya*), 134–5, 156
morality policing: Algerian vigilantes, 235, 256, 258–9, 263 n3; historical roots, 237–9; Indonesia, 36, 234; Iran (*basij*), 234, 248, 250–52; and the Qur'an, 237–8; Saudi Arabia, 244, 246, 247, 310; state strategies, 242–3; transnational phenomenon, 236; and women's participation, 236
mosques: commercialization of men's, 176; women's, 156, 158, 172–3; *see also ahong* (female mosque leaders)
Muhammad, Husein, 30–31
Muhtaseb: Ottoman Empire, 237, 239
Mulia, Musdah, 318–19
mullahs: homoeroticism, 217, 230 n12; *see also ahong* (female mosque leaders)
Musawah, 30
Musdah Mulia, Siti, 41, 44 n38
Muslim diaspora, 151–2
Muslim fundamentalism: definition, 262 n2; and patriarchy, 260–61; spread of, 234–5, 241–2, 261, 263 n3; Tunisia, 327 n27; Wahhabism, 19–21,

239–40, 241, 263 n9; *see also* morality
  policing
Muslim legal tradition: *ahkam* rulings,
  124–5, 129–30; marriage manuals,
  133–5; neo-traditionalist texts,
  135–40; sources of, 143 n3
Muslim Women's Games/Olympics,
  214–16, 228
Muslimness, 2–3
Mutahhari, Morteza, 136, 138–40

nafaqa (maintenance), 128
Najmabadi, Afsaneh, 57
nation-building, 98, 99–100
Natour, Ahmad, 102
Netanyahu, Benjamin, 297, 325 n7
Netherlands: homophobia, 303
NGOs (non-governmental
  organizations): and human rights, 315
Nigeria: sexual crimes, 308
Nissa wa Afaq: Israel, 111–12
Nissa Women Welfare and Social
  Development Organization:
  Pakistan, 94–5

Obama, Barack, 303, 326 n16
Offside (Panahi film), 224–5, 226,
  230 n23
online access, 9, 13 n12
online activism, 74, 230 n17, 246–7, 320;
  see also veiling bloggers
Open Stadiums campaign, 221–7
Organization of the Islamic Conference:
  and homosexuality, 312, 328 n36
Ottoman Empire, 239, 317
Ottoman Law of Family Rights (1917),
  102, 103

Pakistan, 79–97; cultural conceptions of
  honour, 83–4; *hijra* treatment after
  floods, 308; honour killings, 82,
  88–93, 95 n3; Hudud Ordinances,
  140; Islamization of criminal law, 89;
  legal system, 84–6, 93–4, 95;
  marriage and parental consent, 86–8;
  Nissa Women Welfare and Social
  Development Organization, 94–5;
  Saima Waheed case, 86–8, 96 n8
Palestinian women: discrimination in
  Israel, 102–4; family law reform,
  107–11, 117; Islamic texts and
  women's rights, 111–12, 117–18;
  language problems, 109; under-age
  marriage, 118 n4

Palestinians: LGBTTI activism, 319,
  325 n8
Panahi, Jafar: *Offside*, 224–5, 226,
  230 n23
Papanek, H., 157
Pateman, Carole, 85, 98, 124
patriarchy: Bangladesh, 269–70; critique
  of, 141; and the modern state, 133;
  and Muslim fundamentalism,
  260–61; and sacred texts, 100, 101–2,
  125–6; tradition of, 124, 130–31
personal status systems, 99–101, 106, 107,
  132–3
Petchesky, R., 307, 309
Pillsbury, Barbara, 153
Polak, Dr J.E., 60
policing *see* morality policing
polygyny: banned in Tunisia, 133;
  Gerwani opposition to, 26; India,
  120 n20; Indonesia, 22–4, 27–8, 29,
  31; Iran, 55–6, 62, 65, 67, 71; Islamic
  justification for, 23–4; pre-modern
  Iran, 55–6
Pornography Law (2008/Indonesia),
  37–40, 44 n32–33
prayer, 129–30, 158, 197
prostitution *see* sex workers
public space, 208–9, 236, 249–51, 249–52,
  262

QamB activism, 315
'A Question Called *Hijab*' blog,
  186–205
Qur'an: and gender equality in Iran, 72;
  justification for women's sport,
  212–13, 228; and morality policing,
  237–8; and veiling, 196–200

Raja Abdullah, 19
Raja Ali, 19
refugees/asylum seekers, 297, 305–6,
  325 n9, 327 n20
religion: and politics of sexuality, 286,
  313–14, 323; *see also* Muslim
  fundamentalism
resistance strategies: Algeria, 259–60,
  264 n26; civil disobedience in Saudi
  Arabia, 245–7, 264 n12; hermeneutic
  approach, 105–6, 111–12, 113–14, 115,
  116–17; Indonesia, 40–41; LGBTTI
  groups, 314–16, 325 n8; modern Iran,
  73–4, 208–9, 227, 231 n29, 249–52;
  and political alignment, 225; pre-
  modern Iran, 53–4, 56–60; in public

spaces, 236, 262; *see also* online activism

Robinson, Colin, 304

Rohana, Siti, 24

Rothschild, Cynthia, 324 n3

sacred texts: and alternative sexualities, 318–19; Chinese women's knowledge of, 155–6; hermeneutic approach to reform, 105–6, 111–12, 113–14, 115, 116–17; patriarchal readings, 100, 101–2, 125–6; *see also* Qur'an

Sadr, Shadi, 225, 230 n25

Saima Waheed case, 86–8, 96 n8

Salafism, 310, 327 n28

al-Saltaneh, Taj, 60

same-sex sexuality: acceptance of, 284; can be renegotiated, 277–8; criminal sanctions, 313–14, 328 n37; and girls' upbringing, 272–3; homo-sociability as protective cover, 285–8; in Indonesia, 40–41; influence of age and education, 278–9; Iranian penalties, 296–7, 325 n6; middle-class expectations and upbringing, 271, 272–3; and non-hetero sociality, 274–5; pre-modern Iran, 60–61; pressure of heterosexual norms, 273, 285–6; protective cover offered by gender segregation, 284–5; recognition of difference, 276–81; and religion, 286; and sex workers, 271, 275, 279–81, 283, 287; *shomo-kaami* (gay) culture, 282; *shomo-premi* (love for the same) women, 270–71, 276–7, 281–3; types of, 270–71, 275, 283; *see also* homosexuality

Sangh Parivar, 112, 119 n19

Saudi Arabia, 243–8; and Afghanistan, 241; and China, 169, 180 n10; early freedom for women, 243; external support for women, 245, 247; fundamentalism, 235, 242, 263 n3; Internet activism, 246–7; Manal al-Sharif's YouTube video, 246–7; morality police, 244, 246, 247, 310; schoolgirl tragedy, 310; veiling requirements, 244, 310; Wahhabism, 239–40, 241, 263 n9; women's driving ban, 244–7, 263 n11, 264 n15; women's education, 244

Schimmel, Annemarie, 58

schools: and veiling, 33–5

Scott, J.C., 185

Selim I, Sultan of Ottoman Empire, 317

sex segregation *see* gender segregation

sex workers: Iran, 190; and lesbianism, 271, 275, 279–81, 283, 291 n14; street children's reform centres, 279–80

sexual contract, 124

sexual desire (*shahvat*), 134–5, 138–9, 200–201, 278–9

sexual harassment, 29, 193–4

sexual honour (*ghairat*), 135

sexual identities *see* same-sex sexuality

sexual immorality: and communism, 24–6

sexual liaisons: colonial Indonesia, 21; outside marriage *see* adultery; *zina* (sex outside marriage)

sexual scripts, 17, 41, 42

sexual violence: and honour, 84

sexuality: domination and control, 4, 136–40; and family unit, 274; fear of, 82; and personal status systems, 106; political use of, 20; as property in classical *fiqh*, 130–32, 142; and religion, 286, 313–14, 323

Shah Bano case, 104, 119 n7

Shaheed, F., 316

Shahidian, Hammed, 70

Shahri, Jafar, 60

shari'a, 126–7, 141

shari'a courts, 102–3, 109–10

Shari'ati, Ali, 68–9

al-Sharif, Manal: YouTube video, 246–7

sighehs (sisterhoods bonds), 57–8, 58–60

slaves, 130, 131, 197

Smith-Hefner, N., 35

Soviet Union: in Afghanistan, 240–41

sport, 208–233; Iran's provisions for women, 213, 215, 228; Iran's restrictions, 211; in Malaysia, 254; media coverage, 215, 216, 228; morning exercise gatherings, 212; Muslim Women's Games/Olympics, 214–16, 228; Qur'anic justification for, 212–13, 228; Seoul Olympics (1988), 213; *see also* boxing; football

sterilization, 29

Stop Stoning Forever campaign, 73

Sudan, 242, 310

Sufism, 58–9

Suharto, 24, 30

Tabataba'i, Allamah: *al-Mizan*, 138–9

Taia, Abdellah, 320–21

Taiwan: Muslim women, 153
talaq al-tafwiz (delegated divorce), 129
talaq (unilateral divorce), 102
Taleghani, Ayatollah, 186
tamkin (obedience), 128
Tehran University, 65–6
terrorism, 300–301, 325 n12
tomboyism: in Malaysia, 254
transgender people, 303, 310–11, 326 n18
Treki, Ali Abdussalam, 312
triple *talaq* divorce, 104
Tunisia: electoral candidates, 297;
    fundamentalism, 327 n27; lesbian
    discrimination, 312; polygamy
    banned, 133; Salafi activism, 310
Turkey: LGBT activism, 320

ulama: in Iran (Qom Seminary), 219, 224,
    225; in Malaysia, 252–3
United Nations: human rights and
    sexual orientation, 312–13
United States: and LGBTTI people, 303,
    305, 307–8, 326 n16–17, 326 n19;
    support for Islamists in Afghanistan,
    240–41

veiling: anonymity used by Iranian
    women, 56–7; 'bad *hijab*', 182–3;
    banned in Europe, 203–5; ban in
    Pahlavi era, 64–5; *chador*, 56, 194–6;
    citizens' private views (hidden
    transcript), 184–5, 205–6; and
    citizens' rights, 200–205; compulsory
    veiling, Iranians' defiance of, 9,
    13 n13, 73; compulsory veiling in
    Iran, 71, 248, 264 n17; compulsory
    veiling protest rally, 71, 76 n10, 183;
    counter-arguments, 189–96; during
    prayer, 129–30, 197; and fashion, 36;
    hijab covering and seclusion, 129–30;
    improper veiling, 206; Indonesian
    prohibition, 33–4; morality policing,
    36; morality policing (*basij*), 36, 234,
    248, 250–52; opponents of, 188–9,
    198–200; overseas experiences,
    190–92; punishments, 310; in the
    Qur'an, 196–7, 198, 199; religious
    arguments, 196–200; safety issues,
    190–92; Saudi Arabia, 244; in school,
    33–5; self-confidence and self-
    control, 35–6; and sexual harassment,
    193–4; support for, 188, 189
veiling bloggers: 'A Question Called
    Hijab' blog, 186–205; Alireza, 204;

Assal, 202; Atiyeh, 197; B. Eftekhari,
    191–2, 195; Ba-hijab ('the veiled
    one'), 194, 195; Bahar, 192, 194;
    Baran, 200; Bibi Monavvar, 186–7;
    Bita, 197; Darkoob (woodpecker),
    190–91, 194–5, 196, 202, 203; Darya,
    192; Fariba, 198; Ghazal, 199–200;
    Hakimeh Bahmanzadeh, 194; Iraj,
    190; Ley La, 195–6; Man Pesaram (I
    Am A Boy), 201; Mandana, 196;
    Mania, 189–90, 197; Mitra, 196–7;
    Najmeh Vahedi, 193–4; Narjes, 203;
    Payam (male), 199; Sara, 198; Satin,
    193; Sepideh, 198; Shahrzad-e Ghesse
    goo (Shahrzad the Story Teller), 201;
    Shayan, 192; Shirin, 202; Soheila
    Biglarkhan, 204
virginity, 55, 311

Wadud, Amina, 151
Wahhabism, 19–21, 239–40, 241, 263 n9
Wang Daiyu, 154–5, 160, 179 n5
WEMC (Women's Empowerment in
    Muslim Contexts), 6, 11 n2, 79–80,
    95 n1, 180 n7
WLUML (Women Living Under
    Muslim Laws), 12 n8, 229 n2
women: and gender inequality in the
    West, 302–3; gendered power
    structures, 42; in Jewish Orthodox
    communities, 111–12, 311, 328 n31;
    stigmatized for excessive closeness
    (*khalwat*), 36–7; *see also* Chinese
    Muslim women; Iranian women
women drivers, 244–7, 263 n11
women's education: China, 157–8, 164,
    165, 172; Iran, 62–3, 65–6, 249; Saudi
    Arabia, 244
women's empowerment, 2, 11 n2, 94–5,
    170; WEMC project, 11 n2, 6, 79–80,
    95 n1, 180 n7
women's mosques, 156, 158, 172–3;
    see also ahong (female mosque leaders)

Yihewani pai, 179 n3
Yogyakarta Principles, 41, 44 n35
YouTube video, 246–7
Yudhoyono, Susilo Bambang, 31

Zehri, Israrullah, 80–81
zina (sex outside marriage): Indonesia,
    30, 37; Iranian law, 71; and Islamic
    values, 31; reason for divorce, 30;
    see also adultery